21世纪英语专业系列教材

英语综合高级教程
（上 册）

主　编　肖　肃
编　者　（按姓氏笔画排序）
　　　　刘玉梅　肖　肃　杨志亭　钟　毅
　　　　黄四宏　谢　琳　阚哲华

北京大学出版社
PEKING UNIVERSITY PRESS

图书在版编目(CIP)数据

英语综合高级教程.上/肖肃主编.—北京：北京大学出版社，2010.8
21世纪英语专业系列教材
ISBN 978-7-301-17699-3

Ⅰ.英… Ⅱ.肖… Ⅲ.英语-高等学校-教材 Ⅳ.H31

中国版本图书馆CIP数据核字(2010)第167307号

书　　　　名：	英语综合高级教程(上册)
著作责任者：	肖　肃　主编
责任编辑：	李　颖
标准书号：	ISBN 978-7-301-17699-3/H·2626
出版发行：	北京大学出版社
地　　　址：	北京市海淀区成府路205号 100871
网　　　址：	http://www.pup.cn　新浪官方微博：@北京大学出版社
电子信箱：	evalee1770@sina.com
电　　　话：	邮购部 62752015　发行部 62750672　编辑部 62767315　出版部 62754962
印　刷　者：	北京大学印刷厂
经　销　者：	新华书店
	787毫米×1092毫米　16开本　18.75印张　450千字
	2010年8月第1版　2019年7月第3次印刷
定　　　价：	36.00元

未经许可，不得以任何方式复制或抄袭本书之部分或全部内容。
版权所有，侵权必究
举报电话：010-62752024　电子信箱：fd@pup.pku.edu.cn

《21世纪英语专业系列教材》
编写委员会

（以姓氏笔画排序）

王立非	王守仁	王克非
王俊菊	文秋芳	石　坚
申　丹	朱　刚	仲伟合
刘世生	刘意青	殷企平
孙有中	李　力	李正栓
张旭春	张庆宗	张绍杰
杨俊峰	陈法春	金　莉
封一函	胡壮麟	查明建
袁洪庚	桂诗春	黄国文
梅德明	董洪川	蒋洪新
程幼强	程朝翔	虞建华

总 序

  北京大学出版社自2005年以来已出版《语言与应用语言学知识系列读本》多种，为了配合第十一个五年计划，现又策划陆续出版《21世纪英语专业系列教材》。这个重大举措势必受到英语专业广大教师和学生的欢迎。

  作为英语教师，最让人揪心的莫过于听人说英语不是一个专业，只是一个工具。说这些话的领导和教师的用心是好的，为英语专业的毕业生将来找工作着想，因此要为英语专业的学生多多开设诸如新闻、法律、国际商务、经济、旅游等其他专业的课程。但事与愿违，英语专业的教师们很快发现，学生投入英语学习的时间少了，掌握英语专业课程知识甚微，即使对四个技能的掌握也并不比大学英语学生高明多少，而那个所谓的第二专业在有关专家的眼中只是学到些皮毛而已。

  英语专业的路在何方？有没有其他路可走？这是需要我们英语专业教师思索的问题。中央领导关于创新是一个民族的灵魂和要培养创新人才等的指示精神，让我们在层层迷雾中找到了航向。显然，培养学生具有自主学习能力和能进行创造性思维是我们更为重要的战略目标，使英语专业的人才更能适应21世纪的需要，迎接21世纪的挑战。

  如今，北京大学出版社外语部的领导和编辑同志们，也从教材出版的视角探索英语专业的教材问题，从而为贯彻英语专业教学大纲做些有益的工作，为教师们开设大纲中所规定的必修、选修课程提供各种教材。《21世纪英语专业系列教材》是普通高等教育"十一五"国家级规划教材和国家"十一五"重点出版规划项目《面向新世纪的立体化网络化英语学科建设丛书》的重要组成部分。这套系列教材要体现新世纪英语教学的自主化、协作化、模块化和超文本化，结合外语教材的具体情况，既要解决语言、教学内容、教学方法和教育技术的时代化，也要坚持弘扬以爱国主义为核心的民族精神。因此，今天北京大学出版社在大力提倡专业英语教学改革的基础上，编辑出版各种英语专业技能、英语专业知识和相关专业知识课程的教材，以培养具有创新性思维的和具有实际工作能力的学生，充分体现了时代精神。

  北京大学出版社的远见卓识，也反映了英语专业广大师生盼望已久的心愿。由北京大学等全国几十所院校具体组织力量，积极编写相关教材。这就是说，这套教材是由一些高等院校有水平有经验的第一线教师们制定编写大纲，反复讨论，特别是考虑到在不同层次、不同背景学校之间取得平衡,避免了先前的教材或偏难或偏易的弊病。与此同时,一批知名专家教授参与策划和教材审定工作,保证了教材质量。

当然,这套系列教材出版只是初步实现了出版社和编者们的预期目标。为了获得更大效果,希望使用本系列教材的教师和同学不吝指教,及时将意见反馈给我们,使教材更加完善。

航道已经开通,我们有决心乘风破浪,奋勇前进!

胡壮麟
北京大学蓝旗营

前 言

《英语综合高级教程》以《高等学校英语专业英语教学大纲》和《高校英语专业八级考试大纲》为准绳,以英语专业高年级的培养目标和教学原则为指导,充分体现了外语教学始终要"夯实基础、拓宽视野、提升思考、强化表达"这一理念。

英语专业高年级的综合英语学习要继续夯实基础。低年级阶段完成了语音、语法、修辞和基本词汇积累等学习工作,而高年级阶段则需进一步积累语言和吸收知识,把低年级阶段所学内容加以巩固和整合,通过广涉政治、经济、社会、语言、文学、教育、哲学、科技等方面的作品,拓宽学生视野,完善知识结构,提升学生对社会与人生的理解和思考能力,培养学生语篇鉴赏和语篇灵活运用的能力,提高学生分析问题、解决问题的逻辑思维和独立思考的能力,力求达到"自由表达"的外语学习境界。因此,学生"高级英语"的"高级"之处应该体现在这几个方面:其一,常用词汇的灵活化;其二,语法结构的牢固化;其三,概念知识的体系化;其四,语篇鉴赏的能力化;其五,思想见解的独立化;最后,达到准确精要的自由表达。本教程正是针对这些特点而进行编写,核心目标就是帮助学生提升独立思考和自由表达的能力。

本教程所选文章具有以下特点:
- **真实性**:全部材料均用原汁原味的英语资料,少数作了节选或改编。
- **多元化**:涉及科技、教育、文学、社会、语言、政治演讲、情感、人与自然、经济、外交、军事、哲学、历史、国学等内容广泛的题材和体裁。
- **时代性**:经典与前沿信息结合。
- **趣味性**:学生喜闻乐见。
- **深刻性**:内容深刻富有启迪,有利于培养学生独立的思想见解。

本教程的编排,既与《英语综合教程》前四册编排原则上基本一致,又具有自身的特点:
1. **主题式编排内容**。本教程有上、下两册,按主题分为十四个单元。每一单元分两个小节,每一小节由两篇课文构成,这两个小节在语体上独立,在主题上相互联系,有利于学生系统学习语言。
2. **课文的构成**。Text One 和 Text Two 的关系,Text One 为示范性话语材料,供教师学生分析讨论之用。Text Two 主要为学生独立学习之用。题材、体裁、难易程度基本一致,这便于学生模仿学习,建构相应话语,形成相应图式。

Text One 由焦点关注(Focal Consideration)、研究问题(Research Questions)、课文正文(text)、预习助手(Preview Assistant)、参考要点(Referential Points)、巩固练习(Consolidation Work)、短文写作(write a composition)和拓展延伸(Further Development)五个部分构成。
- **焦点关注 (Focal Consideration)**:结合"语言能力、认知能力、自主学习能力、创新能力"四位一体的教学培养目标,设计本小节重点、难点,帮助学生理解和实现学习目标。焦点关注注重引导学生养成语篇鉴赏以及批判性思维能力。
- **调研问题(Research Questions)**:依据课文内容为学生设计课前研究问题,或以任务的形式采用小组研究,撰写研究报告,以利于学生理解课文内涵,文章体裁,主题思想,同时也培养学生搜集、归纳信息的能力、表达思想的能力以及团队协作精神。

- 预习助手(Preview Assistant):注重词汇短语学习。紧扣大纲要求,对重点词汇及短语进行集中注解,同时对一些极为重要的简单词汇进行复现式列出,以提醒学生注意这些词汇的灵活运用。
- 巩固练习(Consolidation Work):注重灵活运用。该项练习注重词汇短语填空练习、派生词汇练习、释义练习、修辞手段识别等,同时也关照TEM-8考试特点,设置有人文知识练习和校对练习。
- 短文写作(Write a Composition):注重学生自由表达。这一练习主要结合课文主题,让学生进行相应思考,把思考所得整理成文。短文写作既是学生"读"的总结,又是学生进行深度"说"的最好准备。
- 拓展延伸(Further Development):在课文内容的基础上拓展相关学科信息。可以问题或任务的形式通过学生交流,教师点评等形式进行讨论分析,拓展学生心智,或采用小组研究,撰写报告等形式延伸课堂内容。

Text Two 主要为学生独立学习之用。题材、体裁、难易程度与 Text One 基本一致,便于学生模仿学习,建构相应话语,形成相应图式。其构成包括:课文正文(text)、自学助手(Independent Study Assistant)、参考要点(Referential Points)、自测练习(Self-test)等。

本教程为英语专业本科高年级阶段的精读教材,也可作为非英语专业学生、英语爱好者达到四级、六级水平后,进一步提高英语语言能力、发展言语能力的精读教材。

本教程的编写并非一朝一夕之事,而是多所高校高年级英语教学队伍长期智慧的结晶。本教程从四川外语学院国家精品课程的实践中来,经过了相当一段时间的考验。本教程的编写者正值中年或"后中年",他们长期工作在英语专业高级英语教学的第一线,比较了解学生的需要。《英语综合高级教程》(上)的编写作者:第一单元,刘玉梅;第二单元,谢琳;第三单元,阚哲华;第四单元,黄四宏;第五单元,肖肃;第六单元,钟毅;第七单元,杨志亭。《英语综合高级教程》(下)的编写作者:第八单元,杜世洪;第九单元,王奇;第十单元,何武;第十一单元,陈喜荣;第十二单元,詹宏伟;第十三单元,肖燕;第十四单元,姜孟。由肖肃对全书进行统一审稿和加工整理。

本教程在编写过程中,参考了不少来自国内外包括杂志、书籍、互联网等的相关资料,在此向作者表示衷心的感谢。

同时,我们还要感谢总主编胡壮麟先生给予的悉心指导,感谢北京大学出版社外语编辑部,特别是张冰主任和李颖编辑,为此书的出版所做的大量的辛勤的工作。

当然,由于一些暂时无法克服的困难以及编者水平有限,本教程仍然存在不少问题。为此,全体编者诚恳希望使用本书的教师和学生多提宝贵意见,以便我们进一步修正、完善。

《英语综合高级教程》编写组

Unit One	Emotion			1
	Section A	Text One	The Woman in the Kitchen	1
		Text Two	A Memoir of Father and Son	13
	Section B	Text One	On Affection	21
		Text Two	On the Nature of Love	32

Unit Two	Literature			41
	Section A	Text One	The Tell-Tale Heart	41
		Text Two	Colonel Cathcart	51
	Section B	Text One	Hills Like White Elephants	59
		Text Two	A Tree, A Rock, A Cloud	69

Unit There	Biography			80
	Section A	Text One	Honor Under Cruel Circumstances	80
		Text Two	Bill Gates Goes Back to School	92
	Section B	Text One	Martin Luther King	101
		Text Two	Nelson Rolihlahla Mandela	113

Unit Four	Public Speaking			124
	Section A	Text One	Radio Broadcast on the German Invasion of Russia	124
		Text Two	40th Anniversary of D-Day Address	136
	Section B	Text One	Harvard Commencement Address	145
		Text Two	Address to the 2005 World Summit United Nations Headquarters	156

Unit Five	Education			166
	Section A	Text One	Education as a Necessity of Life	166
		Text Two	The Use of Leisure	177
	Section B	Text One	Is Rock Music Ruining Education?	185
		Text Two	Literary Study among the Ruins	196

Unit Six Man and Nature **206**
    Section A   Text One   The Obligation to Endure 206
                    Text Two   The Good Earth 216
    Section B   Text One   The Story of an Eyewitness: 226
                              The San Francisco Earthquake
                    Text Two   Dam Brea 236

Unit Seven Science and Technology **246**
    Section A   Text One   The Tale of Albert Einstein's "Greatest Blunder" 246
                    Text Two   Cosmology and 21st-Century Culture 259
    Section B   Text One   A Century of Science 269
                    Text Two   Is Science Evil? 280

Unit 1

Emotion

Section A

Text One The Woman in the Kitchen

Focal Consideration

This article is of the familiar style with the purpose to reflect on the details of everyday life, a reflection shaped and tailored to provide insights into larger truths of the world that the writer sees and understands. In this section, concentration is required for the following discussions:

1. the features of the familiar style;
2. what transitions the author uses to hook up the story of the three stoves, what revelations each tale of the three stoves brings out and what characters are revealed about the mother in each tale;
3. in what ways the author describes his mother as blessing those to call her daughter, sister, wife and mother (in Paragraph 1) and in what ways the stove "stands for simplicity, courage, grace and service (in Paragraph 50)" and "the woman in the kitchen."

Research Questions

Think about the following questions and discuss them with your group members.

1. Who is Dorothea Lange? How is she related to the woman in the kitchen?
2. What is indicated in the title "The Woman in the Kitchen"? What is the purpose of putting the author's realization of his mother at the beginning of the essay?
3. What is true love and how is it found? Which quality of true love is most important to you? State your reasons.
4. What would probably influence your decisions in choosing a life partner? In what ways do your parents contribute to your ideal image?
5. When in a dilemma of love and career, which will you probably give up? State your reasons.

The Woman in the Kitchen

By Gary Allen Sledge

1 My mother looked like a photograph by Dorothea Lange, one of those Depression-era children pinned against a backdrop of bare boards and a denuded landscape. She was fragile boned, with eyes deep and dark as if bruised by sorrow. Yet I realize today, ten years after her death, what uncommon courage she possessed. What pioneer strength she had to transform a life that others would call ordinary into something wonderful for those of us blessed to call her daughter, sister, wife and mother.

2 She never let us look down. Though her own life was filled with harsh circumstances, she believed that the future would be better as soundly as she believed in God. She showed us this conviction daily, and yet the earliest tale I heard her tell about herself was of a little girl who had to give up what she loved best. This is the first story in my mother's "Tale of Three Stoves."

3 "Joanna," her mother said in Hungarian. "You must choose. You can take only one toy with you. There is no room."

4 The girl is eight, maybe nine, and thin as a waif. She is deliberating with great seriousness. "Yes, Mama."

5 Her brother and older sister, running in and out of the plain clapboard cabin, are ecstatic because tomorrow the train will take them away from these West Virginia hills forever.

6 Her brother, John, comes into the kitchen carrying Father's shotgun. He puts it behind the front door so he won't forget it. "Hurry up, little goose," he tells Joanna, who is studying a rag doll and a black cast-iron toy stove.

7 They are her only real toys, and she loves them dearly. They were bought by her father, one each for the last two Christmases. Now she is allowed only one, because the family is carrying everything they own to California, and will be charged by the weight.

8 The year is 1929, and the town they are leaving is Monclo. There, a village of Hungarians work in the coal mines at the end of a railroad line, where the train cannot turn around and has to back up to leave.

9 It is a world I can barely imagine. It is not merely that there was no TV or telephones. Hers was a world of singular things. One pair of shoes, one kind of cereal, one pencil, one schoolbook, one winter coat. It was a world where alternatives were few, choices crucial, and loss a fearful possibility. "Which one did you choose, Mommy?" I used to ask, even after I knew the story.

10 "The doll."

11 "Because you loved it best?"

12 "No, because the stove was heavier and I was afraid there wouldn't be room for things my mother needed to take. I loved the stove best."

13 "What did you do with it?"

14 "The night before we left, we stayed with neighbors, the Demjens. Mary was just my age and my best friend. We used to play together, baking mud pies on my stove. I thought she would take good care of it. So I gave it to her." Mother held out both hands, reenacting the mythic transfer.

15 "And Uncle John left the shotgun behind the door and got a spanking, right?"

16 "Right."

17 She told me these and other stories to teach me the survival skills of self-denial, so I would never fear want. But she also fed me Cream of Wheat, cabbage rolls and a wondrous banquet of books and the Bible, so I would never feel empty. Her Biblical hero was Joseph, who rose from the pit to the pinnacle because he learned how to serve.

18 For three years, while my father was fighting in the Pacific, she raised me alone. It was during this long isolation that she wrote down the story of the stove for her old friend Mary, and as a family keepsake. She wrote with a No.2 pencil on brown grocery bags because paper was scarce during the war.

19 When my father returned, he and a couple of other ambitious young men borrowed money to buy a small stand of timber on a range of hills above the Russian River on the northern California coast. Together, they went into logging.

20 My mother and I went along. It was an ideal situation for a boy of six. We slept in Army-surplus tents and used a two-holer dug behind a thicket of pine. On the opposite side of the camp was a shed where blasting caps and dynamite were stored. I was forever warned to stay away...but forever tantalized by the danger. I played under the six-foot circular saw blade, and heard the whack of the ax into the thick hide of redwood, the dying thunder crack of great trees, and the roar of the diesel tractor belching black smoke. But while I climbed trees and played in the rushing stream, my mother cooked for half a dozen lumberjacks on a Coleman stove, carried water up 57 steep steps from the stream for drinking and washing, and pressed work shirts with flatirons heated in wood-fire coals.

21 I can still see her, a lock of hair loosed from a red kerchief, scrubbing a blackened pot with sand. Or baking potatoes among the pulsing embers in the open pit. Once, my father was paid for an order of redwood with cases of Army-surplus Spam, and for months my mother turned it into breakfast, lunch and dinner in a hundred disguises.

22 For the four years that they struggled on that ridge, my mother created a magic realm for a child. In the evenings she and I would walk out to the knoll and watch the does bring their fawns to drink at our stream. She supplied the commentary to our lives. "Remember the night the mountain lion jumped over the tent?" "Remember how it rained for a week and the cots sank in the mud?" "Remember when you got tick fever?"

23 My father had the right idea. California was throwing up tract houses by the thousands. But the larger mills in the area used threats and extortion to run the little ones out of business. It was a plan that was born to fail, I suppose. And with it, to a certain extent, my parents' youthful expectations failed. My father went to work in the postwar factories that grew up along the San Joaquin River. It was an important sacrifice for both

of them. It meant the displacement of their dreams to assure a future for me and my newly born brother, Robert. It never occurred to them to duck this responsibility. They did what they had to do. Which brings me to the story of my mother's second stove.

24   One morning Mother was cooking outdoors on the Coleman, which sat on a plank table under a tree. The gas tank must have been pumped up too high, because the flames shot several feet in the air. A low-hanging tree limb caught fire. Gasoline must have leaked; the table ignited. A burning branch fell in the dry grass, and the fire spread.

25   "Get back! Run for help!" she called to me. But I couldn't move. What if the fire reached the dynamite shed? I stood there with a cup of water and toothbrush in my hand, feeling cowardly and useless. Mother was 95 pounds dripping wet, but she heaved shovelful after shovelful of dirt on the growing wall of flames. I was afraid the gasoline would explode and she would disappear in a ball of fire. But she kept throwing dirt on the table and stove, and finally the fire went out.

26   Afterward she came to kiss me on the cheek, marked by dried toothpaste. Only then did her fear and relief express themselves. It was the only time I saw her cry.

27   When I was old enough to go to school, she and I moved to Antioch while my father stayed on the mountain. She rented two rooms in a tumbledown, century-old house by the river for $10 a month.

28   There was 50 feet between us and the water, and the Southern Pacific railroad cut right through them. In the late afternoons, we'd take a walk along the tracks. My mother had an abiding love for perspectives. Tops of hills, ocean shores and riverbanks were her natural habitat. We'd sit on the huge stones of the levee and she'd tell me stories about the freighters churning upriver to Sacramento. Sometimes a crewman would come to the rail and wave. "That man probably breathed the air of China or walked the shores of the Philippines," she'd say, "where there are palm tree jungles and butterflies big as kites."

29   Some Sundays we visited my grandmother who lived on the outskirts of town, where the ancient sea-bottom hills rolled up to the flanks of Mount Diablo, one of the highest peaks in the Coast Range. Mother and I would climb the first ridge and look over the town and the San Joaquin Delta.

30   There was something in her demeanor at such times that said: One day this will be all yours. Since she had little to give me, she gave me the world. It was about that time I began to view her as a forlorn creature, one of those maidens imprisoned in some dark tower, or toiling unobserved in the kitchens and ignoring patriarch.

31   I remember her now at a church dinner, with the third stove that marks her story. I was a teenager, already making my own way, self-satisfied with my prospects for which she and my father had sacrificed so much. Suddenly I caught one of those glimpses of adult reality that come to the young as a special revelation.

32   It was a "Church Luau," and the menu was pineapple this and coconut that and egg foo yong. I was a youth representative at the head table, sitting with the pastor and the church leaders. I went into the kitchen to get more to eat. It was jammed with jostling, sweating ladies, and there, working at the hot six-burner stove, was my mother, face

steamed and flush, turning a mess of eggs in a long cake pan. Somehow, with that callow reaction known primarily to teen-agers, it embarrassed me to see her toiling away there. I tiptoed back outside.

33   After dinner, the men and women at the head table had their places cleared, and the minister began his announcements. "First, let's bring out those ladies who made all this possible."

34   There was a round of applause. A hesitant line of women came out. Mother, last of all, was the tiniest one, standing closest to the door. Again it shocked me to realize that my mother—who was everything in my eyes—was not one of those who sat up front on the dais, but was one who served in the kitchen.

35   Why was she never rightly rewarded or recognized? I felt a curious mixture of resentment for the leaders and yet a new appreciation for this woman who, all her life, had given herself away. Counting herself not worthy to sit at the head, she served. The minister was more right than he knew: she was, for me, "one of those ladies who made everything possible."

36   She never had the opportunity to turn her dreams into something entirely her own. Her story was written out on paper bags with a No. 2 pencil, and never saw print. But because of the wealth of imagination she poured into us, my brother and I had the benefit of love, security and the rewards that she and my father squeezed from their livelihood.

37   I went to college, married and moved to New York. In a very short while, Mother got sick. It was an auto-immune disease. Her liver was rebelling against itself.

38   A few years before she died, she planned a trip to New York to see us. Then she began to dream. Maybe she could make a bigger trip of it. Go back to West Virginia. It would be the first time in nearly 50 years she would see her native hills. A quick exchange of letters with her old childhood friend Mary Demjen arranged everything.

39   The reunion completed a circle for my mother. There was cake and coffee, white linen and old silver, and table talk about people and places gone by. The two women lingered, like playmates reluctant to give up their enjoyments in the late-afternoon sun.

40   As they were about to part, Mary pretended to remember something. She went into the other room and brought out a small box wrapped in white paper.

41   My mother made small protests, expecting some local memento of this wonderful occasion. But as she unfolded the paper, her hands began to tremble. A shape out of memory revealed itself. A small black stove. It still had the little burner lids and a skillet to cook mud pies.

42   Her eyes filled with tears, but her face was radiant. "Mary, you didn't forget," she said softly. "It's just as I remembered it. What I always wanted."

43   "My mother kept it all these years," Mary said graciously. "You know how mothers are."

44   The two grown women cried in one another's arms.

45   It's difficult to know what counts in this world. Most of us count credits, honors, dollars. But at the bulging center of midlife, I am beginning to see that the things that

really matter take place not in the board rooms, but in the kitchens of the world. Memory, imagination, love are some of those things. Service to God and the ones we love is another.

46 I once asked my mother, "If you could have anything you ever wanted, what would you ask for?"

47 "Nothing," she said, touching my head in that teasing sort of common benediction mothers give to inquisitive children. "I have you, Rob, Dad. I have everything."

48 At the time, I didn't believe her. Now I have two children of my own, and I finally know.

49 I have a mental snapshot: my mother in her last months sitting outside in the sun, her swollen legs propped up on a pillow. Her chair is sinking into the wet grass. Her head, covered with a floppy red hat, is nodding down. But nearby, almost within reach, on the concrete walk which sparkles in the afternoon sun, is a small black stove with little burner lids, and a skillet for cooking mud pies.

50 My brother, Robert, has it now. It sits in a place of honor, on a shelf in the sun porch of his home in Oakland. It stands for simplicity, courage, grace and service. It stands for the woman in the kitchen.

Preview Assistance

1. **pin** *v.*   to fasten, join, or secure with a pin; to hold fast or immobile; to attach or hang
2. **backdrop** *n.*   backcloth, a large painted cloth hung across the rear of a stage; background
3. **denude** *v.*   to strip of all covering; to make bare or naked; to lay bare by erosion
4. **transform into**   to change in character or condition into; to convert; to change radically in composition or structure into
5. **waif** *n.*   a stray helpless person or animal; homeless child
6. **deliberate** *v.*   to think about carefully
7. **clapboard** *n.*   a wooden board
8. **shotgun** *n.*   a gun fired from the shoulder, usually having two barrels and firing shot especially to kill birds
9. **reenact** *v.*   to act or perform again; to repeat or reconstruct the actions of (an earlier event or incident)
10. **pinnacle** *n.*   peak; highest point; summit; top
11. **keepsake** *n.* souvenir; gift, usually small and often not very costly, that is kept in memory of the giver or previous owner
12. **logging** *n.*   work of cutting down forest trees for timber
13. **thicket** *n.*   bushes; shrubs; mass of trees; undergrowth
14. **dynamite** *n.*   powerful explosive used in blasting and mining
15. **tantalize** *v.*   to tease or torment (a person or an animal) by the sight of sth that is desired but cannot be reached
16. **belch** *v.*   to send out gas from an opening or a funnel; to gush sth
17. **lumberjack** *n.*   esp. in the US and Canada a person who cuts down trees for wood
18. **flatiron** *n.*   iron that can be heated to smooth clothes, etc.
19. **ember** *n.*   ash; small piece of burning or glowing wood or coal in a dying fire
20. **fawn** *n.*   young deer less than a year old

21. **cot** *n.* a small bed for a child, usually with movable sides so that the child cannot fall out
22. **extortion** *n.* obtaining money or something by force or threats
23. **habitat** *n.* the natural home of a plant or animal
24. **levee** *n.* (US) embankment built to protect land from a river in flood
25. **demeanor** *n.* way of behaving; conduct
26. **forlorn** *adj.* lonely and unhappy; uncared for; wretched, eg. forlorn hope
27. **patriarch** *n.* male head of a family or tribe
28. **jostle** *v.* to push roughly against (sb) usually in a crowd
29. **callow** *adj.* inexperienced; unfledged
30. **bulging** *adj.* swelling outward
31. **inquisitive** *adj.* fond of inquiring into other people's affairs
32. **benediction** *n.* blessing
33. **snapshot** *n.* photograph (usually one taken quickly with a hand-held camera)
34. **floppy** *adj.* soft and falling loosely
35. **ignite** *v.* to (cause sth to) catch fire

Referential Points

Dorothea Lange (1895—1965) US journalist and portrait photographer, who documented the change on the homefront, especially among ethnic groups and workers uprooted by the war.

the Depression-era refers to the Great Depression which took place from 1929 to 1933. It followed the collapse of the Stock Market in the US in 1929. Many banks closed down and many shops shut down too. In 1933, 17 million people lost their jobs. Agriculture got worse for the products found no market. Plenty of "extra" products were destroyed.

Army-surplus also called military surplus which are goods, usually material that are sold at public auction when no longer needed by the military. Entrepreneurs often buy these goods and resell them at surplus stores. Military surplus rarely includes weapons or munitions, though they are occasionally found in such stores. Usually the goods sold by the military are clothing, equipment, and tools of a generally useful nature. The largest seller of military surplus in the world is Liquidity Services, Inc., which operates two subsidiaries, Government Liquidation, LLC and Liquidity Services Ltd., which sell military surplus under contracts with the U.S. Department of Defense and the UK Ministry of Defense respectively.

Spam a brand name for chopped or minced ham, spiced, cooked, sold tinned in the form of a loaf, and usually eaten cold.

West Virginia bordered by Ohio, Pennsylvania and Maryland on the north and by Virginia on the south. On the east, the state borders Pennsylvania, Maryland and Virginia, and on the west it is bordered by Ohio and Kentucky. It is the only state in the nation located entirely within the Appalachian Mountain range. The state's nickname is the Mountain State, and West Virginia features some of the most rugged land with heavily forested mountains which hide caverns and underground streams in the United States.

Bible The word Bible is derived from the Greek biblia, meaning "books," and refers to the sacred writings of Judaism and Christianity. The Bible consists of two parts. The first part, called the Old Testament by Christians, consists of the sacred writings of the Jewish people and was written originally in Hebrew, except for some portions in Aramaic. The second part, called the New Testament, was composed in Greek and records the story of Jesus and the beginnings of Christianity. Translated in whole or in part into more than 1,500 languages, the Bible is the most widely distributed book in the world. Its influence on history and culture, including literature and the other arts, is incalculable.

tick fever an acute viral infection transmitted by the bite of a tick or any of various febrile diseases transmitted by ticks, such as Rocky Mountain spotted fever and Texas fever. Tick refers to any of various types of these small parasitic insects that suck blood.

Joseph one of the heroes of the patriarchal narratives of the Book of Genesis. He is presented as the favored son of Jacob and Rachel, sold as a boy into slavery by his brothers, who were jealous of Joseph's dreams and of his coat of many colors given him by Jacob. In Egypt, Joseph gained a position of authority in the household of his master, Potiphar, and was later imprisoned on the false accusations of Potiphar's wife. He was released after interpreting Pharaoh's dream of the lean and fat cows. Pharaoh renamed him Zaphnath-paaneah and took him into favor. Joseph's recognition of his brothers in the famine years when he was governor over Egypt is a famous scene. His wife was Asenath, an Egyptian, and their sons Manasseh and Ephraim were eponymous ancestors of two of the 12 tribes of Israel. The Joseph saga bridges the era of the patriarchs in Canaan and the Hebrews in Egypt.

Cream of Wheat a hot breakfast cereal invented in 1893 by wheat millers in Grand Forks, North Dakota. The cereal is currently manufactured and sold by Kraft Foods. It is similar in texture to grits, but made with farina (ground wheat) instead of ground corn.

auto-immune disease Auto-immune diseases are chronic degenerative and/or inflammatory conditions that result from abnormal immune reactions to compounds absorbed from the environment. Autoimmune diseases are typically considered as connective tissue diseases.

tract house one of numerous houses of similar or complementary design constructed on a tract of land.

blasting cap a small explosive device that generally creates a small explosion that triggers the larger explosion in the dynamite itself.

Spam a canned meat product made by the Hormel Foods Corporation. It has gained a peculiar infamy, along with something of a place in pop culture, and has even entered into folklore and urban legend. Spam is produced in (among other places) Austin, Minnesota, USA (aka *Spam Town USA*). The labeled ingredients in the original variety of Spam are chopped pork shoulder meat with ham meat added salt, water, sugar, and sodium nitrite. Introduced on July 5 1937, the name "Spam" was chosen in the 1930s when the product, whose original name—"Hormel SpicedHam"—was far less memorable, began to lose market share. The name was chosen from multiple entries in a naming contest. A Hormel official once stated that the original meaning of the name spam was "Shoulder of Pork and hAM." According to writer Marguerite Patten in *Spam—The Cookbook*, the name was suggested by Kenneth Daigneau, an actor and the brother of a Hormel vice president. The current official explanation is that the name is a syllabic abbreviation of "SPiced hAM," and that the originator was given a $100 prize for coming up with the name. Many jocular backronyms have been devised, such as "Spare-Parts-Already-Minced," "Something Posing as Meat," and "Specially Processed Artificial Meat."

Coleman a brand name for a cooking instrument.

Antioch a city in California state, an area surrounded by rivers, creeks and open space.

circular saw blade the flat cutting part of a sharpened saw in a circular shape.

diesel tractor also called diesel fuel or diesel oil, referring to a type of heavy oil used instead of petrol used in the diesel engines in tractors.

mountain lion a large powerful wild cat (Felis concolor) of mountainous regions of the

Western Hemisphere, chiefly in western U.S., having an unmarked tawny body; also called catamount, mountain cat; or called panther, puma; or called regionally cougar, painter. Unlike most other desert animals, mountain lions are active during the daytime.

Sacramento   the capital city of California, founded in 1849, and the oldest incorporated city in California.

palm tree   sorts of tree growing in warm climates, with no braches and a mass of large wide leaves at the top.

Church Luau   an elaborate Hawaiian religious feast featuring traditional foods and entertainment.

Egg Foo Yong   also spelled egg fooyung, egg foo yong, egg fu yung, or egg furong. It is a Chinese-American dish made by combining eggs with various foods such as bean, sprouts, water, chestnuts, scallions, ham, chicken or pork. Small, pancake-size portions are poured into a skillet and fried until golden brown. Egg foo yong can also be made in one large round. It is sometimes topped with a sauce of chicken broth, soy sauce and various seasonings.

Consolidation Work

I. Fill in the blanks with the words and expressions provided, making some change when necessary.

transform	denude	floppy	make protests	abiding	prop up
realm	pulse	displace	tantalize	transfer	isolation
deliberate	catch a glimpse of		inquisitive		

1. This friend was different from any other friend they had brought home. She had short stumpy legs and long _____ ears, with a fawn-colored coat and tiny freckles sprinkled across her muzzle.
2. More serious, probably, was the extensive deforestation carried out by neolithic farmers from around 8000 BC onwards: a deforestation which, for example, _____ Scotland in the centuries before the Romans came.
3. But today I want to talk to you—the young people of a great university—about the future, about our future together, and how we can _____ human life on this planet if we bring as much wisdom and curiosity to each other as we bring to our scholarly pursuits.
4. These inspiring structures can _____ and evoke emotions not normally associated with mega structures.
5. In the first place they may want to do no more than ensure that the Constitution is not altered casually or carelessly or by subterfuge or implication; they may want to secure that this important document is not lightly tampered with, but solemnly, with due notice and _____, consciously amended.
6. They fear the new practice could unleash new plagues, by _____ obscure pig pathogens into the human population.
7. The airplane made many more places available for development as resorts, including places that were quite _____.

Unit 1

8. A distant lark, invisible in blue light, was flooding the vast _____ of the sky with glorious song.
9. The smell that rose from the saucepan was so powerful and exciting that they shut the window lest anybody outside should notice it and become _____.
10. Almost the _____ of the town's heart could be felt as the work went forward night and day, pumping the materials of war up the railway arteries to the two battle fronts.
11. Visitors will find a country of dramatic landscapes, pure air, clean water and an _____ respect for tradition.
12. British Telecom is now exploiting its freedom as a commercial company to the full, where Telekom has to hand over all its hard-earned profits to _____ a grossly overmanned and inefficient postal and post-bank service.
13. The last greenish tints had left the sky and a slight chill was _____ the balminess of spring.
14. Children stuck their noses near his windowpane to _____ the weirdo, and a few saw a flash of messy hair atop a pallid face.
15. Rice farmers in central Java have _____ about the compensation they were offered after their village was flooded by a dam development.

II. Use the appropriate form of the words given in the brackets to fill in the blanks.

1. There is little enough of that in the outback and one must search for _____ modes of expression, perhaps among the varieties of modern art which have taught us to see in different ways. (alternate)
2. Under the window was the stained porcelain sink with its wooden draining board, _____ marks on the wood showing evidence of forgotten cigarettes. (black)
3. To make the implications even more salient, this special series includes two _____ from two leading scholars in the field of school psychology. (comment)
4. Once again the prearranged _____ of the clappers alone burst forth; the public, a little out of their depth, sat waiting. (applaud)
5. He was bare-headed, and the leaves had tossed his _____ curls and tangled all their gilded threads. (rebel)
6. Nurse Cramer had a cute nose and a _____, blooming complexion dotted with fetching sprays of adorable freckles. (radiance)
7. Mansell said that recent bone surgery on his left foot to fix a _____ injury was sore occasionally, but should not prove a hindrance. (linger)
8. I'd grown up in a food-phobic home, too, so the idea of producing a serious dessert seemed _____ forbidden and very difficult. (tantalize)
9. A number of studies have clearly documented the adverse impact that snowmobiles have on wildlife. These include _____ from referred habitats, elevated stress and increased use of scarce energy reserves in order to flee from the approaching snowmobiles. (displace)
10. Daisy's face, tipped sideways beneath a three-cornered lavender hat, looked out at me with a bright _____ smile. (ecstasy)

III. Paraphrase the following sentences taken from the text.

1. She was fragile boned, with eyes deep and dark as if bruised by sorrow.

Section A

2. She told me these and other stories to teach me the survival skills of self-denial, so I would never fear want.
3. Mother was 95 pounds dripping wet, but she heaved shovelful after shovelful of dirt on the growing wall of flames.
4. It was about that time I began to view her as a forlorn creature, one of those maidens imprisoned in some dark tower, or toiling unobserved in the kitchens and ignoring patriarch.
5. I caught one of those glimpses of adult reality that come to the young as a special revelation.

IV. Test your general knowledge.

1. The teddy bear is a stuffed toy bear. It is named after President _____.
   A. Abraham Lincoln   B. Theodore Roosevelt
   C. Benjamin Franklin   D. Thomas Jefferson
2. America is often referred to as _____.
   A. the melting pot   B. John Bull
   C. The country of maple leaves D. the country riding on the sheep's back
3. Which of the following is typical of puritan life?
   A. extravagant   B. indulgent
   C. flexible moral or religious principles D. self-denial
4. Which of the following loan words is borrowed from Chinese?
   A. reservoir   B. tea
   C. tsar   D. powwow
5. The Gettysburg Address is a speech by _____ and is one of the most well known speeches in the history of the United States.
   A. Thomas Jefferson   B. Bill Clinton
   C. George Washington   D. Abraham Lincoln
6. Which of the following work is John Milton's masterpiece?
   A. *Songs of Innocence*   B. *Paradise Lost*
   C. *The Rime of the Ancient Mariner* D. *When You Are Old*
7. Which of the following state is not a part of the New England region?
   A. Massachusetts state.   B. Connecticut state.
   C. New Hampshire state.   D. Oklahoma state.
8. The Statue of Liberty, dedicated on October 28, 1886, is a monument commemorating the centennial of the signing of the United States Declaration of Independence, given to the United States by the people of _____.
   A. France   B. Italy
   C. Afghanistan   D. Canada
9. The capital of Massachusetts is _____.
   A. Detroit   B. New York
   C. Houston   D. Boston
10. The capital of Canada is _____.
    A. Vancouver   B. Victoria
    C. Ottawa   D. Toronto
11. The Three Unities, formulated by Renaissance dramatists, are the unities of the following elements but _____.
    A. place   B. time
    C. action   D. character

Unit 1

12. The Hundred Years' War between Britain and France was fought _____.
    A. from 1327 to 1453 B. from 1337 to 1453
    C. from 1347 to 1453 D. from 1357 to 1453
13. *The Old Man and the Sea* is one of the great works by _____.
    A. Jack London B. Charles Dickens
    C. Samuel Coleridge D. Ernest Hemingway
14. _____ was the home of the Lake Poets William Wordsworth, Samuel Taylor, Coleridge and Robert Southey of the 19th century Britain.
    A. Lough Neagh B. Windermere
    C. Lake District D. Coniston Water
15. Washington D.C. is named after _____.
    A. the U.S. President George Washington
    B. Christopher Columbus
    C. both George Washington and Christopher Columbus
    D. none of them

V. Proofread the following passage.

I was now five, and still I showed no real sign of intelligence. I showed some apparent interest in things except with my toes—more especially those of my left foot. Although my natural habits were clean, I could not aid myself, and in this respect my father took care of me. I used to lie on my back all the time in the kitchen or, on bright warm days, out in the garden, a little bundle of crooked muscles and twisted nerves, surrounded with a family that loved me and hoped me and that made me part of their own warmth and humanity. I was lonely, imprisoned in a world of my own, only unable to communicate with others, cut off, separated from them as though a glass wall stood between my existence and them, thrusting me beyond the sphere of their lives and activities. I longed to run about and play with the rest, but I was unable to break loose with my bondage.

1. _____
2. _____
3. _____
4. _____
5. _____
6. _____

Then, suddenly, it happened! In a moment everything is changed, my future life molded into a definite shape, my mother's faith in me rewarding, and her secret fear changed into open triumph.

7. _____
8. _____

It happened so quickly, so simply after all the years of waiting and uncertainty, that I can see and feel the whole scene as if it happened last week. It was the afternoon of a cold, gray December day. The streets outside glistened with snow, the white sparking flakes stuck and melted on the windowpanes and hunged on the boughs of the trees like molten silver. The wind howled dismally, whipped up little whirling columns of snow that rose and fell at every fresh gust. And over all, the dull, murky sky stretched like a dark canopy, a vast infinity of grayness.

9. _____
10. _____

VI. Write a composition.

Read the story again and summarize the tales of the three stoves in the essay in your own words. Do some research on how parental warmth and affection influences a child's character-formation and growth. Share your findings with your group members and work out a report accordingly.

Further Development

1. Reflections on the details of everyday life are helpful for us to discover significance in persons, places, ideas, or experiences that we didn't know of ourselves. In "The Woman in the Kitchen," the author's reflection helps him to move towards larger truths about his mother and his own life. Reflect upon your own life to discover significance in persons, places, ideas, or experiences that you neglect before and then tailor them into an essay.
2. It is said that parental love shapes a child's mind and heart. Conduct a survey to find out how parental love influences children's later happiness, emotional intelligence and self-esteem and finish a report of about 1,000 words.

Section A Text Two

A Memoir of Father and Son

By Adam Hochschild

1   All through my childhood, people would say, "your father? Oh, of course, what a wonderful man. I know him well." But our language is deficient. There should be two words, one for knowing a person as a friend or colleague, the other for knowing someone as a parent. I never felt that way about my mother. For her, one word would do. But Father was different. Others seemed only to see a man of wit, learning and great integrity, someone who generously bestowed gifts and invitations on his wide circle of friends, a world traveler who spoke five languages, a businessman of unusual liberalism, and a self-taught expert on Adirondack history: in his spare time, he wrote a prize-winning book on the subject, and founded a fine museum. A somewhat uncomfortable man, true; shy, a bit distant, sometimes ill at ease, but still, how lucky you must be to have had him, as a father! And besides, Adam, you had everything: Houses, chauffeurs, maids, money—the whole world was yours. How can you complain?

2   All this was true. But there was another side to Father, whose weight only I seemed to feel. Where I most experienced it, even amid all the pleasures of Eagle Nest, was in the recurring outbursts of his intense disapproval. These did not come daily, perhaps not even weekly. But they affected me so powerfully that they colored the time between them as well.

3   Like bouts of a disease, these episodes always followed a set pattern. First was my crime itself. To begin with, Father disapproved of some of my hobbies, tentative as they were, thinking them frivolous. I used to listen to an old shortwave radio that had been his, even, which I found discarded in the attic and fixed up—until one day he solemnly said he thought I was spending too much time on this. Or sometimes my wrongdoing involved my being, in his eyes, too uncommunicative and not polite enough with a guest. Or it was the sin of not being grateful enough for something—not thanking someone with enough enthusiasm, say, for a present I really didn't want. But there was a treacherously narrow path between being not animated enough and being too much so. For, most often of all, my crime would be that of taking too much space, of talking too much: at the table, in a carload of family and guests on route to Eagle Nest, anywhere he and I were together with other people.

4   It was so easy to slip into this pattern, particularly if I had been spending time with my mother: To her I was a precocious, entertaining child; she was endless delighted by my thoughts and questions and fantasies. When I was with her, there was no such thing as talking too much. I could chatter for hours and she loved it. But when Father and a group of his friends were there, I was surrounded by an invisible trip wire. I could never figure out in advance just where it lay, until suddenly I knew, with a sinking-stomach despair, that I had inadvertently stumbled against it. I would be talking and giggling, happily taking center stage, when I would see the moment at which Father found me guilty: a slight pursing of the lips, a raising of one eyebrow, a cryptic word or two which I knew would be expanded on later: "Adam! I think that's enough for now."

5   At this point some valve opened inside me, and I felt a pervasive dread traveling through my whole body as if I had taken some powerful, swift-acting drug. Sometimes I tried desperately to win back his approval by being very affectionate, but it never worked.

6   The next stage, a few hours later, was confirmation of the verdict. Often I overheard my parents talking, when they thought I was asleep, or when I hid behind a tree as they walked from the Club House to the Cottage. Always Father would bring up the subject:

7   "I thought Adam was talking too much at the table today."

8   "Yes, you're probably right, Harold," my mother would agree. She never reprimanded me herself and never seemed angry with me. But she always agreed with him.

9   "I think I better speak to him about it," Father sad.

10   "Yes, dear."

11   I went to sleep subdued. When I woke the next morning, it seemed lie a normal day until, a few moments after opening my eyes, I remembered. In the morning would come the announcement. He would say: "Adam, can I see you in my study at two o'clock, please?" Or perhaps he would be upstairs working, and my mother would be the messenger. "Father wants to see you at two o'clock. O.K., dear?"

12   The morning was long. I could not concentrate when I read. I was cloaked in dread.

13   Two o'clock. I waited until maybe 2:03, but to wait any long would risk the

additional crime of being late, something guaranteed at any time to make Father upset. I knocked on his door.

14   "Come in!"

15   "Hi...you wanted... to talk...to me?"

16   "Sit down, Adam. I'll be with you in a moment."

17   A shuffle of papers: a signature on a document; at last Father put the work in his desk aside, and leaned back in his chair.

18   "I've been meaning to talk to you, Adam, about something that happened yesterday. I thought it was quite rude when you were talking so much at the table last night. Couldn't you see it was preventing people from having their own conversation?"

19   It didn't last long. No speaking. No beating. No raised voice. Maybe just two or three minutes of talk, Father's words were always carefully chosen, balanced, never casual, as if each phrase had been inspected and been found irrefutable before he permitted it to exit his lips.

20   I couldn't bring myself to look at him. I craved for an earthquake to bring the session to an end, what made it so much worse was that Father was always, it seemed, fully reasonable. He spoke in a voice which carried in it the full weight of his authority, of his wide reputation for morality, a voice whose very quietness contained the expectation of unquestioning obedience.

21   After he had finished whatever he had to say—all of which I had know was coming for perhaps a full twenty-four hours—Father would pause for me to respond. He listened, it might be said, in a distinct tone of voice: His right hand, leathery, mottled, crept up to his face to support his chin with its thumb, while first and second fingers bracketed his mouth, as if holding in his own speech while he heard me out. In a way this was the most frightening moment of all, this careful, alert listening from someone whose entire bearing and role in life was that of a man who expected to be listened to. Of course I never really dared argue; his evidence always seemed convincing.

22   At last, to put the seal on the encounter, Father would say, in words which ostensibly dissipated, but in fact thickened, the cloud that hung over me:

23   "All right? I think you now see what I mean, I won't speak about this incident again."

24   Then he motioned for me to come around behind his desk so we could exchange kisses on the cheek, that gesture between us in which there was always an element of submission: Now it was a sign that I had acknowledged my error and would reform. Our session was over.

25   The impact of one these reprimands echoed in my head for days afterward. Take one such incident; multiply it by a hundred. Add to the picture the fact that I had no brothers or sisters, no allies, no witnesses for the defense. Why did this process seem all the worse for his never raising his voice, never striking me? I think because I therefore had no chance to get angry back; I never doubted that he was merciful and that I was guilty.

26   My tendency automatically to assume my own guilt spread from those sessions in

Unit 1

Father's study over the rest of my life.

27   Once, when I was in seventh grade, my history teacher gave me a book to read and report on to the class—a book about the battles of the Civil War. I still remember it: The cover was blue, with crossed swords and a solder's cap. A few days after he gave it to me, I lost the book. I felt complete panic.

28   "What happened to that special report you were going to give us, Hochschild?"

29   "I'm... working on it, sir."

30   Desperately, I searched everywhere: desk, locker, odd corners of the classroom, my room at home. No book. Days went by. I avoided eye contact with the teacher and slipped out of class as soon as the bell rang so I would never find myself alone with him. At one level of awareness, I knew he was an absentminded man and might well have forgotten about the book. But I still lived in fear that he would remember.

31   I searched again and again. The school year ended. The summer was an idyll of Europe and Eagle Nest, but every few day I would remember the lost book, wince, and feel my day darken.

32   Then, one day in the fall, I was studying in the school library. I looked up for a moment, and there, on a shelf at my eye level, was the missing book, crossed swords and all. It had been a library book, and somebody must have seen it lying about and simply returned it. This was the one place I had never thought to look. A vast rush of relief swept through me; I could see the sky again.

Independent Study Assistant

I. Words and Expressions

1. **deficient** adj.   incomplete; inadequate
2. **integrity** n.   quality of being honest and morally upright
3. **bestow** v.   to present sth as a gift (to sb); to confer
4. **chauffeur** n.   person employed to drive a car, esp for sb rich or important
5. **weight** n.   (degree of) importance, seriousness or influence
6. **bout** n.   attack (of an illness)
7. **episode** n.   (description of an) event occurring as part of a long series of events as in a novel, one's life, etc
8. **tentative** adj.   done, said, etc to test sth; hesitant or exploratory; not definite or decisive
9. **frivolous** adj.   (of activities) silly or wasteful
10. **treacherous** adv.   dangerous, esp. when seeming to be safe
11. **animated** adj.   lively
12. **precocious** adj.   (of a child) having developed certain abilities at an earlier age than usual
13. **inadvertent** adj.   (of actions) done without thinking or not deliberately
14. **cryptic** adj.   with a meaning that is hidden or not easily understood; mysterious
15. **verdict** n.   decision reached by a jury on a question of fact in a law case
16. **reprimand** v.   to rebuke sb (for a fault, etc), esp. officially
17. **subdued** adj.   not very loud, intense, noticeable, etc.
18. **shuffle** n.   rearrangement; reordering
19. **irrefutable** adj.   that cannot be proved false

20. **crave** *v.*   to have a strong desire for sth
21. **mottled** *adj.*   marked with patches of different colours without a regular pattern
22. **bearing** *n.*   behaviour
23. **ostensible** *adj.*   stated (as a reason, etc) though perhaps not true; apparent
24. **dissipate** *v.*   to (cause sth to) scatter or vanish
25. **motion** *v.*   to indicate to sb by a gesture
26. **submission** *n.*   state in which one accepts the superior power of sb else
27. **automatic** *adj.*   (of actions) done without thinking, esp. from habit or routine; unconscious
28. **absentminded** *adj.*   with one's mind on other things; forgetful
29. **idyll** *n.*   short piece of poetry or prose that describes a happy and peaceful scene or event, esp. of country life

II. Referential Points

Adam Hochschild   born in New York City. As a college student, he spent a summer working on an anti-government newspaper in South Africa and subsequently worked briefly as a civil rights worker in Mississippi in 1964. Both were politically pivotal experiences about which he would later write in his book *Finding the Trapdoor*. He later was part of the movement against the Vietnam War, and, after several years as a daily newspaper reporter, worked as a writer and editor for the leftwing Ramparts magazine. *Hochschild's first book was a memoir, Half the Way Home: a Memoir of Father and Son* (1986), in which he described the difficult relationship he had with his father. His later books include *The Mirror at Midnight: a South African Journey* (1990), *The Unquiet Ghost: Russians Remember Stalin* (1994), ect. Hochschild's books have been translated into twelve languages.

A Memoir of Father and Son   extracted from *Half the Way Home: a Memoir of Father and Son* (1986).

Adirondack   a place in the northeastern part of New York, a tourist attraction famous for its mountainous beauty. In history, Algonquian and Mohawk Indians used this place for hunting and travel, but they had no settlements in the area. It was merely labeled as "Deer Hunting County" in the 18th century and got its formal name in 1837. Part of the French and Indian War (1754—1763) was played out in some part of this area.

Trip wire   or tripwire, a passive triggering mechanism, usually/originally employed for military purposes, although its principle has been used since prehistory for methods of trapping game.

Eagle Nest   Eagle Nest is a mountain located 2 miles south of Maggie Valley, North Carolina in Haywood County. It is part of the Plott Balsams, a range of the Appalachian Mountains, and less than a mile south of North Eagle Nest Mountain, a higher mountain which used to be called Mount Junaluska and is the highest mountain overlooking Lake Junaluska from the west.

Civil War   The American Civil War (1861—1865), also known as the War Between the States, was a civil war in the United States of America. The war was fought between the Confederacy supported by eleven Southern slave states and the Union supported by all the free states and the five border slave states. It formally started on April 12, 1861, when Confederate forces attacked a US military installation at Fort Sumter in South Carolina and ended after Lee surrendered to Grant at Appomattox Court House on April 9, 1865. The American Civil War was the deadliest war in American history, resulting in the deaths of 620,000 soldiers and an undetermined number of civilian casualties. It legally abolished slavery in the United States, restored the Union and strengthened the role of the federal government. The social, political, economic and racial issues of the war decisively shaped the reconstruction era that lasted to 1877, and brought changes that helped make the country a united superpower.

Idyll　An idyll is a short poem, descriptive of rustic life, named after Theocritus' short pastoral poems, the Idylls. Later imitators included the Roman poets Virgil and Catullus, Italian poet Leopardi, and the English poet Alfred, Lord Tennyson.

the Club House　Club is a kind of association. In the western countries, there are a variety of clubs. For instance, a country club is a private club and it may have a closed membership. Most offer a variety of recreational sports facilities and are located in city outskirts or rural areas. It will usually provide hospitality to members and guests such as a restaurant and bar, and may also provide suitable accommodations for host-catered events, such as weddings. Activities may include, for example, any of golf, tennis, swimming or traditional polo. An athletic club is a similar but is usually located within an urban setting, which may exclude certain activities such as golf or traditional polo. On the other hand, rock climbing practice or a martial art may be available. A service club exists for voluntary or charitable activities.

III. Questions for Comprehension

1. What sort of relationship does Hochschild have with his father? How is the relationship revealed through his language? Does his description win your sympathy? Is he overdramatizing his situation?
2. Do you attribute the unhealthiness of the relationship primarily to the father or the son? What long-term consequences would you expect to result from the relationship described here?
3. Of what social standing is the Hochschild family? Do you think that this has anything to do with the father's behavior?
4. The narrator tells us his father was "A somewhat uncomfortable man, true; shy, a bit distant, sometimes ill at ease," but later he thought "but still, how lucky you must be to have had him, as a father!" Why? What does this indicate?
5. What was the process that the narrator felt the weight of his father?

Self-test

I. Fill in the blanks with the words and expressions provided, making some change when necessary.

episode	bestow on	bout	crave for	treacherous	animate
irrefutable	automatic	dissipate	on route to	inadvertent	tentative
all the worse	cryptic	ill at ease			

1. Her boys had a very reverent remembrance of a most vehement chastisement she once _____ them.

Section A

2. He was disconcertingly reasonable, speaking with a calm even tone, but looked awkwardly stiff in his chair, _____ with being interviewed.
3. When exposed to toxic chemicals, children are not miniature adults. Even small doses can affect their sensitive developing bodies, leaving them vulnerable to allergies and frequent _____ of infections, colds, and even behavior challenges.
4. At least 3,000 local people are "chronically homeless," which means they have long durations or repeated _____ of homelessness.
5. She looked at him anxiously to see how he would take the _____ remark, but he was only astonished.
6. By dawn the weather had abated though the sea was still angry, its surface broken into dark ridges and furrows by a _____ high wind.
7. There is no need to give a prolonged detail of the _____ conversation which ensued during the rest of the banquet.
8. When we visit today's art museums, however, we are often confused. Many museums are altering their buildings, revamping their programs, and spurning the very idea of aesthetic quality _____ the goal of becoming "pluralistic institutions." Yet the result has been anything but pluralistic.
9. What worries many is the potential for violence when a thief and homeowner _____ cross paths.
10. Many caterpillars are _____ colored to match their host plants, making it difficult for birds and reptiles to spot them.
11. She scoured her journals and piles of old snapshots, looking for some spark of memory, _____ indications of love and happiness.
12. One question which will be examined is to what extent increased computerisation and _____ of various aspects of the business might be part of such a strategy.
13. The dog looked foolish, and probably felt so; but there was resentment in his heart, too, and a _____ revenge.
14. The destructive effects of anxiety can sometimes be _____ with reward, undoing the formation of a bad habit, especially if the horse has otherwise been kindly treated.
15. Later that year, he tripped and fell on a boat dock, breaking his left wrist. To make matters _____, his dog chased a deer across his driveway, knocking him off his bicycle.

II. Use the appropriate form of the words given in the brackets to fill in the blanks.

1. A new study by the American Society of Civil Engineers estimates that one-third of major U.S. roads are in poor or mediocre condition, and 26 percent of the nation's bridges are either structurally _____ or functionally obsolete. (deficiency)
2. He asked for streamlined procedures to sift out _____ applications and allow individual board members greater discretion to reduce the number of full hearings. (frivolity)
3. Children's disobedience may include running away from home, disruptive classroom behaviour at school and _____ indulgence in alcohol or addictive substances. (precocity)
4. The fog seemed to hold the moonlight in suspension, rendering it more _____ than in clear air. (pervasion)
5. The _____ decree Emancipation Proclamation, came as a great beacon light of

hope to millions of Negro slaves who had been seared in the flames of withering injustice. (moment)

6. In the political and military conflicts which have arisen as a result of these inequalities, education is not merely a _____ of war but is part of the battlefield. (casual)
7. He is determined to get _____ results, and demands that his associates be similarly single-minded. (authority)
8. The Indian females, when girls, are usually mild and _____, with musical tones, pleasant voices, and merry laughs. (submission)
9. Rather than giving dry statistics about eating disorders, these experts try to present imagery that is _____ and pair it with fragments of personal stories. (impact)
10. Realizing that there was nothing more she could get out of him, she signed that divorce settlement mechanically, and the man gave an exaggerated sigh of _____. (relieve)

III. Translate the short paragraph into Chinese.

Love never just happens. Love needs time to deepen one another's affection, to appreciate one another's differences, to share one another's joys and griefs. This will finally help love to grow. Love also needs the ability to let go so as to grow. Still love needs words to make it real by exchanging our feelings. Otherwise, quarrels can't be resolved, resentment can't come to the surface. We are likely to deprive others of the knowledge of our love and ourselves of the joy that comes from expressing it. Love is not a single act, but a climate in which we live, a lifetime venture in which we are always learning, discovering, growing. It is not destroyed by a single failure, or won by a single caress. Love is a climate—a climate of the heart.

IV. Analyze difficult sentences.

1. But when Father and a group of his friends were there, I was surrounded by an invisible trip wire. I could never figure out in advance just where it lay, until suddenly I knew, with a sinking-stomach despair, that I had inadvertently stumbled against it.
2. He spoke in a voice which carried in it the full weight of his authority, of his wide reputation for morality, a voice whose very quietness contained the expectation of unquestioning obedience.
3. His right hand, leathery, mottled, crept up to his face to support his chin with its thumb, while first and second fingers bracketed his mouth, as if holding in his own speech while he heard me out.
4. In a way this was the most frightening moment of all, this careful, alert listening from someone whose entire bearing and role in life was that of a man who expected to be listened to.

V. Proofread the following passage.

The psychological causes of unhappiness, it is clear, are most and various. But all have something in common. The typical unhappy man is one who, has been deprived in youth of some normal satisfaction, has come to value this one kind of satisfaction more than any other, and has therefore given his life a one-sided direction, together with a quite undue emphasis upon the achievement as opposing to the activities connected with it. There is, however, a

1. _____
2. _____
3. _____
4. _____

further development which is very common in the present day. A
man may feel so completely thwarted that he seeks no form of
satisfaction, and only distraction and oblivion. He then becomes   5. _____
a devotee of "pleasure." That is to say he seeks to make life
bear by becoming less alive. Drunkenness, for example, is   6. _____
temporary suicide; the happiness that it brings is merely positive, 7. _____
a momentary cessation of unhappiness. The narcissist and the
megalomaniac believe that happiness is possible, though they may
adopt mistaken means of achieving it; but the man who seeks
intoxication, in whatever form, had given up hope except   8. _____
in oblivion. In his case, the first thing to be done is to persuade
him that happiness is desirable. Men who are unhappy, like men
who sleep badly, are always proud of the fact. Perhaps their pride is
like that of the fox who had lost their tail; if so, the way to cure it   9. _____
is to point out to them how they can grow a new tail. Very few
men, I believe, will deliberately choose unhappiness if they see
a way of being happy. I do not deny that such men exist, but they
are not sufficient numerous to be important. I shall therefore   10. _____
assume that the reader would rather be happy than unhappy.
Whether I can help him to realize this wish, I do not know; but
at any rate the attempt can do no harm.

VI. Write a composition.

It is natural for young people to be critical of their parents at times and to blame them for most of the misunderstandings between them. They have always complained, more or less justly, that their parents are out of touch with modern ways; that they are possessive and dominant; that they do not trust their children to deal with crises; that they talk too much about certain problems and that they have no sense of humor, at least in parent-child relationships. How do you understand this issue? What may help to develop a better parent-child relationship? Think about the above questions and discuss with your group members, and then finish a report of about 800 words.

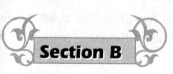

Section B

Text One   On Affection

Focal Consideration

Affection is a "disposition or state of mind or body," which is popularly used to denote a feeling or type of love, amounting to more than goodwill or friendship. Russell's essay, which is profound and thought-provoking, has added to this topic some philosophical overtones. In this

Unit 1

section, concentration is required for the following discussions:
1. the strategies that Russell uses in this essay to expose each type of affection and develop his theme, for instance, exemplification, comparison and contrast, causal analysis and logic reasoning;
2. what virtues true affection calls for;
3. the difference between the familiar style and the prosaic style.

Research Questions

1. Do some research on Bertrand Russell's life, career and publications, and work out a research report and share it with other groups.
2. How many types of affection are mentioned in this essay? What is Russell's attitude towards them?
3. According to Russell, what role does a feeling of security play in a person's life? Why does Russell say "it is affection received, not affection given, that causes this sense of security...?" Do you agree or not? State your opinion.
4. What is the difference between the affection which is received and the affection which is to be given? In what ways does affection achieve its best possibilities? Do you agree with Russell? State your reasons.
5. What are the obstacles to the blossoming of reciprocal affection? What consequences will they lead to in the pursuit of true happiness?

On Affection

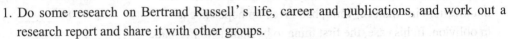

By Bertrand Russell

1   Most men and women sink into a timid despair if they feel themselves unloved. As a rule, the lives of such people become extremely self-centered, and the absence of affection gives them a sense of insecurity from which they instinctively seek to escape by allowing habit to dominate their lives utterly and completely. For those who make themselves the slaves of unvarying routine are generally actuated by fear of a cold outer world, and by the feeling that they will not bump into it if they walk along the same paths that they have walked along on previous days.

2   Those who face life with a feeling of security are much happier than those who face it with a feeling of insecurity, at any rate so long as their sense of security does not lead them to disaster. And in a very great many cases, though not in all, a sense of security will itself help a man to escape dangers to which another would succumb. If you are walking over a chasm on a narrow plank, you are much more likely to fall if you feel fear than if you do not. And the same thing applies to the conduct of life. The fearless man may, of course, meet with sudden disaster, but it is likely that he will pass unscathed through many difficult situations in which a timid man would come to grief. This useful kind of

self-confidence has, of course, innumerable forms. One man is confident on mountains, another on the sea, and yet another in the air. But general self-confidence towards life comes more than anything else from being accustomed to receive as much of the right sort of affection as one has need for.

3   It is affection received, not affection given, that causes this sense of security, though it arises most of all from affection which is reciprocal. Strictly speaking, it is not only affection but also admiration that has this effect. Persons whose trade is to secure public admiration, such as actors, preachers, speakers, and politicians, come to depend more and more upon applause. When they receive their due meed of public approbation their life is full of zest; when they do not, they become discontented and self-centred. The diffused goodwill of a multitude does for them what is done for others by the more concentrated affection of the few. The child whose parents are fond of him accepts their affection as a law of nature. He does not think very much about it, although it is of great importance to his happiness. He thinks about the world, about the adventures that come his way and the more marvelous adventures that will come his way when he is grown up. But behind all these external interests there is the feeling that he will be protected from disaster by parental affection. The child from whom for any reason parental affection is withdrawn is likely to become timid and unadventurous, filled with fears and self-pity, and no longer able to meet the world in a mood of gay exploration. Such a child may set to work at a surprisingly early age to meditate on life and death and human destiny. He becomes an introvert, melancholy at first, but seeking ultimately the unreal consolations of some system of philosophy or theology. The world is a higgledy-piggledy place, containing things pleasant and things unpleasant in haphazard sequence. And the desire to make an intelligible system or pattern out of it is at bottom an outcome of fear, in fact a kind of agoraphobia or dread of open spaces. Within the four walls of his library the timid student feels safe. If he can persuade himself that the universe is equally tidy, he can feel almost equally safe when he has to venture forth into the streets. Such a man, if he had received more affection, would have feared the real world less, and would not have had to invent an ideal world to take its place in his beliefs.

4   By no means all affection, however, has this effect in encouraging adventurousness. The affection given must be itself robust rather than timid, desiring excellence even more than safety on the part of its object, though of course by no means indifferent to safety. The timid mother or nurse, who is perpetually warning children against disasters that may occur, who thinks that every dog will bite and that every cow is a bull, may produce in them a timidity equal to her own, and may cause them to feel that they are never safe except in her immediate neighborhood. To the unduly possessive mother this feeling on the part of a child may be agreeable: she may desire his dependence upon herself more than his capacity to cope with the world. In that case her child is probably worse off in the long run than he would be if he were not loved at all. The habits of mind formed in early years are likely to persist through life. Many people when they fall in love look for a little

haven of refuge from the world, where they can be sure of being admired when they are not admirable, and praised when they are not praiseworthy. To many men home is a refuge from the truth: it is their fear and their timidities that make them enjoy a companionship in which these feelings are put to rest. They seek from their wives what they obtained formerly from an unwise mother, and yet they are surprised if their wives regard them as grown-up children.

5   To define the best kind of affection is not altogether easy, since clearly there will be some protective element in it. We do not feel indifferent to the hurts of people whom we love. I think, however, that apprehension of misfortune, as opposed to sympathy with a misfortune that has actually occurred, should play as small a part as possible in affection. Fear for others is only a shade better than fear for ourselves. Moreover it is very often a camouflage for possessiveness. It is hoped that by rousing their fears a more complete empire over them can be obtained. This, of course, is one of the reasons why men have liked timid women, since by protecting them they came to own them. The amount of solicitude of which a person can be the object without damage to himself depends upon his character: a person who is hardy and adventurous can endure a great deal without damage, whereas a timid person should be encouraged to expect little in this way.

6   Affection received has a twofold function. We have spoken of it hitherto in connection with security, but in adult life it has an even more essential biological purpose, namely parenthood. To be unable to inspire sex love is a grave misfortune to any man or woman, since it deprives him or her of the greatest joys that life has to offer. This deprivation is almost sure sooner or later to destroy zest and produce introversion. Very frequently, however, previous misfortunes in childhood have produced defects of character which are the cause of failure to obtain love in later years. This is perhaps more true where men are concerned than it is as regards women, for on the whole women tend to love men for their character while men tend to love women for their appearance. In this respect, it must be said, men show themselves the inferiors of women, for the qualities that men find pleasing in women are on the whole less desirable than those that women find pleasing in men. I am not at all sure, however, that it is easier to acquire a good character than a good appearance; at any rate, the steps necessary for the latter are better understood and more readily pursued by women than are the steps necessary for the former by men.

7   We have been speaking hitherto of the affection of which a person is the object. I wish now to speak of the affection that a person gives. This also is of two different kinds, one of which is perhaps the most important expression of a zest for life, while the other is an expression of fear. The former seems to me wholly admirable, while the latter is at best a consolation. If you are sailing in a ship on a fine day along a beautiful coast, you admire the coast and feel pleasure in it. This pleasure is one derived entirely from looking outward, and has nothing to do with any desperate need of your own. If, on the other hand, your ship is wrecked and you swim towards the coast, you acquire for it a new kind of love: it represents security against the waves, and its beauty or ugliness becomes an

unimportant matter. The better sort of affection corresponds to the feeling of the man whose ship is secure, the less excellent sort corresponds to that of the ship-wrecked swimmer. The first of these kinds of affection is only possible in so far as a man feels safe, or at any rate is indifferent to such dangers as beset him; the latter kind, on the contrary, is caused by the feeling of insecurity. The feeling caused by insecurity is much more subjective and self-centred than the other, since the loved person is valued for services rendered, not for intrinsic qualities. I do not, however, wish to suggest that this kind of affection has no legitimate part to play in life. In fact, almost all real affection contains something of both kinds in combination, and in so far as affection does really cure the sense of insecurity it sets a man free to feel again that interest in the world which in moments of danger and fear is obscured. But while recognising the part that such affection has to play in life, we must still hold that it is less excellent than the other kind, since it depends upon fear, and fear is an evil, and also because it is more self-centred. In the best kind of affection a man hopes for a new happiness rather than for escape from an old unhappiness.

8 The best type of affection is reciprocally life-giving; each receives affection with joy and gives it without effort, and each finds the whole world more interesting in consequence of the existence of this reciprocal happiness. There is, however, another kind, by no means uncommon, in which one person sucks the vitality of the other, one receives what the other gives, but gives almost nothing in return. Some very vital people belong to bloodsucking type. They extract the vitality from one victim after another, but while they prosper and grow interesting, those upon whom they live grow pale and dim and dull. Such people use others as means to their own ends, and never consider them as ends in themselves. Fundamentally they are not interested in those whom for the moment they think they love; they are interested only in the stimulus to their own activities, perhaps of a quite impersonal sort. Evidently this springs from some defect in their nature, but it is one not altogether easy either to diagnose or to cure. It is a characteristic frequently associated with great ambition, and is rooted, I should say, in an unduly one-sided view of what makes human happiness. Affection in the sense of a genuine reciprocal interest of two persons in each other, not solely as means to each other's good, but rather as a combination having a common good, is one of the most important elements of real happiness, and the man whose ego is so enclosed within steel walls that this enlargement of it is impossible misses the best that life has to offer, however successful he may be in his career. Ambition which excludes affection from its purview is generally the result of some kind of anger or hatred against the human race, produced by unhappiness in youth, by injustices in latter life, or by any of the causes which lead to persecution mania. A too powerful ego is a prison from which a man must escape if he is to enjoy the world to the full. A capacity for genuine affection is one of the marks of the man who has escaped from this prison of self. To receive affection is by no means enough; affection which is received should liberate the affection which is to be given, and only where both exist in equal measure does affection achieve its best possibilities.

Unit 1

9   Obstacles, psychological and social, to the blossoming of reciprocal affection are a grave evil, from which the world has always suffered and still suffers. People are slow to give admiration for fear it should be misplaced; they are slow to bestow affection for fear that they should be made to suffer either by the person upon whom they bestow it or by a censorious world. Caution is enjoined both in the name of morality and in the name of worldly wisdom, with the result that generosity and adventurousness are discouraged where the affections are concerned. All this tends to produce timidity and anger against mankind, since many people miss throughout life what is really a fundamental need, and to nine out of ten an indispensable condition of a happy and expansive attitude towards the world. It is not to be supposed that those who are what is called immoral are in this respect superior to those who are not. In sex relations there is very often almost nothing that can be called real affection; not infrequently there is even a fundamental hostility. Each is trying not to give himself or herself away, each is preserving fundamental loneliness, each remains intact and therefore unfructified. In such experiences there is no fundamental value. I do not say that they should be carefully avoided, since the steps necessary to this end would be likely to interfere also with the occasions where a more valuable and profound affection could grow up. But I do say that the only sex relations that have real value are those in which there is no reticence and in which the whole personality of both becomes merged in a new collective personality. Of all forms of caution, caution in love is perhaps the most fatal to true happiness.

Preview Assistance

1. **sink** *v.*   to fall; to decline; to drop; to submerge
2. **dominate** *v.*   to control; to rule
3. **unvarying** *adj.*   constant; perpetual; lasting; permanent
4. **bump into**   to encounter; to come across
5. **succumb** *v.*   to yield; to give way; to be subject to; to die; to decrease
6. **unscathed** *adj.*   not injured or hurt; unharmed
7. **come to grief** (Colloq.)   to meet with calamity, accident, defeat, ruin, etc., causing grief; to turn out badly
8. **reciprocal** *adj.*   mutual; given and received in return
    reciprocate *(v.)* / reciprocity *(n.)* / reciprocally *(adv.)*
9. **come one's way**   to come across; to meet
10. **withdraw** *v.*   to retreat; to abandon; to quit; to fall back
11. **robust** *adj.*   vigorous; mighty; potent; powerful; sturdy; strong
12. **perpetually** *adv.*   constantly; eternally; unceasingly; permanently; endlessly
    perpetual *(adj.)* / perpetuate *(v.)*
13. **in the long run**   finally; in the end; at last
14. **hitherto**   until now
15. **consolation** *n.*   comfort; relief
    console *(v.)* / consolable *(adj.)* / consolatory *(adj.)* / consolation prize

16. **at best** taking the most hopeful view

  at one's / its best: in the best state or form

17. **desperate** *adj.* frantic; hopeless; wild; reckless. Here it means "imminent or immediate"

18. **in so far as** insomuch as; since; to such an extent or degree as

19. **beset** *v.* to surround on all sides; to threaten; to trouble constantly; to vex; to annoy

20. **spring from** to stem from; to come from

21. **enclose** *v.* to inclose; to fence; to surround; to envelop; to contain

22. **purview** *n.* extent; range; scope

23. **censorious** *adj.* severely critical; tending to find faults in people or things

  censure *(v.)* / censorship *(n.)*

24. **enjoin** *v.* to impose (an action or prohibition) on sb; to order

25. **reticence** *n.* reticent *(adj.)* not revealing one's thoughts or feelings easily; reserved

26. **fatal** *adj.* resulting in someone's death; having a very bad effect, especially making someone fail or stop what they are doing

27. **preserve** *v.* to keep a particular quality, feature, etc.; to keep sth in its original state in good condition

28. **morality** *n.* principles concerning right and wrong or good and bad behaviour; the degree to which sth is right or wrong, good or bad, etc. according to moral principles

29. **bestow** *v.* to give sth to sb, especially to show how much they are respected

30. **timidity** *n.* not having courage or confidence

31. **intact** *adj.* complete and not damaged

32. **indispensable** *adj.* essential; too important to be without

Referential Points

  "On Affection" a piece of essay extracted from *The Conquest of Happiness*, written by Bertrand Arthur William Russell in 1930. The book falls neatly into two halves: the causes of unhappiness and the causes of happiness. The first half includes 9 articles: What Makes People Unhappy?, Byronic Unhappiness, Competition, Boredom and Excitement, Fatigue, Envy, The Sense of Sin, Persecution Mania, Fear of Public Opinion. The second half includes 8 articles: Is Happiness Still Possible?, Zest, Affection, The Family, Work, Impersonal Interests, Effort and Resignation, The Happy Man. The first chapter What Makes People Unhappy? can be viewed as an introduction to the book, and the final chapter The Happy Man as a conclusion.

  Bertrand Arthur William Russell (1872—1970) British philosopher, logician, essayist, and social critic, one of the greatest thinkers of the twentieth century, best known for his work in mathematical logic and analytic philosophy. Along with Moore, Frege, Russell is generally recognized as one of the founders of analytic philosophy. Along with Kurt Gödel, he is also regularly credited with being one of the two most important logicians of the twentieth century. Over the course of his long career, Russell made significant contributions, not just to logic and philosophy, but to a broad range of other subjects including education, history, political theory and religious studies. In addition, many of his writings on a wide variety of topics in both the sciences and the humanities have influenced generations of general readers. He was awarded the Nobel Prize in Literature in 1950. Noted for his many spirited anti-war and anti-nuclear protests, Russell also remained a prominent public figure until his death at the age of 97.

Unit 1

Ego a term used by Sigmund Freud (1856—1940) to analyze the structure of the mind. Freud is creator of Psychoanalysis—"Analyzing the Mind." He proposed the Freudian Structure of the Mind: id, ego, superego. The id (Das Es) refers to the original core of an individual's personality, which is primitive and unchanging because it has no contact with the outside world (primarily unconscious). The id wants its impulses satisfied and does not care how it happens. The ego (Das Ich) refers to self-identity which arises out of the id. The ego controls voluntary motion and self-preservation behaviors. The ego must satisfy the impulsive demands of the id while obeying the standards of the superego. The superego (Das Uber Ich) develops out of the ego, serving as the conscience, which can develop both standards of conduct and inhibitions on prohibited behavior. The superego can be both conscious and unconscious.

subject and object two terms often used in philosophy. A subject is a being which has subjective experiences, subject consciousness or a relationship with another entity (or object). A subject is an observer or perceiver and an object is a thing observed or perceived.

persecution mania According to Russell, in its more extreme forms persecution mania is a recognized form of insanity. Some people imagine that others wish to kill them, or imprison them, or to do them some other grave injury. Often the wish to protect themselves against imaginary persecutors leads them into acts of violence which make it necessary to restrain their liberty.

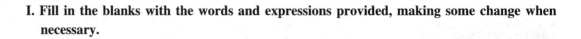

Consolidation Work

I. Fill in the blanks with the words and expressions provided, making some change when necessary.

security	censorious	come to grief	misplace
consequence	psychology	perpetually	zest reciprocal
spring from	vitality	inspire	restraint come one's way
bump into			

1. While the Internet is inherently _____, businesses still need to preserve the privacy of data as it travels over the network.
2. Some of Thomas Hardy's leading characters are relentlessly pursued by fate; they _____ through sequences of evil coincidences no less remarkable than those by means of which the earlier heroes of Evangelical literature had been saved.
3. The _____ of this fray was that the woman who was really the thief made off and got clearly away in the crowd.
4. Rainbows are beautiful, because they have paid the cost of _____; Tears are salty, because they are filled with the bitters of life.
5. It enables men to construct an intellectual vision of a new world, and it preserves the _____ of life by the suggestion of satisfying purpose.
6. The metacognitive strategies were manifested through the use of self-instruction strategies of the students. Strategic planning guided students' efforts to control learning and was affected _____ by feedback from these efforts.
7. Education is the foundation of success, Robert said. Just as scholastic skills are _____

important, so are financial skills and communication skills.
8. Armstrong's theory of life was very simple. He appreciated what had _____, worked hard for it, and what he wanted to do, he always said, was make people happy.
9. It was not compunction that _____ him, but an inherent sense of economy that objected to seeing time and effort and pain squandered uselessly.
10. Children at this stage spend a lot of their waking hours moving around and tend to _____ things as they do.
11. Language is not merely a neutral medium for the conveying of information; it can trigger emotional responses which may _____ prejudice, stereotyping or misunderstanding.
12. The correspondence between Marx and Engels was for me not a theoretical one, but a _____ revelation.
13. The theologians used to assert that the proof of the divine _____ of the Bible rested on miracles and prophecies.
14. Every effort has been made to keep this list accurate. However, _____ and misspelling of names and unreported errors in the catalogs may have resulted in some inaccuracies.
15. The waitress brought our food on a tray, giving me a moderately _____ glance as she set the chowder, sweet potatoes, and BLT down in front of me.

II. Use the appropriate form of the words given in the brackets to fill in the blanks.
1. If Ms. Mann, herself a playwright of some _____, has bold designs for her theater, she must be holding them in reserve for later endeavors. (adventure)
2. Then, out of pure _____ and fear, he did the only thing he could think of at that moment. (desperate)
3. Around noon Bruce angled the canoe into a back channel, looking for a green island he knew, while she kept her _____ rhythm, dip, dip, the water falling from her paddle in strands. (vary)
4. Voters rarely give lawmakers high marks, so the poll's positive rating is another sign of the public's unusually _____ attitude toward politicians in Washington. (expand)
5. The _____ of the powers and pretensions of government gives administrative law great practical importance, while tax law creates continual problems for business and industry. (large)
6. Richard Baxter saw this as an illustration of the vanity of this life as both rich and poor alike had to stand by helplessly as their houses and all their _____ goods went up in flames before their eyes. (world)
7. In San Diego, the group life with my new friends gradually enticed me out of the stony _____ I had constructed around myself. (enclose)
8. To become like angels, people had to abandon their _____ attachment to worldly things. (possess)
9. Whatever means of training you choose, it is important to listen to as many recordings as possible, as these will provide _____ guidance for you and students. (dispense)
10. An early lesson that may be _____ from both experiences is that building regional partnership capacity is a prerequisite for developing greater cooperation and coordination. (derivation)

Unit 1

III. Paraphrase the following sentences taken from the text.

1. But general self-confidence towards life comes more than anything else from being accustomed to receive as much of the right sort of affection as one has need for.
2. It is a characteristic frequently associated with great ambition, and is rooted, I should say, in an unduly one-sided view of what makes human happiness.
3. Evidently this springs from some defect in their nature, but it is one not altogether easy either to diagnose or to cure.
4. and the man whose ego is so enclosed within steel walls that this enlargement of it is impossible misses the best that life has to offer, however successful he may be in his career.
5. ...affection which is received should liberate the affection which is to be given, and only where both exist in equal measure does affection achieve its best possibilities.

IV. Test your general knowledge.

1. Bertrand Russell is generally recognized as one of the founders of _____.
   A. analytic philosophy   B. hermeneutic philosophy
   C. modern philosophy   D. social philosophy
2. Who founded the psychoanalytic school of psychology?
   A. B. Spinoza.   B. S. Freud.
   C. F. Bacon.   D. J. Locke.
3. _____ is the writer of *Common Sense* and *The Rights of Man*.
   A. William Godwin   B. Thomas Paine
   C. Thomas Jefferson   D. George Washington
4. Which of the following is not written by Percy B. Shelley?
   A. Ode to the West Wind.   B. The Call to Freedom.
   C. Prometheus Unbounded.   D. *Don Juan*.
5. Which of the following is not included in the key figures of the Romantic Movement in British literature?
   A. Lord Byron.   B. Charles Dickens.
   C. Percy Shelley.   D. John Keats.
6. Who is the author of *Thoughts on Man, his Nature, Productions, and Discoveries*?
   A. William Godwin.   B. Mary Wollstonecraft.
   C. John Milton.   D. T. S. Elio.t.
7. *Paradise Lost* is an epic poem in _____.
   A. rhymed verse   B. blank verse
   C. free verse   D. ballad
8. _____ refers to a movement of the working class for realizing the "people's charter" which was about universal suffrage.
   A. The Reform of Bill   B. The Enlightenment
   C. The Chartist Movement   D. The Downing Street Declaration
9. The Norman Conquest happened in _____.
   A. 55 B. C.   B. 1066
   C. 700   D. the 7th century
10. The first woman Prime Minister in British history was _____, who had her administration for two terms from 1979 to 1990.
    A. Diana Spenser   B. Condoleezza Rice

    C. Margaret Thatcher   D. Alice Thomson
11. _____ was signed at the Paris Peace Conference in 1919, according to which Britain took Palestine and Mesopotamia from Turkey and seized a large number of German colonies in Africa and in the Pacific Ocean.
    A. The Townshend Acts   B. The Potsdam Conference
    C. The Warsaw Pact   D. The Treaty of Versailles
12. The British North America Act of 1867 established _____ as a domain.
    A. Australia   B. Canada
    C. New Zealand   D. India
13. _____ is the world's largest exporter of lamb and mutton.
    A. New Zealand   B. Australia
    C. Canada   D. America
14. Who was lauded as the "greatest American humorist of his age," and "the father of American literature"?
    A. William Faulkner.   B. Ralph Waldo Emerson.
    C. Ernest Hemingway.   D. Mark Twain.
15. The term "Father of Waters" is used to refer to _____.
    A. the Amazon River   B. the Mississippi River
    C. the Nile River   D. the Hudson River

V. Proofread the following passage.

One of the chief causes of lack of zest is the feeling that one is unloved, when conversely the feeling of being loved promotes   1. _____
zest more than anything else does. A man may have the feeling of being unloved for a variety of reasons. He may consider himself
such a dreadful person what no one could possibly love him; he   2. _____
may in childhood have had to accustom himself to receiving less love than fell to the share of other children; or he may in fact
be a person who nobody loves. But in this latter event the cause   3. _____
probably lies in a lack of self-confidence owing to early misfortune. 4. _____
The man who feels himself unloved may take various attitudes as a result. He may make desperate efforts to win affection, probably
by means of exceptional acts of kindness. In this, however, he is
very likely to be successful, since the motive of the kindnesses   5. _____
is easily perceived by their beneficiaries, and human nature is so
constructed that it gives affection most ready to those who seem   6. _____
least to demand it. The man, therefore, who endeavours to purchase
affection by benevolent actions become disillusioned by experience   7. _____
of human ingratitude. It never occurs to him that the affection
which he is trying to buy is far more value than the material   8. _____
benefits which he offers as its price, and yet the feeling that this is
so is at the basis of his actions. Another man, observing that he is
unloved, may seek revenge upon the world, neither by stirring up   9. _____
wars and revolutions, or by a pen dipped in gall, like Dean Swift.

This is a heroic reaction to misfortune, requiring a force of character sufficient to enable a man to pit himself on the rest of the world.   10. _____

Further Development

1. Both "The Woman in the Kitchen" and "On Affection" deal with the subject matter of affection, but differ in diction, syntax, style, etc. Compare the two articles in these aspects and finish a report of about 600 words.
2. Both Wells and Russell discussed the obstacles or enemies of love and affection. Do you agree with them? Do some research in the field of philosophy, psychology, literature, or biology, and finish a report on the possible obstacles or enemies of love and affection.

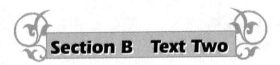
Section B Text Two

On the Nature of Love

By H. G. Wells

1   It has been most convenient to discuss all that might be generalized about conduct first, to put in the common background, the vistas and atmosphere of the scene. But a man's relations are of two orders, and these questions of rule and principle are over and about and round more vivid and immediate interests. A man is not simply a relationship between his individual self and the race, society, the world and God's Purpose. Close about him are persons, friends and enemies and lovers and beloved people. He desires them, lusts after them, craves their affection, needs their presence, abhors them, hates and desires to limit and suppress them. This is for most of us the flesh and blood of life. We go through the noble scene of the world neither alone, nor alone with God, nor serving an undistinguishable multitude, but in a company of individualized people. It is well perhaps to look a little into the factors that make up Love.

2   Love does not seem to me to be a simple elemental thing. It is, as I have already said, one of the vicious tendencies of the human mind to think that whatever can be given a simple name can be abstracted as a single something in a state of quintessential purity. I have pointed out that this is not true of Harmony or Beauty, and that these are synthetic things. You bring together this which is not beautiful and that which is not beautiful, and behold! Beauty! So also Love is, I think, a synthetic thing. One observes this and that, one is interested and stirred; suddenly the metal fuses, the dry bones live! One loves.

3   Almost every interest in one's being may be a factor in the love synthesis. But apart from the overflowing of the parental instinct that makes all that is fine and delicate and young dear to us and to be cherished, there are two main factors that bring us into love

with our fellows. There is first the emotional elements in our nature that arise out of the tribal necessity, out of a fellowship in battle and hunting, drinking and feasting, out of the needs and excitements and delights of those occupations; and there is next the intenser narrower desirings and gratitudes, satisfactions and expectations that come from sexual intercourse. Now both these factors originate in physical needs and consummate in material acts, and it is well to remember that this great growth of love in life roots there, and, it may be, dies when its roots are altogether cut away.

4   At its lowest, love is the mere sharing of, or rather the desire to share, pleasure and excitement, the excitements of conflict or lust or what not. I think that the desire to partake, the desire to merge one's individual identity with another's, remains a necessary element in all personal loves. It is a way out of ourselves, a breaking down of our individual separation, just as hate is an intensification of that. Personal love is the narrow and intense form of that breaking down, just as what I call Salvation is its widest, most extensive form. We cast aside our reserves, our secrecies, our defences; we open ourselves; touches that would be intolerable from common people become a mystery of delight, acts of self-abasement and self-sacrifice are charged with symbolical pleasure. We cannot tell which of us is me, which you. Our imprisoned egoism looks out through this window, forgets its walls, and is for those brief moments released and universal.

5   For most of us the strain of primordial sexual emotion in our loves is very strong. Many men can love only women, many women only men, and some can scarcely love at all without bodily desire. But the love of fellowship is a strong one also, and for many, love is most possible and easy when the thought of physical lovemaking has been banished. Then the lovers will pursue interests together, will work together or journey together. So we have the warm fellowships of men for men and women for women. But even then it may happen that men friends together will talk of women, and women friends of men. Nevertheless we have also the strong and altogether sexless glow of those who have fought well together, or drunk or jested together or hunted a common quarry.

6   Now it seems to me that the Believer must also be a Lover, that he will love as much as he can and as many people as he can, and in many moods and ways. As I have said already, many of those who have taught religion and morality in the past have been neglectful or unduly jealous of the intenser personal loves. They have been, to put it by a figure, urgent upon the road to the ocean. To that they would lead us, though we come to it shivering, fearful and unprepared, and they grudge it that we should strip and plunge into the wayside stream. But all streams, all rivers come from this ocean in the beginning, lead to it in the end.

7   It is the essential fact of love as I conceive it, that it breaks down the boundaries of self. That love is most perfect which does most completely merge its lovers. But no love is altogether perfect, and for most men and women love is no more than a partial and temporary lowering of the barriers that keep them apart. With many, the attraction of love seems always to fall short of what I hold to be its end, it draws people together in the most momentary of self-forgetfulnesses, and for the rest seems rather to enhance their

egotisms and their difference. They are secret from one another even in their embraces. There is a sort of love that is egotistical lust almost regardless of its partner, a sort of love that is mere fleshless pride and vanity at a white heat. There is the love-making that springs from sheer boredom, like a man reading a story-book to fill an hour. These inferior loves seek to accomplish an agreeable act, or they seek the pursuit or glory of a living possession, they aim at gratification or excitement or conquest. True love seeks to be mutual and easy-minded, free of doubts, but these egotistical mockeries of love have always resentment in them and hatred in them and a watchful distrust. Jealousy is the measure of self-love in love.

8   True love is a synthetic thing, an outcome of life, it is not a universal thing. It is the individualized correlative of Salvation; like that it is a synthetic consequence of conflicts and confusions. Many people do not desire or need Salvation, they cannot understand it, much less achieve it; for them chaotic life suffices. So too, many never, save for some rare moment of illumination, desire or feel love. Its happy abandonment, its careless self-giving, these things are mere foolishness to them. But much has been said and sung of faith and love alike, and in their confused greed these things also they desire and parody. So they act worship and make a fine fuss of their devotions. And also they must have a few half-furtive, half-flaunting fallen love-triumphs prowling the secret backstreets of their lives, they know not why.

9   In setting this down be it remembered I am doing my best to tell what is in me because I am trying to put my whole view of life before the reader without any vital omissions. These are difficult matters to explain because they have no clear outlines; one lets in a hard light suddenly upon things that have lurked in warm intimate shadows, dim inner things engendering motives. I am not only telling quasi-secret things but exploring them for myself. They are none the less real and important because they are elusive.

10   True love I think is not simply felt but known. Just as Salvation as I conceive it demands a fine intelligence and mental activity, so love calls to brain and body alike and all one's powers. There is always elaborate thinking and dreaming in love. Love will stir imaginations that have never stirred before.

11   Love may be, and is for the most part, one-sided. It is the going out from oneself that is love, and not the accident of its return. It is the expedition whether it fail or succeed.

12   But an expedition starves that comes to no port. Love always seeks mutuality and grows by the sense of responses, or we should love beautiful inanimate things more passionately than we do. Failing a full return, it makes the most of an inadequate return. Failing a sustained return it welcomes a temporary coincidence. Failing a return it finds support in accepted sacrifices. But it seeks a full return, and the fullness of life has come only to those who, loving, have met the lover.

13   I am trying to be as explicit as possible in thus writing about Love. But the substance in which one works here is emotion that evades definition, poetic flashes and figures of speech are truer than prosaic statements. Body and the most sublimated ecstasy pass into

one another, exchange themselves and elude every net of words we cast.

14   I have put out two ideas of unification and self-devotion, extremes upon a scale one from another; one of these ideas is that devotion to the Purpose in things I have called Salvation; the other that devotion to some other most fitting and satisfying individual which is passionate love, the former extensive as the universe, the latter the intensest thing in life. These, it seems to me, are the boundary and the living capital of the empire of life we rule.

15   All empires need a comprehending boundary, but many have not one capital but many chief cities, and all have cities and towns and villages beyond the capital. It is an impoverished capital that has no dependent towns, and it is a poor love that will not overflow in affection and eager kindly curiosity and sympathy and the search for fresh mutuality. To love is to go living radiantly through the world. To love and be loved is to be fearless of experience and rich in the power to give. Love is a thing to a large extent in its beginnings voluntary and controllable, and at last quite involuntary. It is so hedged about by obligations and consequences, real and artificial, that for the most part I think people are overmuch afraid of it. And also the tradition of sentiment that suggests its forms and guides it in the world about us, is far too strongly exclusive. It is not so much when love is glowing as when it is becoming habitual that it is jealous for itself and others. Lovers a little exhausting their mutual interest find a fillip in an alliance against the world. They bury their talent of understanding and sympathy to return it duly in a clean napkin. They narrow their interest in life lest the other lover should misunderstand their amplitude as disloyalty.

16   Our institutions and social customs seem all to assume a definiteness of preference, a singleness and a limitation of love, which is not psychologically justifiable. People do not, I think, fall naturally into agreement with these assumptions; they train themselves to agreement. They take refuge from experiences that seem to carry with them the risk at least of perplexing situations, in a theory of barred possibilities and locked doors. How far this shy and cultivated irresponsive lovelessness towards the world at large may not carry with it the possibility of compensating intensities, I do not know. Quite equally probable is a starvation of one's emotional nature.

17   The same reasons that make me decide against mere wanton abstinences make me hostile to the common convention of emotional indifference to most of the charming and interesting people one encounters. In pleasing and being pleased, in the mutual interest, the mutual opening out of people to one another, is the key of the door to all sweet and mellow living.

Independent Study Assistance

I. Words and Expressions

1. **abstract** *v.* to remove sth from somewhere; to make a written summary of a book, etc.
2. **quintessential** *adj.* being a perfect example of a particular type of person or thing
3. **behold** *v.* to see or to look at something
4. **overflow** *v.* sth to be so full that the contents go over the sides; to have too many people in it
5. **instinct** *n.* a natural tendency for people and animals to behave in a particular way using the knowledge and abilities that they were born with rather than thought
6. **tribal** *adj.* connected with a tribe or tribes
7. **necessity** *n.* the fact that sth must happen or be done; the need for sth; a thing that you must have and cannot manage without
8. **gratitude** *n.* the feeling of being grateful and wanting to express your thanks
9. **consummate** *adj.* extremely skilled; perfect
10. **partake** *v.* to eat or drink sth especially sth that is offered to you
11. **intensification** *n.* enhancement
12. **abasement** *n.* noun form of abase (*v.*). to behave in a way that shows you accept that someone has complete power over you)
13. **egoism** *n.* to behave in a way that shows you accept that someone has complete power over you
14. **strain** *n.* pressure on sb/sth because they have too much to do or manage, or sth very difficult to deal with; the problems, worry or anxiety that this produces
15. **banish** *v.* to order sb to leave a place, especially a country, as a punishment
16. **quarry** *n.* a place where large amounts of stone, etc. are dug out of the ground
17. **unduly** *adv.* more than you think is reasonable or necessary
18. **shiver** *v.* to shake slightly because you are cold, frightened, excited, etc.
19. **grudge** *n.* not giving enough care or attention to sb/sth
20. **strip** *v.* to take off all or most of your clothes
21. **suffice** *v.* to be enough for sb/sth
22. **parody** *n.* a piece of writing, music, acting, etc. that deliberately copies the style of sb/sth in order to be amusing
23. **furtive** *adj.* a piece of writing, music, acting, etc. that deliberately copies the style of sb/sth in order to be amusing
24. **flaunt** *v.* to show sth you are proud of to other people, in order to impress them
25. **prowl** *v.* to move quietly and carefully around an area, especially when hunting
26. **lurk** *v.* to wait somewhere secretly, especially because you are going to do sth bad or illegal
27. **elude** *v.* to manage to avoid or escape from sb/sth, especially in a clever way

II. Referential Points

Herbert George Wells (1866—1946) an English author, best known for his work in the science fiction genre. He was also a prolific writer in many other genres, including contemporary novels, history, politics and social commentary. Together with Jules Verne, Wells has been referred to as "The Father of Science Fiction." His works include non-fictions, such as *The Fate of Man, Little Wars, The Future in American: A Search After Realities*, ect, and fictions, such as *The Invisible Man, The First Men in the Moon, The Time Machine*, ect, and some short stories and collections.

The Nature of Love extracted from *Some Personal Things in First and Last Things: A Confession of Faith and Rule of Life* which is written by H.G. Wells. This book falls into four separate parts: Metaphysics, Of Belief, Of General Conduct, and Some Personal Things. *First and Last Things* is widely considered to be one of the top 100 greatest books of all time.

Salvation In religion, salvation is the concept that God or other Higher Power, as part of Divine Providence, saves humanity from spiritual death or Eternal Damnation by providing for them an eternal life or afterlife. Salvation may also be called "deliverance" or "redemption" from sin and its effects. The world's religions agree that humanity needs salvation from its present condition. However, they hold irreconcilable positions on what it means from an eternal perspective to become saved, the actual way to get saved, and the resources needed to attain salvation.

III. Questions for Comprehension

1. What is the nature of love according to Wells and what are the factors that make up love?
2. In Wells' view, what are the two main factors that bring us into love with our fellows and where do they come from?
3. Why does the author say "True love is a synthetic thing, an outcome of life, it is not a universal thing"? Do you agree with him or not? State your reasons.
4. Did Russell and Wells suggest how to break down the boundaries of self? If not, provide your own understanding.
5. Compare Wells' definition of true love and Russell's best type of affection.

Self-test

I. Fill in the blanks with the words and expressions provided, making some change when necessary.

vanity	neglect	engender	sublimate	salvation	sustain
animate	chaos	apart from	harmonious	associate	synthetic
flesh	elude	impoverished	trust		

1. A gathering to _____ and promote love, as for the satisfaction of the participants or as a form of social activism.
2. A more realistic concern is that farmland prices will become so high that it will be impossible to _____ owner-operated farms.
3. Down below where he lived was the ignoble, and he wanted to purge himself of the ignoble that had soiled all his days, and to rise to that _____ realm where dwelt the upper classes.
4. Some _____ flavors are safer than natural ones, he noted, adding that some natural toxins occur where preservatives and antioxidants are excluded by consumer demand.
5. If one acquires English without getting to its cultural core, his cultural world will be shabby and _____.

Unit 1

6. From this _____ skyful of crowding flakes the mead and moor momentarily received additional clothing, only to appear momentarily more naked thereby.
7. The hope for national _____, Roosevelt thought, lay in quick action to overcome the menace of national economic collapse.
8. The Fairy palaces burst into _____, before pale morning showed the monstrous serpents of smoke trailing themselves over Coketown.
9. I have given away my whole soul to some one who treats it as if it were a flower to put in his coat, a bit of decoration to charm his _____, an ornament for a summer's day.
10. With strong evidence that the disclosures to date represent only the tip of the iceberg, the State President's claim that a commission of inquiry would create a climate of _____ verges on self-parody.
11. Quite _____ the adverse opinion polls, they were conscious that Britain was in the midst of its second deep recession in little more than a decade.
12. Similarly, white is _____ with purity and peace in the West, and with funerals and death in Asia.
13. The greater the beauty, the greater the loneliness, for at the back of beauty was _____, and at the back of harmony was union.
14. The chap's countenance was yellow and _____, and the dented cheeks had accented his nose to be as high and straight as that of a Greek.
15. Plato first raised these questions and asserted the independence of _____ from religion.

II. Use the appropriate form of the words given in the brackets to fill in the blanks.

1. _____ silence is, of course, the most perfect means of maintaining the powerful integrity of the institutional boundaries against any criticisms. (neglect)
2. Whilst there are no satisfactory measures of capital stock for this sector its capital needs are large and include a substantial proportion of the real but _____ element of human capital. (elude)
3. Getting out of breath he finally desisted and dragged the apparently _____ body on to the settle. (animate)
4. In contrast, the researchers say holding a more _____ view of your loved one means you are less likely to be disappointed, and therefore more satisfied with your marriage. (prose)
5. I have sought love, first, because it brings _____ —so great that I would often have sacrificed all the rest of my life for a few hours of this joy. (ecstatic)
6. A huge slab lies just outside the tomb entrance, part of a stone _____ about 122 centimeters high. (bound)
7. Dora had never received such a gift; she had no finery except her wedding ring. Speechless, she smiled _____ and gathered her son into her arms. (radiance)
8. Praise or blame has but a _____ effect on the man whose love of beauty in the abstract makes him a severe critic on his own works. (moment)
9. Both sides also exchanged views on relevant problems such as the security situation and economic development in Asia, the _____ of Europe, etc. (unify)

10. Every unit of production must enjoy independence as the _____ of centralization if it is to develop more vigorously. (correlate)

III. Translate the short paragraph into Chinese.

This passion hath his floods, in very times of weakness; which are great prosperity, and great adversity; though this latter hath been less observed: both which times kindle love, and make it more fervent, and therefore show it to be the child of folly. They do best, who if they cannot but admit love, yet make it keep quarters; and sever it wholly from their serious affairs, and actions, of life; for if it check once with business, it troubleth men's fortunes, and maketh men, that they can noways be true to their own ends. There is in man's nature, a secret inclination and motion, towards love of others, which if it be not spent upon some one or a few, doth naturally spread itself towards many, and maketh men become humane and charitable; as it is seen sometime in friars.

IV. Analyze difficult sentences.

1. It is a way out of ourselves, a breaking down of our individual separation, just as hate is an intensification of that. Personal love is the narrow and intense form of that breaking down, just as what I call Salvation is its widest, most extensive form.
2. With many, the attraction of love seems always to fall short of what I hold to be its end, it draws people together in the most momentary of self-forgetfulnesses, and for the rest seems rather to enhance their egotisms and their difference.
3. True love is a synthetic thing, an outcome of life, it is not a universal thing.
4. Failing a full return, it makes the most of an inadequate return. Failing a sustained return it welcomes a temporary coincidence. Failing a return it finds support in accepted sacrifices. But it seeks a full return, and the fullness of life has come only to those who, loving, have met the lover.
5. Body and the most sublimated ecstasy pass into one another, exchange themselves and elude every net of words we cast.

V. Proofread the following passage.

The lives of most men are determined by their environment. They
accept the circumstances amid which fate has thrown them
not only with resignation but even with a good will. They   1. _____
are like streetcars running contentedly on their rails and they despise
the sprightly flivver that dashes in and out the traffic and speeds   2. _____
so jaunty across the open country. I respect them; they are good   3. _____
citizens, good husbands, and good fathers, and of course somebody
has to pay the taxes; but I do find them exciting. I am fascinated   4. _____
by the men, few enough in all conscience, who take life in their
own hands and seem to mould it to their own likings. It may be   5. _____
that we have no such thing as free will, but at all events we have
the illusion of it. As a cross-road it does seem to us what we might 6. _____
go either to the right or the left and, the choice once made, it is
easy to see the whole course of the world's history obliged us to   7. _____
take the turning we did.

I never met a more interesting man than Mayhew. He was a
lawyer in Detroit. He was an able and a successful one.
For the time he was thirty-five he had a large and lucrative   8. _____
practice, he had amassed a competence, and he stood on
the threshold of a distinguishing career. He had an acute   9. _____
brain, an attractive personality, and uprightness. There was
no reason why he should not become, financially or politically,
a power in the land. One evening he was sitting in his club with a
group of friends and they were perhaps a little worse (or the better)
for liquor. One of them had recently come from Italy and he told
them of a house he had seen at Capri, a house on the hill,
overlooked the Bay of Naples, with a large and shady garden. He   10. _____
described to them the beauty of the most beautiful island in the
Mediterranean.

VI. Write a composition.

Both Wells and Russell talked about self or ego in love. According to Wells, "it is the essential fact of love as I conceive it, that it breaks down the boundaries of self." In Russell's opinion, "a too powerful ego is a prison from which a man must escape if he is to enjoy the world to the full." How do you understand the relationship between self or ego with love or affection? Finish a composition under this topic with about 600 words.

Unit 2

Literature

Section A

Text One The Tell-Tale Heart

Focal Consideration

Poe's writing reflects his literary theories. He believed that meaning in literature should be an undercurrent just beneath the surface, and works with obvious meaning cease to be art. According to Poe, quality work should be brief and focus on a specific single effect. To that end, he believed that the writer should carefully calculate every sentiment and idea. Therefore, the discussion on this story will be focused on the following topics:

1. the literary elements such as the point of view, irony, foreshadowing and symbolism in *The Tell-Tale Heart;*
2. the specific literary and linguistic devices Poe employed in this story in order to create a particular atmosphere;
3. the rich thematic meanings embodied in the story.

Research Questions

You are supposed to collect information on the following topics and be sure that you are able to give an oral presentation on any of the topics in class.

1. Make an introduction to Allan Poe including his life, career, main literary works, etc.
2. What are the major literary elements of a story?
3. *The Tell-Tale Heart* is widely considered as a classic of the Gothic fiction genre. What are the features of Gothic fiction?

The Tell-Tale Heart

By Edgar Allan Poe

1. True!—Nervous—very, very dreadfully nervous I had been and am; but why will you say that I am mad? The disease had sharpened my senses—not destroyed—not dulled them. Above all was the sense of hearing acute. I heard all things in the heaven and in the earth. I heard many things in hell. How, then, am I mad? Hearken! and observe how healthily—how calmly I can tell you the whole story.

2. It is impossible to tell how first the idea entered my brain; but once conceived, it haunted me day and night. Object there was none. Passion there was none. I loved the old man. He had never wronged me. He had never given me insult. For his gold I had no desire. I think it was his eye! Yes, it was this! One of his eyes resembled that of a vulture—a pale blue eye, with a film over it. Whenever it fell upon me, my blood ran cold; and so by degrees—very gradually—I made up my mind to take the life of the old man, and thus rid myself of the eye forever.

3. Now this is the point. You fancy me mad. Madmen know nothing. But you should have seen me. You should have seen how wisely I proceeded—with what caution—with what foresight—with what dissimulation I went to work!

4. I was never kinder to the old man than during the whole week before I killed him. And every night, about midnight, I turned the latch of his door and opened it—oh, so gently! And then, when I had made an opening sufficient for my head, I put in a dark lantern, all closed, closed, so that no light shone out, and then I thrust in my head. Oh, you would have laughed to see how cunningly I thrust it in! I moved it slowly—very, very slowly, so that I might not disturb the old man' sleep. It took me an hour to place my whole head within the opening so far that I could see him as he lay upon his bed. Ha!—would a madman have been so wise as this? And then, when my head was well in the room, I undid the lantern cautiously—oh, so cautiously—cautiously (for the hinges creaked)—I undid it just so much that a single thin ray fell upon the vulture eye. And this I did for seven long nights—every night just at midnight—but I found the eye always closed; and so it was impossible to do the work; for it was not the old man who vexed me, but his Evil Eye. And every morning, when the day broke, I went boldly into the chamber, and spoke courageously to him, calling him by name in a hearty tone, and inquiring how he had passed the night. So you see he would have been a very profound old man, indeed, to suspect that every night, just at twelve, I looked in upon him while he slept.

5. Upon the eighth night I was more than usually cautious in opening the door. A watch's minute hand moves more quickly than did mine. Never before that night had I felt the extent of my own powers—of my sagacity. I could scarcely contain my feelings of triumph. To think that there I was, opening the door, little by little, and he not even to

dream of my secret deeds or thoughts. I fairly chuckled at the idea; and perhaps he heard me; for he moved on the bed suddenly, as if startled. Now you may think that I drew back—but no. His room was as black as pitch with the thick darkness (for the shutters were close fastened, through fear of robbers), and so I knew that he could not see the opening of the door, and I kept pushing it on steadily, steadily.

6   I had my head in, and was about to open the lantern, when my thumb slipped upon the tin fastening, and the old man sprang up in bed, crying out: "Who's there?"

7   I kept quite still and said nothing. For a whole hour I did not move a muscle, and in the meantime I did not hear him lie down. He was still sitting up in the bed listening;—just as I have done, night after night, hearkening to the death watches in the wall.

8   Presently I heard a slight groan, and I knew it was the groan of mortal terror. It was not a groan of pain or grief—oh no!—it was the low stifled sound that arises from the bottom of the soul when overcharged with awe. I knew the sound well. Many a night, just at midnight, when all the world slept, it has welled up from my own bosom, deepening, with its dreadful echo, the terrors that distracted me. I say I knew it well. I knew what the old man felt, and pitied him, although I chuckled at heart. I knew that he had been lying awake ever since the first slight noise, when he had turned in the bed. His fears had been ever since growing upon him. He had been trying to fancy them causeless, but could not. He had been saying to himself: "It is nothing but the wind in the chimney—it is only a mouse crossing the floor," or "it is merely a cricket which has made a single chirp." Yes, he had been trying to comfort himself with these suppositions; but he had found all in vain. All in vain; because Death, in approaching him had stalked with his black shadow before him, and enveloped the victim. And it was the mournful influence of the unperceived shadow that caused him to feel—although he neither saw nor heard—to feel the presence of my head within the room.

9   When I had waited a long time, very patiently, without hearing him lie down, I resolved to open a little—a very, very little crevice in the lantern. So I opened it—you cannot imagine how stealthily, stealthily—until, at length, a single dim ray, like the thread of the spider, shot from out the crevice and fell upon the vulture eye.

10 It was open—wide, wide open—and I grew furious as I gazed upon it. I saw it with perfect distinctness—all a dull blue, with a hideous veil over it that chilled the very marrow in my bones; but I could see nothing else of the old man's face or person: for I had directed the ray, as if by instinct, precisely upon the damned spot.

11 And now—have I not told you that what you mistake for madness is but over–acuteness of the senses?—now, I say, there came to my ears a low, dull, quick sound, such as a watch makes when enveloped in cotton. I knew that sound well too. It was the beating of the old man's heart. It increased my fury, as the beating of a drum stimulates the soldier into courage.

12 But even yet I refrained and kept still. I scarcely breathed. I held the lantern motionless. I tried how steadily I could maintain the ray upon the eye. Meantime the

hellish tattoo of the heart increased. It grew quicker and quicker, and louder and louder every instant. The old man's terror must have been extreme! It grew louder, I say, louder every moment!—do you mark me well? I have told you that I am nervous: so I am. And now at the dead hour of night, amid the dreadful silence of that old house, so strange a noise as this excited me to uncontrollable terror. Yet, for some minutes longer I refrained and stood still. But the beating grew louder, louder! I thought the heart must burst. And now a new anxiety seized me—the sound would be heard by a neighbor! The old man's hour had come! With a loud yell, I threw open the lantern and leaped into the room. He shrieked once—once only. In an instant I dragged him to the floor, and pulled the heavy bed over him. I then smiled gaily, to find the deed so far done. But, for many minutes, the heart beat on with a muffled sound. This, however, did not vex me; it would not be heard through the wall. At length it ceased. The old man was dead. I removed the bed and examined the corpse. Yes, he was stone, stone dead. I placed my hand upon the heart and held it there many minutes. There was no pulsation. He was stone dead. His eye would trouble me no more.

13   If still you think me mad, you will think so no longer when I describe the wise precautions I took for the concealment of the body. The night waned, and I worked hastily, but in silence. First of all I dismembered the corpse. I cut off the head and the arms and the legs.

14   I then took up three planks from the flooring of the chamber, and deposited all between the scantlings. I then replaced the boards so cleverly, so cunningly, that no human eye—not even his—could have detected anything wrong. There was nothing to wash out—no stain of any kind—no blood-spot whatever. I had been too wary for that. A tub had caught all—ha! ha!

15   When I had made an end of these labors, it was four o'clock—still dark as midnight. As the bell sounded the hour, there came a knocking at the street door. I went down to open it with a light heart—for what had I now to fear? There entered three men, who introduced themselves, with perfect suavity, as officers of the police. A shriek had been heard by a neighbor during the night: suspicion of foul play had been aroused; information had been lodged at the police office, and they (the officers) had been deputed to search the premises.

16   I smiled—for what had I to fear? I bade the gentlemen welcome. The shriek, I said, was my own in a dream. The old man, I mentioned, was absent in the country. I took my visitors all over the house. I bade them search—search well. I led them, at length, to his chamber. I showed them his treasures, secure, undisturbed. In the enthusiasm of my confidence, I brought chairs into the room, and desired them here to rest from their fatigues, while I myself, in the wild audacity of my perfect triumph, placed my own seat upon the very spot beneath which reposed the corpse of the victim.

17   The officers were satisfied. My manner had convinced them. I was singularly at ease. They sat, and while I answered cheerily, they chatted familiar things. But, ere long, I felt

myself getting pale and wished them gone. My head ached, and I fancied a ringing in my ears: but still they sat and still chatted. The ringing became more distinct:—it continued and became more distinct: I talked more freely to get rid of the feeling: but it continued and gained definiteness—until, at length, I found that the noise was not within my ears.

18   No doubt I now grew very pale,—but I talked more fluently, and with a heightened voice. Yet the sound increased—and what could I do? It was a low, dull, quick sound—much such a sound as a watch makes when enveloped in cotton. I gasped for breath—and yet the officers heard it not. I talked more quickly—more vehemently; but the noise steadily increased. Why would they not be gone? I paced the floor to and fro with heavy strides, as if excited to fury by the observation of the men—but the noise steadily increased. Oh, God! what could I do? I foamed—I raved—I swore! I swung the chair upon which I had been sitting, and grated it upon the boards, but the noise arose over all and continually increased. It grew louder—louder—louder! And still the men chatted pleasantly, and smiled. Was it possible they heard not? Almighty God!—no, no! They heard!—they suspected—they knew!—they were making a mockery of my horror!—this I thought, and this I think. But anything was better than this agony! Anything was more tolerable than this derision! I could bear those hypocritical smiles no longer! I felt that I must scream or die!—and now—again!—hark! louder! louder! louder!

19   "Villains!" I shrieked, "dissemble no more! I admit the deed!—tear up the planks! —here, here!—it is the beating of his hideous heart!"

Preview Assistance

1. **acute** *adj.*   sharp; able to notice small differences
2. **hearken** *v.*   (literary use) to listen
3. **conceive** *v.*   to think of something such as a new idea, plan, or design
4. **vulture** *n.*   a large ugly tropical bird with an almost featherless head and neck, which feeds on dead animals
5. **by degrees**   gradually; in a gradual manner
6. **dissimulation** *n.*   noun form of dissimulate. Dissimulation is a form of deception in which one conceals the truth. It commonly takes the form of concealing one's ability in order to gain the element of surprise over an opponent. Synonyms are dissemblance, deception, etc.
7. **thrust** *v.*   to push forcefully and suddenly
8. **look in upon**   to pay a short visit to; call on briefly
9. **sagacity** *n.*   (formal or literary use) good judgment and understanding; wisdom that cannot be reached
10. **chuckle** *v.*   to laugh quietly
11. **spring up**   to arise, develop, grow quickly; to sit up
12. **stifled** *adj.*   choked; suffocated; smothered; suppressed
13. **distract** *v.*   usu. to distract from, to take sb or their attention off something
14. **stalk** *v.*   to walk stiffly, proudly, or with long steps
15. **crevice** *n.*   a narrow opening

16. **well up**   to rise like water in a well
17. **stone dead**   completely dead
18. **pulsation** *n.*   a beat of the heart or any regular beat that can be measured; pulsating movement
19. **dismember** *v.*   to cut or tear (a body) apart
20. **foul play** *n.*   violence or criminal actions that cause someone's death; behaviour that is not fair or honest or that does not keep to accepted rules
21. **depute** *v.*   to appoint sb to do sth
22. **repose** *v.*   to place (an object or part of a body) on
23. **foam** *v.*   to produce foam; produce a whitish mass of very small bubbles
24. **rave** *v.*   to talk wildly as if mad
25. **dissemble** *v.*   to hide one's feeling; to dissimulate; to deceive

Referential Points

The Tell-Tale Heart is a short story by Edgar Allan Poe first published in 1843. It follows an unnamed narrator who insists on his sanity after murdering an old man with a "vulture eye." The murder is carefully calculated, and the murderer hides the body by dismembering it and hiding it under the floorboards. Ultimately the narrator's guilt manifests itself in the hallucination that the man's heart is still beating under the floorboards. The story was first published in James Russel Lowell's *The Pioneer* in January 1843. *The Tell-Tale Heart* is widely considered a classic of the Gothic fiction genre and one of Poe's most famous short stories.

Edgar Allan Poe (1809—1849) an American writer, poet, editor and literary critic, considered part of the American Romantic Movement. Best known for his tales of mystery and the macabre, Poe was one of the earliest American practitioners of the short story and is considered the inventor of the detective-fiction genre. He is further credited with contributing to the emerging genre of science fiction. He was the first well-known American writer to try to earn a living through writing alone, resulting in a financially difficult life and career. Poe and his works influenced literature in the United States and around the world, as well as in specialized fields, such as cosmology and cryptography.

Detective Story often called a **whodunit**. It did not spring into being in its current form. Rather, it evolved over time, beginning with stories in which the reader is not a participant at all, but a witness, so to speak, looking over the detective's shoulder. The detective story is a tale that features a mystery and/or the commission of a crime, emphasizing the search for a solution. The detective story is distinguished from other forms of fiction by the fact that it is a puzzle. Although a crime usually has been committed, the reader's attention is directed to baffling circumstances surrounding the crime rather than to the event itself. The tale's climax is the solution of the puzzle, and the bulk of the narrative concerns the logical process by which the investigator follows a series of clues to this solution. Very often the detective solves the mystery by means of deductive reasoning from facts known both to the character and the reader.

Section A 47

Consolidation Work

I. Fill in the blanks with the words and expressions provided, making some change when necessary.

cut off	foul play	chuckle	depute	by degrees	dismember
spring up	at length	rid... of	well up	by instinct	refrain from
conceive	at ease	look in upon			

1. When my bosom holds the most beautiful flowers in this world, my eyes _____ with warm tears.
2. Every student shall be honor bound to _____ cheating (including plagiarism).
3. Could Sir Thomas _____ us just now, he would bless himself.
4. No one calls for justice; no one pleads his case with integrity. They rely on empty arguments and speak lies; they _____ trouble and give birth to evil.
5. The writer depicts a young woman struggling to _____ herself _____ the painful influence of her abusive father.
6. At New York's World Trade Center, many bodies were burned, _____ or crushed below collapsing steel and concrete.
7. We choose our friends _____, but we keep them by judgment.
8. The small girl was crying so hard that her father had to lean down to put her _____.
9. The hiring party will _____ against their representative at the main entry gate of the hall to ensure that only invited persons enter the hall.
10. I am sorry to have gone on _____ such _____, but I think this is an important issue.
11. Then _____ a cold light crept through the Venetian blinds, until at length it revealed the objects in the room.
12. I thought the title was rather funny and had hoped that at least some people would get a good _____ out of it.
13. Russia said on Sunday it would _____ gas supplies to Ukraine within hours over a price row that strikes at the heart of relations between the two ex-Soviet states.
14. Buildings are upgraded frequently, and the skyline is characterized with dense, tall constructions that _____ thick and fast.
15. Your watchword is fair play; your hatred, _____.

II. Use the appropriate form of the words given in the brackets to fill in the blanks.

1. Her tears helped her really to _____, for she had instantly, in so public a situation, to recover herself. (dissimulation)
2. Attempts during the past 20 years have largely failed to solve the _____ problem of software integration, due mostly to a lack of industry support. (vexation)
3. Though your abilities are small, yet a _____ good-will is sufficient to supply all defects. (heart)
4. When a scandal breaks, the discovery of an attempt to cover up or _____ the

evidence of wrongdoing is often regarded as even more scandalous than the original deeds. (concealment)
5. We witness how each one _____ outwits the super-predators in its own special way, with extra-sharp senses and other strategies for survival. (cunning)
6. The Internet is the widest possible _____ because it lets you wander so far afield that getting work done—if you are, like me, the distractible sort of person—is almost impossible. (distract)
7. As we have taken _____ measures the degree of destruction has been kept in a minimal rate. (precaution)
8. The baby's heart was _____ again after the surgeon massaged it. (pulsation)
9. China's economy and China's financial system was not directly impacted. Currently, the RMB exchange rate was stable, the economy still rapidly grew _____ as planned, and the inflation rate was controlled to a relatively low level. (health)
10. Even this white stone bridge beneath his feet seemed abnormally deserted and so white that even the street lamps shed a _____ light. (mourn)

III. Paraphrase the following sentences taken from the text.
1. The disease had sharpened my senses—not destroyed—not dulled them.
2. I was never kinder to the old man than during the whole week before I killed him.
3. It took me an hour to place my whole head within the opening so far that I could see him as he lay upon his bed.
4. I saw it with perfect distinctness—all a dull blue, with a hideous veil over it that chilled the very marrow in my bones...
5. ...suspicion of foul play had been aroused; information had been lodged at the police office, and they (the officers) had been deputed to search the premises.

IV. Test your general knowledge.
1. _____ was regarded the master of the tightly wound tale of psychological horror, such as *The Fall of the House of Usher*.
   A. Edgar Allan Poe   B. James Joyce
   C. Jack London   D. Theodore Dreiser
2. Of Old English literature, five relics are still preserved among which _____ is regarded as the national epic of the English people.
   A. *Piers the Plowman*   B. *Beowulf*
   C. *The Canterbury Tales*   D. *History of the Kings of Britain*
3. _____ is regarded as the founder of modern science and the first essayist in England, whose essays cover a wide variety of subjects such as love, truth, friendship, parents and children, beauty, studies...
   A. Leigh Hunt   B. John Bunyan
   C. Francis Bacon   D. Christopher Marlowe
4. _____ is a psychological term indicating "the flux of conscious and subconscious thoughts and impressions moving in the mind at any given time independently of the person's will."
   A. The stream of consciousness B. The psychoanalysis

C. The Oedipus Complex   D. The Stimulus-Response

5. Which of the following poems by T. S. Eliot is hailed as a landmark and a model of the 20th century English poetry?
   A. The Hollow Men.
   B. The Waste Land.
   C. The Loving Song of J. Alfred Prufrock.
   D. Preludes.

6. The Romantic Period in American literature began with the publication of Washington Irving's _____ and ended with Whitman's _____ .
   A. *The Legend of Sleepy Hollow* and *Leaves of Grass*
   B. *Tales of a Traveler* and *Song of Myself*
   C. *The Sketch Book* and *Leaves of Grass*
   D. *The History of New York* and *Song of Myself*

7. _____ refers to a philosophical and literary movement, flourished in New England from 1830s to the Civil War.
   A. Romanticism   B. Sentimentalism
   C. Regionalism   D. Transcendentalism

8. The Age of Realism from 1865 to 1914 is also what Mark Twain referred to as "_____."
   A. The Gilded Age   B. The Realistic Age
   C. The Jazz Age   D. The Victorian Age

9. In *The Sound and The Fury,* Faulkner used a technique called _____ in which the whole story was told through the thoughts of one character.
   A. Psychoanalysis   B. Stream of Consciousness
   C. Symbolism   D. Imagism

10. Which of the following characters does NOT appear in Hawthorne's *The Scarlet Letter*?
    A. Pearl.   B. Hester.
    C. Arthur.   D. Nick.

11. _____ refers to a literary trend that attempts to apply scientific principles of objectivity and detachment to its study of human beings.
    A. Naturalism   B. Realism
    C. Regionalism   D. Romanticism

12. Which of the following novel has been called the first modern war novel?
    A. *The Blue Hotel.*   B. *A Farewell to Arms.*
    C. *Crime and Punishment.*   D. *The Red Badge of Courage.*

13. Abraham Lincoln was said to comment that _____ had been a catalyst for the Civil War.
    A. *Song of Myself*   B. *The Red Badge of Courage*
    C. *Uncle Tom's Cabin*   D. *Babbitt*

14. _____ refers to a type of literature which aims to capture the special atmosphere, the "local color," of the area and people the fiction portrays.
    A. Realism   B. Regionalism
    C. Modernism   D. Post-modernism

15. A novel can best be defined as a book-length prose fiction. Early novels in English fall into

three categories: the picaresque novel; the novel of sentiment; and _____.
A. the romance novel   B. the modern novel
C. the gothic novel   D. the entertainment novel

V. Proofread the following passage.

There is at present a high degree of uncertainty about the role of literature in a school foreign-language course. Changes in educational and social conditions have shaken the once unquestioning status of literary study amongst our educational goals, and it also plays an ever problematic role in a new pattern of language teaching which aims primarily to impart practical communicative skills. Recent discussions in advanced courses in schools have generally advocated less emphasis on literature in favor of language, and a revision of the principles governing the selection of texts in order to include great consideration of pupils' actual ability, experience, and interests.

Nevertheless, there is still comparative little clarity about what role these texts should perform, and it is not uncommon to find a situation that the teacher translates passages and dictates notes, in an examination-centered approach which largely ignores the deeper insights or skills that pupils might gain from their confrontation with literature. On the other hand, it is clearly not possible to think in the terms of one singe role which literature should perform. A group of pupils aiming at a functional command of a language may read a modern novel because of its linguistic content, unless a group of future academic specialists may discuss the basic human issues portrayed in a classical play. These are the two different activities in two different situations, each equally justifiable in its context but not to be confused: different pupils' aims require literature to serve different functions, which is best performed by different literary works.

1. _____
2. _____
3. _____
4. _____
5. _____
6. _____
7. _____
8. _____
9. _____
10. _____

VI. Write a composition.

Allan Poe is believed to be a writer who is expert at symbolism. Refer to the preview assistant about the introduction of symbolism. Write a composition. List and define the symbols employed in "*The Tell-Tale Heart*" and explicate how the symbols create meaning and effect in it.

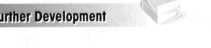

Further Development

It is said that human nature is a delicate balance of light and dark or good and evil. Once that balance is broken, the dark or evil side of human nature will be released and overbear the light or good side.

1. In your eyes, what is significant to keep the delicate balance of light and dark side of human nature? Support your view with reasons.

2. Does Allan Poe tell readers the protagonist "I" in "The Tell-Tale Heart" is insane directly? Does he explain the reason for his insaneness? What kind of reason would be to explain the protagonist's insaneness?

Section A Text Two

Colonel Cathcart

(Excerpt from Catch 22)
By Joseph Heller

1 Colonel Cathcart was a slick, successful, slipshod, unhappy man of thirty-six who lumbered when he walked and wanted to be a general. He was dashing and dejected, poised and chagrined. He was complacent and insecure, daring in the administrative stratagems he employed to bring himself to the attention of his superiors and craven in his concern that his schemes might all backfire. He was handsome and unattractive, a swashbuckling, beefy, conceited man who was putting on fat and was tormented chronically by prolonged seizures of apprehension. Colonel Cathcart was conceited because he was a full colonel with a combat command at the age of only thirty-six; and Colonel Cathcart was dejected because although he was already thirty-six he was still only a full colonel.

2 Colonel Cathcart was impervious to absolutes. He could measure his own progress only in relationship to others, and his idea of excellence was to do something at least as well as all the men his own age who were doing the same thing even better. The fact that there were thousands of men his own age and older who had not even attained the rank of major enlivened him with foppish delight in his own remarkable worth; on the other hand, the fact that there were men of his own age and younger who were already generals contaminated him with an agonizing sense of failure and made him gnaw at his fingernails with an unappeasable anxiety that was even more intense than Hungry Joe's.

3 Colonel Cathcart was a very large, pouting, broad-shouldered man with close-cropped curly dark hair that was graying at the tips and an ornate cigarette holder that he purchased the day before he arrived in Pianosa to take command of his group. Hedisplayed the cigarette holder grandly on every occasion and had learned to manipulate it adroitly. Unwittingly, he had discovered deep within himself a fertile aptitude for smoking with a cigarette holder. As far as he could tell, his was the only cigarette holder in the whole Mediterranean theater of operations, and the thought was both flattering and disquieting. He had no doubts at all that someone as debonair and intellectual as General Peckem approved of his smoking with a cigarette holder, even though the two were in each other's presence rather seldom, which in a way was very lucky, Colonel Cathcart recognized with relief, since General. Peckem might not have approved of his cigarette holder at all. When such misgivings assailed Colonel Cathcart, he choked back a sob and

wanted to throw the damned thing away, but he was restrained by his unswerving conviction that the cigarette holder never failed to embellish his masculine, martial physique with a high gloss of sophisticated heroism that illuminated him to dazzling advantage among all the other full colonels in the American Army with whom he was in competition although how could he be sure?

4   Colonel Cathcart was indefatigable that way, an industrious, intense, dedicated military tactician who calculated day and night in the service of himself. He was his own sarcophagus, a bold and infallible diplomat who was always berating himself disgustedly for all the chances he had missed and kicking himself regretfully for all the errors he had made. He was tense, irritable, bitter and smug. He was a valorous opportunist who pounced hoggishly upon every opportunity Colonel Korn discovered for him and trembled in damp despair immediately afterward at the possible consequences he might suffer. He collected rumors greedily and treasured gossip. He believed all the news he heard and had faith in none. He was on the alert constantly for every signal, shrewdly sensitive to relationships and situation that did not exist. He was someone in the know who was always striving pathetically to find out what was going on. He was a blustering, intrepid bully who brooded inconsolably over the terrible ineradicable impressions he knew he kept making on people of prominence who were scarcely aware that he was even alive.

5   Everybody was persecuting him. Colonel Cathcart lived by his wits in an unstable, arithmetical world of black eyes and feathers in his cap, of overwhelming imaginary triumphs and catastrophic imaginary defeats. He oscillated hourly between anguish and exhilaration, multiplying fantastically the grandeur of his victories and exaggerating tragically the seriousness of his defeats. Nobody ever caught him napping. If word reached him that General Dreedle or General Peckem had been seen smiling, frowning, or doing neither, he could not make himself rest until he had found an acceptable interpretation and grumbled mulishly until Colonel Korn persuaded him to relax and take things easy.

6   Lieutenant Colonel Korn was a loyal, indispensable ally who got on Colonel Cathcart's nerves. Colonel Cathcart pledged eternal gratitude to Colonel Korn for the ingenious moves he devised and was furious with him afterward when he realized theymight not work. Colonel Cathcart was greatly indebted to Colonel Korn and did not like him at all. The two were very close. Colonel Cathcart was jealous of Colonel Korn's intelligence and had to reminded himself often that Colonel Korn was still only a lieutenant colonel, even though he was almost ten years older than Colonel Cathcart, and that Colonel Korn had obtained his education at a state university Colonel Cathcart bewailed the miserable fate that had given him for an invaluable assistant someone as common as Colonel Korn. It was degrading to have to depend so thoroughly on a person who had been educated at a state university. If someone did have to become indispensable to him, Colonel Cathcart lamented, it could just as easily have been someone wealthy and well groomed, someone from a better family who was more mature

than Colonel Korn and who did not treat Colonel Cathcart's desire to become a general as frivolously as Colonel Cathcart secretly suspected Colonel Korn secretly did.

7   Colonel Cathcart wanted to be a general so desperately he was willing to try anything, even religion, and he summoned the chaplain to his office late one morning the week after he had raised the number of missions to sixty and pointed abruptly down toward his desk to his copy of The Saturday Evening Post. The colonel wore his khaki shirt collar wide open, exposing a shadow of tough black bristles of beard on his egg-white neck, and had a spongy banging underlip. He was a person who never tanned, and he kept out of the sun as much as possible to avoid burning. The colonel was more than a head taller than the chaplain and over twice as broad, and his swollen, overbearing authority made the chaplain feel frail and sickly by contrast.

8   "Take a look, Chaplain," Colonel Cathcart directed, screwing a cigarette into his holder and seating himself affluently in the swivel chair behind his desk. "Let me know what you think."

9   The chaplain looked down at the open magazine compliantly and saw an editorial spreads dealing with an American bomber group in England whose chaplain said prayers in the briefing room before each mission. The chaplain almost wept with happiness when he realized the colonel was not going to holler at him. The two had hardly spoken since the tumultuous evening Colonel Cathcart had thrown him out of the officers' club at General Dreedle's bidding after Chief White Halfoat had punched Colonel Moodus in the nose. The chaplain's initial fear had been that the colonel intended reprimanding him for having gone back onto the officer's club without permission the evening before. He had gone there with Yossarian and Dubar after the two had come unexpectedly to his tent in the clearing in the woods to ask him to join them. Intimidated as he was by Colonel Cathcart, he nevertheless found it easier to brave his displeasure than to decline the thoughtful invitation of his two new friends, whom he had met on one of his hospital visits just a few weeks before and who had worked so effectively to insulate him against the myriad social vicissitudes involved in his official duty to live on closest terms of familiarity with more than nine hundred unfamiliar officers and enlisted men who thought him anodd duck.

10 The chaplain glued his eyes to the pages of the magazine. He studied each photograph twice and read the captions intently as he organized his response to the colonel's question into a grammatically complete sentence that he rehearsed and reorganized in his mind a considerable number of times before he was able finally to muster the courage to reply.

11 "I think that saying prayers before each mission is a very moral and highly laudatory procedure, sir," he offered timidly, and waited.

12 "Yeah," said the colonel, "But I want to know if you think they'll work here."

13 "Yes, sir," answered the chaplain after a few moments, "I should think they would."

14 "Then I'd like to give it a try." The Colonel's ponderous, farinaceous cheeks were

tinted suddenly with glowing patches of enthusiasm. He rose to his feet and began walking around excitedly. "Look how much good they've done for these people in England. Here's a picture of a colonel in The Saturday Evening Post whose chaplain conducts prayers before each mission. If the prayers work for him, they should work for us. Maybe if we say prayers, they'll put my picture in The Saturday Evening Post."

15   The colonel sat down again and smiled distantly in lavish contemplation.

Independent Study Assistant

I. Words and Expressions

1. **slipshod** *adj.*   done in a careless way, casual
2. **lumber** *v.*   to walk slowly because of being large and heavy
3. **dejected** *adj.*   someone who is dejected has lost all their hope or enthusiasm, especially because they have failed at something
4. **chagrin** *n.*   a feeling of being very annoyed, disappointed, or embarrassed
5. **complacent** *adj.*   too confident and relaxed because you think you can deal with something easily, even though this may not be true
6. **stratagem** *n.*   a plan for achieving something or for tricking someone
7. **craven** *adj.*   not brave, cowardly
8. **backfire** *v.*   if a plan or idea backfires, it has the opposite effect of the one that you wanted
9. **swashbuckling** *adj.*   used about a character in a story, movie, etc. who has a lot of fights and exciting experiences
10. **beefy** *adj.*   a beefy person has a large heavy body and strong muscles
11. **apprehension** *n.*   a feeling of worry or fear that something bad might happen
12. **enliven** *v.*   to make something more interesting or lively
13. **gnaw** *v.*   to keep biting something
14. **debonair** *adj.*   a man who is debonair wears fashionable clothes and is attractive, relaxed, and confident
15. **assail** *v.*   to make someone feel worried or upset
16. **embellish** *v.*   to make a story more interesting by adding details, especially ones that are not completely true; to make something more beautiful by decorating it
17. **sarcophagus** *n.*   a stone box, used in some ancient cultures for putting a dead body in
18. **berate** *v.*   to talk to someone in an angry way because they have done something wrong
19. **bluster** *v.*   to speak or behave angrily
20. **intrepid** *adj.*   not afraid to do dangerous things
21. **brood** *v.*   to think and worry about something a lot
22. **oscillate** *v.*   to continuously change your feelings, opinions, or decisions from one extreme position to the other
23. **bewail** *v.*   to complain strongly about something that makes you sad, disappointed, or upset
24. **groom** *v.*   to take care of your appearance by keeping your hair, body, and clothes clean and neat
25. **holly** *v.*   to shout very loudly
26. **tumultuous** *adj.*   noisy and excited; involving a lot of noise, excitement, activity, or violence

27. **reprimand** *v.*   to tell someone officially and in a serious way that something they have done is wrong
28. **insulate** *v.*   to protect someone from unpleasant knowledge or harmful experiences
29. **myriad** *adj.*   very many, especially too many to count
30. **vicissitudes** *n.*   changes and unexpected difficulties
31. **laudatory** *adj.*   expressing praise or admiration

II. Referential Points

Joseph Heller   (1923—1999) an American satirical novelist, short story writer and playwright. He wrote the influential novel *Catch-22* about American servicemen during World War II. The title of this work entered the English lexicon to refer to absurd, no-win choices, particularly in situations in which the desired outcome of the choice is an impossibility, and regardless of choice, the same negative outcome is a certainty. Heller is widely regarded as one of the best post-World War II satirists. Although he is remembered primarily for *Catch-22*, his other works center on the lives of various members of the middle class and remain exemplars of modern satire.

Catch-22   a satirical, historical novel by the American author Joseph Heller, first published in 1961. The novel, set during the later stages of World War II from 1943 onwards, is frequently cited as one of the great literary works of the twentieth century. It has a distinctive non-chronological style where events are described from different characters' points of view and out of sequence so that the time line develops along with the plot. The novel follows Yossarian, a U.S. Army Air Forces B-25 bombardier, and a number of other characters. Most events occur while the airmen of the fictional Fighting 256th (or "two to the fighting eighth power") Squadron are based on the island of Pianosa, in the Mediterranean Sea west of Italy. The text is an excerpt from Chapter 19 of *Catch 22*.

The Chaplain   Albert Taylor Tappman (usually simply referred to as "The Chaplain" in the novel.) He is a naïve Anabaptist minister from Kenosha, Wisconsin, who is tormented throughout the novel by his atheist assistant, Corporal Whitcomb. While easily intimidated by the cruelty of others, the chaplain is a kind, gentle and sensitive man who worries constantly about his wife and children at home. He is the only character in the book Yossarian truly trusts.

Colonel Cathcart   A full colonel, Cathcart is a group commander at the U.S. Army Air Corps base in Pianosa and is obsessed with becoming a general. As such, he does whatever it takes to please his superiors—in particular, by repeatedly raising the number of missions the men have to fly to complete a tour of duty, beyond that normally ordered by other outfits. This becomes the bane of Yossarian's life, as every time he comes close to obtaining the target number of missions for being sent home, Colonel Cathcart raises the required number again. The concept of Catch-22 is also represented in the character of Colonel Cathcart, as he consists entirely of irreconcilable oppositions and maintains an illogical thought process that echoes that of the catch. Cathcart is a master of political doublespeak, often completely contradicting what he says seconds after he says it, usually when a superior officer disagrees with him.

General Peckem   a personification of bureaucracy. General Peckem wants to replace General Dreedle as the head of combat operations in Pianosa.

Lieutenant Colonel Korn   the assistant to Colonel Cathcart. Korn is sadistic, cynical, and humorless.

General Dreedle the commander of the U.S. Army Air Corps base in Pianosa, Dreedle is an exceedingly blunt and ill-tempered man. He is an archetypal no-nonsense military man who does not care what the men under his command do as long as they fight and die unquestioningly when given orders. His arch-rival is General Peckem, head of Special Services in Rome; the two men frequently have their disputes mediated without their knowledge by the desk clerk, ex-P.F.C. Wintergreen.

Colonel Moodus General Dreedle's son-in-law, whom the general hates.

Captain John Yossarian a fictional character in Joseph Heller's novel *Catch-22* and its sequel *Closing Time*, and the protagonist of both books. In *Catch-22*, Yossarian is a 28-year-old Captain and B-25 bombardier in the 256th squadron of the Army Air Corps, stationed on the small island of Pianosa off the Italian mainland during World War II. Yossarian's exploits are based on the experiences of the author: Heller was also a bombardier in the Air Corps, stationed on an island off the coast of Italy during World War II.

Dunbar an airman stationed at the same base as Yossarian, on the island of Pianosa. He and Yossarian seem to have similar personalities, and so they make fast friends. Like Yossarian, Dunbar's chief goal is to prolong his life to whatever extent possible.

III. Questions for Comprehension

1. There are always two sides in Colonel Cathcart's character. Take some instances from this excerpt and illustrate his two sides.
2. What was Colonel Cathcart's idea of excellence?
3. What feelings did he hold about his cigarette holder?
4. How did Colonel Korn stand in his eyes?
5. Why did Colonel Cathcart call the chaplain to his office?
6. Find all the important indicators relevant to Colonel Cathcart and place them under separate columns in such a way as to highlight his contradictory character.

Self-test

I. Fill in the blanks with the words and expressions provided, making some change when necessary.

insulate against	indebted to	backfire	enliven	contaminate
take command of	embellish	on the alert	indispensable	get on... nerves
impervious to	apprehension	furious	aptitude for	vicissitudes

1. Being pushy will _____ and leave you in an uncertain and awkward position.
2. Some were wounded, one and all were _____ at their ill-success and long exposure.
3. You follow rules until they _____ your _____, then you throw out the rule book and start shooting.
4. Wall vines and ground cover _____ summer heat and reduce reflected radiation.
5. They had come this far through successive acts of faith that had enabled them to transcend the _____ of history.

6. In the followings considerations we are heavily dependent on Schutz in the prolegomena concerning the foundations of knowledge in everyday life and greatly _____ his work in various important places of our main argument thereafter.
7. We may _____ a story, forget a word of the song, adapt an old technology or concoct a new theory out of old ideas.
8. He has an unfortunate _____ saying the wrong thing.
9. You will learn lessons here, such as responsibility and limitlessness, which will lead you to the life you were meant to live. These lessons provide you with the essential tools you need in order to _____ your life.
10. Dinitz was so _____ personal appeals as he had been impenetrable in the face of official approaches.
11. I am _____ for the first signs of spring, to hear the chance note of some arriving bird, or the striped squirrel's chirp, for his stores must be now nearly exhausted, or see the woodchuck venture out of his winter quarters.
12. If you don't get rid of hooligans and rowdies who won't study, they'll _____ the general atmosphere of the school.
13. Even though countless human pursuits require water, it is only when we experience a water shortage or pay a water bill that we think much about this _____ fluid.
14. Life would be dull without stories to _____ our imaginations and fire up our dreams.
15. It is risky to restrict all activities of the population by introducing law after law. Too much restriction may cause pressure, tension and lasting _____ not only in the relations among individuals, but also in those between citizens, society, and the state.

II. Use the appropriate form of the words given in the brackets to fill in the blanks.

1. My most precious abilities are mainly _____ ones, I have a happy facility forgetting different people to agree. (administrate)
2. Because of its thinness the mouth and eyes looked disproportionately large, and the eyes seemed filled with a murderous, _____ hatred of somebody or something. (appease)
3. Then he descended with cautious and slow step, for he dreaded lest an accident similar to that he had so _____ feigned should happen in reality. (adroit)
4. By your _____ defense of these principles you have made a constructive contribution to the evolution of a world order. (swerve)
5. Remember that workers are human and not _____, so devise methods and devices that prevent them from making errors. (fallible)
6. This love story as related by Bai Juyi in Song of Eternal Sorrow is indeed _____ touching. (pathetic)
7. Typically, the more specific the target, the better. Trying to create a design solution that simultaneously serves the needs of even three or four personas can be quite an _____ task. (overwhelm)
8. Now we are promoting pro-creativity teaching and encouraging our teachers to work _____ so as to bring up a young generation full of original ideas. (ingenious)
9. Author Yoshizaki attributes the change to Japanese parents' over-indulgence of their children, material _____, and growing concern for private matters. (affluent)

10. Before we reached home, Catherine's _____ softened, into a perplexed sensation of pity and regret. (pleasure)

III. Translate the short paragraph into Chinese.

Colonel Cathcart was a slick, successful, slipshod, unhappy man of thirty-six who lumbered when he walked and wanted to be a general. He was dashing and dejected, poised and chagrined. He was complacent and insecure, daring in the administrative stratagems he employed to bring himself to the attention of his superiors and craven in his concern that his schemes might all backfire. He was handsome and unattractive, a swashbuckling, beefy, conceited man who was putting on fat and was tormented chronically by prolonged seizures of apprehension. Colonel Cathcart was conceited because he was a full colonel with a combat command at the age of only thirty-six; and Colonel Cathcart was dejected because although he was already thirty-six he was still only a full colonel.

IV. Analyze difficult sentences.
1. Unwittingly, he had discovered deep within himself a fertile aptitude for smoking with a cigarette holder.
2. He was his own sarcophagus, a bold and infallible diplomat who was always berating himself disgustedly for all the chances he had missed and kicking himself regretfully for all the errors he had made.
3. He was a valorous opportunist who pounced hoggishly upon every opportunity
4. He was someone in the know who was always striving pathetically to find out what was going on.
5. Colonel Cathcart lived by his wits in an unstable, arithmetical world of black eyes and feathers in his cap, of overwhelming imaginary triumphs and catastrophic imaginary defeats.

V. Proofread the following passage.

Although important events often reflect themselves quickly in the literature of a country, the effect of World War I with American writing was delayed. The War promptly produced some mediocre prose and poetry, and distinguished work—mainly in the form of novels—appeared only some years later. The best came from Ernest Hemingway. He had already written some very good short stories and one first-class novel, *The Sun Also Rises*, but he did not publish a novel fully involved in the war till 1929. It proved worth waiting for. *A Farewell to Arms*, the moving story of the love affair of a wounded American lieutenant and an English nurse, outstanding among literary works relating to World War I. Hemingway had served with an ambulance group in France and then transferred to the Italian infantry, where he stayed till the close of the war. In this novel, his two characters pass idyllic Italian summer together. She becomes pregnant, and they go to Switzerland where she

1. _____
2. _____

3. _____

4. _____
5. _____

6. _____

has her baby. But both she and the baby died, and the American is left desolate. The war plays a principal part in the book. The American has taken part in a combat in the disastrous withdrawal of the Italian army after an overwhelmed defeat. Because of his aversion of the cruelties of World War I, Hemingway made a cult of the courage necessary to survive such an ordeal.

7. _____
8. _____
9. _____
10. _____

VI. Write a composition.

Joseph Heller is regarded as a master of the absurd school. Write briefly on Joseph Heller's point of view on Colonel Cathcart and your views about Colonel Cathcart.

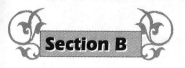

Text One Hills Like White Elephants

Focal Consideration

Hemingway's distinctive writing style is characterized by economy and understatement, and has a significant influence on the development of twentieth-century fiction writing. The study of the story *Hills like White Elephant* will be focused on:

1. the effect of Hemingway's Iceberg Theory. Hemingway once suggested that his purpose in such a story is to tell the reader as little as possible directly yet to reveal characters' motives and their conflict. We are going to discuss how this principle operates in this story;
2. the implied meanings of the story in perspective of the literary elements. We are going to explore how the interweaving of the setting and symbolism helps Hemingway juice each sentence to provide maximum detail;
3. the possible themes contained in this thematically-rich story.

Research Questions

Students are supposed to do research on the following topics and report their findings in groups:

1. Hemingway's life, writing careers and major contributions to literature;
2. America in 1920s and Lost Generation writers;
3. Hemingway's Iceberg Theory and prose style.

Hills like White Elephants

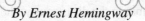

By Ernest Hemingway

1   The hills across the valley of the Ebro were long and white. On this side there was no shade and no trees and the station was between two lines of rails in the sun. Close against the side of the station there was the warm shadow of the building and a curtain, made of strings of bamboo beads, hung across the open door into the bar, to keep out flies. The American and the girl with him sat at a table in the shade, outside the building. It was very hot and the express from Barcelona would come in forty minutes. It stopped at this junction for two minutes and went to Madrid.

2   "What should we drink?" the girl asked. She had taken off her hat and put it on the table.

3   "It's pretty hot," the man said.

4   "Let's drink beer."

5   "Dos cervezas," the man said into the curtain.

6   "Big ones?" a woman asked from the doorway.

7   "Yes. Two big ones."

8   The woman brought two glasses of beer and two felt pads. She put the felt pads and the beer glasses on the table and looked at the man and the girl. The girl was looking off at the line of hills. They were white in the sun and the country was brown and dry.

9   "They look like white elephants," she said.

10 "I've never seen one," the man drank his beer.

11 "No, you wouldn't have."

12 "I might have," the man said. "Just because you say I wouldn't have doesn't prove anything."

13 The girl looked at the bead curtain. "They've painted something on it," she said. "What does it say?"

14 "Anis del Toro. It's a drink."

15 "Could we try it?"

16 The man called "Listen" through the curtain. The woman came out from the bar.

17 "Four reales." "We want two Anis del Toro."

18 "With water?"

19 "Do you want it with water?"

20 "I don't know," the girl said. "Is it good with water?"

21 "It's all right."

22 "You want them with water?" asked the woman.

23 "Yes, with water."

24 "It tastes like liquorice," the girl said and put the glass down.

25 "That's the way with everything."

26   "Yes," said the girl. "Everything tastes of liquorice. Especially all the things you've waited so long for, like absinthe."
27   "Oh, cut it out."
28   "You started it," the girl said. "I was being amused. I was having a fine time."
29   "Well, let's try and have a fine time."
30   "All right. I was trying. I said the mountains looked like white elephants. Wasn't that bright?"
31   "That was bright."
32   "I wanted to try this new drink. That's all we do, isn't it – look at things and try new drinks?"
33   "I guess so."
34   The girl looked across at the hills.
35   "They're lovely hills," she said. "They don't really look like white elephants. I just meant the coloring of their skin through the trees."
36   "Should we have another drink?"
37   "All right."
38   The warm wind blew the bead curtain against the table.
39   "The beer's nice and cool," the man said.
40   "It's lovely," the girl said.
41   "It's really an awfully simple operation, Jig," the man said. "It's not really an operation at all."
42   The girl looked at the ground the table legs rested on.
43   "I know you wouldn't mind it, Jig. It's really not anything. It's just to let the air in."
44   The girl did not say anything.
45   "I'll go with you and I'll stay with you all the time. They just let the air in and then it's all perfectly natural."
46   "Then what will we do afterwards?"
47   "We'll be fine afterwards. Just like we were before."
48   "What makes you think so?"
49   "That's the only thing that bothers us. It's the only thing that's made us unhappy."
50   The girl looked at the bead curtain, put her hand out and took hold of two of the strings of beads.
51   "And you think then we'll be all right and be happy."
52   "I know we will. Yon don't have to be afraid. I've known lots of people that have done it."
53   "So have I," said the girl. "And afterwards they were all so happy."
54   "Well," the man said, "if you don't want to you don't have to. I wouldn't have you do it if you didn't want to. But I know it's perfectly simple."
55   "And you really want to?"
56   "I think it's the best thing to do. But I don't want you to do it if you don't really want to."

57 "And if I do it you'll be happy and things will be like they were and you'll love me?"
58 "I love you now. You know I love you."
59 "I know. But if I do it, then it will be nice again if I say things are like white elephants, and you'll like it?"
60 "I'll love it. I love it now but I just can't think about it. You know how I get when I worry."
61 "If I do it you won't ever worry?"
62 "I won't worry about that because it's perfectly simple."
63 "Then I'll do it. Because I don't care about me."
64 "What do you mean?"
65 "I don't care about me."
66 "Well, I care about you."
67 "Oh, yes. But I don't care about me. And I'll do it and then everything will be fine."
68 "I don't want you to do it if you feel that way."
69 The girl stood up and walked to the end of the station. Across, on the other side, were fields of grain and trees along the banks of the Ebro. Far away, beyond the river, were mountains. The shadow of a cloud moved across the field of grain and she saw the river through the trees.
70 "And we could have all this," she said. "And we could have everything and every day we make it more impossible."
71 "What did you say?"
72 "I said we could have everything."
73 We can have everything."
74 "No, we can't."
75 "We can have the whole world."
76 "No, we can't."
77 "We can go everywhere."
78 "No, we can't. It isn't ours any more."
79 "It's ours."
80 "No, it isn't. And once they take it away, you never get it back."
81 "But they haven't taken it away."
82 "We'll wait and see."
83 "Come on back in the shade," he said. "You mustn't feel that way."
84 "I don't feel any way," the girl said. "I just know things."
85 "I don't want you to do anything that you don't want to do—"
86 "Nor that isn't good for me," she said. "I know. Could we have another beer?"
87 "All right. But you've got to realize—"
88 "I realize," the girl said. "Can't we maybe stop talking?"
89 They sat down at the table and the girl looked across at the hills on the dry side of the valley and the man looked at her and at the table.

90   "You've got to realize," he said, "that I don't want you to do it if you don't want to. I'm perfectly willing to go through with it if it means anything to you."
91   "Doesn't it mean anything to you? We could get along."
92   "Of course it does. But I don't want anybody but you. I don't want anyone else. And I know it's perfectly simple."
93   "Yes, you know it's perfectly simple."
94   "It's all right for you to say that, but I do know it."
95   "Would you do something for me now?"
96   "I'd do anything for you."
97   "Would you please please please please please please please stop talking?"
98   He did not say anything but looked at the bags against the wall of the station. There were labels on them from all the hotels where they had spent nights.
99   "But I don't want you to," he said, "I don't care anything about it."
100   "I'll scream," the girl said.
101   The woman came out through the curtains with two glasses of beer and put them down on the damp felt pads. "The train comes in five minutes," she said.
102   "What did she say?" asked the girl.
103   "That the train is coming in five minutes."
104   The girl smiled brightly at the woman, to thank her.
105   "I'd better take the bags over to the other side of the station," the man said. She smiled at him.
106   "All right. Then come back and we'll finish the beer."
107   He picked up the two heavy bags and carried them around the station to the other tracks.
108   He looked up the tracks but could not see the train. Coming back, he walked through the bar-room, where people waiting for the train were drinking. He drank an Anis at the bar and looked at the people. They were all waiting reasonably for the train. He went out through the bead curtain. She was sitting at the table and smiled at him.
109   "Do you feel better?" he asked.
110   "I feel fine," she said. "There's nothing wrong with me. I feel fine."

Preview Assistance

1. **keep out**   to remain outside
2. **junction** *n.*   a place where two or more highways, railroad lines, or rivers join together
3. **felt pad**   a pat made with thick firm cloth of wool, hair, or fur that has been pressed flat
4. **Dos cervezas**   (Spanish), two glasses of beer.
5. **white elephant**   an object that is useless and may have cost a lot of money; an important project that has failed very badly and may have cost a lot of money
6. **Anis del Toro**   (Spanish) an alcoholic drink that is dark in color and tastes like licorice, first

produced in 1904 under the name Anis del Juliano or Julian's Anise. Anise is the herb that gives the drink its flavor

7. **reales**   Its singular form is real, the currency for Spanish in the past
8. **liquorice**   also licorice; a Mediterranean perennial plant having blue flowers, pinnately compound leaves, and a sweet, distinctively flavored root; the root of this plant, used as a flavoring in candy, liqueurs, tobacco, and medicines
9. **absinthe** *n.*   a green liqueur having a bitter anise or licorice flavor and a high alcohol content, prepared from absinthe and other herbs, and now prohibited in many countries because of its toxicity
10. **coloring** *n.*   something that produces color
11. **rest on**   to lie on, to depend on
12. **take hold of**   to grasp or seize
13. **let the air in**   an old-fashioned induced abortion operation during which air should be let in or puff in the womb or uterus
14. **get along**   if people get along, they like each other and are friendly to each other

Referential Points

Ernest Hemingway (1898—1961)   American short story writer and novelist. Hemingway, who himself owes a debt to Mark Twain, Sherwood Anderson, and Gertrude Stein, has exerted an influence on the direction of American fiction which is perhaps greater than all of these other writers combined. His greatest contribution, as the Nobel Prize committee acknowledged, was in the area of "prose style." In his use of the "zero ending," which goes counter to the traditional "well-made" ending, Hemingway has influenced the form of the modern short story. He himself a great sportsman, liked to portray soldiers, hunters, bullfighters—tough, at times primitive people whose courage and honesty are set against the brutal ways of modern society, and who in this confrontation lose hope and faith. By depicting the plight of the disenchanted, lost group of Post-World-War I expatriates, he influenced an entire generation of writers and artists, bringing into print for the first time, in the epigraph to *The Sun Also Rises* (1926), the phrase "The Lost Generation." His important works are also "*A Farewell to Arms*" (1929), "*For Whom the Bell Tolls*" (1940), "*The Old Man and the Sea*" (1952).

The Iceberg Theory   After the publication of his last major work, *The Old Man and the Sea*, Ernest Hemingway explained his "iceberg" theory of fiction writing in a Paris Review interview: "If it is any use to know it, I always try to write on the principle of the iceberg. There is seven-eighths of it underwater for every part that shows. Anything you know you can eliminate and it only strengthens your iceberg. It is the part that doesn't show. If a writer omits something because he does not know it then there is a hole in the story."

It is indeed of use on several counts to the Hemingway reader to approach any Hemingway story with an understanding of this "iceberg" theory, the principles of aesthetics that it embodies, and the assumptions about life that it entails. What is below the water level of the Hemingway iceberg? First, there is a conviction that man's awareness of death is one of the guiding forces in life. Beneath every surface activity, then, is the awareness of death. Secondly, there is also the notion that conventional and traditional ways of coping with the fact of man's mortality are based on romantic illusions which cause one to avoid thinking about the central fact of existence: that one must eventually die.

Ebro A river rising in the Cantabrian Mountains of northern Spain and flowing about 925 km (575 mi) to the Mediterranean Sea southwest of Barcelona

Barcelona Seaport city, capital of of Catalonia autonomous region, northeastern Spain. Spain's largest port and second largest city, it is the country's principal industrial and commercial centre, as well as a major cultural and educational centre.

Madrid The capital and largest city of Spain, on the central plateau north-northeast of Toledo. Built on the site of a Moorish fortress captured in the 10th century, it became the capital in 1561 during the reign of Philip II and grew in importance and magnificence under the Bourbons in the 18th century. Madrid was a Loyalist stronghold during the Spanish Civil War (1936—1939).

Consolidation Work

I. Fill in the blanks with the words and expressions provided, making some change when necessary.

| rest on | white elephant | beyond | taste of | get along | take hold of |
| keep out | care about | junction | string | shade | go through |

1. She looked at the clouds _____ the mountain top, without noticing danger was approaching her.
2. If they _____ themselves together into any sort of structure, then they are no longer monomers, they are polymers.
3. Do you _____ her heart as much as we do?
4. Many established landscapes have large areas of partial shade, where sections of the yard are _____ by mature trees.
5. The pyramids were designed to _____ people _____ , but wound up attracting them instead.
6. I would _____ Hellfire if I could but get free from sin at last.
7. Samson _____ the two middle pillars upon which the house rested, and leaned upon them, the one with his right hand, and the other with his left.
8. The research institute of a university, however, is the place for preliminary scholarship. But even there you get only the first _____ learning and the emphasis is on research methodology and practice.
9. Huludao, as the first city outside Shanhai Pass, is situated at such a key _____ that it serves as the west gate of the Northeast.
10. Maybe a transaction can only be completed if the termination date is extended two weeks _____ the official limit. Most companies would rather fudge on the termination date than see a million-dollar deal go up in smoke.
11. The economist J. M. Keynes once remarked that those economists who disliked theory, or claimed to _____ better without it, were simply in the grip of an older theory.
12. They gave us a number of very large pictures as a wedding present; but as we lived in a very small flat the present was a _____.

Unit 2

II. Use the appropriate form of the words given in the brackets to fill in the blanks.

1. Is there a real _____ the US could face fighting two wars at once? (impossible)
2. Under the plan, commercial banks will be allowed to _____ credit procedure for small enterprises and offer more flexibility on interest charges and repayment schemes. (simple)
3. Descartes started his line of _____ by doubting everything, so as to assess the world from a fresh perspective. (reasonably) 4. In some pictures, a lot of important information is conveyed by variations in reds and greens. This is a real problem for _____ blind people who will miss this information. (coloring)
5. They _____ glass making and introduced the technology for coloring it with metal oxides. (perfectly)
6. Please see the _____ policy and strategy sections for more details and the full documents. (operation)
7. *Reader's Digest* may pay hundreds of dollars for an _____ anecdote that it accepts for publication. (amused)
8. One of the best ways to move yourself toward the _____ of your dreams is to visualize yourself doing what your dream is about. (realize)
9. The missile _____ is mounted alongside the operator's _____ telescope and is collimated to it. (track)
10. New York is an amazing city; the Grand Canyon is an awe-inspiring sight; the awesome complexity of the universe; this sea, whose gently _____ stirrings seem to speak of some hidden soul beneath- Melville; Westminster Hall's _____ majesty, so vast, so high, so silent.... (awe)

III. Paraphrase the following sentences taken from the text.

1. "That's the way with everything."
2. I just meant the coloring of their skin through the trees."
3. "I know. But if I do it, then it will be nice again if I say things are like white elephants, and you'll like it?"
4. "No, it isn't. And once they take it away, you never get it back."
5. "... I'm perfectly willing to go through with it if it means anything to you."

IV. Test your general knowledge.

1. _____ refers to the disillusioned intellectuals and aesthetes of the years following World War I, who rebelled against what America had become by the 1900's.
   A. The Beat Generation   B. The Lost Generation
   C. The Angry Young Man   D. Youth
2. What best summarizes the artistic characteristics in Hemingway's short stories?
   A. The Iceberg Analogy   B. Realism
   C. Shortness   D. Simplicity
3. Which of the following work brought the term "the lost generation" into print?
   A. *A Farewell to Arms*   B. *For Whom the Bell Tolls*
   C. *The Sound and the Fury*   D. *The Sun Also Rises*
4. F. Scott Fitzgerald is often acclaimed literary spokesman of _____.

A. The Beat Generation B. The Lost Generation
C. The Jazz Age D. The Modern Literature

5. Which of the following writers does not belong to "The Lost Generation"?
   A. Ernest Hemingway B. F. Scott Fitzgerald
   C. Emily Dickinson D. John Dos Passos
6. Which of the following novels does not belong to John Dos Passos?
   A. *U.S.A., Trilogy* B. *The Big Times*
   C. *The Big Money* D. *The Grapes of Wrath*
7. Fitzgerald produced a summary of the experiences and attitudes of the 1920 decade in U.S. in his masterpiece novel _____.
   A. *The Great Gatsby* B. *Tender is the Night*
   C. *The Rich Boy* D. *The Side of Paradise*
8. In which of the following writings does Hemingway presents his philosophy about life and death through the depiction of the bull-fight as a kind of microcosmic tragedy?
   A. *The Snows of Kilimanjaro* B. *The Old Man and the Sea*
   C. *Death in the Afternoon* D. *The Sun Also Rises*
9. _____ is considered as a leading spokesman of the "Imagist Movement."
   A. Emile Zola B. Emily Dickinson
   C. Ezra Pound D. Ralph Waldo Emerson
10. Which of the following books refers to what Hemingway commented as "all modern American literature comes"?
    A. *The Adventures of Huckleberry Finn* B. *The Great Gatsby*
    C. *Moby-Dick* D. *The Red Badge of Courage*
11. Whose work is said to show a unique synthesis of realism, the "stream of consciousness" and symbolism and his master piece has been regarded as "modern prose epic" in the 20th century?
    A. James Joyce B. Virginia Woolf
    C. Ezra Pound D. Thomas Hardy
12. _____ is regarded as a forerunner of the "stream of consciousness" literature in the 20th century whose novels reveal a fundamental theme of the innocence of the New World and the corruption of the Old.
    A. James Joyce B. Henry James
    C. Katharine Mansfield D. Samuel Butler
13. Whose literary work marks the transition from romanticism to realism in English literature of the 19th century?
    A. Walter Scott B. Charles Lamb
    C. William Wordsworth D. Charles Dickens
14. _____, as the founder of the English realistic novel, was once called "the prose Homer of Human Nature" in Byron's famous phrase.
    A. William Morris B. William Thackeray
    C. Henry Fielding D. Charles Lamb
15. Who introduced the rhymed stanza of various types to English poetry and was regarded as the founder of English literature?
    A. Geoffrey Chaucer B. William Shakespeare
    C. Thomas More D. Christopher Marlowe

Unit 2

V. Proofread the following passage.

If it is true that characterization is as important as conflict
in fiction, it is also true that characterization places certainly demands   1. _____
on the reader which conflict does not. In order to understand what
these demands are and they exist, let us look briefly at the basic   2. _____
nature of the reading process.

Most readers (particularly readers of fiction) think of reading   3. _____
a passive process; the relationship between the reader and the writer is
the one in which the writer does all the work and the reader simply enjoys   4. _____
the product. In the handling of action, this is largely true; if somebody
does something in a story, the writer simply tells us that he does, and   5. _____
all the reader has to do is translate the words that symbolize the action
to a concept. In other words, action in fiction is handled directly. But   6. _____
as soon as a writer goes beyond the simple narration of action, he must
rather be handled directly. Another way of putting this is to say that the   7. _____
writer shows rather than tells; he handles character, theme, and emotion by
implication or suggestion. The writer knows that handle these elements   8. _____
otherwise does not work; it fails to convince and it may even fail to
communicate at all. But implication or dramatization is enough; it is   9. _____
simply a method of presenting characters in such a way as to engage
our attention and interest, and beyond it characters in a story must be
credible, and must seem real. When we believe in the people in a   10. _____
story, we cannot believe in what happens to them, and, consequently,
we stop believing in the story.

VI. Write a composition.

Lewis Weeks claimed in 1980 that "although subject, setting, point of view, characterization, dialog, irony, and compression all make '*Hills like White Elephants*' one of Hemingway's most brilliant short stories, the symbolism implicit in the title and developed in the story contributes more than any other single quality to the powerful impact." In your composition, you are expected to explore all the symbols used in *Hills like White Elephant*.

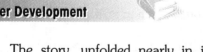
Further Development

1. The story, unfolded nearly in its entirety through dialogue, is a conversation between a young woman and a man waiting for a train in Spain. Through their tight, brittle conversation, much is revealed about their personalities. However, much about their relationship remains hidden. At the end of the story it is still unclear as to what decision has or has not been made, or what will happen to these two characters waiting for a train on a platform in Spain. Reread the story and work out an ending for the story on your own. The style of your work must conform to that of Hemingway's.

2. Put on a role-play: Students are chosen to act out Hills like White Elephants.

Section B Text Two

A Tree, A Rock, A Cloud

By Carson McCullers

1. It was raining that morning, and still very dark. When the boy reached the streetcar café he had almost finished his route and he went in for a cup of coffee. The place was an all-night café owned by a bitter and stingy man called Leo. After the raw, empty street, the café seemed friendly and bright: along the counter there were a couple of soldiers, three spinners from the cotton mill, and in a corner a man who sat hunched over with his nose and half his face down in a beer mug. The boy wore a helmet such as aviators wear. When he went into the café he unbuckled the chin strap and raised the right flap up over his pink little ear; often as he drank his coffee someone would speak to him in a friendly way. But this morning Leo did not look into his face and none of the men were talking. He paid and was leaving the café when a voice called out to him:

2. "Son! Hey Son!"

3. He turned back and the man in the corner was crooking his finger and nodding to him. He had brought his face out of the beer mug and he seemed suddenly very happy. The man was long and pale, with a big nose and faded orange hair.

4. "Hey Son!"

5. The boy went toward him. He was an undersized boy of about twelve, with one shoulder drawn higher than the other because of the weight of the paper sack. His face was shallow, freckled, and his eyes were round child eyes.

6. "Yeah Mister?"

7. The man laid one hand on the paper boy's shoulders, then grasped the boy's chin and turned his face slowly from one side to the other. The boy shrank back uneasily.

8. "Say! What's the big idea?"

9. The boy's voice was shrill; inside the café it was suddenly very quiet.

10. The man said slowly: "I love you."

11. All along the counter the men laughed. The boy, who had scowled and sidled away, did not know what to do. He looked over the counter at Leo, and Leo watched him with a weary, brittle jeer. The boy tried to laugh also. But the man was serious and sad.

12. "I did not mean to tease you, Son," he said. "Sit down and have a beer with me. There is something I have to explain."

13. Cautiously, out of the corner of his eye, the paper boy questioned the men along the counter to see what he should do. But they had gone back to their beer or their breakfast and did not notice him. Leo put a cup of coffee on the counter and a little jug of cream.

14. "He is a minor," Leo said.

15   The paper boy slid himself up onto the stool. His ear beneath the upturned flap of the helmet was very small and red. The man was nodding at him soberly. "It is important," he said. Then he reached in his hip pocket and brought out something which he held up in the palm of his hand for the boy to see.

16   "Look very carefully," he said.

17   The boy stared, but there was nothing to look at very carefully. The man held in his big, grimy palm a photograph. It was the face of a woman, but blurred, so that only the hat and the dress she was wearing stood out clearly.

18   "See?" the man asked.

19   The boy nodded and the man placed another picture in his palm. The woman was standing on a beach in a bathing suit. The suit made her stomach very big, and that was the main thing you noticed.

20   "Got a good look?" He leaned over closer and finally asked: "You ever seen her before?"

21   The boy sat motionless, staring slantwise at the man. "Not so I know of."

22   "Very well." The man blew on the photographs and put them back into his pocket. "That was my wife."

23   "Dead?" the boy asked.

24   Slowly the man shook his head. He pursed his lips as though about to whistle and answered in a long-drawn way: "Nuuu—" he said. "I will explain."

25   The beer on the counter before the man was in a large brown mug. He did not pick it up to drink. Instead he bent down and, putting his face over the rim, he rested there for a moment. Then with both hands he tilted the mug and sipped.

26   "Some night you'll go to sleep with your big nose in a mug and drown," said Leo. "Prominent transient drowns in beer. That would be a cute death."

27   The paper boy tried to signal to Leo. While the man was not looking he screwed up his face and worked his mouth to question soundlessly: "Drunk?" But Leo only raised his eyebrows and turned away to put some pink strips of bacon on the grill. The man pushed the mug away from him, straightened himself, and folded his loose crooked hands on the counter. His face was sad as he looked at the paper boy. He did not blink, but from time to time the lids closed down with delicate gravity over his pale green eyes. It was nearing dawn and the boy shifted the weight of the paper sack.

28   "I am talking about love," the man said. "With me it is a science."

29   The boy half slid down from the stool. But the man raised his forefinger, and there was something about him that held the boy and would not let him go away.

30   "Twelve years ago I married the woman in the photograph. She was my wife for one year, nine months, three days, and two nights. I loved her. Yes..." He tightened his blurred, rambling voice and said again: "I loved her. I thought also that she loved me. I was a railroad engineer. She had all home comforts and luxuries. It never crept into my brain that she was not satisfied. But do you know what happened?"

31   "Mgneeow!" said Leo.

32   The man did not take his eyes from the boy's face. "She left me. I came in one night and the house was empty and she was gone. She left me."

33   "With a fellow?" the boy asked.

34   Gently the man placed his palm down on the counter. "Why naturally, Son. A woman does not run off like that alone."

35   The café was quiet, the soft rain black and endless in the street outside. Leo pressed down the frying bacon with the prongs of his long fork. "So you have been chasing the floozie for eleven years. You frazzled old rascal!"

36   For the first time the man glanced at Leo. "Please don't be vulgar. Besides, I was not speaking to you." He turned back to the boy and said in a trusting and secretive undertone: "Let's not pay any attention to him. O.K.?"

37   The paper boy nodded doubtfully.

38   "It was like this," the man continued. "I am a person who feels many things. All my life one thing after another has impressed me. Moonlight. The leg of a pretty girl. One thing after another. But the point is that when I had enjoyed anything there was a peculiar sensation as though it was laying around loose in me. Nothing seemed to finish itself up or fit in with the other things. Women? I had my portion of them. The same. Afterwards laying around loose in me. I was a man who had never loved."

39   Very slowly he closed his eyelids, and the gesture was like a curtain drawn at the end of a scene in a play. When he spoke again his voice was excited and the words came fast—the lobes of his large, loose ears seemed to tremble.

40   "Then I met this woman. I was fifty-one years old and she always said she was thirty. I met her at a filling station and we were married within three days. And you know what it was like? I just can't tell you. All I had ever felt was gathered together around this woman. Nothing lay around loose in me any more but was finished up by her."

41   The man stopped suddenly and stroked his long nose. His voice sank down to a steady and reproachful under-tone: "I'm not explaining this right. What happened was this. There were these beautiful feelings and loose little pleasures inside me. And this woman was something like an assembly line for my soul. I run these little pieces of myself through her and I come out complete. Now do you follow me?"

42   "What was her name?" the boy asked.

43   "Oh," he said. "I called her Dodo. But that is immaterial."

44   "Did you try to make her come back?"

45   The man did not seem to hear. "Under the circumstances you can imagine how I felt when she left me."

46   Leo took the bacon from the grill and folded two strips of it between a bun. He had a gray face, with slitted eyes, and a pinched nose saddled by faint blue shadows.

47   One of the mill workers signaled for more coffee and Leo poured it. He did not give refills on coffee free. The spinner ate breakfast there every morning, but the better Leo knew his customers the stingier he treated them. He nibbled his own bun as though he grudged it to himself.

48 "And you never got hold of her again?"

49 The boy did not know what to think of the man, and his child's face was uncertain with mingled curiosity and doubt. He was new on the paper route; it was still strange to him to be out in the town in the black, queer early morning.

50 "Yes," the man said. "I took a number of steps to get her back. I went around trying to locate her. I went to Tulsa where she had folks. And to Mobile. I went to every town she had ever mentioned to me, and I hunted down every man she had formerly been connected with. Tulsa, Atlanta, Chicago, Cheehaw, Memphis… For the better part of two years I chased around the country trying to lay hold of her."

51 "But the pair of them had vanished from the face of the earth!" said Leo.

52 "Don't listen to him," the man said confidentially. "And also just forget those two years. They are not important. What matters is that around the third year a curious thing began to happen to me."

53 "What?" the boy asked.

54 The man leaned down and tilted his mug to take a sip of beer. But as he hovered over the mug his nostrils fluttered slightly; he sniffed the staleness of the beer and did not drink. "Love is a curious thing to begin with. At first I thought only of getting her back. It was a kind of mania. But then as time went on I tried to remember her. But do you know what happened?"

55 "No," the boy said.

56 "When I laid myself down on a bed and tried to think about her my mind became a blank. I couldn't see her. I would take out her pictures and look. No good. Nothing doing. A blank. Can you imagine it?"

57 "Say Mac!" Leo called down the counter. "Can you imagine this bozo's mind a blank!"

58 Slowly, as though fanning away flies, the man waved his hand. His green eyes were concentrated and fixed on the shallow little face of the paper boy.

59 "But a sudden piece of glass on a sidewalk. Or a nickel tune in a music box. A shadow on a wall at night. And I would remember. It might happen in a street and I would cry or bang my head against a lamppost. You follow me?"

60 "A piece of glass…" the boy said.

61 "Anything. I would walk around and I had no power of how and when to remember her. You think you can put up a kind of shield. But remembering don't come to a man face forward—it corners around sideways. I was at the mercy of everything I saw and heard. Suddenly instead of me combing the countryside to find her, she began to chase me around in my very soul. She chasing me mind you! And in my soul."

62 The boy asked finally: "What part of the country were you in then?"

63 "Ooh," the man groaned. "I was a sick mortal. It was like smallpox. I confess, Son, that I boozed. I fornicated. I committed any sin that suddenly appealed to me. I am loath to confess it but I will do so. When I recall that period it is all curdled in my mind, it was so terrible."

64   The man leaned his head down and tapped his forehead on the counter. For a few seconds he stayed bowed over in this position, the back of his stringy neck covered with orange furze, his hands with their long warped fingers held palm to palm in an attitude of prayer. Then the man straightened himself; he was smiling and suddenly his face was bright and tremulous and old.

65   "It was in the fifth year that it happened," he said. "And with it I started my science."

66   Leo's mouth jerked with a pale, quick grin. "Well none of we boys are getting any younger," he said. Then with sudden anger he balled up a dishcloth he was holding and threw it down hard on the floor. "You draggletailed old Romeo!"

67   "What happened?" the boy asked.

68   The old man's voice was high and clear: "Peace," he answered.

69   "Huh?"

70   "It is hard to explain scientifically, Son," he said. "I guess the logical explanation is that she and I had fled around from each other for so long that finally we just got tangled up together and lay down and quit. Peace. A queer and beautiful blankness. It was spring in Portland and the rain came every afternoon. All evening I just stayed there on my bed in the dark. And that is how the science come to me."

71   The windows in the streetcar were pale blue with light. The two soldiers paid for their beers and opened the door—one of the soldiers combed his hair and wiped off his muddy puttees before they went outside. The three mill workers bent silently over their breakfasts. Leo's clock was ticking on the wall.

72   "It is this. And listen carefully. I meditated on love and reasoned it out. I realized what is wrong with us. Men fall in love for the first time. And what do they fall in love with?"

73   The boy's soft mouth was partly open and he did not answer.

74   "A woman," the old man said. "Without science, with nothing to go by, they undertake the most dangerous and sacred experience in God's earth. They fall in love with a woman. Is that correct, Son?"

75   "Yeah," the boy said faintly.

76   "They start at the wrong end of love. They begin at the climax. Can you wonder it is so miserable? Do you know how men should love?"

77   The old man reached over and grasped the boy by the collar of his leather jacket. He gave him a gentle little shake and his green eyes gazed down unblinking and grave.

78   "Son, do you know how love should be begun?"

79   The boy sat small and listening and still. Slowly he shook his head. The old man leaned closer and whispered:

80   "A tree. A rock. A cloud."

81   It was still raining outside in the street: a mild, gray, endless rain. The mill whistle blew for the six o'clock shift and the three spinners paid and went away. There was no one in the café but Leo, the old man, and the little paper boy.

82   "The weather was like this in Portland," he said. "At the time my science was begun.

I meditated and I started very cautious. I would pick up something from the street and take it home with me. I bought a goldfish and I concentrated on the goldfish and I loved it. I graduated from one thing to another. Day by day I was getting this technique. On the road from Portland to San Diego—"

83   "Aw shut up!" screamed Leo suddenly. "Shut up! Shut up!"

84   The old man still held the collar of the boy's jacket; he was trembling and his face was earnest and bright and wild. "For six years now I have gone around by myself and built up my science. And now I am a master. Son. I can love anything. No longer do I have to think about it even. I see a street full of people and a beautiful light comes in me. I watch a bird in the sky. Or I meet a traveler on the road. Everything, Son. And anybody. All stranger and all loved! Do you realize what a science like mine can mean?"

85   The boy held himself stiffly, his hands curled tight around the counter edge. Finally he asked: "Did you ever really find that lady?"

86   "What? What say, Son?"

87   "I mean," the boy asked timidly. "Have you fallen in love with a woman again?"

88   The old man loosened his grasp on the boy's collar. He turned away and for the first time his green eyes had a vague and scattered look. He lifted the mug from the counter, drank down the yellow beer. His head was shaking slowly from side to side. Then finally he answered: "No, Son You see that is the last step in my science. I go cautious. And I am not quite ready yet."

89   "Well!" said Leo. "Well well well!"

90   The old man stood in the open doorway. "Remember," he said. Framed there in the gray damp light of the early morning he looked shrunken and seedy and frail. But his smile was bright. "Remember I love you," he said with a last nod. And the door closed quietly behind him.

91   The boy did not speak for a long time. He pulled down the bangs on his forehead and slid his grimy little forefinger around the rim of his empty cup. Then without looking at Leo he finally asked:

92   "Was he drunk?"

93   "No," said Leo shortly.

94   The boy raised his clear voice higher. "Then was he a dope fiend?"

95   "No."

96   The boy looked up at Leo, and his flat little face was desperate, his voice urgent and shrill. "Was he crazy? Do you think he was a lunatic?" The paper boy's voice dropped suddenly with doubt. "Leo? Or not?"

97   But Leo would not answer him. Leo had run a night café for fourteen years, and he held himself to be a critic of craziness. There were the town characters and also the transients who roamed in from the night. He knew the manias of all of them. But he did not want to satisfy the questions of the waiting child. He tightened his pale face and was silent.

98   So the boy pulled down the right flap of his helmet and as he turned to leave he made the only comment that seemed safe to him, the only remark that could not be laughed down and despised:

99   "He sure has done a lot of traveling."

Independent Study Assistance

I. Words and Expressions

1. **crook** *v.*   to bend a part of your body inwards, especially your finger
2. **scowle** *v.*   to twist your face into an expression that shows you are angry
3. **sidle** *v.*   to move slowly in a particular direction, usually because you are nervous or do not want to be noticed
4. **brittle** *adj.*   weak, fragile, flimsy. A brittle laugh or smile does not show real humour or happiness.
5. **purse one's lips**   to press one's lips together and outwards because one is angry or is thinking
6. **transient** *n.*   someone who does not have a permanent home or job and moves from one place to another
7. **prong** *n.*   a long sharp point, especially one of the points on a fork
8. **floozy** *n.*   an insulting word for a woman who likes to attract men and have sex
9. **frazzled** *adj.*   extremely tired, annoyed, and unable to deal with things
10. **undertone** *n.*   something that suggests a particular idea or feeling without directly saying or showing it
11. **stingy** *adj.*   unwilling to spend, give, or use a lot of money
12. **slit** *v.*   to make a long thin cut in something
13. **hover** *v.*   to be in a state or situation that may change at any time.
14. **bozo** *n.*   a stupid person
15. **smallpox** *n.*   a serious disease in which your skin becomes covered in spots that can leave permanent marks
16. **booze** *v.*   to drink alcohol, or to be drunk
17. **fornicate** *v.*   to have sex with someone that you are not married to. This word shows you think this is morally wrong.
18. **loath** *adj.*   very unwilling to do something
19. **curdle** *v.*   if milk or another liquid curdles, or if something makes it curdle, lumps begin to form in it.
20. **ball up**   to become a small round shape, or to make something into a small round shape
21. **tangle** or **tangle up**   if something tangles, or if you tangle it, its parts become twisted around each other or around something else so that they look messy and are difficult to separate
22. **shrunken** *adj.*   smaller than before, or smaller than is natural
23. **seedy** *adj.*   connected with activities that are illegal or morally wrong, and often looking dirty or unpleasant
24. **dope** *n.*   a stupid person; an illegal drug, especially marijuana
25. **fiend** *n.*   (mainly literary) a very evil person; informally someone who is extremely enthusiastic about something

II. Referential Points

Carson McCullers (1917—1967) considered to be among the most significant American writers of the twentieth century. She wrote novels, short stories, and two plays, as well as essays and some poetry. Carson McCullers is best known for her novels *The Heart Is a Lonely Hunter, The Ballad of the Sad Café, Reflections in a Golden Eye*, and *The Member of the Wedding*. Her first novel *The Heart is a Lonely Hunter* explores the spiritual isolation of misfits and outcasts of the South. Her other novels have similar themes and are all set in the South. *The Ballad of the Sad Café* (1951) is a short story collection comprising: a novella of the same title which was later made into a Merchant Ivory Film, *Wunderkind* (1936), *The Jockey* (1941), *Madame Zilensky and the King of Finland* (1941), *The Sourner* (1950), *A Domestic Dilemma* (1941), *A Tree, a Rock, a Cloud* (1942).

Psychological Novel, also called **psychological realism** a work of prose fiction which places more than the usual amount of emphasis on interior characterization, and on the motives, circumstances, and internal action which springs from, and develops, external action. The psychological novel is not content to state what happens but goes on to explain the motivation of this action. In this type of writing, character and characterization are more than usually important, and they often delve deeper into the mind of a character than novels of other genres. The psychological novel can be called a novel of the "inner man," so to say. In some cases, the stream of consciousness technique, as well as interior monologues, may be employed to better illustrate the inner workings of the human mind at work. Flashbacks may also be featured. *The Tale of Genji* written in 11th century Japan, has often been considered the first psychological novel.

III. Questions for Comprehension

1. Draw a character sketch of the man, the paper boy and Leo.
2. From the old man's tale, how much do you know about the woman?
3. What is the theme of the story? How is every character related to it?
4. The topic of *A Tree, A Rock, A Cloud* is love. How is the title of the story related to this topic?
5. What does the old man mean by "science"?
6. Why did the transient tell his story to the boy instead of other people in the Café?
7. What is the lesson learnt by the old man from his experience?

Self-test

I. Fill in the blanks with the words and expressions provided, making some change when necessary.

stand out	at the mercy of	transient	tangle	shrunken	creep into
undertone	get hold of	appeal to	hover	be loath to	stingy
reason... out	build up	curdle			

1. It's my position that gentlemen should _____ things _____ rather than resort to force.

Section B

2. And at the same instant Dants felt himself flung into the air like a wounded bird, falling, falling, with a rapidity that made his blood _____ .
3. Most people are _____ spend their days in ceaseless conflict with authority, especially when it can only end in the defeat of the isolated individual.
4. The feather gorgeous birds nobly and gracefully _____ in the all colors variegated jungle sky.
5. Contrasts in value are something people perceive quickly and easily, so value can be a good tool for drawing attention to elements that need to _____ .
6. Doubt and mistrust could _____ our lives, corroding personal and professional relationship.
7. Heaven and earth are a lodging house for the ten thousand things of creation; time is a _____ guest for all generations.
8. He takes the road of collective prosperity instead of trying to _____ family fortunes.
9. There were old men with grizzled beards and sunken eyes, men who were comparatively young but _____ by diseases, men who were middle-aged.
10. The latter film with anti-Nazi _____ was banned by Nazi party which then demanded Lang's collaboration.
11. Joel had been traveling a lot lately too—to Iceland to interview Bjork; to Hollywood for the Oscars—but he was _____ with details.
12. What was needed to _____ the floating voters was the ability to inspire them with a sense of conviction.
13. This fully indicates that the law governing science exists objectively, and people all over the world can _____ it sooner or later no matter what method is used.
14. One's happiness must in some measure be always _____ chance.
15. You are currently in a muddle where financial and emotional concerns are _____ together.

II. Use the appropriate form of the words given in the brackets to fill in the blanks.
1. But in the Zen meditation hall, they would meditate on the Zen, and they have even achieved advanced levels of _____ . (meditate)
2. He said, turning to Alice: he had taken his watch out of his pocket, and was looking at it _____ , shaking it every now and then, and holding it to his ear. (easy)
3. The body is material but the soul is _____ . (material)
4. The gap between us these days is of my own making, but to me it is an incalculable loss. Yet while I mean to _____ his hold on me, I've only helped tighten it. (loose)
5. Two days later, Nancy was seated in her car, observing the house which Davey Birdsony had visited so _____ . (secret)
6. Again Chueh-hui happened to catch Chueh-hsin's gaze. Chueh-hsin was looking at him in a melancholy and somewhat _____ manner. (reproach)
7. While communication is not a big problem on the internet, you can't assume _____ , so exercise caution in sending certain financial, personnel, or proprietary information. (confidential)
8. My happy eye was upon it always, and I sat _____ , steeped in satisfaction, drunk with enjoyment. (motion)
9. In the summer of 1958 the pianist had a _____ triumphant return. (sensation)
10. History is a combination between permanence and _____ . (transient)

Unit 2

III. Translating the short paragraph into Chinese.

The old man reached over and grasped the boy by the collar of his leather jacket. He gave him a gentle little shake and his green eyes gazed down unblinking and grave.

"Son, do you know how love should be begun?"

The boy sat small and listening and still. Slowly he shook his head. The old man leaned closer and whispered:

"A tree. A rock. A cloud."

It was still raining outside in the street: a mild, gray, endless rain. The mill whistle blew for the six o'clock shift and the three spinners paid and went away. There was no one in the café but Leo, the old man, and the little paper boy.

"The weather was like this in Portland," he said. "At the time my science was begun. I meditated and I started very cautious. I would pick up something from the street and take it home with me. I bought a goldfish and I concentrated on the goldfish and I loved it. I graduated from one thing to another. Day by day I was getting this technique. On the road from Portland to San Diego—"

IV. Analyze difficult sentences.

1. Nothing lay around loose in me any more but was finished up by her.
2. And this woman was something like an assembly line for my soul. I run these little pieces of myself through her and I come out complete.
3. When I recall that period it is all curdled in my mind, it was so terrible.
4. For the better part of two years I chased around the country trying to lay hold of her.
5. "A woman," the old man said. "Without science, with nothing to go by, they undertake the most dangerous and sacred experience in God's earth."
6. I graduated from one thing to another.

V. Proofread the following passage.

As if you didn't know, Stephen King just may be the world's most popular author. He has certainly gone far beyond being recognized solely as the most successful horror writer in history.

Since 1974, more than 300 million copies of his approximate 45 novels and collections have been published in 33 languages, include "The Dark Tower" series and "The Dead Zone." King started off on the road to scary stories early, becoming something of an expert of horror films.

His interest was first sparked by a collection of fantasy novels which belonged to his father, who deserted the family when Stephen was a toddler. King started writing when he was still a child, and as a teenager he sold a couple of short stories to a mysterious magazine. But it was not all blood and guts; the young Stephen also played in a rock band and for his high school football team. After graduation from the University of Maine, King briefly taught high school English. When "Carrie" pushed him in the big time, King was just 27 years old. Then his brand of storytelling

1. _____
2. _____
3. _____
4. _____
5. _____
6. _____

captured the public imagination tight away, he proved he had come to stay as a thriller writer on his next two books, "Salem's Lot," a modern vampire story, and "The Shining," about the Queen Mother of haunted houses. Right now he has won several important literary awards including British Fantasy Award for Short Fiction of "The Breathing Method" in 1993 and the O'Henry Award for "Different Seasons," in 1996.

7. _____
8. _____
9. _____
10. _____

VI. Write a composition.

Read the story again and then write a plot summary of the story.

Unit 3

Biography

Section A

Text One Honor Under Cruel Circumstances

Focal Consideration

1. Marie Curie was historically and is still remembered by most people as Madam Curie rather than in her full name. Some say that it was not an honorific title or an accident, rather it was a contempt, scorn, and obliteration of her contribution to science. Give your comment on this in connection with the hardships that Marie Curie experienced.
2. This text, an excerpt from *Marie Curie: And the Science of Radioactivity*, is written in a style of biography. Concentration will be on the characteristics of bibliographical style as reflected in this text.

Research Questions

Think about the following questions and discuss them with your group members. After your discussion, work out a research report and share it with students of other groups.
1. How much do you know about Madame Curie? Work out a brief report about her life and main achievements.
2. Before Pierre Curie joined his wife in the study of radioactivity, he had codiscovered piezoelectricity (producing an electrical field by applying stress to crystals) and invented the quartz balance. Why did Pierre Curie leave his own work, then?
3. What cruel circumstances did Madame Curie sustain after Pierre Curie's death?

Honor Under Cruel Circumstances

By Naomi Pasachoff

1   When Pierre left the house on Thursday, April 19, 1906, there was no way for

Marie to know that she would never again see him alive. The family had just spent a delightful Easter holiday in the country, where Pierre had enjoyed the attempts of $8\frac{1}{2}$-year-old Irène to catch butterflies in a little green net, and of 14-month-old Ève to remain surefooted on the bumpy terrain.

2   Despite his illness and depression of the past several years, Pierre was once again feeling involved in his work. Decades later, in her biography of her mother, Ève quoted a letter he wrote five days before his death, expressing guarded optimism that a new joint project with Marie was finally showing signs of success: "Madame Curie and I are working to dose radium with precision by the amount of emanation [the name Ernest Rutherford had given to the radioactive gas emitted by a radioactive substance] it gives off. That might seem to be nothing, and yet here we have been at it for several months and are only now beginning to obtain regular results."

3   Pierre had several engagements to attend on his last day—a luncheon of the Association of Professors in the Faculty of Science, a visit to his publisher to correct proofs, one appointment in the afternoon, and another that evening with his physicist colleague and next-door neighbor Jean Perrin. He was fated to keep only the first engagement. Lunch with his fellow professors over, he went out into the rain and headed for his publisher, only to discover that the offices were shut because of a strike. As he walked on, fumbling with his umbrella, he slipped while crossing a busy street. The driver of a heavy horse-drawn cart pulled on his reins, but to no avail. The cart's rear wheel hit Pierre's head, crushing his skull. Death was instantaneous.

4   News of the fatal accident arrived shortly thereafter at the Curie home, but only Pierre's father was there to receive it. According to Ève, when he saw the faces of the bearers of bad news, her grandfather said, "My son is dead." After learning the circumstances of Pierre's death, he added, "What was he dreaming of this time?"

5   Marie did not return home from the lab until six o'clock that evening, only to discover the two visitors—Professor Perrin and the dean of faculty, Paul Appell—still sitting with her father-in-law. Paul Appell repeated the facts. After standing silently for what seemed an eternity, the 38-year-old widow said, "Pierre is dead? Dead? Absolutely dead?" Ève was later to analyze the transformation that occurred in that moment: "Mme Curie, on that day in April, became not only a widow, but at the same time a pitiful and incurably lonely woman."

6   Marie nonetheless took charge. She asked Madame Perrin to take Irène next door for a few days, where she could be with the Perrin children. She sent a telegram to her family in Poland: "Pierre dead result accident." She arranged to have Pierre's body brought back to the house. Only when Pierre's older brother, Jacques, arrived the next day from Montpellier did she allow herself to break down. The emotional outburst was brief.

7   Telegrams and letters began to arrive. Newspapers around the world carried the story. To enable those, like Lord Kelvin, her brother Joseph, and her sister Bronya, who

set out hastily for Paris, to attend the funeral, she scheduled it for that Saturday, in the same cemetery where his mother lay. After the funeral and burial, she began a diary into which, for an entire year, she poured her emotions, addressing herself to her deceased husband in intimate terms. (The contents of the diary, which the family entrusted after Marie's death to the French National Library, were closed to researchers until 1990.)

8   The day after the funeral the French government officially offered to support Marie and the children with a state pension, as had been done for the widow of the great chemist and bacteriologist Louis Pasteur (1822—95). When Jacques informed her of the offer, she flatly rejected it, asserting her conviction that she could perfectly well support herself and her daughters.

9   Accompanied by Jacques, Marie returned to her research that very day. Ève later quoted Marie's diary entry describing that first attempt to resume productive work: "On the Sunday morning after your death, Pierre, I went to the laboratory with Jacques for the first time. I tried to make a measurement, for a graph on which we had each made several points. But I felt the impossibility of going on."

10   In her Autobiographical Notes, Marie summarized the emotional turmoil of those days: "It is impossible for me to express the profoundness and importance of the crisis brought into my life by the loss of the one who had been my closest companion and best friend. Crushed by the blow, I did not feel able to face the future. I could not forget, however, what my husband used to say, that, even deprived of him, I ought to continue my work."

11   Less than a month after Pierre's death, on May 13, 1906, the University of Paris, which had never before had a female professor, made an unprecedented offer to Marie. Pierre's academic position was hers, if she would have it. As she reported in her Autobiographical Notes, she hesitated before accepting. "The honor that now came to me was deeply painful under the cruel circumstances of its coming." Her sense that she could best pay homage to her deceased husband by resuming their research was instrumental in overcoming her hesitancy. In Pierre Curie she wrote, "I accepted this heavy heritage, in the hope that I might build up some day, in his memory, a laboratory worthy of him, which he had never had, but where others would be able to work to develop his idea."

12   The summer following Pierre's death was a busy one for Marie. She sent the girls off to the country with relatives and set about several tasks. She decided to move, together with her father-in-law, to Sceaux, where Pierre had lived with his parents when the couple first met, and where he and his mother were now buried. The move would mean a half-hour commute to work, but she felt it would be better for the family to be in new surroundings. She also faced two formidable professional challenges: to prepare a course justifying her professorial position and to refute a devastating criticism of her work from an unexpected quarter—Pierre's longtime supporter, Lord Kelvin.

13   The first challenge was the less daunting of the two. In the course of the summer,

Marie went over Pierre's teaching notes, as well as other professional materials. An hour and a half before her first lecture at the Sorbonne, on November 5, 1906—15 years to the day after she had first enrolled there as a student—Marie stood in the cemetery at Sceaux by Pierre's tomb. Meanwhile, crowds began to fill the lecture hall, not only students but also many curious onlookers who, having been alerted by the press, were eager to hear what the Sorbonne's first woman professor would say, and how the mourning wife would acquit herself. Those expecting high drama were doubtlessly disappointed when the small woman entered the room and, waiting for the spontaneous applause to die down, began to speak. Picking up Pierre's course exactly where he had left it, she began, "When one considers the progress that has been made in physics in the past ten years, one is surprised at the advance that has taken place in our ideas concerning electricity and matter...."

14   The second challenge was issued in an unconventional manner. Lord Kelvin had decided that radium was not an element at all, but more likely a compound of lead and five helium atoms. Because of the popular interest in radium, he published his theory not in a scientific journal but in the "Letters to the Editor" column on the front page of the London Times. Lord Kelvin's theory threatened to undermine not only Marie's entire scientific career but also Rutherford's work in explaining the phenomenon of radioactivity. Marie responded not in words but by setting out to prove in the laboratory that radium indeed merited its own spot in the periodic table. With the help of André Debierne, who had been a colleague of the Curies from the earliest days in the SIPC storeroom, she succeeded in 1910 in isolating pure radium metal. To do so meant separating radium from its salts, even though radium was only stable as long as it was chemically combined in a salt. The difficult process, which risked the loss of precious radium, was never again repeated, but it proved its point. Lord Kelvin, having died in 1907, spared himself the embarrassment of being proved wrong.

15   While the determination to vindicate her claims about radium propelled her forward in the months after Pierre's death, other professional satisfactions came her way. Two in particular advanced her goal of building a laboratory worthy of Pierre. In the winter of 1907, some months after meeting Marie Curie in Paris, the American philanthropist Andrew Carnegie sent Dean Paul Appell $50,000 to found the Curie Scholarships. These fellowships, which would enable promising scientists to devote themselves full-time to research, helped Marie put together a research staff. In choosing the Curie scholars, she always had an eye out for talented Poles and talented women. Then, in 1909, the Pasteur Institute—interested in radium's medical applications—and the University of Paris began discussions about founding a Radium Institute. Within a few years the arrangements were made. The two institutions would share equally in the cost of establishing the Institute, which would consist of two divisions—a radioactivity laboratory under Marie's supervision, and a medical research laboratory under the supervision of an eminent physician.

16   Her intensive laboratory work and teaching preparations made it necessary for Marie to give up her teaching at the school in Sèvres for women teachers-in-training, where her friend and colleague Paul Langevin replaced her. But Marie in these years undertook another course of teaching closer to home. Dissatisfied with the methods of the schools she looked at for Irène, she decided with a group of like-minded professional parents to run a cooperative school, with the parents teaching the children in their fields of specialization. For two years, Irène, along with eight or nine other children, thus studied mathematics, chemistry, physics, French history and literature, art history, and studio art, taught by some of the great practitioners of the time.

17   The death of Pierre's father in February 1910 dealt a severe blow to Marie. Dr. Curie had been instrumental not only in caring for both girls but also in imbuing Irène, the older of the two, with his values. For the next several years, Marie would share the responsibilities of the girls' upbringing with a succession of Polish governesses, some more successful than others.

18   But that year of intense mourning also was a year of achievement. In addition to her triumph in isolating pure radium metal, Marie was awarded five honorary titles, as well as a medal from the Royal Society of Arts in London. That fall, at an international professional meeting in Belgium, Marie was given the prestigious responsibility of defining the international standard for measuring radium. Such a standard was needed in order to ensure the success of radium therapy, as well as for industrial purposes and scientific research. Although not everyone agreed, Marie insisted that since it had already been determined that the standard unit was to be called a "curie," she and she alone should define it. Using a carefully weighed amount of pure radium salt, she prepared the standard curie the following year. Although originally defined as the amount of radiation emitted by 1 gram of radium, a curie is now defined as 37 billion atomic decays per second. Shortly after returning to Paris, Marie also took pleasure in the publication of her monumental Treatise on Radioactivity. Rutherford reviewed the two-volume work favorably, although privately he questioned its long-term utility, since it was heavy on specific details and short on critical analysis.

19   Marie Curie was able to go on living after the devastating blow dealt her in April 1906 because of her work. In Pierre Curie, Marie described conversations she and Pierre sometimes had in the early days of their marriage, when one or the other entertained thoughts of irreparable loss. According to Marie, Pierre always offered the same response: "Whatever happens, even if one should become like a body without a soul, still one must always work." By taking Pierre's advice to heart, Marie was able to continue functioning—if never to give up grieving—after his untimely death.

Section A

Preview Assistance

1. **surefooted** *adj.*   able to walk without sliding or falling, in a place where it is not easy to do this
2. **bumpy** *adj.*   (of a surface) not even; with a lot of bumps
3. **emanation** *n.*   any of several radioactive gases that are isotopes of radon and are products of radioactive decay
4. **fumble** *v.*   to use your hands in an awkward way when you are doing sth or looking for sth
5. **eternity** *n.*   a period of time that seems to be very long or to never end
6. **break down**   to lose control of your feelings and start crying
7. **deceased** *adj.*   dead
8. **pension** *n.*   an amount of money paid regularly by a government or company to sb who is considered to be too old or too ill/sick to work
9. **flatly** *adv.*   in a way that is very definite and will not be changed
10. **conviction** *n.*   the feeling or appearance of being confident or very certain about sth
11. **turmoil** *n.*   a state of excitement or uncontrolled activity
12. **deprive (of)** *v.*   to prevent sb from having or doing sth, especially sth important
13. **unprecedented** *adj.*   that has never happened, been done or been known before
14. **pay homage to** *phr.*   to say or do sth that shows you respect and admire someone a lot
15. **instrumental** *adj.*   involved in an important way in making sth happen
16. **commute** *n.*   the journey that a person makes when they commute to work
17. **formidable** *adj.*   difficult to deal with and needing a lot of effort or skill
18. **refute** *v.*   to prove that sth is wrong
19. **devastating** *adj.*   causing a lot of damage and destruction
20. **to the day** *phr.*   used for saying that sth happened on the same day in a different year
21. **acquit oneself well/honourably** *phr.*   to behave or do sth well, especially sth difficult that you do for the first time in front of other people
22. **vindicate** *v.*   to prove that sth is true or that you were right to do sth, especially when other people had a different opinion
23. **eminent** *adj.*   (of people) famous and respected, especially in a particular profession
24. **practitioner** *n.*   a person who works in a profession, especially medicine or law
25. **deal a blow to**   to harm, upset, or shock someone or sth
26. **imbue (with)** *v.*   to fill someone or sth with a particular quality or emotion
27. **a succession of**   a number of people or things of the same kind, following, coming, or happening one after the other
28. **prestigious** *adj.*   respected and admired as very important or of very high quality
29. **treatise** *n.*   a long and serious piece of writing on a particular subject
30. **entertain** *v.*   to consider or allow yourself to think about an idea, a hope, a feeling, etc.

Referential Points

    Biography as a genre is a description or account of someone's life and the times, which is usually published in the form of a book or an essay, or in some other form, such as a film. A biography is more than a list of impersonal facts (education, work, relationships, and death), it also portrays the subject's experience of those events. Unlike a profile or curriculum vitae (résumé), a biography presents the subject's story, highlighting various aspects of his or her life, including intimate details of experiences, and may include an analysis of the subject's personality.

Marie Skłodowska Curie (1867—1934) was a physicist and chemist of Polish upbringing and subsequent French citizenship. She was a pioneer in the field of radioactivity and the first person honored with two Nobel Prizes — in physics and chemistry. She was also the first woman professor at the University of Paris.

Pierre Curie (1859—1906) was a French physicist, a pioneer in crystallography, magnetism, piezoelectricity and radioactivity, and Nobel laureate. In 1903 he received the Nobel Prize in Physics with his wife, Maria Skłodowska-Curie, and Henri Becquerel, "in recognition of the extraordinary services they have rendered by their joint researches on the radiation phenomena discovered by Professor Henri Becquerel."

Easter the most important annual religious feast in the Christian liturgical year. According to Christian scripture, Jesus was resurrected from the dead on the third day of his crucifixion. Christians celebrate this resurrection on Easter Day or Easter Sunday (also Resurrection Day or Resurrection Sunday), two days after Good Friday and three days after Maundy Thursday.

Jean Perrin (1870—1942) was a French physicist and Nobel laureate. After Albert Einstein published (1905) his theoretical explanation of Brownian motion in terms of atoms, Perrin did the experimental work to test and verify Einstein's predictions, thereby settling the century-long dispute about John Dalton's atomic theory. He received the Nobel Prize in Physics in 1926 for this and other work on the discontinuous structure of matter, which put a definite end to the long struggle regarding the question of the physical reality of molecules.

Ève Curie Labouisse (1904—2007) was a French-American author and writer. She was the second daughter of Marie and Pierre Curie and wrote an acclaimed biography of her mother, Madame Curie, in 1937. Her life was intimately connected with the Nobel Prize: both of her parents and her sister, Irène Curie, were awarded Nobel Prizes for sciences and her husband, Henry Richardson Labouisse, Jr., accepted a Nobel Peace Prize on behalf of UNICEF.

Irène Joliot-Curie (1897—1956) was a French scientist, the daughter of Marie Curie and Pierre Curie and the wife of Frédéric Joliot-Curie. Jointly with her husband, Joliot-Curie was awarded the Nobel Prize for chemistry in 1935 for their discovery of artificial radioactivity. This made the Curies the family with most Nobel laureates to date. Both children of the Joliot-Curies, Hélène and Pierre, are also esteemed scientists.

Paul-Jacques Curie (1856—1941) was a French physicist and professor at the University of Montpellier. He and his brother, Pierre Curie, studied pyroelectricity in the 1880s, leading to their discovery of some of the mechanisms behind piezoelectricity.

Lord Kelvin, or William Thomson, 1st Baron Kelvin of Largs (1824—1907), was a British mathematical physicist and engineer. For his work on the transatlantic telegraph project he was Knighted by Queen Victoria, becoming Sir William Thomson. Lord Kelvin is widely known for developing the basis of Absolute Zero, and for this reason a unit of temperature measure is named after him. On his ennoblement in honour of his achievements in thermodynamics he adopted the title Baron Kelvin of Largs and is therefore often described as Lord Kelvin.

Louis Pasteur (1822—1895) was a French chemist and microbiologist born in Dole. He is remembered for his remarkable breakthroughs in the causes and preventions of disease. His discoveries reduced mortality from puerperal fever, and he created the first vaccine for rabies. His experiments supported the germ theory of disease. He was best known to the general public for inventing a method to stop milk and wine from causing sickness, a process that came to be called pasteurization.

André-Louis Debierne (1874—1949) was a French chemist and is considered the discoverer of the element actinium. He was a close friend of Pierre and Marie Curie and was associated with their work. In 1899, he discovered the radioactive element actinium, as a result of continuing the work with pitchblende that the Curies had initiated.

Andrew Carnegie (1835—1919) was an American industrialist, businessman, entrepreneur, and a major philanthropist. He is one of the most famous captains of industry of the late 19th and early 20th centuries. With the fortune he made from business, he later turned to philanthropy and interests in education, founding the Carnegie Corporation of New York, Carnegie Endowment for International Peace, Carnegie Mellon University and the Carnegie Museums of Pittsburgh.

Consolidation Work

I. Fill in the blanks with the words and expressions provided, making some change when necessary.

surefooted	entertain	prestigious	a succession of	imbue
deal a blow to	vindicate	undermine	acquit	to the day
instrumental	deprive	conviction	pay homage to	unprecedented

1. For national salvation and self emancipation, Chinese women, along with the entire nation, waged a dauntless struggle that lasted for over a century. They also launched _____ movements for women's liberation.
2. He went to London's _____ Westminster School where, aged 14, he earned his first fee for a satirical piece about Von Ribbentrop's son, a fellow pupil for the Evening Standard newspaper.
3. She wanted her children to feel loved and lovable, creative and imaginative, _____ with a sense that there was magic in the world and beauty even in the face of adversity.
4. Each of the major peasant uprisings and wars _____ the feudal regime of the time, and hence more or less furthered the growth of the social productive forces.
5. We are vigorous and energetic, with _____ working attitude, can satisfy all of your demands, and create more competitive marketing for you.
6. A large number of economic crimes were dealt with in accordance with the law, and criminals found to have seriously _____ the market order were punished.
7. His involvement in the recent government scandal has evaporated any hopes that he might have _____ regarding his future political life.
8. This fired the people with soaring enthusiasm for building a new China and a new life,

Unit 3

emancipated the social productive forces and set the economy on the track of _____ growth.

9. Then why—since the choice was with himself—should the individual, whose connexion with the fallen woman had been the most intimate and sacred of them all, come forward to _____ his claim to an inheritance so little desirable?

10. I take much pleasure in recommending to you Miss Susan Keyser and am confident that, if appointed, she will _____ herself most creditably.

11. Five hundred years ago, almost _____, the world of art discovered a subtle solution to an iconographic puzzle with which it had been struggling for several centuries.

12. Under the patronage of the king and his wives, Buddhism spread quickly in Tibet and devout worshippers began flocking to Lhasa to _____ Buddha.

13. Since then, the poor fellow had seemed _____ of reason, wandering aimlessly about and supported by public charity—an object of universal pity.

14. While most scientists agree that the greenhouse effect is coming, there aren't enough data yet to say with absolute _____ what its consequences will be.

15. The launching of euro and the completion of the EMU will be _____ in reshaping the international monetary system, principally by making it more balanced and symmetrical.

II. Use the appropriate form of the words given in the brackets to fill in the blanks.

1. He seemed to undergo a _____, to stiffen physically, to thrust his chin forward aggressively, and to glint harshly in his eyes. (transform)

2. Chaco is remarkable for its _____ public and ceremonial buildings and its distinctive architecture—it has an ancient urban ceremonial centre that is unlike anything constructed before or since. (monument)

3. The elegant design, exquisite craftsman, noble quality show up the _____ of culture and charm of fashion that a metropolitan embraced. (profound)

4. In all but these few and (except in the very commencement of human society) unimportant cases, the objects supplied by nature are only _____ to human wants, after having undergone some degree of transformation by human exertion. (instrument)

5. But old friends are dwindling away year by year. They are originally few in number, so the disappearance of any of them is an _____ loss to me. (repair)

6. After six months of arguing and final 16 hours of hot parliamentary debates, Australia's Northern Territory became the first legal authority in the world to allow doctors to take the lives of _____ ill patients who wish to die. (cure)

7. During the last century, while achieving _____ results in material and spiritual civilization, mankind also went through the tribulation of tragic wars and prolonged Cold War. (precede)

8. At Eton, he proved a good classical scholar, But was not very happy, for he was by nature revolutionary and _____. (convention)

9. There is nothing inchoate, it says, about this universe of ours, all that was or is or shall be actual in it having been from _____ virtually there. (eternal)

10. The Chinese people are _____ but also skeptical, aspiring but also conscious that no one man's intuition, however tremendous, can provide the answer to the dilemmas of history. (talent)

Section A

III. Paraphrase the following sentences taken from the text.

1. Marie responded not in words but by setting out to prove in the laboratory that radium indeed merited its own spot in the periodic table.
2. The difficult process, which risked the loss of precious radium, was never again repeated, but it proved its point. Lord Kelvin, having died in 1907, spared himself the embarrassment of being proved wrong.
3. While the determination to vindicate her claims about radium propelled her forward in the months after Pierre's death, other professional satisfactions came her way.
4. In choosing the Curie scholars, she always had an eye out for talented Poles and talented women.
5. For the next several years, Marie would share the responsibilities of the girls' upbringing with a succession of Polish governesses, some more successful than others.

IV. Test your general knowledge.

1. In 1891, at the age of twenty-four, Curie enrolled at _____ and became one of the few women in attendance at the university.
   A. Warsaw University   B. Sorbonne University
   C. the University of Paris   D. the University of Montpellier
2. In 1898, _____ extracted a new element, which was much more radioactive than even pure uranium, and named it polonium in honor of Marie's native Poland.
   A. Marie Curie   B. Pierre Curie
   C. the Curies   D. Henri Becquerel
3. Pitchblende contained another new element, one that was thousands of times more radioactive than uranium; to this element the Curies in 1898 gave the name _____.
   A. radium   B. polonium
   C. radioactivity   D. thorium
4. The Nobel Prize was established in 1895 by a Swedish chemist and inventor Alfred Nobel. It was first awarded in Physics, Chemistry, Physiology or Medicine, Literature, and Peace in _____.
   A. 1895   B. 1896   C. 1898   D. 1901
5. The Curies and _____ shared the 1903 Nobel Prize for Physics for their contributions to the new science of radioactivity.
   A. Henri Becquerel   B. Lord Kelvin
   C. Paul Appell   D. Jean Perrin
6. Madam Curie was the first person to receive twice the Nobel Prize, first in _____ in 1903, and the second in _____ in 1911.
   A. Chemistry ... Physics   B. Physics ... Chemistry
   C. Chemistry ... Chemistry, too D. Physics ... Physics, too
7. Albert Einstein remarked that "_____ is, of all celebrated beings, the only one whom fame has not corrupted."
   A. Marie Curie   B. Pierre Curie
   C. Henri Becquerel   D. Paul Appell
8. *Madame Curie,* a biography published by Gallimard (Paris) in 1938, was written by _____.

A. Pierre Curie B. Ève Curie
C. Irène Curie D. Paul Langevin

9. _____ and her husband was jointly awarded the Nobel Prize for chemistry in 1935 for their discovery of artificial radioactivity.
   A. Irène Curie B. Ève Curie
   C. Hélène Joliot-Curie D. Bronya Sklodowska

10. _____ findings about the relationship between temperature and magnetism became known as Curie's law. The temperature above which magnetic properties disappear is called the Curie point.
    A. Pierre Curie's B. Marie Curie's
    C. Irène Curie's D. Hélène Joliot-Curie's

11. Which of the following statements is NOT true? _____
    A. Pierre Curie was killed in an accident.
    B. Pierre Curie died from radioactivity.
    C. Pierre Curie had two daughters.
    D. Pierre Curie attended a luncheon at his last day.

12. Why did Madam Curie think it was a heavy heritage to accept the offer to assume Pierre's academic position?
    A. Because she was too sad to continue research work.
    B. Because she was afraid that she could not acquit herself.
    C. Because she was not sure that she could build up some day a laboratory where others would work to develop Pierre's idea.
    D. Because the University of Paris had never before had a female professor.

13. On hearing Madam Curie's first lecture at the Sorbonne, on November 5, 1906, many other persons besides students went to the lecture hall mainly _____.
    A. to protest the female professor to give lectures
    B. to encourage Madam Curie
    C. to see how the female professor would acquit herself
    D. to listen to Madam Curie's lecture on the progress of physics

14. Which of the followings is NOT written by Madam Curie? _____
    A. *Autobiographical Notes*. B. *Pierre Curie*.
    C. *Madam Curie*. D. *Treatise on Radioactivity*.

15. A number of families have included multiple laureates, and the Curie family claim the most Nobel Prizes, _____ in total.
    A. two B. three C. four D. five

V. Proofread the following passage.

The Curies and Becquerel shared the 1903 Nobel Prize for Physics for their contributions to the new science of radioactivity, but the couple did not attend the ceremony, for they were ill to make the trip. Pierre Curie was also offered a 1. _____ professorial position in the Sorbonne's research laboratory, with his wife as his lab superintendent. In 1906, Pierre Curie was killed in a traffic accident, and his wife took over his position,

continued his lectures at the exact point at which they were
interrupted. She was the first woman to teach at the Sorbonne.

In the years after her husband's death, Marie Curie
conducted extensively work at the new Paris Institute of
Radium; because its mysterious properties, radium was used as
a medicinal aid. Though it was often used indiscriminately,
Curie's assistance proved that there were certain illnesses which
radium was an effective therapy. In particular, radium played an
important role in the treatment of cancer, and still does. Marie
Curie also introduced the use of radium and X-ray technology
in medicine. For the discover of radium and polonium, she was
awarded the 1911 Nobel Prize for Chemistry, the only person to
win two Nobel laureates in the sciences.

Except World War I, during which she drove an ambulance,
Curie spent the remainder of her life studying the role of
radium therapy. Though the process was wildly successful for
many years, she received no royalties from its use, since she and
her husband had chosen not to besmirch the scientific purity of
her discovery by patenting it. Instead, she lived—rather
comfortable—on the Nobel Prize money, as well as on income
from other accolades.

Late in her life, the dangerous nature of radioactivity
became tragically evident: her long years of expose to radium
had resulted in leukemia, leading to her death in 1934. She is
historically recognized as an outstanding female scientist, as
well as one of the greatest researchers.

2. _____

3. _____
4. _____

5. _____

6. _____

7. _____
8. _____

9. _____

10. _____

VI. Write a composition.

Read the text again and summarize Madame Curie's work and life after Pierre Curie's death in no more than 300 words.

Further Development

1. The work of the Curies contributed substantially to shaping the world of the twentieth and twenty-first centuries. Cornell University professor L. Pearce Williams observes:

    The result of the Curies' work was epoch-making. Radium's radioactivity was so great that it could not be ignored. It seemed to contradict the principle of the conservation of energy and therefore forced a reconsideration of the foundations of physics.... In medicine, the radioactivity of radium appeared to offer a means by which cancer could be successfully attacked.

Search in the library or in the internet to find whether the radioactivity of radium contributes to the solving of cancer.

2. Marie Curie was honored as a feminist precursor. She was ahead of her time, emancipated, independent, and in addition uncorrupted. She not only contributed much to science but had an equally profound effect in the societal sphere. In order to attain her scientific achievements, she had to overcome barriers that were placed in her way because she was a woman, in both her native and her adoptive country. Read stories or biographies of Marie Curie to find more materials to evidence her honors under cruel circumstances.

Section A Text Two

Bill Gates Goes Back to School

By Lev Grossman

1   There's a great photo of Bill Gates from 1977, the year he would have graduated from Harvard if he hadn't dropped out. He was 22 at the time and looks all of 16. He's got a flowered collar, tinted glasses and feathered blond hair, and he looks so happy, you'd swear he knew what the rest of his life was going to be like. He also has a sign around his neck: it's a mug shot. "I was out driving Paul [Allen]'s car," Gates says, flashing that same smile 30 years later. "They pulled me over, and I didn't have my license, and they put me in with all the drunks all night long. And that's why the rest of my life, I've always tried to have a fair amount of cash with me. I like the idea of being able to bail myself out."

2   It is the destiny of revolutionaries—the successful ones, anyway—to end their careers as part of the Establishment they once sought to overthrow. This is true of Gates, whose success has been so total, it has annihilated all memory of the cocky, visionary, deeply weird teenager he once was, a child of the moneyed élite who threw away a Harvard education to found a company in an industry that at the time consisted of a few shut-ins with full beards in Albuquerque, N.M.

3   Now, at 51, Gates has gone back to Harvard, effectively closing the loop between Bills 1.0 and 2.0. He delivers the commencement address at Harvard on June 7 at 3:30 p.m. and acceptsan honorary degree. But on some level he's still that grinning, cocky kid in the mug shot, and to prove it, he's dropping out all over again. He is transitioning out of Microsoft to become a full-time philanthropist-at-arge, directing his formidable intelligence and ridiculous wealth at improving global education and global health. But who is this new Gates, Bill 3.0? And what makes him think a software guy has the answers to humanity's oldest, toughest, messiest problems?

4   Gates' life is a classic American riches-to-even-more-riches story. Growing up the son of a successful Seattle-area attorney, he was a curious fusion of nerd and bad boy.

He was a straight-arrow student, but it was never enough to be the best. He had to push everything a little too far—he wanted to win the game and break the rules at the same time to show he was even smarter than the guy who wrote the rules. In high school, he and Allen, with whom Gates would later co-found Microsoft, were obsessed with programming a mainframe owned by a local company. But mastering it wasn't enough. "We did this thing where we proved you could steal the password file," Gates says. "Paul and I were banned from using the computer for a year."

5   The same was true at Harvard. A brilliant math student, Gates would blow off his classes to go to ones he hadn't registered for. He would slack all semester, then cram at the last minute and ace the final. He met Steve Ballmer, Microsoft's current CEO, when they both talked their way into a graduate course in microeconomics. (Gates says he came away with the top grade on the final exam.) "The only computer-science course that I ever signed up for was the one that had the most prerequisites in the whole catalog—and I signed up for the second half of the year," Gates says. "So my freshman year I show up, and it's all graduate students, and two days into the course I tell the professor, Hey, you know, this thing is wrong ... My social skills weren't that great."

6   Pretty soon Gates and Allen twigged that there was a bigger game going on, even bigger than Harvard. "We'd agreed the microprocessor was going to change the world," Gates remembers. "It was weird that people didn't see that." A Popular Mechanics cover story about an early personal computer called the Altair was what doomed Gates' career at Harvard. "The thing that Paul and I had been talking about happening was happening," he says, "and we're sitting there going, Oh, no, it's happening without us!" Gates had realized that there was a future in writing and selling software for personal computers. It was one of the great technology and business insights of the century. Harvard wasn't impressed. When Gates and Allen sold the Altair folks a version of BASIC—which they wrote without ever having seen an Altair—the school brought him up on disciplinary charges for running a business out of his dorm room. So Gates turned on, booted up and dropped out.

7   Gates wasn't just the nascent titan of a new industry. He was the harbinger of that quintessential fin-de-millennium American type, the power nerd. He didn't have social skills, but then again, he wasn't running for prom king. The forces that were reshaping the world weren't political or cultural anymore; they were technological, and if you knew where the bits and bytes were buried, you had the power. Long before the dotcom boom, long before it was hip to besquare, Gates crossed over to the dork side.

8   Gates' social skills still aren't all that great. He may omit to shake your hand when you meet him. His voice has one setting: high and loud. He still has that much remarked–upon habit of rocking back and forth while he's thinking, and he sometimes jumps up, rather startlingly, to pace while he's talking.

9   But there's a warmth to him and a weird but genuine charm. It's always a pleasure to interview Gates, not because he's a good talker but because he isn't: he doesn't talk

you around, doesn't spin you or snow you, or if he does, he does it so badly that you can see it coming a mile off. It's just how his mind works—he can't help answering your questions seriously and literally. There are tales, probably true, of his brutally breaking down employees in meetings. He likes the truth, and he likes things to be clear. I sit in on a meeting in which he works through the kinks in his Harvard speech. He stumbles on a superfluous phrase: more fully. "That's the kind of stuff I hate," he says, pausing for a minute to riff. "I delete stuff like that all the time. The word truly—whenever I see it, I tend to delete it. Why say 'truly X'? Is 'X' not enough?"

10   That's typical of Gates: he takes an engineer's approach—a literal, analytical, hacker's approach—to everything, whether it's an engineering problem or not. This isn't always the best approach. On the one hand, it's worked out pretty well for making software. On the other hand, look at Gates' haircut.

11   And take another look at that software. Microsoft makes efficient business tools, but they've never enjoyed the same reputation for simplicity and elegance as, say, Apple. For all his drive and intelligence, Gates doesn't see things with an artist's eye for those human intangibles. In May, Gates made a rare and instructive public appearance with his longtime frenemy Steve Jobs. An audience member asked each of them what he had learned from the other. "Well, I'd give a lot to have Steve's taste," Gates said. "You know, we sat in Mac product reviews where there were questions about software choices, how things would be done, that I viewed as an engineering question. That's just how my mind works. And I'd see Steve make the decision based on a sense of people and product that is even hard for me to explain. The way he does things is just different, and you know, I think it's magical." The audience cracked up. But Gates wasn't joking.

12   So it'll be interesting to watch Gates try his Vulcan approach on challenges like curing AIDS and fixing America's public schools. In July 2008, his primary focus will become the Bill & Melinda Gates Foundation, which he and his wife founded to address health and education issues. It has an endowment of more than $33 billion, making it by far the largest charitable foundation in the world. In 2006 his close friend Warren Buffett committed to transferring to the foundation much of his wealth too, which will eventually add about $30 billion more. Gates' foundation makes him one of the most powerful nonelected actors on the global stage.

13   The worst grade Gates ever got at Harvard, a C+, was in organic chemistry. Now he has to study it all the time. He monitors clinical research, talks to doctors, sits in classrooms, flies to nfectious hot zones. As a foe of disease and ignorance, he is fearsome.

14   Gates refers to his philanthropic work as "solving inequity," as if it were a long-division problem. When Gates looks at the world, a world in which millions of preventable deaths occur each year, he sees an irrational, inefficient, broken system, an application that needs to be debugged. It shocks him—his word—that people don't see this, the same way it shocked him that nobody but he and Allen saw the microchip for what it was. "We had just assumed that if millions of children were dying and they could

be saved, the world would make it a priority to discover and deliver the medicines to save them," he said in his Harvard speech. "But it did not."

15 Gates isn't just focused on specific diseases and educational deficits. To him, that's thinking small. Like the high school password stealer he once was, the cocky Harvard kid, Gates wants to rewrite the rules of the whole system. He's all for capitalism—it has treated him well—but he gets that it's not going to take care of everybody. The financial incentives to take care of the disadvantaged just aren't there.

16 So capitalism itself needs to be re-engineered. In his Harvard speech he introduces an idea he calls creative capitalism. "That may be the most important phrase in there," he says, "in the sense that capitalism has really triumphed in this incredible way, and certainly for at least a billion people, it's done a spectacular job, and alternative systems have not. Yet there's this strong feeling that getting that system to direct itself to the right problem—there's more that can be done." In the speech he exhorts the students and faculty to do something about it: to hack the system and add the features it needs to address these problems. He cites a practice called advance market commitment, in which governments band together to guarantee orders for an expensive and otherwise financially risky vaccine. "That's the kind of idea. It's about using competition and market incentives but directing it the right way."

17 If there's a limit to what Gates can do, it's always going to be found in that human element, the messy, fallible, unquantifiable stuff that doesn't respond to engineering. His limitations as a technologist will be his limitations as a philanthropist. But he knows he's not writing software anymore. "There are some [problems], like discovering a vaccine for malaria, that actually are surprisingly similar," he says. "That is, a bit like a software project. Some things like designing high schools and new high school curricula and the way that you need to have the community and the teachers, particularly their union, feel like they need to participate in that ... that's a very tough thing."

18 Gates is probably getting out of technology at the right time. Funnily enough, it's not really a business for nerds anymore. Gates was at the center of the personal-computer revolution and the Internet revolution, but now the big innovations are about exactly the things he's bad at. The iPod was an aesthetic revolution. MySpace was a social revolution. YouTube was an entertainment revolution. This is not what Gates does. Technology doesn't need him anymore.

19 Now education and health care—those are areas in which the bedrock problems, the bits and bytes, have yet to be solved. All that pretty, fluffy stuff, that can come later. That's for thecool kids to figure out. Sickness, death, ignorance, illiteracy—those are the problems that need nerds. That's where Gates 3.0 needs to be, and that's where he's going.

Independent Study Assistant

I. Words and Expressions

1. **annihilate** *v.*   to destroy a group of people or things completely
2. **cocky** *adj.*   too confident about yourself and your abilities, especially in a way that annoys other people
3. **visionary** *adj.*   characterized by vision or foresight; with clear ideas or hopes of how sth should be done or how things will be in the future
4. **weird** *adj.*   strange and unusual, sometimes in a way that upsets you
5. **shut-in** *n.*   someone who is living secludedly, disposed to avoid social contact; excessively withdrawn or introverted; a person confined indoors by illness or disability
6. **mug** *n.*   a cup with straight sides and no saucer, used mainly for hot drinks
7. **mug shot**   a photograph of someone's face, taken by the police for their records
8. **bail out**   to give money to a court when someone is allowed to stay out of prison while they wait for their trial
9. **nerd** *n.*   a person who is single-minded or accomplished in scientific or technical pursuits but is felt to be socially inept: a computer nerd
10. **formidable** *adj.*   very impressive in size, power, or skill and therefore deserving respect and often difficult to deal with
11. **obsess** *v.*   to think about sth or someone much more than is necessary or sensible—used to show disapproval.
12. **blew off**   to not do sth one has agreed or arranged to do
13. **slack** *v.*   to try to avoid working; to work less hard than you usually do or should do
14. **cram** *v.*   to learn a lot of things in a short time, in preparation for an exam
15. **twig** *v.*   to suddenly understand or realize sth
16. **BASIC** (Beginner's All-purpose Symbolic Instruction Code)   *n.* a family of high-level programming languages.
17. **frenemy** *n.*   someone who you have a friendly relationship with but is really an enemy or competitor
18. **crack up** *v.*   to suddenly laugh a lot at sth; to laugh unrestrainedly
19. **address** *v.*   1. to make a formal speech to; 2. *(formal)* to try to deal with a problem or question
20. **microchip** *n.*   a very small piece of silicon containing a set of electronic parts, which is used in computers and other machines
21. **debug** *v.*   to remove the bugs (= mistakes) from a computer program
22. **exhort** *v.*   to try very hard to persuade someone to do sth
23. **fallible** *adj.*   able to make mistakes or be wrong
24. **philanthropist** *n.*   a rich person who gives a lot of money to help poor people
25. **philanthropic** *adj.*   a philanthropic person or institution gives money and help to people who are poor or in trouble
26. **aesthetic** *adj.*   connected with beauty and the study of beauty
27. **fluffy** *adj.*   made of sth very soft such as wool
28. **bedrock** *n.*   the basic ideas, features, or facts on which sth is based

II. Referential Points

Melinda Gates (1964—) is an American philanthropist. She is the co-founder and co-chair of the Bill & Melinda Gates Foundation and a former unit manager for several Microsoft products such as Publisher, Microsoft Bob, Encarta, and Expedia. In 1994, she married Bill Gates, founder, chairman, and former chief software architect of Microsoft. They have three children: Jennifer Katharine Gates, Rory John Gates and Phoebe Adele Gates.

Paul Allen (1953—) is an American entrepreneur and philanthropist who co-founded Microsoft with Bill Gates and is one of the wealthiest people in the world. He is the founder and chairman of Vulcan Inc., which is his private asset management company, and is chairman of Charter Communications. Allen also has a multi-billion dollar investment portfolio which includes stakes in Digeo, Kiha Software, real estate holdings, and more than 40 other technology, media, and content companies.

Steven Ballmer (1956—) is an American businessman who has been the chief executive officer of Microsoft Corporation since January 2000. Ballmer was ranked the 43rd richest person in the world, with an estimated wealth of $11 billion.

Steve Jobs (1955—) is an American businessman, and the co-founder and chief executive officer of Apple Inc. In the late 1970s, Jobs, with Apple co-founder Steve Wozniak, created one of the first commercially successful personal computers. In 1985, Jobs resigned from Apple and founded NeXT, a computer platform development company specializing in the higher education and business markets. NeXT's subsequent 1997 buyout by Apple Computer Inc. brought Jobs back to the company he co-founded, and he has served as its CEO since then. Jobs is currently a member of Walt Disney Company's Board of Directors.

Warren Buffett (1930—) is an American investor, businessman, and philanthropist. In 2007, he was listed among *Time's* 100 Most Influential People in the world. He is one of the most successful investors in history, the primary shareholder and CEO of Berkshire Hathaway, and in 2008 was ranked by Forbes as the richest person in the world with an estimated net worth of approximately $62 billion. Buffett is often called the "Oracle of Omaha" or the "Sage of Omaha" and is noted for his adherence to the value investing philosophy and for his personal frugality despite his immense wealth. Buffett is also a notable philanthropist, having pledged to give away 85 percent of his fortune to the Gates Foundation.**Vulcan** in Roman mythology, the god of fire and metalworking; He was the son of Jupiter and Juno, and husband of Maia and Venus. He was worshipped at an annual festival on August 23 known as the Volcanalia.

III. Questions for Comprehension

1. What does the title of this passage probably mean?
2. How much do you know about Bill Gates and how do you like him?
3. How much do you know about Microsoft? Work out a brief report about its founder, development, achievements and influences.
4. Why does the author think Gates' going back to Harvard at 51 effectively closed the loop between Bills 1.0 and 2.0? What is it that makes Bill 3.0?
5. What is the difference between capitalism and creative capitalism advocated in Gates' Harvard speech?

Unit 3

Self-test

I. Fill in the blanks with the words and expressions provided, making some change when necessary.

annihilate	visionary	cocky	shut-in
weird	nerd	formidable	obsess
aesthetic	philanthropic	debug	address
fallible	exhort	bedrock	superfluous

1. Arguably the most important and radical influence on the world of modern dance came around the turn of the 20th century with the _____ American Isadora Duncan.
2. That member is Peter Novilio— _____, impetuous, risk loving.
3. Ngũgĩ wa Thiong'o describes the largest weapon of imperialism as the "cultural bomb". The effect of a cultural bomb is to _____ a people's belief in their names, in their languages, in their environment, in their heritage of struggle, in their unity, in their capacities and ultimately in themselves.
4. If you are undecided at this point, it might be better to stay home, as you most likely are intentionally ill-informed, a _____, have no access to media or the Internet, and you simply are someone who will not like any candidate and can't take a stand on any issue, let alone your next preference for president.
5. He didn't move, his eyes on the roiling gray-black clouds. He was feeling a chill that had nothing to do with the temperature. His chest was tight, and he was experiencing a _____ panicky sensation. It was as if those threatening clouds were alive and stalking him.
6. "But you get somebody like Step Fletcher to design you some real software—I mean, this guy isn't just a computer _____, he's got a Ph.D. in history! He knows something!" Step couldn't believe that Cranes knew that about him.
7. As it is in other developing regions of the world, achieving progress in governance in Africa will be a _____ task. But in recent years, a growing number of Africa's leaders have established or started participating in major regional initiatives to deal with the continent's governance problems.
8. "You can only keep one thought in your mind at a time," Mercer argues, "Happy, optimistic people _____ on cheerful thoughts of what they want, their aspirations, and indulge in dwelling on their successes, but unhappy, pessimistic people on gloomy thoughts of how they could fall down and not get up."
9. Every other condition in which we can live refers us to a previous condition, and requires for its solution a following condition; only the _____ is a complete whole in itself, for it unites in itself all conditions of its source and of its duration.
10. Gates stepped down as chairman of Microsoft last year to devote his attention to the Bill & Melinda Gates Foundation, focusing on health care and other _____ issues.
11. The combined MNETS, graphical editor, and VHDL system provide a widely available, versatile set of tools that can be used to enter, edit, modify, simulate, _____, check, and capture a design in a highly modular, easily understood fashion.

12. Surprisingly, most evaluations of after-school programs neglected this question. Results from two studies that did _____ the issue demonstrated that simply enrolling students in after-school programs does not automatically reduce the number of unsupervised youth during the hours after the school day ends.
13. It is the American story—a story of flawed and _____ people, united across the generations by grand and enduring ideals.
14. It aims to glorify and to instill pride in their ancestors and to _____ the future generations to emulate their illustrious forebears.
15. Visual noise within an interface is caused by _____ visual elements that distract from the primary objective of directly communicating software function and behavior.

II. Use the appropriate form of the words given in the brackets to fill in the blanks.

1. He had obviously been disguised, and had removed whatever had given his skin a pale color, and whatever—_____ glasses of the contact type which fitted on the eyeballs, probably—had given his eyes a nondescript brown shade. (tint)
2. You might say it comes with the territory: when you're a _____, an innovator, you follow your own star—you don't stop to ask what other people think. (vision)
3. Bernie Madoff is probably not a household name for most investors, but on Wall Street and among sort of elite, _____ investors in New York, and sort of in Florida, Palm Beach area, he's a legend, almost a hero. (money)
4. Thirty hours later, with the sun still _____ high in the sky, the hurricane just an hour away, and the winds beginning to rise, there wasn't a cloud to be seen. (formidable)
5. Hamlet, in his intellectual unrest, morbid brooding, cynical self-analysis and dislike of bloodshed, is much more _____ of the nineteenth or twentieth century than of the sixteenth. (type)
6. All of them were so young looking, even with their sweeping yellow mustaches and full black and brown beards, so handsome, so reckless, with their arms in slings, with head bandages _____ white across sun-browned faces. (startle)
7. I used to wonder why the Americans attached so much importance to the graduation ceremony and why the graduation ceremony was called _____ ceremony. (commence)
8. Too many educators today excuse teachers, principals, and school superintendents who fail to substantially raise the performance of low-income minority students by claiming that schools can not really be held accountable for student achievement because _____ students bear multiple burdens of poverty. (advantage)
9. In the past three years, records show, at least 17 casinos have faced _____ action for alleged offenses such as improper use of slot machines and accounting irregularities. (discipline)
10. Evolutionary analysis is really the basic tool that we use to understand and explore the human genome, among other things. Its the basic tool that we use to control _____ disease, to develop new drugs, and a host of other scientific applications. (infect)

III. Translate the short paragraph paragraphs into Chinese.

It is the destiny of revolutionaries—the successful ones, anyway—to end their careers as part of the Establishment they once sought to overthrow. This is true of Gates, whose success has been so total, it has annihilated all memory of the cocky, visionary, deeply weird teenager he once was, a child of the moneyed élite who threw away a Harvard education to found a company in an industry that at the time consisted of a few shut-ins with full beards in Albuquerque, N.M..

IV. Analyze difficult sentences.
1. A brilliant math student, Gates would blow off his classes to go to ones he hadn't registered for. He would slack all semester, then cram at the last minute and ace the final.
2. Gates wasn't just the nascent titan of a new industry. He was the harbinger of that quintessential fin-de-millennium American type, the power nerd.
3. He cites a practice called advance market commitment, in which governments band together to guarantee orders for an expensive and otherwise financially risky vaccine.
4. He's all for capitalism—it has treated him well—but he gets that it's not going to take care of everybody. The financial incentives to take care of the disadvantaged just aren't there.
5. He doesn't talk you around, doesn't spin you or snow you, or if he does, he does it so badly that you can see it coming a mile off. It's just how his mind works—he can't help answering your questions seriously and literally.

V. Proofread the following passage.

William Henry Gates III was born October 28, 1955, in Seattle, Washington. He was the second child and only son of William Henry Gates Jr., a prominent Seattle attorney, and Mary Maxwell, a formerly   1. _____
school teacher. Although Gates's parents had in mind a legal career for their son, he developed an early interest in computer science and began studying computers in the seventh grade at Seattle's Lakeside School. At Lakeside, Gates became acquaint with Paul Allen, a teenager with a   2. _____
similar interest in technology who would eventually become his future business partner.

Gates's early experience with computers included debugging (or   3. _____
eliminating errors from) programs for the Computer Center Corporation's PDP-10, helping to computerize electric power grids for the Bonneville Power Administration, and—while still in high school—found with Allen a firm named Traf-O-Data. Their small   4. _____
company earned them $20 thousand in fees for analyzing local traffic patterns.

While working with the Computer Center's PDP-10, Gates was responsible for that was probably the first computer virus, which is a   5. _____
program that copies itself into other programs and ruins data. Discovered   6. _____
that the machine was hooked up to a national network of computers, called Cybernet, Gates invaded the network and installed a program on the main computer that sent itself to the rest of the network's computers. Cybernet crashed. When Gates found out, he was severely reprimanded   7. _____
and he kept away from computers for his entire junior year at Lakeside. Without the lure of computers, Gates made plans in 1970 for college and

law school. In 1971, however, he was back help Paul Allen write a class scheduling program for their school's computer. 8. _____

   Gates entered Harvard University in 1973 and pursued his studies for the next year and a half. His life was to change, however, in January of 1975 when the magazine *Popular Electronics* carried a cover story on a three hundred-fifty dollar microcomputer, the Altair, was made by a firm called MITS in New Mexico. When Allen excitedly showed him the story, Gates knew what he wanted to be: at the forefront of computer software design.

9. _____

10. _____

VI. Write a composition.

   Review and compare the three versions of Bill Gates, Bill 1.0, Bill 2.0 and Bill 3.0. Summarize the differences between these three versions. Write a composition in which you have to show how much you have known about the connections between them.

Section B

Text One   Martin Luther King

Focal Consideration

1. There are some controversial views about the death of Martin Luther King:
   a. He died from overdose.
   b. He wasn't shot by a jealous lover.
   b. He was politically assassinated.
      Find out more information from the library or internet about the death of Martin Luther King, and present your argument over the cause of his death.
2. We are going to explore the reason why Dexter Scott King, the second son of Martin Luther King, publicly stated his belief that James Earl Ray was innocent.

Research Questions

   Think about the following questions and discuss them with your group members. After your discussion, work out the research report and share it with the students of other groups.
   1. How much do you know about Martin Luther King? Work out a brief report about his life and main activities or achievements.
   2. Why did Martin Luther King repeat in his Memphis speech, "I've seen the promised land. I may not get there with you. But I want you to know tonight, that we, as a people, will get to the promised land"?
   3. What are the significances of Martin Luther King's political activities?

Martin Luther King

By Roger Bruns

1   On the evening of April 3, 1968, at the Masonic Temple in Memphis, King, facing an injunction by Memphis city officials preventing him from leading another march, delivered an unusual speech—inspiring, defiant, but pensive. He talked about how far these people surrounding him that night had come together in the movement, how overwhelming had been the odds, and how daunting remained the challenges ahead.

2   He told them to hold together for the cause of social equality, no matter what happened. "We got some difficult days ahead," King told the overflowing crowd, "But it really doesn't matter to me now, because I've been to the mountaintop. I've seen the promised land. I may not get there with you. But I want you to know tonight, that we, as a people, will get to the promised land."

3   And then, in a remarkably prescient moment, he looked forward: "But it doesn't matter with me now. Because I've been to the mountaintop. And I don't mind. Like anybody, I would like to live a long life. Longevity has its place. But I'm not concerned about that now. I just want to do God's will. And He's allowed me to go up to the mountain. And I've looked over. And I've seen the promised land. I may not get there with you. But I want you to know tonight, that we, as a people, will get to the promised land. And I'm happy, tonight. I'm not worried about anything. I'm not fearing any man. Mine eyes have seen the glory of the coming of the Lord."

4   Early the following morning, there was good news for King and his associates. The injunction against the march had been lifted. At midday, preparing to leave the Lorraine Motel to meet with march organizers, King stepped out from his room onto the balcony. King and Jesse Jackson, standing in the parking lot below, exchanged a few remarks.

5   And then there was the crack of the rifle shot. Hit in the face and neck, King crumpled on the balcony floor. Andrew Young, Reverend Samuel Kyles, and others raced to his side. Ralph Abernathy, his closest friend, cradled him. Blood covered the balcony.

6   Kyles, pastor of the Monumental Baptist Church in Memphis and long-time civil rights activist, was with King and Abernathy in King's room of the Lorraine for the last hour of King's life. Kyles had helped arrange for the upcoming march and had been working on the sanitation workers strike since the beginning. That evening King was to have had dinner at Kyles's home, along with Jackson.

7   "About a quarter of 6:00 we walked out onto the balcony," Kyles remembered. "He was greeting people he had not seen. Somebody said, 'It's going to be cold, Doc, get your coat.' He didn't go back in the room. He went to the door and said, 'Ralph, get my coat.' Ralph was in the room putting on shaving lotion. Ralph said, 'I'll get your coat.' He went back to the railing of the balcony and was greeting people again. He said something to Jesse Jackson and saidsomething to some other people. We stood together.

I said, 'Come on, guys. Let's go.'" Since that day, Kyles reflected on why he happened to be at that place at that time. He concluded that he was there to be a witness. "Martin Luther King, Jr., didn't die in some foolish, untoward way," Kyles said. "He didn't overdose. He wasn't shot by a jealous lover. He died helping garbage workers."

8   Kyles also pointed out, as did others, that King had mentioned on occasion that he might never reach age 40. When the bullet ended his life that day in Memphis, he was 39. During a speech at Kansas State University in January 1968, just a few months before his death, King looked back over the civil rights movement with a sense of pride and awe that so many people—thousands in city after city, march after march—had managed to hurdle great psychological and economic barriers to come together in a mass movement for change. The movement had not been simply to gain the right to sit with whites in classrooms or in buses, he said; it was emblematic of a broader sense that a just society might be possible for them after all. They would have to scratch and fight for every gain and, most importantly, they would have to remain a unified force. But even with the setbacks and disappointments of recent months and years, King still had faith that they would, indeed, overcome.

9   As King in the last months of his life joined the black sanitation workers under their banner "I Am a Man," he saw their protest as perfectly geared for the kind of national challenge that lay ahead in the Poor People's Campaign. Here were exploited and class-bound workers fighting for their proper chance in the system. The Memphis strike was not a diversion from King's larger plan, he believed, but a starting place for demonstrating the need for systemic reform, for action to create jobs and income for those trapped in an unfair ghetto of economic limitations.

10 Memphis sanitation workers did win their strike. King's death forced the segregationist mayor of Memphis to allow a strike settlement, which may have benefited the city's black middle class most of all. As sanitation worker Taylor Rogers pointed out recently, "city hall is full of blacks, even to the mayor," and organized public workers who vote helped to put them there. Blacks with city and county jobs and in clerical positions as well, he says, "wouldn't be in the position they're in now if it had not been for King comin' here and dyin'."

11 The success of the Memphis strike opened the way to unionization of the working poor in government jobs across the country, a major area in which unions have expanded for the past 30-plus years.

12 News of the assassination swept many of the nation's towns and cities into a whirl of fire and rage. In more than 125 locations across the country, entire sections of inner cities were engulfed in rioting and arson. A harried President Johnson dispatched military troops and national guardsmen to several cities. By late April, nearly 50 people had perished in the frenzy. The irony and sadness was towering; the death of the man who had preached nonviolence had provoked retaliatory ferocity, against which he had preached all his life.

13 Finally, the lawlessness subsided, as if the violent pressure within the inner cities had

finally, in a futile burst, spent the last of its energy. The nation turned to mourning. There werememorials and rallies. Public facilities closed for a day in honor of King. On April 8, a bereaved Reverend Ralph Abernathy was chosen to succeed King as SCLC president. He led 42,000 silent marchers, including King's widow, Coretta, and other family members in Memphis, to honor King and to support the sanitation workers.

14 On April 9, at Ebenezer Baptist Church, pastor King and his family, surrounded by many of the nation's political and civil rights leaders, gathered to pay tribute. Thousands stood outside in the streets weeping.

15 Two Georgia mules pulled King's mahogany coffin on a rickety farm wagon for over three miles through Atlanta's streets to Southview Cemetery. Former Morehouse College president Benjamin Mays, now 70 years old, had a mutual agreement with his former prize student. Whoever survived, Mays said, would deliver the eulogy. Mays, over 30 years King's senior, sadly fulfilled his part of the agreement.

16 King was "more courageous than those who advocate violence as a way out," Mays told the mourners. "Martin Luther faced the dogs, the police, jail, heavy criticism, and finally death; and he never carried a gun, not even a knife to defend himself. He had only his faith in a just God to rely on... If physical death was the price he had to pay to rid America of prejudice and injustice," Mays said of King, "nothing could be more redemptive."

17 An international manhunt in the coming months resulted in the capture of white segregationist James Earl Ray, who fled to England after the assassination. Tennessee prosecutors agreed to a plea bargain in which Ray admitted guilt in return for a sentence of life imprisonment rather than the death penalty. Over the years, Ray attempted various legal maneuvers to reverse his conviction—retracting his confession, claiming that he was framed, and insisting that a larger conspiracy lay behind the death of King. By the time of Ray's death in 1998, many members of the King family supported Ray's appeal for a new trial, and King's son, Dexter Scott King, publicly stated his belief that Ray was innocent. As in the case of the assassination of President Kennedy in 1963, conspiracy theories continue to surround the shooting of King.

18 In 1962 Ralph Allen was a student at Connecticut's Trinity College. Inspired by the civil rights marches, Allen and some of his friends decided to travel to Albany, Georgia to help in the voter registration drive. Working with local civil rights leaders and members of King's organization, they canvassed neighborhoods and organized meetings to help spread the message about voting rights.

19 During that summer and the next, Allen met King, Andrew Young, Stokely Carmichael, James Farmer and many other prominent civil rights leaders. Allen and his friends avoided most of the sit-ins and mass demonstrations and concentrated on the less confrontational aspects of voter registration. Nevertheless, they were arrested numerous times in general roundups by local police attempting to slow down progress being made in signing up black voters.

20   At the Mt. Olive Baptist Church in Sasser, the group held weekly meetings on canvassing and other aspects of the voter registration campaign and gathered to pray and sing freedom songs. In mid-July, one of the weekly meetings was suddenly visited by Sheriff Zeke T. Mathews and 15 or 20 deputized white citizens with nightsticks. The sheriff proceeded to go from person to person interrogating them in a mockingly friendly but threatening manner. To the leader of the gathering, Lucius Holloway, the sheriff remarked that none of the blacks in the room that night, including Holloway, had ever wanted to vote until the outside agitators had arrived and stirred things up and "put these dang fool ideas in your head."

21   In late August, Mt. Olive Church was firebombed to the ground early one Sunday morning. The civil rights leaders called King in Atlanta. Although he was scheduled to preach at Ebenezer that morning, he and some friends drove to Alabama to be with the people who had lost their church.

22   Ralph Allen remembered the camaraderie and comfort that King engendered, the sense that they were all in this together, like a congregation. They gathered in the open near a cotton field and King preached. "We will rebuild this church," King declared. "They prayed and sang freedom songs," said Allen. "At the end we all gathered in a circle and crossed our arms, each person holding hands with the person on either side and sang 'We Shall Overcome.' In Southwest Georgia the way it ends is everybody hums the song and anybody who's moved to say or pray anything goes ahead and does it. Rev. Wells from Albany, who would later go to work for Dr. King's Southern Christian Leadership Conference, he prayed, and Sherrod prayed. My friend Chris Potter... describes good friends as those who 'you can call late, and they'll come early.' That's the kind of person Dr. King was. That's the point I want to make about him. In addition to being a visionary, a deeply inspiring writer and speaker, and a man of such courage he could walk daily joking with the shadow of death, he was a 'call late and come early' friend to whole communities of people he didn't even know."

23   Friend, leader, and, eventually, a symbol, Martin Luther King, Jr. was first and foremost a preacher. His roots, talents, and the way he viewed the world all sprang from the earliest lessons from his family and the African American church ministers that he, often reluctantly, listened to in the pews of Ebenezer and other churches. Although his inclinations in his early years veered away from simple faith and unquestioned scriptural truths, he remained, throughout his life, a preacher, one who saw possibilities in the midst of despair and the chance for justice in a world of injustice.

24   In his speech at the Lincoln Memorial in 1963, King melded religious belief with a call for national mobilization. In the middle of the speech, he brushed aside his notes, locked his eyes squarely on the thousands gathered around the reflecting pool, and offered his vision. Mostly it was a vision squarely from the gospel, this dream of God's children, black and white, rich and poor, gathered in respect and love. A dream unattainable it might have been, but the message left an impression of mutual kinship

both powerful and lasting. All of it, King said—the vision, the gains large and small, the steps toward reconciliation—all of it was worth the commitment to try.

25   They could never be satisfied, he said, as long as blacks were still denied their rights as God's people. And, using the words of the Prophet Amos as he had done that first night of the Montgomery Bus Boycott, he said that they could never be satisfied until "justice rolls down like waters, and righteousness like a mighty stream."

Preview Assistance

1. **injunction** n.   an order from a court that prevents someone from doing something; the act or an instance of enjoining; a command, directive, or order
2. **defiant** adj.   refusing to obey a person or rule
3. **pensive** adj.   seeming to be thinking carefully about something, especially something sad or serious
4. **daunting** adj.   frightening in a way that makes you feel less confident
5. **prescient** adj.   (formal) knowing or appearing to know about things before they happen
6. **crumple** v.   to fall to the ground suddenly, with your body, legs, and arms bent, because you are injured, ill, or upset
7. **Reverend** n.   a title of respect used before the name of a minister in the Christian church
8. **pastor** n.   a Christian priest in some Protestant churches
9. **untoward** adj.   unusual and unexpected, and usually unpleasant
10. **hurdle** v.   to jump over something while you are running
11. **emblematic** adj.   (formal) seeming to represent or be a sign of something
12. **arson** n.   the crime of deliberately setting fire to a building
13. **harried** adj.   (formal) annoyed or upset by continuously asking questions or for sth
14. **frenzy** n.   a state of great activity and strong emotion that is often violent or frightening and not under control
15. **retaliatory** adj.   done against someone because they have harmed you
16. **subside** v.   to become calmer or quieter
17. **rally** adj.   not strong or well made; likely to break
18. **mahogany** n.   the hard reddish-brown wood of a tropical tree, used for making furniture
19. **rickety** adj.   a rickety structure or piece of furniture is likely to break if you put any weight on it, often because it is old
20. **redemptive** adj.   making someone free from the power of evil, especially in the Christian religion
21. **plea bargain**   a process by which someone may be allowed to avoid punishment for a serious crime if they admit they have committed a less serious crime
22. **maneuver** n.   a skilful or carefully planned action intended to gain an advantage for yourself
23. **conviction** n.   a decision by a court of law that someone is guilty of a crime
24. **retract** v.   to say that something that you previously said or wrote is not true
25. **frame** v.   to produce false evidence against an innocent person so that people think he or she is guilty
26. **canvass** v.   to try to persuade people to support a political party, politician, plan etc by going to see them and talking to them, especially when you want them to vote for you in an election
27. **deputize** v.   to do something that sb in a higher position than you would usually do

28. **dang** *adj.* (informal) a mild swear word, used instead of "damn"
29. **camaraderie** *n.* friendship and trust between people in a group
30. **engender** *v.* to make a feeling or situation exist
31. **pews** *n.* a long wooden seat in a church
32. **veer** *v.* to change in a sudden or noticeable way, for example in your opinion or mood
33. **gospel** *n.* a set of ideas that sb believes in and tries to persuade others to accept

Referential Points

Martin Luther King, Jr. (1929—1968) was an American clergyman, activist and prominent leader in the African-American civil rights movement. He led the 1955 Montgomery Bus Boycott and helped found the Southern Christian Leadership Conference in 1957, serving as its first president. King's efforts led to the 1963 March on Washington, where King delivered his "I Have a Dream" speech. In 1964, King became the youngest person to receive the Nobel Peace Prize for his work to end racial segregation and racial discrimination through civil disobedience and other non-violent means. By the time of his death in 1968, he had refocused his efforts on ending poverty and opposing the Vietnam War, both from a religious perspective. King was assassinated on April 4, 1968, in Memphis, Tennessee. Martin Luther King, Jr. Day was established as a U.S. national holiday in 1986.

Jesse Jackson, Sr. (1941—) is an American civil rights activist and Baptist minister. He was a candidate for the Democratic presidential nomination in 1984 and 1988 and served as shadow senator for the District of Columbia from 1991 to 1997. He was the founder of both entities that merged to form Rainbow/PUSH.

Andrew Young (1932—) is a civil rights activist, an American politician, diplomat and pastor from Georgia who has served as Mayor of Atlanta, a Congressman from the 5th district, and United States Ambassador to the United Nations. He served as President of the National Council of Churches USA, and was a supporter and friend of the Rev. Dr. Martin Luther King, Jr.

Ralph Abernathy (1926—1990) was a leader of the American Civil Rights Movement of the 20th Century, a minister, civil rights leader and a close associate of Martin Luther King, Jr. in the Southern Christian Leadership Conference. Following King's assassination, Dr. Abernathy took up the leadership of the SCLC Poor People's Campaign and led the March on Washington, D.C. that had been planned for May 1968.

Samuel Kyles (1934—) is a longtime leader in the civil rights movement in the USA, and the only living person that actually spent the last hour of Dr. King's life with him.

Coretta Scott King (1927—2006) was an American author, activist, and civil rightsleader. The widow of Martin Luther King, Jr., Coretta Scott King helped lead the African-American Civil Rights Movement in the 1960s. Mrs. King's most prominent role may have been in the years after her husband's 1968 assassination when she took on the leadership of the struggle for racial equality herself and became active in the Women's Movement.

James Earl Ray (1928—1998) confessed to the assassination of American civil rights leader Dr. Martin Luther King, Jr. on April 4, 1968, in Memphis, Tennessee, and pled guilty in legal proceedings, forgoing a jury trial. A habitual criminal, Ray was sentenced to 99 years in prison. Later he recanted his confession and unsuccessfully tried to gain a trial. He died in prison of hepatitis C.

Stokely Carmichael (1941—1998), also known as Kwame Toure, was a Trinidadian-American black activist active in the 1960s American Civil Rights Movement. He rose to prominence first as a leader of the Student Nonviolent Coordinating Committee (SNCC, pronounced "Snick") and later as the "Honorary Prime Minister" of the Black Panther Party. Initially an integrationist, Carmichael later became affiliated with black nationalist and Pan-Africanist movements.

James Farmer, Jr. (1920—1999) was a civil rights activist, a leader of the American civil rights movement of the 1940s, '50s and '60s, and the initiator and organizer of the 1961 Freedom Ride which eventually led to the desegregration of inter-state busing in the United States.

The Montgomery Bus Boycott was a political and social protest campaign started in 1955 in Montgomery, Alabama, USA, intended to oppose the city's policy of racial segregation on its public transit system. Many historically significant figures of the civil rights movement were involved in the boycott, including Martin Luther King, Jr. and others. The struggle lasted from December 1, 1955, when Rosa Parks, an African American woman, was arrested for refusing to surrender her seat to a white person, to December 20, 1956 when a federal ruling took effect, and led to a United States Supreme Court decision that declared the Alabama and Montgomery laws requiring segregated buses to be unconstitutional.

Consolidation Work

I. Fill in the blanks with the words and expressions provided, making some change when necessary.

injunction	daunting	prescient	untoward	hurdle	odds	retaliatory
manhunt	crumple	redemptive	rickety	subside	canvass	engender
veer						

1. I look at the pictures of the car after the crash, with the passenger-side floor sill and roof _____ and distorted and my seat moved forward, which helped trap me in the car.
2. The court could, for example, issue an _____, forbidding specified acts in order to prevent further injury, or it could decree specific performance, ordering performance of an obligation.
3. In the Macphails' there was nothing but a poor, worn bed with a ragged mosquito net, a _____ chair, and a washstand.
4. The European Commission spokesman Gooch said at a press conference that after the European Commission has officially notified the WTO, "the EU can feel free to impose _____ tariffs on US products."
5. Heavy-weights like Sotheby's or Christie's may seem _____ to outsiders, but one made its reputation selling books and the other sold horses at a time when the business had the social status of selling second-hand cars.
6. They knew something very bad was going to happen because they were quite _____. So they did something about it when nobody else did.

7. It seemed heartless to leave a woman with two young children, so weak and helpless, without anyone to rely on. How could he be sure nothing _____ would happen to them?
8. Sergeant Terry Lawton, of British Transport Police, said yesterday: "The train was approaching and if all 450 runners had _____ the barriers and any had fallen, there could have been a mass slaughter on the line."
9. Lourdes, one of the Marian shrines most loved by the Christian people, is both a place and a symbol of hope and grace, characterised by accepting and offering up _____ suffering.
10. Other incidents of violence during the campaign include an attack on Mr Christopher Chope, the roads minister, who was punched in the face as he _____ in his Southampton Itchen, and the punching of Mr Owen Paterson, the Conservative candidate in Wrexham.
11. China's WTO accession will _____ challenges as well as benefits and how best to bolster the benefits and mitigate the risks remains a subject of considerable debate among policy planners, business people, and consumers.
12. Whenever his thoughts _____ off in that direction, he would hurriedly change his line of thinking, though not before he felt a twinge of shame.
13. A massive _____ for the missing men has severely taxed military resources and morale at a time when the U.S. is under pressure at home over troop deployment.
14. While the Government's plans to double spending on roads were at _____ with its proclaimed conversion to green issues, Labour's new policies recognised the need to drastically cut congestion and pollution from vehicle emissions.
15. Once the initial infection has _____, the body keeps some of these antibodies around, so that it can respond to a future infection much more quickly.

II. Use the appropriate form of the words given in the brackets to fill in the blanks.
1. He sank down in his chair, resting his chin in his hand—mere sensation, without thought, holding him. Then something like a _____ affection and self-pity swept over him. (bereave)
2. They were unprepared for his _____ and could not match it simply because the rewards being fought over were not, to their minds, worth so much bloodshed. (ferocious)
3. She could recognize her wild, desperate, _____ mood, the flightiness of her temper, and even some of the very cloud-shapes of gloom and despondency that had brooded in her heart. (defy)
4. Despite significant progress in preventing and treating infectious diseases, they remain a major cause of illness and death, particularly in regions of poor _____, poor nutrition, and crowding. (sanitate)
5. This _____ building forms part of the history and heritage of Football Club Barcelona, and is an ancient country residence built in 1702. (emblem)
6. The historical significance of its architecture is being effaced every day. Monuments are becoming rarer and rarer, and one seems to see them gradually _____, by the flood of houses. (gulf)
7. The capacious soul of Shakespeare had an intuitive and _____ sympathy with whatever could enter into the heart of man in all possible circumstances. (might)

Unit 3

8. By this time the Coxes too had completed their spat and their _____, and were turning in—to think, to think, and toss, and fret, and worry over what the remark could possibly have been which Goodson made to the stranded derelict. (reconcile)
9. Tom, remembering the pickets outside the camp, went out at night to investigate. He found Casy, who was the leader of the _____. (agitate)
10. He sees with one eye closed and with one eye opened the _____ of much that goes on around him and of his own endeavors, but barely retains enough sense of reality to determine to go through with it. (futile)

III. Paraphrase the following sentences taken from the text.
1. As King in the last months of his life joined the black sanitation workers under their banner "I Am a Man," he saw their protest as perfectly geared for the kind of national challenge that lay ahead in the Poor People's Campaign.
2. News of the assassination swept many of the nation's towns and cities into a whirl of fire and rage. In more than 125 locations across the country, entire sections of inner cities were engulfed in rioting and arson.
3. Finally, the lawlessness subsided, as if the violent pressure within the inner cities had finally, in a futile burst, spent the last of its energy.
4. "If physical death was the price he had to pay to rid America of prejudice and injustice," Mays said of King, "nothing could be more redemptive."
5. Tennessee prosecutors agreed to a plea bargain in which Ray admitted guilt in return for a sentence of life imprisonment rather than the death penalty.

IV. Test your general knowledge.
1. Martin Luther King, Jr., was born on January 15, 1929, in _____. He was the son of the Reverend Martin Luther King, Sr. and Alberta Williams King.
   A. Atlanta, Georgia   B. Huston, Texas
   C. Seattle, Washington   D. Chicago, Illinois
2. In 1948, King graduated from _____ with a Bachelor of Arts degree in sociology, and enrolled in Crozer Theological Seminary in Chester, Pennsylvania, from which he graduated with a Bachelor of Divinity degree in 1951.
   A. University of Georgia   B. Boston University
   C. Morehouse College   D. University of Chicago
3. King then began doctoral studies in systematic theology at _____ and received his Doctor of Philosophy on June 5, 1955.
   A. Boston University   B. University of Pennsylvania
   C. Montgomery College   D. Yale University
4. Inspired by _____'s success with non-violent activism, King visited the Gandhi family in India in 1959, with assistance from the Quaker group—the American Friends Service Committee.
   A. Gandhi   B. Rustin
   C. Jackson   D. Abernathy
5. On December 1, 1955, Rosa Parks was arrested for refusing to give up her seat to a white passenger in compliance with the Jim Crow Laws. _____, urged and planned by Nixon and led by King, soon followed.

A. The Montgomery Bus Boycott   B. The Albany Movement
  C. The Birmingham Campaign   D. The Opposition to the Vietnam War
6. _____ for Jobs and Freedom was a large political rally that took place in Washington, D.C. on August 28, 1963. Martin Luther King, Jr. delivered his historic "I Have a Dream" speech advocating racial harmony at the Lincoln Memorial during the march.
  A. The March on Washington   B. The Poor People's Campaign
  C. The Birmingham Campaign   D. Southern Christian Leadership Conference
7. On October 14, 1964, King became the youngest recipient of _____, which was awarded to him for leading non-violent resistance to end racial prejudice in the United States.
  A. American Liberties Medallion   B. the Nobel Peace Prize
  C. the Presidential Medal of Freedom.   D. Congressional Gold Medal
8. King organized and led marches for blacks' right to vote, desegregation, labor rights and other basic civil rights. Most of these rights were successfully enacted into the law of the United States with the passage of the _____ of 1964.
  A. Civil Rights Act   B. Voting Rights Act
  C. Emancipation Proclamation   D. Declaration of the Rights of Man and the Citizen
9. On March 29, 1968, King went to _____, Tennessee in support of the black sanitary public works employees, who had been on strike since March 12 for higher wages and better treatment.
  A. Nashville   B. Memphis
  C. Clarksville   D. Shelbyville
10. On April 3, 1968, King addressed a rally and delivered his "I've Been to the Mountaintop" address at _____, the world headquarters of the Church of God in Christ.
  A. Mason Temple   B. the Lorraine Motel
  C. the Kennedy Airport   D. Lincoln Memorial
11. _____, where King was assassinated, is now the site of the National Civil Rights Museum.
  A. Mason Temple   B. The Lorraine Motel
  C. the Kennedy Airport   D. Lincoln Memorial
12. Presidential nominee _____ was on his way to Indianapolis for a campaign rally when he was informed of King's death. He gave a short speech to the gathering of supporters informing them of the tragedy and asking them to continue King's idea of non-violence.
  A. Robert Kennedy   B. Ronald Reagan
  C. Lyndon B. Johnson   D. Hubert Humphrey
13. Two months after King's death, escaped convict _____ was captured at London Heathrow Airport while trying to leave the United Kingdom on a false Canadian passport in the name of Ramon George Sneyd on his way to white-ruled Rhodesia.
  A. James Earl Ray   B. Ralph Abernathy
  C. Jesse Jackson   D. Stokely Carmichael
14. In 1997, King's son _____ met with Ray, and publicly supported Ray's efforts to obtain a new trial.
  A. Yolanda Kingg   B. Martin Luther King III
  C. Dexter Scott Kin   D. Bernice King

Unit 3

15. *The New York Times* reported a church minister, Rev. Ronald Denton Wilson, claimed his father, Henry Clay Wilson—not James Earl Ray—assassinated Martin Luther King, Jr., as he thought Martin Luther King was connected with _____, and he wanted to get him out of the way.

   A. communism   B. capitalism
   C. feudalism   D. chauvinism

V. Proofread the following passage.

During the last half of the twentieth century in the United States, Martin Luther King, Jr. (1929—1968), emerged as the major leader of the modern civil rights movement. He organized large numbers of African Americans in 1960s to aggressively   1. _____
pursue non-violent civil disobedience in pursuit of racial justice and economic equality. Until his assassination in 1968, King remained a steadfast leader committing   to the radical transfor-   2. _____
mation of society through persistent, non-violent activism.

King grew up during the Great Depression, was a direct   3. _____
witness not only to racism in the South but to bread lines and social injustice. These experiences heightened his awareness of economic inequalities. He watched his father campaigned   4. _____
against racial discrimination in voting and in salary differences between white and African-American teachers. His father's activism provided a model for King's own political engaged   5. _____
ministry.

King attended Morehouse College from 1944 to 1948. The president of Morehouse, Benjamin E. Mays, strongly influenced King's spirit development by encouraging him to view   6. _____
Christianity as a potential force for social change in the secular world. King struggled with mixed feelings about religion during his college years, but decided to enter the ministry after graduation, respond to what he called an "inner urge" calling   7. _____
him "to serve God and community." He was ordained during his final semester at Morehouse.

King later continued his religious education at Boston University's School of Theology, there he completed a   8. _____
doctorate in theology in 1955.   In 1960, King was known nationwidely for his book on civil rights advocacy, *Stride*   9. _____
Toward Freedom. And in 1963, in front of 200,000 people gathered in Washington, D.C., King delivered a speech, known today as the "I Have A Dream" speech. It marked a high point in King's crusade and served as an inspiration for civil rights supporters. Televising throughout the world, his speech   10. _____
electrified those who heard those words and saw the thousands who had marched on Washington in support ofivil rights movement.

VI. Write a composition.

Review the text and write a summary of Martin Luther King's life and struggle in no less than 400 words.

Further Development

1. Starting in 1965, King began to express doubts about the United States' role in the Vietnam War. On April 4, 1967, King delivered a speech titled "Beyond Vietnam". In the speech, he spoke strongly against the U.S.'s role in the war, insisting that the U.S. was in Vietnam "to occupy it as an American colony" and calling the U.S. government "the greatest purveyor of violence in the world today." Consult reference books or visit websites for more information about King's opposition to the Vietnam War. Write a composition not less than 300 words about the connection of civil rights and anti-Vietnam War.
2. In December 1963, FBI officials who were gathered to a special conference alleged that King was "knowingly, willingly and regularly cooperating with and taking guidance from communists" whose long-term strategy was to create a "Negro-labor" coalition detrimental to American security. Work in groups and present in class your research result of the so-called allegations of King's communist connections.

Section B Text Two

Nelson Rolihlahla Mandela

By Suzanne Michele Bourgoin and Paula Kay Byers

1   Nelson Rolihlahla Mandela (born 1918) was a South African resistance leader who, after years of imprisonment for opposing apartheid, emerged to become the first president of a black-majority-ruled South Africa and a winner of the Nobel Peace Prize.

2   The father of Nelson Mandela was a Xhosa chief in the Transkei, where Mandela was born. He studied law at Witwatersrand University and set up practice in Johannesburg in 1952. The years between 1951 and 1960 were marked by turbulence. The younger nationalists, led by Mandela and others, were coming to the view that nonviolent demonstrations against apartheid invited state violence against the Africans. There was also criticism of the type of collaboration with the non-Africans which the African National Congress (ANC) practiced. These nationalists were not unanimous on the alternative to nonviolence.

3   Unlike the young leaders with whom he grew up, Mandela was ready to try every possible technique to destroy apartheid peacefully, though he, too, realized the futility of nonviolence in view of the conditions which prevailed in his country. His attitude enabled him to

support Albert Luthuli when some of the militants walked out of the ANC.

Mandela had joined the ANC in 1944, at a time of crisis for the movement. Its younger members had opposed African participation in World War II and had demanded the declaration of South Africa's war aims for the black people. The Old Guard, led by Dr. Alfred Batini Xuma, was reluctant to embarrass the Jan Smuts government by pressing the African people's demands for the abolition of segregation. The militants, led by Anton M. Lembede, formed the ANC Youth League in 1943. Mandela was elected its president in 1951 and campaigned extensively for the repeal of discriminatory laws. He was appointed volunteer in chief in the resistance movement which the ANC led in 1951—1952, and he was subsequently banned for 6 months and later sentenced to 9 months for his leadership of the defiance campaign.

5　　Mandela was one of the leaders arrested with Luthuli and charged with treason in 1956. The case against him and others collapsed in 1961. He was arrested again during the state of emergency which followed the Sharpeville shootings in 1960. Both the Pan-Africanist Congress, which had organized the demonstrations which led to the shootings, and the ANC were banned.

6　　Sharpeville had made it clear that the days of nonviolent resistance were over. A semi-underground movement, the All-African National Action Council, came into being in 1961. Mandela was appointed its honorary secretary and later became head of Umkhonto we Sizwe (the Spear of the Nation), which used sabotage in its fight against apartheid.

7　　Mandela traveled for a while in free Africa. On his return he was arrested for leaving the country illegally and for inciting the Africans to strike in protest against the establishment of the Republic of South Africa. He was sentenced to 5 years in jail. At the trial, he told the court, "I want at once to make it clear that I am not a racialist and do not support any racialism of any kind, because to me racialism is a barbaric thing whether it comes from a black man or a white man."

8　　Mandela subsequently figured in the Rivonia trial with other leaders of Umkhonto we Sizwe on a charge of high treason and was given a life sentence, which he began serving on Robben Island.

9　　During the 27 years that Mandela spent in prison, hidden from the eyes of the world while he quarried limestone and harvested seaweed, his example of quiet suffering was just one of numerous pressures on the apartheid government. Public discussion of Mandela was illegal, and he was allowed few visitors. But as the years dragged on, he assumed the mantle of a martyr. In 1982 Mandela was moved to the maximum security Pollsmoor Prison outside Cape Town. This move apparently stemmed from fears by the South African authorities that Mandela was exerting too great an influence on the other prisons at Robben Island. Mandela spent much of the next sixyears in solitary confinement, during which he was allowed a weekly 30-minute visit by his wife, Winnie. He was offered a conditional freedom in 1984 on the condition that he settle in the officially designated black "homeland" of Transkei, an offer Mandela refused with an affirmation of his allegiance to the African National Congress. In 1988, Mandela was hospitalized with tuberculosis, and after his recovery he was returned to prison under somewhat less stringent circumstances. By this time, the situation within South Africa was becoming desperate for the ruling powers. Civil unrest had spread, and international boycotts and diplomatic pressures were increasing. More and more, South Africa was isolated as a racist state. It was against this backdrop that F.W. de Klerk, the President of South Africa and leader of the white-dominated National party, finally heeded the calls from around the world to release Mandela.

10   On Feb. 11, 1990, Mandela, grey and thin but standing erect and appearing in surprisingly good health, walked out of Verster Prison. He received tumultuous welcomes wherever he went. He visited the United States in July 1990 to raise funds for his cause and received overwhelming acclaim at every turn. In 1991 Mandela assumed the presidency of the African National Congress, by then restored to legal status by the government. Both Mandela and deKlerk realized that only a compromise between whites and blacks could avert a disastrous civil war in South Africa. In late 1991 a multiparty Convention for a Democratic South Africa convened to establish a Democratic government. Mandela and deKlerk led the negotiations, and their efforts later won them the Nobel Peace Prize in 1993. In September 1992 the two leaders signed a Record of Understanding that created a freely elected constitutional assembly to draft a new constitution and act as a transition government. On April 27, 1994, the first free elections open to all South African citizens were held. The ANC won over 62 percent of the popular vote and Mandela was elected president.

11   Mandela's agenda as president consisted of defusing the still dangerous political differences and building up the South African economy. The former he attempted to achieve by forming a coalition cabinet with representatives of different groups included. The latter he attempted to attain by inviting new investment from abroad, setting aside some government contracts for black entrepreneurs, and initiating action to return to blacks land seized in 1913. Mandela ran into some personal sorrow during this period in the downfall of his wife, Winnie. After all his years of imprisonment, the Mandelas were separated in 1993 and divorced in 1996. Mandela had appointed his then-wife to his cabinet, but she was forced to exit in 1995 after evidence of her complicity in civil violence was revealed.

12   However, Mandela's presidency for the most part was successful to a remarkable degree. Mandela's skill as a consensus builder, plus his enormous personal authority, helped him lead the transition to a majority democracy and what promised to be a peaceful future. He backed the establishment of a Truth and Reconciliation Commission which offered amnesty to those who had committed crimes during the apartheid era in the interests of clearing up the historical record. The elderly statesman even gave rise to a new style of dress in South Africa known as "Madiba smart." "Madiba" was Mandela's

Xhosa clan title, by which he was informally known. And "smart" was local slang for nicely turned out. The style became popular after Mandela traded his business suits for brightly patterned silk shirts, carefully buttoned at the neck and wrists, worn with dress slacks and shoes.

13   Mandela without question was both the leading political prisoner of the late 20th century and one of Africa's most important reformers. The man who spent nearly three decades in prison out of dedication to his cause became an international symbol of human rights. That he proved to be an effective negotiator and practical politician as well only added to his reputation and proved a blessing to his nation. Mandela retired from the presidency in June 1999, choosing not to challenge Thabo Mbeki, his vice president, in elections. Mbeki won the election in another strong showing for the ANC and was inaugurated as president on June 16, 1999. Mandela quickly took on the role of statesman after leaving office, acting as mediator in the peace process in Burundi in 1999, and in negotiations to end a stalemate between Libya and Western powers over the 1988 Lockerbie, Scotland, bombing in 2000.

14   Mandela also proved to be a man of surprises on his 80th birthday in 1998. He appeared at his birthday party with his new wife Graça Machel, whom he had married that very day.

15   Mandela's office announced on July 16, 2000, that a power-sharing agreement aimed at ending the conflict between the Tutsi-dominated army and Hutu rebels in Burundi would be signed by the end of August. Mandela was facilitating negotiations to try to end Burundi's seven-year civil war.

16   On December 2, 2000, Mandela received a lifetime achievement award from the Congress of South African Trade Unions. The organization is the largest trade federation in South Africa. Mandela was honored for his contribution to the struggle of workers. During his presidency, the government introduced legislation requiring workplace safety, overtime pay and minimum wages.

17   In 2002, the 84-year-old Mandela was in the news after he condemned the United State's attitude toward Iraq, referred to the U.S. vice-president as a dinosaur, and accused the U.S. of threatening world peace. On President George W. Bush's war on terrorism, Mandela said, "If you look at these matters, you will come to the conclusion that the attitude of the United States of America is a threat to world peace." Although U.S. Vice-President Dick Cheney recommended against releasing Mandela from jail in 1986 on the grounds that the South African supported terrorism, Mandela insisted he was not motivated by any sense of revenge when he said, "Quite clearly we are dealing with an arch-conservative in Dick Cheney ... my impression of the president is that this is a man with whom you can do business. But it is the men around him who are dinosaurs, who do not want him to belong to the modern age."

18   In late 2002, a group of South African businessmen announced a plan to build a 210-ft statue of Mandela—larger than the Statue of Liberty—in Port Elizabeth, South

Africa. The project was expected to create 9,000 jobs, and plans were to use melted-down guns in the statue's steel frame.

19   In 2005, Mandela faced perhaps his greatest tragedy when his son, Makgatho, died of AIDS. Mandela announced his son's death in a press conference and urged South Africans to be more open about the disease. In March of 2005 Mandela hosted a concert in George, South Africa, to raise money for South African women with HIV. Performers at the concert, which was called "46664" after Mandela's number while he was in prison, included Will Smith, Annie Lennox, and Queen. In 2005 Mandela made his fifth trip to the White House, where he was received by President Bush. While he was in America, on May 12, 2005, Mandela, addressed Amherst College students and faculty in New York. He discussed the importance of U.S. universities improving their methods of educating talented students of modest means. He received an honorary degree from the college at St. Bartholomew's Church in New York.

Independent Study Assistance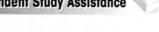

I. Words and Expressions

1. **apartheid** *n.*   the former political and social system in South Africa, in which only white people had full political rights and people of other races, especially black people, were forced to go to separate schools, live in separate areas etc.
2. **turbulence** *n.*   a political or emotional situation that is very confused
3. **invite** *v.*   to make sth, especially sth bad or unpleasant, likely to happen
4. **unanimous** *adj.*   a group of people who are unanimous about sth all agree about it
5. **discriminatory** *adj.*   treating a particular group of people unfairly because of their religion, race, or other personal features
6. **high treason** *n.*   a crime against your country
7. **sabotage** *n.*   things that are done to stop someone from achieving sth or to prevent a plan or process from being successful
8. **incite** *v.*   to encourage people to be violent or commit crimes by making them angry or excited
9. **barbaric** *adj.*   extremely violent and cruel
10. **figure** *v.*   to be an important part of sth
11. **quarry** *v.*   to dig stone out of the ground
12. **limestone** *n.*   a type of white or grey stone containing calcium, used for building and making cement
13. **mantle** *n.*   the authority or responsibility connected with someone's position, duties, or beliefs
14. **martyr** *n.*   someone who suffers or is killed because of their religious or political beliefs
15. **confinement** *n.*   a situation in which someone is forced to stay in a place, especially a prison, and not allowed to leave
16. **allegiance** *n.*   strong loyalty to a person, group, belief, or country
17. **tuberculosis** *n.*   a serious infectious disease affecting your lungs
18. **stringent** *adj.*   constricted; tight
19. **unrest** *n.*   angry or violent behaviour by people who are protesting against sth

20. **backdrop** *n.*   the situation or place in which sth happens
21. **heed** *v.*   to consider someone's advice or warning and do what they suggest
22. **erect** *n.*   in a straight upright position
23. **tumultuous** *adj.*   very loud; involving strong feelings, especially feelings of approval: tumultuous applause/a tumultuous welcome
24. **avert** *v.*   to prevent sth bad or harmful from happening
25. **convene** *v.*   to arrange a formal meeting, or to gather for a meeting
26. **coalition** *n.*   a temporary union of different political parties that agree to form a government together
27. **entrepreneur** *n.*   someone who uses money to start businesses and make business deals.
28. **complicity** *n.*   the fact that someone is involved in or knows about sth bad that happens
29. **consensus** *n.*   agreement among all the people involved
30. **amnesty** *n.*   a situation in which a government agrees not to punish, or to no longer punish, people who have committed a particular crime
31. **reconciliation** *n.*   a way of making it possible for ideas, beliefs, needs etc that are opposed to each other to exist together
32. **clan** *n.*   a large group of families that are related to each other, especially in Scotland
33. **stalemate** *n.*   a situation in which progress is impossible because the people or groups involved cannot agree
34. **HIV**   abbreviation for "human immunodeficiency virus", which can cause AIDS

II. Referential Points

The African National Congress (ANC)   has been South Africa's governing party, supported by its tripartite alliance with the Congress of South African Trade Unions (COSATU) and the South African Communist Party (SACP), since the establishment of non-racial democracy in April 1994.

Albert Luthuli,   also known by his Zulu name "Mvumbi" (1898—1967), was a South African teacher and politician. Luthuli was elected president of the African National Congress (ANC), at the time an umbrella organisation that led opposition to the white minority government in South Africa. He was awarded the 1960 Nobel Peace Prize for his role in the non-violent struggle against apartheid.

Alfred Batini Xuma (1893—1962)   was a South African leader and activist and president-general of the African National Congress (ANC) from 1940 to 1949. He was a member of Alpha Phi Alpha, the first intercollegiate Greek-letter fraternity established for African Americans.

Jan Smuts (1870—1950)   was a prominent South African and British Commonwealth statesman, military leader and philosopher. In addition to holding various cabinet posts, heserved as Prime Minister of the Union of South Africa from 1919 until 1924 and from 1939 until 1948. For most of his public life, Smuts advocated segregation between the races and was opposed to the unilateral enfranchisement of the black majority in South Africa.

Umkhonto we Sizwe,   translated "Spear of the Nation," was the active military wing of the African National Congress (ANC) in cooperation with the South African Communist Party in their fight against the South African apartheid government.

Robben Island (Afrikaans Robbeneiland)   is an island in Table Bay, some seven kilometres off the coast of Cape Town, South Africa. It was here that former South African

President and Nobel Laureate Nelson Mandela and former South African President Kgalema Motlanthe, alongside many other political prisoners, spent decades imprisoned during the apartheid era.

Winnie Mandela (born 1936), South Africa's first black professional social welfare worker, chose service to needy people and devotion of her energy and skill to the struggle for equality and justice for all people in South Africa. After her marriage to Nelson Mandela in 1958 she suffered harassment, imprisonment, and periodic banishment for her continuing involvement in that struggle.

Frederik Willem de Klerk (born 1936), often known as F. W. de Klerk, was the last State President of apartheid-era South Africa, serving from September 1989 to May 1994. De Klerk is best known for engineering the end of apartheid, South Africa's racial segregation policy, and supporting the transformation of South Africa into a multi-racial democracy by entering into the negotiations that resulted in all citizens, including the country's black majority, having equal voting and other rights. He shared the Prince of Asturias Awards in 1992 and the Nobel Peace Prize in 1993 along with Nelson Mandela for his role in the ending of apartheid.

Thabo Mvuyelwa Mbeki (born 1942) is a South African politician who served almost two terms as the second post-apartheid President of South Africa from 14 June 1999 to 24 September 2008. On 20 September 2008, he announced his resignation after being recalled by the African National Congress's National Executive Committee, following a conclusion by Judge Nicholson of improper interference in the National Prosecuting Authority (NPA), including the prosecution of Jacob Zuma for corruption. On 12 January 2009, the Supreme Court of Appeal unanimously overturned Judge Nicholson's judgment but the resignation stood.

Graça Machel (born 1945) is the third wife of former South African president Nelson Mandela and the widow of the late Mozambican president Samora Machel. She is the only person in the world to have been married to the presidents of two different nations. She is an international advocate for women's and children's rights.

III. Questions for Comprehension

1. How much do you know about Nelson Mandela? Work out a brief report about his life and main achievements.
2. Why did Nelson Mandela commit himself to civil rights via non-violent disobedience even confronted with armed forces?
3. Concerning their struggle for civil rights and freedom for the people, is there any difference between Nelson Mandela and Mohandas Gandhi, the pre-eminent political and spiritual leader of India during the Indian independence movement?
4. South African archbishop Desmond Tutu, recipient of the Nobel Peace Prize, has said of the Mandelas: "[They] have become a symbolic couple with their incredible strength and refusal to be broken." Not long after Mandelas' release from prison in 1993, however, they were divorced. Why? Illustrate your points with evidence.

Unit 3

Self-test

I. Fill in the blanks with the words and expressions provided, making some change when necessary.

apartheid	heed	invite	unanimous
clan	complicity	segregation	stalemate
figure	sabotage	incite	tumultuous
quarry	allegiance	backdrop	

1. Negotiations on the dismantling of _____ will have to address the overwhelming demand of our people for a democratic, non-racial and unitary South Africa.
2. All state organs and functionaries must rely on the support of the people, keep in close touch with them, _____ their opinions and suggestions, accept their supervision and work hard to serve them.
3. "We must not let that boy be with Alois so often," he said to his wife that night, "because it may _____ trouble. He is fifteen now and she is twelve. And the boy is handsome."
4. The decision was not _____; three justices dissented, Justice Harlan roundly attacking his six colleagues for violating another basic American principle-separation of powers.
5. They prayed for a mere girl, thinking a large dowry would buy the daughter a husband from a poor family who would take their _____ name.
6. She was never tried for this; and although she was held in detention by the Allies between 1945 and 1950, four separate investigations cleared her of _____ with the regime.
7. The riots that swept American cities in the 1960s occurred shortly after congress passed a whole series of civil rights acts that destroyed the legal basis of _____, particularly in the South.
8. The current _____ can not be broken nor can the overall negotiations be pushed forwarded unless developed members with high subsidy, high support and high tariffs make major and substantial reduction commitments.
9. The writing of moral literature would be perfectly suitable for women according to Genlis's stipulations, and indeed, moral tales and didactic works _____ prominently in writing done by women in the nineteenth century.
10. According to Strauss, he stayed in Nazi Germany because he thought that someone should be there to protect the culture from Hitler's barbaric _____.
11. I must stress that I'm not trying to _____ any social disharmony here, but my point is: the passion that charged the twenty-somethings 50 years ago, when they fought for their cause, is almost non-existent in the people of the same age group today.
12. The Enlightenment and the Industrial Revolution that followed caused a _____ transformation in Europe. Shaking off its feudal shackles in ideology and social systems, Europe created a brave new world for itself.
13. And sometimes he walked as far as the town of Corleone, its eighteen thousand people strung out in dwellings that pitted the side of the nearest mountain, the mean hovels built out of black rock _____ from that mountain.

14. Although naturalism had not become an obsession among American writers by 1914, it clearly commanded the _____ of a majority of serious young writers.
15. Meanwhile, against the _____ of new economy and globalization, integration of markets gave consumers more choices and raised their demand for higher quality, all of which have poised a higher demand for technological upgrading and product development.

II. Use the appropriate form of the words given in the brackets to fill in the blanks.
1. People may have different opinions while setting a valuation on his world outlook and his writings, but _____ agree that his style is unique in the literary circles of the world. (unanimous)
2. Blunkett's ruling means that this "Dr. Death" will probably die of old age in prison because cases of life _____ will only be reevaluated after a service of 25 years. After that, evaluation will be given every five years. (prison)
3. In the current field of international trade, technical barriers to trade as a both rational, _____, convert and powerful non-tariff barriers have posed the great obstacle to China's export trade objectively. (discriminate)
4. She concluded by thanking him for his kindness in a crude way, then puzzled over the formality of signing her name, and finally decided upon the severe, winding up with a "Very truly," which she _____ changed to "Sincerely." (subsequence)
5. Fanny's emotion, which but now had been that of _____ and anger, have turned to dismay and supplication. (defy)
6. Her mere experience and the free out-of-door life of the country caused her nature to revolt at such _____. Dirt had never been her share. (confine)
7. She had suffered a stroke that left half of her body paralyzed, had been _____ for treatment of a brain tumor, and had recently lost her father, her mother and her home. (hospital)
8. In Paris, the beauty and charm of the ages have remained intact not by accident but by _____ enforced city planning regulations. (stringent)
9. Because I wanted to bask in her unfailing concern for me, and because of those tears of _____ she shed over her inability to comfort me, I would bury my face in my arms and cry over trivialities. (desperate)
10. Three passions, simple but _____ strong, have governed my life: the longing for love, the search for knowledge, and the unbearable pity for the suffering of mankind. (overwhelm)
11. Cardiff Hill, beyond the village and above it, was green with vegetation and it lay just far enough away to seem a Delectable Land, dreamy, reposeful, and _____ (invite).
12. Xiangzi managed to keep his temper, unable to think of any _____ to sticking it out until he had his own rickshaw, when things would work out all right. (alter)
13. They had come to hate Sonny for his bloodthirstiness, which they considered _____. Also not good business sense. Nobody wanted the old days back again with all its turmoil and trouble. (barbarian)
14. Although naturalism had not become an obsession among American writers by 1914, it clearly commanded the _____ of a majority of serious young writers. (allege)
15. Kazakhstan, China, Kirgizstan, Russia, Tadzhikistan and Uzbekistan formally founded the Shanghai Cooperation Organization and started this regional economic cooperative

organization with the trade and investment _____ as the mainstay. (facile)

III. Translating the short paragraph into Chinese.

However, Mandela's presidency for the most part was successful to a remarkable degree. Mandela's skill as a consensus builder, plus his enormous personal authority, helped him lead the transition to a majority democracy and what promised to be a peaceful future. He backed the establishment of a Truth and Reconciliation Commission which offered amnesty to those who had committed crimes during the apartheid era in the interests of clearing up the historical record. The elderly statesman even gave rise to a new style of dress in South Africa known as "Madiba smart." "Madiba" was Mandela's Xhosa clan title, by which he was informally known. And "smart" was local slang for nicely turned out. The style became popular after Mandela traded his business suits for brightly patterned silk shirts, carefully buttoned at the neck and wrists, worn with dress slacks and shoes.

IV. Analyze difficult sentences.

1. The younger nationalists, led by Mandela and others, were coming to the view that nonviolent demonstrations against apartheid invited state violence against the Africans.
2. There was also criticism of the type of collaboration with the non-Africans which the African National Congress (ANC) practiced. These nationalists were not unanimous on the alternative to nonviolence.
3. Mandela was ready to try every possible technique to destroy apartheid peacefully, though he, too, realized the futility of nonviolence in view of the conditions which prevailed in his country. His attitude enabled him to support Albert Luthuli when some of the militants walked out of the ANC.
4. The Old Guard, led by Dr. Alfred Batini Xuma, was reluctant to embarrass the Jan Smuts government by pressing the African people's demands for the abolition of segregation.
5. Mandela subsequently figured in the Rivonia trial with other leaders of Umkhonto we Sizwe on a charge of high treason and was given a life sentence, which he began serving on Robben Island.

V. Proofread the following passage.

Nelson Mandela has spent a lifetime fighting for the rights of black South Africans, endured trial and incarceration for his principles. A political prisoner in his native South Africa for more than 25 years, eloquent and statesman-like Mandela became the human embodiment of the struggle against government-mandated discrimination. His courage and determination through decades of imprison galvanized not only South African blacks, but also concerned citizens on every continent. After his release from prison in 1990, Mandela reclaimed his position in the once-banned African National Congress (ANC) and fought tireless for democratic reform in his troubled homeland.

With his magnetic personality and calm demeanor, Mandela was widely regarded the last best hope for conciliating

1. _____

2. _____

3. _____

4. _____

5. _____

a peaceful transition to a South African government that would enfranchise all of their citizens. "For whites," wrote John F. Burns in the *New York Times*, "a man once present to them as a threat to everything they prize is now widely viewed as the best hope for a political settlement that will guarantee them a future. For blacks, Mr. Mandela has achieved a legendary stature, towering above most other leaders in the way that Lenin dominated the revolutionary cause in Russia, and Churchill the fight for England's survival in World War II."

6. _____

Time magazine contributor Richard Lacayo characterized Mandela a figure who is "unique among heroes because he is a live embodiment of black liberation.... His soft-spoken manner and unflappable dignity bespeak his background as a lawyer, a single-minded political organizer and a longtime prisoner still blinked a bit in the spotlight." Lacayo continued: "For the many blacks who have begun to call themselves African Americans, [Mandela] is a flesh-and-blood exemplar of what an African can be. For Americans of all colors, were weary of their nation's perennial racial standoffs, [he] offers the opportunity for a full-throat expression of their no less perennial hope for reconciliation."

7. _____

8. _____

9. _____

10. _____

VI. Write a composition.

Review the text and write a summary of Nelson Mandela's life and struggles in no more than 400 words.

Unit 4

Public Speaking

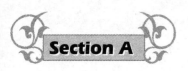
Section A

Text One
Radio Broadcast on the German Invasion of Russia

Focal Consideration

Churchill's passionate war speech, which implored British soldiers to fight on the beaches, is regarded as one of the finest addresses in history. In this section, concentration is required for the following discussions:
1. information of WWII;
2. linguistic and rhetorical styles of Churchill;
3. skills needed in speech delivery.

Research Questions

1. What climacterics of the war urged Churchill to deliver this speech?
2. According to the text, how did Hitler attack Russia? Why did Churchill say he was not surprised at the attack?
3. How did Churchill describe Hitler, his soldier and the Russian people? What effect does the description bring about?
4. Why did Churchill regard the German invasion of Russia as a prelude? Do you agree with him?
5. Do you think Churchill successfully persuades his people to support his policy? How?

Radio Broadcast on the German Invasion of Russia

By Winston Churchill

1. I have taken occasion to speak to you tonight because we have reached one of the climacterics of the war. In the first of these intense turning points, a year ago, France fell prostrate under the German hammer and we had to face the storm alone.

2. The second was when the Royal Air Force beat the Hun raiders out of the daylight air raid and thus warded off the Nazi invasion of our islands while we were still ill-armed and ill-prepared.

3. The third turning point was when the President and Congress of the United States passed the lease and lend enactment, devoting nearly 2,000,000,000 sterling of the wealth of the New World to help us defend our liberties and their own.

4. Those were the three climacterics.

5. The fourth is now upon us.

6. At 4 o'clock this morning Hitler attacked and invaded Russia. All his usual formalities of perfidy were observed with scrupulous technique. A non-aggression treaty had been solemnly signed and was in force between the two countries. No complaint had been made by Germany of its non-fulfillment. Under its cloak of false confidence the German armies drew up in immense strength along a line which stretched from the White Sea to the Black Sea and their air fleets and armoured divisions slowly and methodically took up their stations.

7. Then, suddenly, without declaration of war, without even an ultimatum, the German bombs rained down from the sky upon the Russian cities; the German troops violated the Russian frontiers and an hour later the German Ambassador, who till the night before was lavishing his assurances of friendship, almost of alliance, upon the Russians, called upon the Russian Foreign Minister to tell him that a state of war existed between Germany and Russia.

8. Thus was repeated on a far larger scale the same kind of outrage against every form of signed compact and international faith which we have witnessed in Norway, in Denmark, in Holland, in Belgium and which Hitler's accomplice and jackal, Mussolini, so faithfully imitated in the case of Greece.

9. All this was no surprise to me. In fact I gave clear and precise warnings to Stalin of what was coming. I gave him warnings, as I have given warnings to others before. I can only hope that these warnings did not fall unheeded.

10. All we know at present is that the Russian people are defending their native soil and that their leaders have called upon them to resist to the utmost.

11. Hitler is a monster of wickedness, insatiable in his lust for blood and plunder. Not content with having all Europe under his heel or else terrorized into various forms of abject submission, he must now carry his work of butchery and desolation among the vast

multitudes of Russia and of Asia. The terrible military machine which we and the rest of the civilized world so foolishly, so supinely, so insensately allowed the Nazi gangsters to build up year by year from almost nothing—this machine cannot stand idle, lest it rust or fall to pieces. It must be in continual motion, grinding up human lives and trampling down the homes and the rights of hundreds of millions of men.

12 Moreover, it must be fed not only with flesh but with oil. So now this bloodthirsty guttersnipe must launch his mechanized armies upon new fields of slaughter, pillage and devastation. Poor as are the Russian peasants, workmen and soldiers, he must steal from them their daily bread. He must devour their harvests. He must rob them of the oil which drives their ploughs and thus produce a famine without example in human history.

13 And even the carnage and ruin which his victory, should he gain it—though he's not gained it yet—will bring upon the Russian people, will itself be only a stepping stone to the attempt to plunge four or five hundred millions who live in China and the 350,000,000 who live in India into that bottomless pit of human degradation over which the diabolic emblem of the swastika flaunts itself.

14 It is not too much to say here this pleasant summer evening that the lives and happiness of a thousand million additional human beings are now menaced with brutal Nazi violence. That is enough to make us hold our breath.

15 But presently I shall show you something else that lies behind and something that touches very nearly the life of Britain and of the United States.

16 The Nazi regime is indistinguishable from the worst features of Communism. It is devoid of all theme and principle except appetite and racial domination. It excels in all forms of human wickedness, in the efficiency of its cruelty and ferocious aggression. No one has been a more consistent opponent of Communism than I have for the last twenty-five years. I will unsay no words that I've spoken about it. But all this fades away before the spectacle which is now unfolding.

17 The past, with its crimes, its follies and its tragedies, flashes away. I see the Russian soldiers standing on the threshold of their native land, guarding the fields which their fathers have tilled from time immemorial. I see them guarding their homes; their mothers and wives pray, ah yes, for there are times when all pray for the safety of their loved ones, for the return of the breadwinner, of the champion, of their protectors.

18 I see the 10,000 villages of Russia, where the means of existence was wrung so hardly from the soil, but where there are still primordial human joys, where maidens laugh and children play I see advancing upon all this, in hideous onslaught, the Nazi war machine, with its clanking, heel-clicking, dandified Prussian officers, its crafty expert agents, fresh from the cowing and tying down of a dozen countries. I see also the dull, drilled, docile brutish masses of the Hun soldiery, plodding on like a swarm of crawling locusts. I see the German bombers and fighters in the sky, still smarting from many a British whipping, so delighted to find what they believe is an easier and a safer prey. And behind all this glare, behind all this storm, I see that small group of villainous men who

planned, organized and launched this cataract of horrors upon mankind.

19   And then my mind goes back across the years to the days when the Russian armies were our Allies against the same deadly foe when they fought with so much valor and constancy and helped to gain a victory, from all share in which, alas, they were, through no fault of ours, utterly cut off.

20   I have lived through all this and you will pardon me if I express my feelings and the stir of old memories. But now I have to declare the decision of His Majesty's Government, and I feel sure it is a decision in which the great Dominions will, in due course, concur. And that we must speak of now, at once, without a day's delay. I have to make the declaration, but can you doubt what our policy will be?

21   We have but one aim and one single irrevocable purpose. We are resolved to destroy Hitler and every vestige of the Nazi regime. From this nothing will turn us. Nothing. We will never parley; we will never negotiate with Hitler or any of his gang. We shall fight him by land; we shall fight him by sea; we shall fight him in the air, until, with God's help, we have rid the earth of his shadow and liberated its people from his yoke.

22   Any man or State who fights against Nazism will have our aid. Any man or State who marches with Hitler is our foe. This applies not only to organized States but to all representatives of that vile race of Quislings who make themselves the tools and agents of the Nazi regime against their fellow-countrymen and against the lands of their births. These Quislings, like the Nazi leaders themselves, if not disposed of by their fellow–countrymen, which would save trouble, will be delivered by us on the morrow of victory to the justice of the Allied tribunals. That is our policy and that is our declaration.

23   It follows, therefore, that we shall give whatever help we can to Russia and to the Russian people. We shall appeal to all our friends and Allies in every part of the world to take the same course and pursue it as we shall, faithfully and steadfastly to the end.

24   We have offered to the Government of Soviet Russia any technical or economic assistance which is in our power and which is likely to be of service to them. We shall bomb Germany by day as well as by night in ever-increasing measure, casting upon them month by month a heavier discharge of bombs and making the German people taste and gulp each month a sharper dose of the miseries they have showered upon mankind.

25   It is noteworthy that only yesterday the Royal Air Force, striking inland over France, cut down with very small loss to themselves twenty-eight of the Hun fighting machines in the air above the French soil they have invaded, defiled and profess to hold.

26   But this is only a beginning. From now henceforward the main expansion of our air force proceeds with gathering speed. In another six months the weight of the help we are receiving from the United States in war materials of all kinds, especially in heavy bombers, will begin to tell. This is no class war. It is a war in which the whole British Empire and Commonwealth of Nations is engaged without distinction of race, creed or party.

27   It is not for me to speak of the action of the United States, but this I will say: If Hitler

imagines that his attack on Soviet Russia will cause the slightest division of aims or slackening of effort in the great democracies, who are resolved upon his doom, he is woefully mistaken. On the contrary, we shall be fortified and encouraged in our efforts to rescue mankind from his tyranny. We shall be strengthened and not weakened in our determination and in our resources.

28   This is no time to moralize upon the follies of countries and governments which have allowed themselves to be struck down one by one when by united action they could so easily have saved themselves and saved the world from this catastrophe.

29   But, when I spoke a few minutes ago of Hitler's bloodlust and the hateful appetites which have impelled or lured him on his Russian adventure, I said there was one deeper motive behind his outrage. He wishes to destroy the Russian power because he hopes that if he succeeds in this he will be able to bring back the main strength of his army and air force from the East and hurl it upon this island, which he knows he must conquer or suffer the penalty of his crimes.

30   His invasion of Russia is no more than a prelude to an attempted invasion of the British Isles. He hopes, no doubt, that all this may be accomplished before the Winter comes and that he can overwhelm Great Britain before the fleets and air power of the United States will intervene. He hopes that he may once again repeat upon a greater scale than ever before that process of destroying his enemies one by one, by which he has so long thrived and prospered, and that then the scene will be clear for the final act, without which all his conquests would be in vain, namely, the subjugation of the Western Hemisphere to his will and to his system.

31   The Russian danger is therefore our danger and the danger of the United States just as the cause of any Russian fighting for his hearth and home is the cause of free men and free peoples in every quarter of the globe.

32   Let us learn the lessons already taught by such cruel experience. Let us redouble our exertions and strike with united strength while life and power remain.

Preview Assistance

1. **perfidy** *n.*   behavior which is not loyal. Its adjective form is perfidious.
2. **formalities** *n.*   although it is a plural form of the word formality, their connotation or stress is different. Formality means something which has to be done but which has no real importance, while formalities refers to something that the law or an official process says must be done.
3. **observe** *v.*   to adhere to; abide by. It stresses respectful adherence, as to law or tradition, often in the form of compliance with prescribed rites
4. **under the cloak of**   cloak in this phrase meaning something which hides, covers or keeps something else secret
5. **methodically** *adv.*   the word methodical is used to describe people who do things in a very ordered, careful way, e.g. a very methodical person. Methodically means proceeding in a regular and systematic order.

Section A

6. **ultimatum** *n.*   a final statement of terms or a threat in which a person or group of people are warned that if they do not do a particular thing, something unpleasant will happen to them.
7. **lavish** *v.*   to give someone too much of something. Usually we say lavish something on somebody or something.
8. **outrage** *n.*   an act of extreme violence or viciousness
9. **to the utmost**   the word utmost in the phrase means the greatest possible amount, degree, or extent; the maximum
10. **insatiable** *adj.*   impossible to satiate or satisfy:
11. **be devoid of**   to be completely lacking
12. **excel in**   to surpass others in a certain aspect
13. **unsay** *v.*   to retract something said
14. **fade away**   to disappear gradually; vanish
15. **wring** *v.*   extract by twisting or compressing
16. **primordial** *adj.*   existing at or since the beginning of the world or the universe
17. **onslaught** *n.*   a violent attack
18. **tie down**   to compel; to constrain; to pin down
19. **plod** *v.*   to move or walk heavily
20. **crawl** *v.*   to be or feel as if swarming or covered with moving things
21. **smart from**   when it is used as a verb, the word smart means to sting or to cause someone to feel a stinging pain.
22. **stir** *v.*   when it is used as a verb, it means to cause to feel a strong emotion. In the text it is used as a noun, thus meaning a lot of interest or excitement.
23. **in due course**   at a suitable time in the future
24. **resolve** *v.*   make a firm decision about; be resolved to do means to be determined to do
25. **parley** *n.*   a discussion or conference, especially one between enemies over terms of truce or other matters
26. **dispose of sb/sth**   to get rid of someone or something.
27. **It follows that...**   It comes/happens after something as a natural result
28. **appeal to**   to make a request for help or ask for support
29. **divergence** *n.*   difference about opinions
30. **impel** *v.*   to drive forward; propel.
31. **prelude** *n.*   an introductory performance, event, or action preceding a more important one; a preliminary or preface
32. **in every quarter of the globe**   quarter in this phrase means area or place
33. **exertion** *n.*   the act of making a strenuous effort

Referential Points

Churchill, Sir Winston Leonard Spencer (1874—1965) British politician and prime minister of the United Kingdom, widely regarded as the greatest British leader for the 20th century. Churchill is celebrated for his leadership during World War II (1939—1945). His courage, decisiveness, political experience, and enormous vitality enabled him to lead his country through the war, one of the most desperate struggles in British history. He is also known for the many books on British history and politics he wrote throughout his lifetime. His command of the English language not only made him a great orator but earned him the Nobel Prize for literature in 1953.

Today some Britons regard Churchill as a disturbing emblem of the old regime of class privilege and colonial empire. Others admire his efforts to adapt the British tradition of self-government, liberty, civility, and the rule of law to a new world made by democracy and science in the 20th century. Churchill once wrote that "a man's life must be nailed to a cross either of thought or of action." His own choice was clearly the active life of politics and, at its climax, he led his country in its "finest hour."

It is hard to avoid the conclusion that Churchill himself was bigger than Britain. People are still fascinated by this man who was "easily satisfied with the very best." They marvel at his boundless energy and his tremendous power of concentration. They are also struck by his daily naps, his fondness for Harrow School songs, his witty remarks, his love of animals, and his taste for cigars and Pol Roger champagne. Even after his death, readers can consider his example as a statesman and his reflections in his books.

German-Soviet non-aggression treaty On August 23, 1939, a non-aggression treaty was signed in Moscow by representatives of the German Reich and the Union of Soviet Socialist Republics. The exchange of the documents of ratification took place in Berlin on September 24, 1939. The treaty became effective on August 23, 1939 in accordance with its Article VII. Both Stalin and Hitler pledged not to attach one another and agreed to divide the territory that lay between them into German and Soviet spheres of influence. Hitler betrayed the agreement, however, and in June 1941 he launched his armies against the USSR. Britain and the United States rallied to the USSR's defense, which produced the coalition that would defeat Germany over the next four years.

the White Sea White Sea, arm of the Barents Sea, forming an indentation in the coast of northwestern Russia, and partly enclosed on the north by Kola Peninsula. It is 590 km long and has an area of 90,000 sq km. The White Sea receives the waters of numerous rivers, notably the Northern Dvina, the Onega, and the Mezen, and partly because of the resultant low salinity, a large part of its surface is frozen from November to May annually. The sea contains highly productive herring, cod, and seal fisheries. It is linked to the Baltic Sea by an inland waterway.

the Black Sea Black Sea, inland sea, lying between southeastern Europe and Asia Minor. It is connected with the Aegean Sea by the Bosporus, the Sea of Marmara, and the Dardanelles. Romania, Bulgaria, and the European portion of Turkey bound it on the west. The northern and eastern shores are bordered by Ukraine, Russia, and Georgia; the entire southern shore is Turkish territory.

British Isles A group of islands off the northwest coast of Europe comprising Great Britain, Ireland, and adjacent smaller islands.

Commonwealth of Nations An association comprising the United Kingdom, its dependencies, and many former British colonies that are now sovereign states with a common allegiance to the British Crown. It was formally established by the Statute of Westminster in 1931.

Huns a group of nomadic Asian people, probably of Turkish, Tataric, or Ugrian origins, who made repeated attacks to Europe in the 300s and 400s A.D. This group was described as an aggressive people of great vigor and comparatively low cultural achievement. They developed considerable skill in the techniques of warfare, particularly in military horsemanship. Hun later is used as a disparaging term for a German, especially a German soldier in World War I.

Prussia former kingdom and state of Germany. At the height of its expansion, in the late 19th century, Prussia extended along the coasts of the Baltic and North seas, from Belgium, the Netherlands, France, and Luxembourg on the west to the Russian Empire on the east, to Austria-Hungary on the east, southeast, and south, and to Switzerland on the south. Prussia began as the German district of Brandenburg. It became the Kingdom of Prussia in 1701, and a strong army was created. By 1871, Prussian King Wilhelm I had made the German Empire the mightiest in Europe. Prussian soldiers were the best educated and most well trained of any European army.

Quisling Vidkun Quisling (1887—1945), head of Norway's government during the Nazi occupation (1940—1945). It refers to a traitor who serves as the puppet of the enemy occupying his or her country.

Dominions a self-governing member of the British Commonwealth of Nations.

Consolidation Work

I. Fill in the blanks with the words and expressions provided, making some change when necessary.

be crawling with	die down	dispose of	rid of	to the utmost
excel in	complain	impel	assure	aggress
declare	invade	dead	cruel	solemn
diverge				

1. Such a thing never happened to this house that the kitchen floor _____ ants.
2. "How hard it is that we have to die"— a strange _____ that comes from the mouths of people who have had to live.
3. When the war broke out she took down the signed photograph of the Kaiser and, with some _____, hung it in the menservants' lavatory; it was her one combative action.
4. A decent respect to the opinions of mankind requires that they should declare the causes which _____ them to the separation.
5. The course of events justified the fact that the _____ of war against Japan was made in the usual diplomatic language.
6. Organic life, we are told, has developed gradually from the protozoon to the philosopher, and this development, we are _____, is indubitably an advance. Unfortunately it is the philosopher, not the protozoon, who gives us this _____.
7. My pacifism is not based on any intellectual theory but on a deep antipathy to every form of _____ and hatred.
8. The car has become the carapace, the protective and _____ shell, of urban and suburban man.
9. The world is _____ of Lord Byron, but the slime of his touch still remains.
10. We may find in the long run that tinned food is a _____ weapon than the machine-gun.

11. Music creates order out of chaos; for rhythm imposes unanimity upon the _____, melody imposes continuity upon the disjointed, and harmony imposes compatibility upon the incongruous.
12. In World War II he became supreme commander and was responsible for the D-day _____ of Europe.
13. It took a mere five minutes for the world champion to _____ of his opponent.
14. When the speaker appeared on the stage, people became so enthusiastic that it was several minutes before the applause _____ down.
15. Ellen worked to her _____ in her study and _____ all the courses in her class.

II. Use the appropriate form of the words given in the brackets to fill in the blanks.

1. Once they've switched their diets, they become much more receptive to the ethical message. When they hear about animal cruelty, they're no longer supporting it, so they lose their _____. (defend)
2. The _____ in the man's tone suddenly brought her wide awake. Something was wrong somewhere. (solemnly)
3. The order was precise, and I'd repeat it with an addict's talent for turning _____ into ritual. (repeat)
4. Home currency was to be devalued or revalued only in the case of persistent deficits or surpluses, respectively. In practice, however, countries were _____ to any adjustment in the parity. (resist)
5. We believe, however, that those researchers who did present and the articles that make up this journal issue provide an _____ overview of the progress in various areas of drug abuse research. (excel)
6. Such gray-market microenterprises _____ a spirit of dynamism and creativity straining to be fully unleashed. (example)
7. He is participating in an increasingly _____ discourse that represents the role of religion in one's life in this objectified way. (domination)
8. I hear the information echoed on the police scanner as the emboldened bank manager, my deputy and new best friend, rescued from despair after seven _____ and bursting now with hope for civilization, scurries around the parking lot telling people to stand away from the crime scene and suddenly here comes the chopper and all faces turn toward the sky. (rob)
9. With one hand she smoothed her skirt, feeling _____ dowdy, all too aware that her wardrobe and hairstyle were basic, practical, no nonsense. She'd never been a fashionista to start with, and nine years in the classroom had reduced both her wardrobe and her sense of style to nil. (misery)
10. This extreme high country, famous for its 54 peaks above 14,000-foot elevation, attracts the _____ who aim to make marks of achievement, or merely to breathe rare air. (adventure)

III. Paraphrase the following sentences taken from the tex.

1. All his usual formalities of perfidy were observed with scrupulous technique.
2. The Nazi regime is devoid of all theme and principle except appetite and racial domination.

3. I see the German bombers and fighters in the sky, still smarting from many a British whipping, delighted to find what they believe is an easier and a safer prey.
4. We have rid the earth of his shadow and liberated its people from his yoke.
5. Let us redouble our exertions, and strike with united strength while life and powerremain.

IV. Test your general knowledge.
1. From September 1940 to July 1941, London suffered severe damage from German air attacks. Known as _____, this period of World War II resulted in many British casualties.
   A. the London Blitz   B. the London Battle
   C. the London Attack   D. the London disaster
2. In February 1945 the leaders of the _____ known as the Big Three, met at Yalta on the Crimean Peninsula to discuss Allied military strategy in the final months of World War II.
   A. the Axis Powers   B. the Central Powers
   C. the Allied Powers   D. the Kernel Powers
3. The leaders of Allied Powers included British Prime Minister Winston Churchill, _____ Franklin Roosevelt, and Soviet Premier Joseph Stalin.
   A. American General   B. American Premier
   C. American Chairman   D. American President
4. In 1945 nations determined to maintain the hard-won peace of the Second World War founded the _____. which is an association of sovereign nations that provides the machinery to cope with international disputes and to find solutions to problems that exceed the boundaries and means of national states.
   A. the NATO   B. the UN
   C. the Warsaw Pact   D. CENTO
5. World War II, global military conflict that, in terms of lives lost and material destruction, was the most devastating war in human history. It began in 1939 as a European conflict between _____ but eventually widened to include most of the nations of the world. It ended in 1945, leaving a new world order dominated by the United States and the USSR.
   A. Germany and Britain   B. Italy and France
   C. Germany and an Anglo-French coalition   D. Italy and an Anglo-French coalition
6. On June 6, 1944, _____, the day of invasion for Overlord, the U.S. First Army, under General Omar N. Bradley, and the British Second Army, under General Miles C. Dempsey, established beachheads in Normandy, on the French channel coast. The German resistance was strong, and the footholds for Allied armies were not nearly as good as they had expected.
   A. Degree-Day   B. Dominion Day
   C. D-Day   D. Day-O
7. A few minutes before 8 am, on Sunday, December 7, 1941, Japanese aircraft initiated a surprise attack on the United States Pacific Fleet at Hawaii's Pearl Harbor. As a result of the attack, and at the request of U.S. President Franklin D. Roosevelt, the Congress of the United States _____ the following day.
   A. declared war on Japan   B. declared war on Germany and Japan
   C. made a strong protest to Japan D. made a strong protest to Germany and Japan

Unit 4

8. _____ (United Kingdom) originated in 1900, when the Trades Union Congress at Plymouth adopted a resolution calling for a conference of trade unions, as well as socialistic, cooperative, and other labor bodies, to consider the problem of securing adequate parliamentary representation for labor.
   A. Whig Party   B. Democratic Party
   C. Liberal Party   D. Labor Party

9. The United Kingdom is bordered on the south _____ which separates it from the continent of Europe. It is bordered on the east by the North Sea, and on the west by the Irish Sea and the Atlantic Ocean. The United Kingdom's only land border with another nation is between Northern Ireland and Ireland.
   A. by the North Sea   B. by the Irish Sea
   C. by the English Channel   D. by the Celtic Sea

10. United Kingdom is officially called the United Kingdom of Great Britain and Northern Ireland. Great Britain is the largest island in the cluster of islands known as the British Isles. _____ is the largest and most populous division of the island of Great Britain, making up the south and east.
    A. Scotland   B. England
    C. Wales   D. Northern Ireland

11. The major Axis powers were composed of Germany, Japan, and _____ in World War II.
    A. Romania   B. Italy
    C. Hungary   D. Bulgaria

12. Leaving aside the honour of a state funeral, Churchill received a wide range of awards and other honours. For example, he was the first person to become an Honorary Citizen of.
    A. Scotland   B. England
    C. the United States   D. China

13. Churchill received the _____ in 1953 "for his mastery of historical and biographical description as well as for brilliant oratory in defending exalted human values".
    A. one of the most influential leaders in history by *Time*
    B. Nobel Prize in Literature
    C. Nobel Prize in Peace
    D. one of the 100 Greatest Britons

14. In June 1944, the _____ invaded Normandy and pushed the Nazi forces back into Germany on a broad front over the coming year.
    A. the Axis Powers   B. the Central Powers
    C. the Allied Powers   D. the Kernel Powers

15. The Prime Minister of the United Kingdom is responsible for nominating all other members of the government, chairing _____ meetings and deciding when to call a new general election for the House of Commons.
    A. Her Majesty's   B. Cabinet
    C. House of Representatives   D. Senator's

V. Proofread the following passage.

There are many similarities between public speaking and daily conversation. In conversation, almost without thinking about it,

you employ wide range of skills. You organize your ideas logically. 1._____
You tailor your message to your audience. You tell a story for
maximum impact. You adapt feedback from your listener. These are 2._____
among the most important skills you will need for public speaking.
Of course, public speaking is also different from conversation.
  First, public speaking is more highly structure than conversation. It 3._____
usually imposes strict time limitations on the speaker, and it requires
more detail preparation than ordinary conversation does. Second, 4._____
public speaking requires more formal language. Listeners react
negatively to speeches loading with slang, jargon, and bad grammar. 5._____
Third, public speaking demands a different method of delivery.
Effective speakers adjust their voices to the larger audience but 6._____
work at avoiding distracting physical mannerisms and verbal habits.
  One of the major concern of students in any speech class is stage 7._____
fright. Actually, most successful speakers are nervous before making
a speech. Your speech class will give you an opportunity to gain
confidence and make you nervousness work for you rather than 8._____
against you. You will take a big step toward overcoming stage fright
if you think negatively, choose speech topics you really care about, 9._____
prepare thoroughly, and concentrate on communicating with your
audience. Like the other students over the years, you too can develop 10._____
confidence in your speechmaking abilities.

VI. Write a composition.

Churchill's speech is vivid and powerful. Read the speech again and summarize his main arguments within 200 words. And then write a comment on this speech, explaining from a linguistic and rhetoric perspective how Churchill made this one of the finest speeches in history.

Further Development

1. Speech delivery requires quite a number of skills. Conduct a survey to find out what makes a successful speaker and finish a report of about 300 words.
2. Read Churchill's other speeches delivered during the war and pick out one to discuss in your group. Importance should be attached to his linguistic and rhetoric styles.

Section A Text Two

40th Anniversary of D-Day Address

By Ronald Reagan

1   We're here to mark that day in history when the Allied armies joined in battle to reclaim this continent to liberty. For four long years, much of Europe had been under a terrible shadow. Free nations had fallen, Jews cried out in the camps, millions cried out for liberation. Europe was enslaved and the world prayed for its rescue. Here, in Normandy, the rescue began. Here, the Allies stood and fought against tyranny, in a giant undertaking unparalleled in human history.

2   We stand on a lonely, windswept point on the northern shore of France. The air is soft, but forty years ago at this moment, the air was dense with smoke and the cries of men, and the air was filled with the crack of rifle fire and the roar of cannon. At dawn, on the morning of the 6th of June, 1944, two hundred and twenty-five Rangers jumped off the British landing craft and ran to the bottom of these cliffs.

3   Their mission was one of the most difficult and daring of the invasion: to climb these sheer and desolate cliffs and take out the enemy guns. The Allies had been told that some of the mightiest of these guns were here, and they would be trained on the beaches to stop the Allied advance.

4   The Rangers looked up and saw the enemy soldiers at the edge of the cliffs, shooting down at them with machine guns and throwing grenades. And the American Rangers began to climb. They shot rope ladders over the face of these cliffs and began to pull themselves up. When one Ranger fell, another would take his place. When one rope was cut, a Ranger would grab another and begin his climb again. They climbed, shot back, and held their footing. Soon, one by one, the Rangers pulled themselves over the top, and in seizing the firm land at the top of these cliffs, they began to seize back the continent of Europe. Two hundred and twenty-five came here. After two days of fighting, only ninety could still bear arms.

5   And behind me is a memorial that symbolizes the Ranger daggers that were thrust into the top of these cliffs. And before me are the men who put them there. These are the boys of Pointe du Hoc. These are the men who took the cliffs. These are the champions who helped free a continent. And these are the heroes who helped end a war. Gentlemen, I look at you and I think of the words of Stephen Spender's poem. You are men who in your "lives fought for life and left the vivid air signed with your honor."

6   I think I know what you may be thinking right now—thinking "we were just part of a bigger effort; everyone was brave that day." Well everyone was. Do you remember the story of Bill Millin of the 51st Highlanders? Forty years ago today, British troops were pinned down near a bridge, waiting desperately for help. Suddenly, they heard the sound

of bagpipes, and some thought they were dreaming. Well, they weren't. They looked up and saw Bill Millin with his bagpipes, leading the reinforcements and ignoring the smack of the bullets into the ground around him.

7 Lord Lovat was with him—Lord Lovat of Scotland, who calmly announced when he got to the bridge, "Sorry, I'm a few minutes late," as if he'd been delayed by a traffic jam, when in truth he'd just come from the bloody fighting on Sword Beach, which he and his men had just taken.

8 There was the impossible valor of the Poles, who threw themselves between the enemy and the rest of Europe as the invasion took hold; and the unsurpassed courage of the Canadians who had already seen the horrors of war on this coast. They knew what awaited them there, but they would not be deterred. And once they hit Juno Beach, they never looked back.

9 All of these men were part of a roll call of honor with names that spoke of a pride as bright as the colors they bore: The Royal Winnipeg Rifles, Poland's 24th Lancers, the Royal Scots' Fusiliers, the Screaming Eagles, the Yeomen of England's armored divisions, the forces of Free France, the Coast Guard's "Matchbox Fleet," and you, the American Rangers.

10 Forty summers have passed since the battle that you fought here. You were young the day you took these cliffs; some of you were hardly more than boys, with the deepest joys of life before you. Yet you risked everything here. Why? Why did you do it? What impelled you to put aside the instinct for self-preservation and risk your lives to take these cliffs? What inspired all the men of the armies that met here? We look at you, and somehow we know the answer. It was faith and belief. It was loyalty and love.

11 The men of Normandy had faith that what they were doing was right, faith that they fought for all humanity, faith that a just God would grant them mercy on this beachhead, or on the next. It was the deep knowledge—and pray God we have not lost it—that there is a profound moral difference between the use of force for liberation and the use of force for conquest. You werehere to liberate, not to conquer, and so you and those others did not doubt your cause. And you were right not to doubt.

12 You all knew that some things are worth dying for. One's country is worth dying for, and democracy is worth dying for, because it's the most deeply honorable form of government ever devised by man. All of you loved liberty. All of you were willing to fight tyranny, and you knew the people of your countries were behind you.

13 The Americans who fought here that morning knew word of the invasion was spreading through the darkness back home. They fought—or felt in their hearts, though they couldn't know in fact, that in Georgia they were filling the churches at 4:00 am. In Kansas they were kneeling on their porches and praying. And in Philadelphia they were ringing the Liberty Bell.

14 Something else helped the men of D-day; their rock-hard belief that Providence would have a great hand in the events that would unfold here; that God was an ally in this

great cause. And so, the night before the invasion, when Colonel Wolverton asked his parachute troops to kneel with him in prayer, he told them: "Do not bow your heads, but look up so you can see God and ask His blessing in what we're about to do." Also, that night, General Matthew Ridgway on his cot, listening in the darkness for the promise God made to Joshua: "I will not fail thee nor forsake thee."

15 These are the things that impelled them; these are the things that shaped the unity of the Allies.

16 When the war was over, there were lives to be rebuilt and governments to be returned to the people. There were nations to be reborn. Above all, there was a new peace to be assured. These were huge and daunting tasks. But the Allies summoned strength from the faith, belief, loyalty, and love of those who fell here. They rebuilt a new Europe together. There was first a great reconciliation among those who had been enemies, all of whom had suffered so greatly. The United States did its part, creating the Marshall Plan to help rebuild our allies and our former enemies. The Marshall Plan led to the Atlantic alliance—a great alliance that serves to this day as our shield for freedom, for prosperity, and for peace.

17 In spite of our great efforts and successes, not all that followed the end of the war was happy or planned. Some liberated countries were lost. The great sadness of this loss echoes down to our own time in the streets of Warsaw, Prague, and East Berlin. The Soviet troops that came to the center of this continent did not leave when peace came. They're still there, uninvited, unwanted, unyielding, almost forty years after the war. Because of this, allied forces still stand on this continent. Today, as forty years ago, our armies are here for only one purpose: to protect and defend democracy. The only territories we hold are memorials like this one and graveyards where our heroes rest.

18 We in America have learned bitter lessons from two world wars. It is better to be here ready to protect the peace, than to take blind shelter across the sea, rushing to respond only after freedom is lost. We've learned that isolationism never was and never will be an acceptable response to tyrannical governments with an expansionist intent. But we try always to be preparedfor peace, prepared to deter aggression, prepared to negotiate the reduction of arms, and yes, prepared to reach out again in the spirit of reconciliation. In truth, there is no reconciliation we would welcome more than a reconciliation with the Soviet Union, so, together, we can lessen the risks of war, now and forever.

19 It's fitting to remember here the great losses also suffered by the Russian people during World War II. Twenty million perished, a terrible price that testifies to all the world the necessity of ending war. I tell you from my heart that we in the United States do not want war. We want to wipe from the face of the earth the terrible weapons that man now has in his hands. And I tell you, we are ready to seize that beachhead. We look for some sign from the Soviet Union that they are willing to move forward, that they share our desire and love for peace, and that they will give up the ways of conquest. There must be a changing there that will allow us to turn our hope into action.

20   We will pray forever that someday that changing will come. But for now, particularly today, it is good and fitting to renew our commitment to each other, to our freedom, and to the alliance that protects it.

21   We're bound today by what bound us 40 years ago, the same loyalties, traditions, and beliefs. We're bound by reality. The strength of America's allies is vital to the United States, and the American security guarantee is essential to the continued freedom of Europe's democracies. We were with you then; we're with you now. Your hopes are our hopes, and your destiny is our destiny.

22   Here, in this place where the West held together, let us make a vow to our dead. Let us show them by our actions that we understand what they died for. Let our actions say to them the words for which Matthew Ridgway listened: "I will not fail thee nor forsake thee."

23   Strengthened by their courage and heartened by their value [valor] and borne by their memory, let us continue to stand for the ideals for which they lived and died.

24   Thank you very much, and God bless you all.

Independent Study Assistant

I. Words and Expressions

1. **tyranny** *n.* cruel and unfair treatment by people with power over others
2. **unparalleled** *adj.* not found elsewhere; never seen or experienced before
3. **windswept** *adj.* exposed to strong winds
4. **ranger** *n.* a soldier in the U.S. Army who has special training especially in fighting at close range
5. **grenade** *n.* a small bomb that is designed to be thrown by someone or shot from a rifle
6. **memorial** *n.* something (such as a monument or ceremony) that honors a person who has died or serves as a reminder of an event in which many people died
7. **pin down** to cause or force (someone) to make a definite statement or decision about something
8. **bagpipe** *n.* a musical instrument that is played especially in Scotland and that has a bag, a tube for blowing air into the bag, and pipes where the air leaves and makes sounds
9. **reinforcements** *n.* people and supplies that are sent to help or support an army, military force, etc.
10. **smack** *n.* a loud noise that is made when something hits something else in a forceful way
11. **valor** *n.* courage or bravery
12. **take hold** to become effective, established, or popular
13. **deter** *v.* to cause (someone) to decide not to do something
14. **roll call** a list of people or things
15. **armored** *adj.* having soldiers and vehicles that are protected with armor
16. **beachhead** *n.* a beach on an enemy's shore that an invading army takes and controls in order to prepare for the arrival of more soldiers and supplies—often used figuratively to mean a place or position that serves as a base for future action or progress

17. **Providence** *n.*   God or fate thought of as the guide and protector of all human beings
18. **cot** *n.*   a narrow, light bed often made of cloth stretched over a folding frame
19. **forsake** *v.*   to give up or leave (someone or something) entirely
20. **daunting** *adj.*   tending to make people afraid or less confident: very difficult to do or deal with
21. **reconciliation** *n.* the act of causing two people or groups to become friendly again after an argument or disagreement
22. **shield** *n.*   something that defends or protects someone or something
23. **unyielding** *adj.*   not changing or stopping
24. **perish** *v.*   to die or be killed

II. Referential Points

D-day   June 6, 1944 — the day of the Normandy Landings— initiating the Western Allied effort to liberate mainland Europe from Nazi occupation during World War II. The operation was the largest amphibious invasion of all time, with 175,000 troops landing on 6 June 1944. 195,700 Allied naval and merchant navy personnel in over 5,000 ships were involved. The invasion required the transport of soldiers and material from the United Kingdom by troop-laden aircraft and ships, the assault landings, air support, naval interdiction of the English Channel and naval fire-support. The landings took place along a 50-mile (80 km) stretch of the Normandy coast.

Ronald Reagan (1911—2004)   the 40th President of the United States (1981—1989) and the 33rd Governor of California (1967—1975). As president, Reagan implemented sweeping new political and economic initiatives. His supply-side economic policies, dubbed "Reaganomics," advocated reduced business regulation, controlling inflation, reducing growth in government spending, and spurring economic growth through tax cuts.

Stephen Spender (1909—1995)   an English poet, novelist and essayist who concentrated on themes of social injustice and the class struggle in his work. He was appointed the seventeenth Poet Laureate Consultant in Poetry to the United States Library of Congress in 1965.

Pointe du Hoc   a clifftop location on the coast of Normandy in northern France. It lies 4 miles (6.4 km) west of Omaha Beach, and stands on 100 ft (30 m) tall cliffs overlooking the sea. It was a point of attack by the United States Army Ranger Assault Group during Operation Overlord in World War II (i.e. the invasion of western Europe during World War II by Allied forces).

Lord Lovat (1911—1995)   Brigadier Simon Christopher Joseph Fraser, the 25th Chief of the Clan Fraser and a prominent British Commando during the Second World War. His clan referred to him as MacShimidh, his Gaelic patronym, meaning Son of Simon. Simon is the favoured family name for the Chiefs of Clan Fraser. He is commonly known as the 15th Lord Lovat.

Bill Millin   commonly known as Piper Bill, personal piper to Lord Lovat, commander of 1 Special Service Brigade at D-Day. Millin is most famous for being one of the few pipers to play during a World War II battle. Pipers had traditionally led Scottish troops into battle however the death toll among pipers in World War I was so high that the practice was banned by the British high command. Lord Lovat, however, ignored these orders and Millin, aged 21, played "Hielan' Laddie" and "The Road to the Isles" as his comrades fell around him on Sword Beach. As German soldiers later attested, they did not target Millin because they believed him to be mad.

Sword Beach   the codename of one of the five main landing beaches in Operation

Neptune, which was the initial assault phase of Operation Overlord (the Allied invasion of Normandy on 6 June 1944). Stretching 8 km from Ouistreham to Saint-Aubin-sur-Mer it was the farthest east of the landing points and around 15 km from Caen. The initial landings were achieved with low casualties, but the British forces ran into heavily defended areas behind the beachhead. The British landings were the only Allied sectors that faced attack by German Panzer Divisions on 6 June 1944.

Juno Beach one of the five main landing sites of the Allied invasion of the coast of Normandy on D-Day during World War II. It was situated between Sword Beach and Gold Beach. It is also known as the Canadian beach, as it was assigned to the 3rd Canadian Infantry Division. Juno Beach stretched from Saint-Aubin-sur-Mer on the east to Courseulles-sur-Mer on the west. The 3rd Canadian Division was placed under the command of British I Corps for the initial phase of the invasion, and did not come under Canadian command again until July 1944 and the establishment of II Canadian Corps headquarters in Normandy. Despite being assigned to the Canadians, significant British forces were also present at Juno Beach. The naval component of the invasion force was known as Force J.

The Royal Winnipeg Rifles a Primary Reserve one-battalion infantry regiment of the Canadian Forces. Nicknamed the "Little Black Devils", they are based at Minto Armouries inWinnipeg, Manitoba. The Royal Winnipeg Rifles are part of Land Force Western Area's 38 Canadian Brigade Group.

The Royal Scots' Fusiliers a Regiment of the British Army.

The Screaming Eagles the nickname of The 101st Airborne Division, a U.S. Army modular infantry division trained for air assault operations. During World War II, it was renowned for action during the Normandy Landings and in the Battle of the Bulge. It is the only U.S. Army division with two aviation brigades. It is one of the most decorated divisions in the U.S. Army.

The Forces of Free France French fighters in World War II who decided to continue fighting against Axis forces after the surrender of France and subsequent German occupation.

Matchbox Fleet the nickname of a 60-cutter flotilla of wooden 83-foot (25 m) US Coast Guard cutters. During the Normandy invasion of June 6, 1944, it cruised off all five landing beaches as combat search-and-rescue boats, saving 400 Allied airmen and sailors.

Liberty Bell situated in Philadelphia, Pennsylvania, one of the most prominent symbols of the American Revolutionary War. It is a familiar symbol of independence within the United States and has been described as an icon of liberty and justice. According to tradition, its most famous ringing occurred on July 8, 1776, to summon citizens of Philadelphia for the reading of the Declaration of Independence. Historians today consider this highly doubtful, as the steeple in which the bell was hung had deteriorated significantly by that time. The bell had also been rung to announce the opening of the First Continental Congress in 1774 and after the Battle of Lexington and Concord in 1775. The Liberty Bell was known as the "Independence Bell"or the "Old Yankee's Bell"until 1837, when it was adopted by the American Anti-Slavery Society as a symbol of the abolitionist movement.

Joshua an Israelite leader who succeeded Moses (according to the Hebrew Bible). His story is told chiefly in the books Exodus, Numbers and Joshua. He was one of the twelve spies sent by Moses to explore the land of Canaan. He would later lead the conquest of that land, known in the Bible as the "Promised Land."Joshua also holds a position of respect to Muslims; Sunnis consider him a prophet, while the Shi'ah believe he was an Imam. According to conventional Bible chronology, Joshua lived between 1450—1370 B.C., or sometime in the late Bronze Age.

Marshall Plan   officially the European Recovery Program, the primary plan of the United States for rebuilding and creating a stronger foundation for the countries of Western Europe, and repelling communism after World War II. The initiative was named for Secretary of State George Marshall and was largely the creation of State Department officials, especially William L. Clayton and George F. Kennan. George Marshall spoke of the administration's desire to help European recovery in his address at Harvard University in June 1947.

The Atlantic alliance   the North Atlantic Treaty Organization (NATO), an intergovernmental military alliance based on the North Atlantic Treaty which was signed on April 4, 1949. The NATO headquarters are in Brussels, Belgium, and the organization constitutes a system of collective defense whereby its member states agree to mutual defense in response to an attack by any external party.

III. Questions for Comprehension

1. How much do you know about President Reagan? Work out a brief report about his life and main achievements.
2. What was much of Europe like before D-day? What was Reagan's view on the significance of Normandy landings?
3. How did the American Rangers behave on D-day?
4. According to President Reagan, what contributed to the success of the men of Normandy?
5. How was the new Europe rebuilt after the World War II?
6. What lessons have the United States and the world learned from the world wars? What does the President anticipate for the future?

Self-test

I. Fill in the blanks with the words and expressions provided, making some change when necessary.

testify	unsurpassed	never look back	forsake	unyielding
take hold	tyranny	memorial	smack	roll call
shield	reconciliation	valor	deter	pin down

1. Utah woman uses wedgie and headlock to _____ man suspected of breaking into a car.
2. It had set into stone her heart's conviction. She would marry Lucas. And she would _____.
3. In 2003, not long after the U.S. invaded Iraq, a rumor _____ around Kano that the polio campaign was, in fact, a U.S.-led conspiracy against Muslims.
4. On the way, _____ in the middle of the lobby, was an octagonal enclosure about twenty feet wide.
5. Finally, it is in our moral interests to save lives, to fight _____ and injustice and to

end conflicts that destabilize and destroy chances for human progress and prosperity.
6. And the _____ itself, shaped like a towering candle with a golden eternal flame, seemed to him in some sense a culmination of this effort.
7. A century later, Americans embraced a system of religious liberty that remains _____ in history.
8. He was awarded an Army Commendation Medal of _____ for his bravery and leadership saving the lives of two soldiers.
9. Something cold was spreading through Sarah's body, and she took two more steps back, deliberately removing herself from the other woman's protective _____.
10. Insurgent presence has markedly diminished since the offensive and _____ efforts, which took place last month.
11. It's clear that women who don't want to be pregnant won't be _____ by limited access to providers or to clinics.
12. Darnell, do you take this woman whose hand you now hold to be your lawfully wedded wife, before these witnesses, _____ all others till death do you part?
13. In February 2007, right after Anna Nicole died, Howard K. Stern _____ under oath about Anna Nicole's drug use.
14. Christa was determined to become a star, and she had the energy and _____ ambition to make it happen.
15. It's a _____ of the patients who we would want to target extra resources at, for example, people who have mental health problems, anyone who has an addiction, a single parent or somebody who doesn't speak English or has learning disabilities.

II. Use the appropriate form of the words given in the brackets to fill in the blanks.

1. He turned back to the window and gestured _____ across the face of the globe below them. (expansionist)
2. Most other _____ states and nations also relegate minority languages to a secondary status. (democracy)
3. From a Western _____ humanist perspective, begging thus often became the focus of an overall indictment of Confucian morality, exemplified by what we might term the lack of regard for beggars as strangers. (liberty)
4. After he was paroled in 1992, he _____ three bank robberies before being re-incarcerated. (commitment)
5. The smallest, basic settlement unit is a village, including _____ concentrations of several housing units clustered in relative proximity. (isolationism)
6. The military _____ of the land of Canaan by the Hebrews in about 1200 B.C.E. is often characterized as "genocide" and has all but become emblematic of biblical violence and intolerance. (conquer)
7. The 1947 _____ proved to be the high point of the Cardinals' time in Chicago-or anywhere else. (champion)
8. I think that, that is a key point. I think you're much more likely to see tremendous _____ across the spectrum of foreign policy issues, whether it's on how to deal with, with rogue states. (continue)
9. In the late 19th century, many imperialist countries waged _____ war against China. (invasion)

10. He could be angry with her without wanting to forever live in the _____ he had felt when she seemed to have walked out of his life forever. (desolate)

III. Translate the short paragraph into Chinese.

I tell you from my heart that we in the United States do not want war. We want to wipe from the face of the earth the terrible weapons that man now has in his hands. And I tell you, we are ready to seize that beachhead. We look for some sign from the Soviet Union that they are willing to move forward, that they share our desire and love for peace, and that they will give up the ways of conquest. There must be a changing there that will allow us to turn our hope into action.

IV. Analyze difficult sentences.

1. The Americans who fought here that morning knew word of the invasion was spreading through the darkness back home.
2. It is better to be here ready to protect the peace, than to take blind shelter across the sea, rushing to respond only after freedom is lost.
3. In truth, there is no reconciliation we would welcome more than a reconciliation with the Soviet Union, so, together, we can lessen the risks of war, now and forever.

V. Proofread the following passage.

Only a few days in each month were suitable for launching the operation, because of both a full moon and a spring tide were required: the former to illuminate navigational landmarks for the crews of aircraft, gliders and landing craft, and the latter provided the deepest possible water to help safe navigation over defensive obstacles placed from the Germans in the surf on the seaward approaches to the beaches. Allied Expeditionary Force Supreme Commander Dwight D. Eisenhower had tentative selected 5 June as the date for the assault. Most of May had fine weather, but this deteriorated in early June. On 4 June, conditions clearly unsuitable for a landing; wind and high seas would make it impossible to launch landing craft, and low clouds would prevent aircraft to find their targets. The Allied troop convoys already at sea were forced to take shelter in bays and inlets on the south coast of Britain for the night.

It seemed possible that everything would have to cancel and the troops returned to their camps (a vast undertaking because the enormous movement of follow-up formations was already proceeding). The next full moon period would be nearly a month away that. At a vital meeting on 5 June, Eisenhower's chief meteorologist (Group Captain J.M. Stagg) forecast a brief improvement for 6 June. General Bernard Montgomery and Eisenhower's Chief of Staff General Walter Bedell Smith wished to proceed with the invasion. Leigh Mallory was doubted, but Admiral Bertram Ramsay believed that conditions would be marginally favorable. On the strength of Stagg's forecast, Eisenhower ordered the invasion to proceed.

The Germans meanwhile took comfort from the existing poor conditions, which were worse over Northern France than over the

1. _____
2. _____
3. _____
4. _____
5. _____
6. _____
7. _____
8. _____
9. _____

Channel itself, and believed no invasion would be impossible for
several days. Some troops stood down, and many senior officers were
away for the weekend. General Erwin Rommel, for example, took a
few days' leave to celebrate his wife's birthday, while dozens of
division, regimental, and battalion commanders were away from
their posts at war games.

10. _____

VI. Write a composition.

Review the address in groups. Summarize the main points of the address. Write a composition in which you are expected to show how much you have known about the history relevant to D-day as well as President Reagan's purpose and significance of delivering the speech.

Section B

Text One Harvard Commencement Address

Focal Consideration

1. Problems such as inequities, disasters, poverty, etc. are some of the most serious and critical problems that the whole world is being confronted. Many speakers have focused on these relevant issues. Gates in this text also shows his concern about inequities. The discussion of the text will be focused on:
   a. the serious inequities existing in the world
   b. how to solve the problem of inequities
2. We are going to explore the most outstanding rhetorical devices Gates employs to make his speech so persuasive and convincing.

Research Questions

Think about the following questions and discuss them with your group members. Each group reports your ideas through discussion to the whole class.
  1. How much do you know about Bill Gates? Work out a brief report about his life and main achievements.
  2. How much do you know about the inequities of the world? What are the main causes of inequities?
  3. How can human society solve the problem of inequity?

Harvard Commencement Address

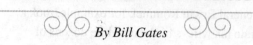

By Bill Gates

1   President Bok, former President Rudenstine, incoming President Faust, members of the Harvard Corporation and the Board of Overseers, members of the faculty, parents, and especially, the graduates:

2   I've been waiting more than 30 years to say this: "Dad, I always told you I'd come back and get my degree."

3   I want to thank Harvard for this timely honor. I'll be changing my job next year ... and it will be nice to finally have a college degree on my resume.

4   I applaud the graduates today for taking a much more direct route to your degrees. For my part, I'm just happy that the Crimson has called me "Harvard's most successful dropout." I guess that makes me valedictorian of my own special class ... I did the best of everyone who failed.

5   But I also want to be recognized as the guy who got Steve Ballmer to drop out of business school. I'm a bad influence. That's why I was invited to speak at your graduation. If I had spoken at your orientation, fewer of you might be here today.

6   Harvard was just a phenomenal experience for me. Academic life was fascinating.

7   What I remember above all about Harvard was being in the midst of so much energy and intelligence. It could be exhilarating, intimidating, sometimes even discouraging, but always challenging. It was an amazing privilege—and though I left early, I was transformed by my years at Harvard, the friendships I made, and the ideas I worked on.

8   But taking a serious look back ... I do have one big regret.

9   I left Harvard with no real awareness of the awful inequities in the world—the appalling disparities of health, and wealth, and opportunity that condemn millions of people to lives of despair.

10 I learned a lot here at Harvard about new ideas in economics and politics. I got great exposure to the advances being made in the sciences.

11 But humanity's greatest advances are not in its discoveries—but in how those discoveries are applied to reduce inequity. Whether through democracy, strong public education, quality health care, or broad economic opportunity—reducing inequity is the highest human achievement.

12 I left campus knowing little about the millions of young people cheated out of educational opportunities here in this country. And I knew nothing about the millions of people living in unspeakable poverty and disease in developing countries.

13 It took me decades to find out. You graduates came to Harvard at a different time. You know more about the world's inequities than the classes that came before. In your years here, I hope you've had a chance to think about how—in this age of accelerating technology—we can finally take on these inequities, and we can solve them.

14   We can make market forces work better for the poor if we can develop a more creative capitalism—if we can stretch the reach of market forces so that more people can make a profit, or at least make a living, serving people who are suffering from the worst inequities. We also can press governments around the world to spend taxpayer money in ways that better reflect the values of the people who pay the taxes.

15   If we can find approaches that meet the needs of the poor in ways that generate profits for business and votes for politicians, we will have found a sustainable way to reduce inequity in the world. This task is open-ended. It can never be finished. But a conscious effort to answer this challenge will change the world.

16   I am optimistic that we can do this, but I talk to skeptics who claim there is no hope. They say: "Inequity has been with us since the beginning, and will be with us till the end—because people just ... don't ... care." I completely disagree.

17   I believe we have more caring than we know what to do with.

18   All of us here in this Yard, at one time or another, have seen human tragedies that broke our hearts, and yet we did nothing—not because we didn't care, but because we didn't know what to do. If we had known how to help, we would have acted.

19   The barrier to change is not too little caring; it is too much complexity.

20   To turn caring into action, we need to see a problem, see a solution, and see the impact. But complexity blocks all three steps.

21   Even with the advent of the Internet and 24-hour news, it is still a complex enterprise to get people to truly see the problems. When an airplane crashes, officials immediately call a press conference. They promise to investigate, determine the cause, and prevent similar crashes in the future.

22   But if the officials were brutally honest, they would say: "Of all the people in the world who died today from preventable causes, one half of one percent of them were on this plane. We're determined to do everything possible to solve the problem that took the lives of the one half of one percent."

23   The bigger problem is not the plane crash, but the millions of preventable deaths.

24   We don't read much about these deaths. The media covers what's new—and millions of people dying is nothing new. So it stays in the background, where it's easier to ignore. But even when we do see it or read about it, it's difficult to keep our eyes on the problem. It's hard to look at suffering if the situation is so complex that we don't know how to help. And so we look away.

25   If we can really see a problem, which is the first step, we come to the second step: cutting through the complexity to find a solution.

26   Finding solutions is essential if we want to make the most of our caring. If we have clear and proven answers anytime an organization or individual asks "How can I help?", then we can get action—and we can make sure that none of the caring in the world is wasted. But complexity makes it hard to mark a path of action for everyone who cares — and that makes it hard for their caring to matter.

27   Cutting through complexity to find a solution runs through four predictable stages: determine a goal, find the highest-leverage approach, discover the ideal technology for that approach, and in the meantime, make the smartest application of the technology that you already have—whether it's something sophisticated, like a drug, or something simpler, like a bednet.

28   Yes, inequity has been with us forever, but the new tools we have to cut through complexity have not been with us forever. They are new—they can help us make the most of our caring—and that's why the future can be different from the past.

29   The defining and ongoing innovations of this age—biotechnology, the computer, the Internet—give us a chance we've never had before to end extreme poverty and end death from preventable disease.

30   Sixty years ago, George Marshall came to this commencement and announced a plan to assist the nations of post-war Europe. Thirty years after his address, as my class graduated without me, technology was emerging that would make the world smaller, more open, more visible, less distant.

31   The emergence of low-cost personal computers gave rise to a powerful network that has transformed opportunities for learning and communicating.

32   The magical thing about this network is not just that it collapses distance and makes everyone your neighbor. It also dramatically increases the number of brilliant minds we can have working together on the same problem—and that scales up the rate of innovation to a staggering degree.

33   At the same time, for every person in the world who has access to this technology, five people don't. That means many creative minds are left out of this discussion—smart people with practical intelligence and relevant experience who don't have the technology to hone theirtalents or contribute their ideas to the world.

34   We need as many people as possible to have access to this technology, because these advances are triggering a revolution in what human beings can do for one another. They are making it possible not just for national governments, but for universities, corporations, smaller organizations, and even individuals to see problems, see approaches, and measure the impact of their efforts to address the hunger, poverty, and desperation George Marshall spoke of 60 years ago.

35   Members of the Harvard Family: Here in the Yard is one of the great collections of intellectual talent in the world.

36   What for?

37   There is no question that the faculty, the alumni, the students, and the benefactors of Harvard have used their power to improve the lives of people here and around the world. But,can we do more? Can Harvard dedicate its intellect to improving the lives of people who will never even hear its name?

38   Let me make a request of the deans and the professors—the intellectual leaders here at Harvard: As you hire new faculty, award tenure, review curriculum, and determine degree requirements, please ask yourselves:

39   Should our best minds be dedicated to solving our biggest problems?

40   Should Harvard encourage its faculty to take on the world's worst inequities? Should Harvard students learn about the depth of global poverty... the prevalence of world hunger ... the scarcity of clean water ...the girls kept out of school ... the children who die from diseases we can cure?

41   Should the world's most privileged people learn about the lives of the world's least privileged?

42   These are not rhetorical questions—you will answer with your policies.

43   My mother never stopped pressing me to do more for others. A few days before my wedding, she hosted a bridal event, at which she read aloud a letter about marriage that she had written to Melinda. My mother was very ill with cancer at the time, but she saw one more opportunity to deliver her message, and at the close of the letter she said: "From those to whom much is given, much is expected."

44   When you consider what those of us here in this Yard have been given—in talent, privilege, and opportunity—there is almost no limit to what the world has a right to expect from us.

45   In line with the promise of this age, I want to exhort each of the graduates here to take on an issue—a complex problem, a deep inequity, and become a specialist on it. If you make it the focus of your career, that would be phenomenal. But you don't have to do that to make an impact. For a few hours every week, you can use the growing power of the Internet to get informed, find others with the same interests, see the barriers, and find ways to cut through them.

46   Don't let complexity stop you. Be activists. Take on the big inequities. It will be one of the great experiences of your lives.

47   You graduates are coming of age in an amazing time. As you leave Harvard, you have technology that members of my class never had. You have awareness of global inequity, which we did not have. And with that awareness, you likely also have an informed conscience that will torment you if you abandon these people whose lives you could change with very little effort. You have more than we had; you must start sooner, and carry on longer.

48   Knowing what you know, how could you not?

49   And I hope you will come back here to Harvard 30 years from now and reflect on what you have done with your talent and your energy. I hope you will judge yourselves not on your professional accomplishments alone, but also on how well you have addressed the world's deepest inequities ... on how well you treated people a world away who have nothing in common with you but their humanity.

50   Good luck.

Preview Assistance

1. **valedictorian** *n.* a person, usually the most outstanding graduate, who delivers a farewell speech at a graduation ceremony
2. **orientation** *n.* a course, programme, lecture, etc. introducing a new situation or environment
3. **phenomenal** *adj.* very good or great; unusual in a way that is very impressive
4. **exhilarate** *v.* to make lively and cheerful; gladden; elate
5. **intimidate** *v.* to make timid or frightened; scare
6. **appalling** *adj.* very bad in a way that causes fear, shock, or disgust
7. **disparity** *n.* a noticeable and often unfair difference between people or things
8. **inequity** *n.* lack of fairness; unfair treatment
9. **accelerate** *v.* to move faster; to gain speed
10. **take on** to compete against, oppose, or fight; to agree to do; undertake
11. **sustainable** *adj.* able to be used without being completely used up or destroyed; able to last or continue for a long time
12. **barrier** *n.* a law, rule, problem, etc., that makes something difficult or impossible
13. **advent** *n.* the time when something begins or arrives
14. **sophisticated** *adj.* highly developed and complex
15. **give rise to** to cause, to result in
16. **scale up** to increase proportionally
17. **staggering** *adj.* very large, shocking, or surprising
18. **hone** *v.* make (something, such as a skill) better or more effective
19. **trigger** *v.* to cause (something) to start or happen
20. **alumni** *n.* the plural form of alumnus, i.e., someone who was a student at a particular school, college, or university; all of the men and women who are former students of a school, college, or university
21. **benefactor** *n.* someone who helps another person, group, etc., by giving money
22. **intellect** *n.* the ability to think in a logical way
23. **tenure** *n.* the right to keep a job (especially the job of being a professor at a college or university) for as long as you want to have it
24. **curriculum** *n.* the courses that are taught by a school, college, etc.
25. **prevalence** *n.* the quality of prevailing generally; being widespread
26. **rhetorical** *adj.* (of a question) asked in order to make a statement rather than to get an answer
27. **in line with** in agreement with
28. **exhort** *v.* to try to influence (someone) by words or advice; to strongly urge (someone) to do something

Referential Points

Bill Gates (1955—) an American business magnate, philanthropist, and chairman of Microsoft, the software company he founded with Paul Allen. He is ranked consistently one of the world's wealthiest people and the wealthiest overall as of 2009. During his career at Microsoft, Gates held the positions of CEO and chief software architect, and remains the largest individual shareholder with more than 8 percent of the common stock. He has also authored or co-authored several books.

Harvard   Harvard University, a private university located in Cambridge, Massachusetts and a member of the Ivy League. Founded in 1636 by the colonial Massachusetts legislature, Harvard is the oldest institution of higher learning in the United States and currently comprises ten separate academic units. It is also the first and oldest corporation in the United States.

Harvard Corporation   (also known as the President and Fellows of Harvard College) the more fundamental of Harvard University's two governing boards. (The other is the Harvard Board of Overseers.) On 9 June 1650, at the request of President Henry Dunster, the Great and General Court of Massachusetts (i.e., the colonial legislature) issued the body's charter, making it the oldest corporation in The Americas. In fact, due to the history of the Harvard Corporation, its set of laws is written into the laws of the Commonwealth of Massachusetts. (Note that although Harvard is today generally referred to as a "University" the corporation's legal title still formally refers to "Harvard College.")

Melinda (1964—)   Melinda French Gates (born Melinda Ann French). An American philanthropist. She is the co-founder and co-chair of the Bill & Melinda Gates Foundation and a former unit manager for several Microsoft products such as Publisher, Microsoft Bob, Encarta, and Expedia. In 1994, she married Bill Gates, founder, chairman, and former chief softwarearchitect of Microsoft. She has been known to play bridge competitively with her partner Helene Fornia in Bellevue, Washington. They have three children: Jennifer Katharine Gates (born 26 April, 1996), Rory John Gates (b. 23 May, 1999) and Phoebe Adele Gates (b. 14 September, 2002).

Biotechnology   technology based on biology, agriculture, food science, and medicine. Modern use of the term usually refers to genetic engineering as well as cell- and tissue culture technologies. However, the concept encompasses a wider range and history of procedures for modifying living things according to human purposes, going back to domestication of animals, cultivation of plants and "improvements" to these through breeding programs that employ artificial selection and hybridization. By comparison to biotechnology, bioengineering is generally thought of as a related field with its emphasis more on mechanical and higher systems approaches to interfacing with and exploiting living things. United Nations Convention on Biological Diversity defines biotechnology as: "Any technological application that uses biological systems, dead organisms, or derivatives thereof, to make or modify products or processes for specific use."

George Marshall (1880—1959)   an American military leader, Chief of Staff of the Army, Secretary of State, and the third Secretary of Defense. Once noted as the "organizer of victory" by Winston Churchill for his leadership of the Allied victory in World War II, Marshall served as the U.S. Army Chief of Staff during the war and as the chief military adviser to President Franklin D. Roosevelt. In early 1947, he became the spokesman for the State Department's ambitious plans to rebuild Europe. On June 5, 1947 in a speech at Harvard University, he outlined the American plan. The European Recovery Program, as it was formally known, became known as the Marshall Plan. The Marshall plan would help Europe quickly rebuild and modernize its economy along American lines. He was awarded the Nobel Peace Prize in 1953.

Consolidation Work

I. Fill in the blanks with the words and expressions provided, making some change when necessary.

privilege	accelerate	trigger	exhilarate	benefactor
sustainable	advent	appalling	intimidate	give rise to
exhort	in line with	prevalence	staggering	take on

1. They are accused of illegally giving Anna Nicole a _____ combination of drugs, thousands of pills.
2. They love the _____ of having an outdoor picnic while not getting dressed right away.
3. I have found myself increasingly at odds with the Republican philosophy and more _____ the philosophy of the Democratic Party.
4. As a parent, I found this to be so _____, so disgusting that a young man who had been nurtured like I nurture my kids.
5. She raised her face to the rain, to the dark sky, _____ rather than frightened by this sudden wildness coming up from nothing around her.
6. I felt my heart stutter a bit, the beat _____, trying to catch up and stay even.
7. While he never had an operational role at Citi, the company still _____ massive risks that resulted in losses of $18.7 billion in 2008.
8. It was with the _____ of realism in the latter 18th century and especially 19th century that the plein air "snapshot" acquired value for its own sake.
9. Recent studies have shown that the _____ of daily smoking among university students was approximately 50%.
10. I had the privilege of sitting near a fantastically successful local area businessman and his wife, Mr. and Mrs. Forcht. They are immense _____ of the school and had brought me there.
11. Ecotechnology and, more specifically, ecological engineering and self-design are appropriate bases for _____ ecosystem management.
12. In jail, he was able to avoid floggings because the jail attendants were _____ by his tattoos.
13. The toothless carter leaned to one side, whipping the pair of draft horses and _____ them to move.
14. Fat _____ the release of a digestive hormone that seems to provoke a brain slump called postprandial somnolence.
15. Some said that he was of a long line of prophets, whose deeds _____ the town's name, which meant "inspiration" in our tongue.

II. Use the appropriate form of the words given in the brackets to fill in the blanks.

1. The isolated facility was called Victory Christian _____ and was located in the desert town of Ramona in San Diego County, California. (academic)
2. The idea was to persuade venture _____ to empty their wallets, hire like it was going

out of style, and bank on a successful IPO. (capitalism)
3. What I would hate to do is make a _____ of what the technology is going to look like 20 years ago. (predictable)
4. In my lifetime, I've witnessed man's _____ from centuries of darkness. (emerge)
5. We ask Paul to leave the room, giving our _____ time to read the fine print, which gets stranger and stranger. (application)
6. The relationship between creativity and the economy is complex and _____, for the value of the creative process can not be explained in economic terms and can not be directlyinduced by policy. (problem)
7. The spirit of modern social science, by contrast, draws on a brash _____ that the secrets to life can be laid bare. (optimistic)
8. It is a retaliation over the U.N. Security Council's _____ of North Korea's recent rocket launch. (condemn)
9. The association between low self-esteem and drug use is too small to be of practical value for explanation or _____. (preventable)
10. The poor darling was claustrophobic. He had to be _____ fighting down feelings of suffocation along with fear of an accident. (desperation)

III. Paraphrase the following sentences taken from the text.
1. If I had spoken at your orientation, fewer of you might be here today.
2. I left Harvard with no real awareness of the awful inequities in the world—the appalling disparities of health, and wealth, and opportunity that condemn millions of people to lives of despair.
3. The magical thing about this network is not just that it collapses distance and makes everyone your neighbor.
4. It also dramatically increases the number of brilliant minds we can have working together on the same problem—and that scales up the rate of innovation to a staggering degree.

IV. Test your general knowledge.
1. In June, 2006, Gates announced that he would be transitioning from full-time work at _____ to part-time work and full-time work at _____.
   A. Microsoft, Harvard University
   B. Microsoft, the Bill & Melinda Gates Foundation
   C. the Bill & Melinda Gates Foundation, Harvard University
   D. Harvard University, Microsoft
2. Bill Gates stepped down as chief executive officer of Microsoft in January, _____.
   A. 2000   B. 2002   C. 2004   D. 2006
3. The primary aims of the Bill & Melinda Gates Foundation are, globally, to enhance healthcare and reduce extreme poverty, and in America, to expand educational opportunities and access to _____.
   A. Microsoft   B. information technology
   C. employment   D. healthcare center
4. Which of the following is not a member of the Ivy League of the United States?
   A. Brown University   B. Princeton University
   C. New York University   D. Dartmouth College

5. In 2007 the founders of the Bill & Melinda Gates Foundation were ranked as the second most generous _____ in America.
   A. economists   B. capitalists
   C. politicians   D. philanthropists
6. What was Harvard University initially called?
   A. Harvard College   B. New College
   C. Massachusetts College   D. Towne College
7. During his _____ tenure as Harvard president, Charles William Eliot radically transformed Harvard into the pattern of the modern research university.
   A. 40-year   B. 35-year
   C. 30-year   D. 25-year
8. Modern biological sciences (including even concepts such as molecular ecology) are intimately entwined and dependent on the methods developed through biotechnology and what is commonly thought of as _____.
   A. the molecular industry
   B. the chemical engineering industry
   C. the information technology
   D. the life sciences industry
9. Biotechnology can be defined as "any technological application that uses _____ systems, dead organisms, or derivatives thereof, to make or modify products or processes for specific use."
   A. ecological   B. chemical
   C. biological   D. genetic
10. Headquartered in Redmond, Washington, USA, the most profitable products of Microsoft are the Microsoft Windows operating system and the _____ suite of productivity software.
    A. Microsoft SQL Server   B. Microsoft Visual Studio
    C. Microsoft Office   D. Windows Vista
11. On his return in early 1947, President Truman appointed George Marshall _____. He became the spokesman for the State Department's ambitious plans to rebuild Europe.
    A. Vice President   B. Secretary of State
    C. Chief of Staff of the Army D. president of the American National Red Cross
12. In the later stages of his career, Gates has pursued a number of philanthropic endeavors, donating large amounts of money to various _____ and scientific research programs.
    A. charitable organizations   B. educational institutes
    C. environmental organizations D. computer companies
13. George Marshall was awarded the Nobel Peace Prize in 1953 for _____.
    A. his work for American National Red Cross
    B. his work in China
    C. his achievements during the World War II.
    D. his post-war work
14. _____ is a term popularized by American entrepreneur and Microsoft chairman Bill Gates at the 2008 World Economic Forum in Davos, Switzerland. The ideology calls for a new form of capitalism that works both to generate profits and solve the world's inequities, using market forces to better address the needs of the poor.

A. Creative Capitalism   B. Equal Capitalism
C. Beneficial Capitalism   D. New Capitalism

15. Melinda Gates was listed in Forbes magazine as one of the 100 Most Powerful Women in _____.

A. 2006, 2007 and 2008   B. 2005, 2006 and 2007
C. 2004, 2005 and 2006   D. 2002, 2003 and 2005

V. Proofread the following passage.

The world is getting better, but it's not getting better fast enough, and it's not getting better for everyone. The great advances in the world have often aggravated the inequities in the world. The lest needy see the most improvement, and the most needy see the least—in particular the billion people who live on less than a dollar a day.

1. _____

There are rough a billion people in the world who don't get enough food, who don't have clean drinking water, who don't have electricity, the things that we take for granted. Diseases like malaria that kill over a million people a year get far less attention than drugs to help with baldness. Not only these people miss the benefits of the global economy – they will suffer from the positive effects of economic growth they missed out on. Climate change will have the biggest effect on people who have done the least to cause it.

2. _____

3. _____
4. _____

Why do people benefit in inverse proportion in their need? Market Incentives make that happen. In a system of pure capitalism, as people's wealth rises, the financial incentive to serve them to rise. As their wealth falls, the financial incentive to serve them falls—until it becomes zero. We have to find a way to make the aspects of capitalism that serves wealthier people serve poorer people as well.

5. _____

6. _____

7. _____

The genius of capitalism lies in its ability to make self-interest serve the wider interest. The potential of a big financial return for innovation leashes a broad set of talented people in pursuit of many different discoveries. This system driven by self-interest is responsible for the great innovations what have improved the lives of billions. But to harness this power so it benefits everyone—we need refining the system. As I see it, there are two great forces of human nature: self-interest, and caring for others.

8. _____

9. _____

10. _____

VI. Write a composition.

Review and discuss the main points of Bill Gates' address in groups. Summarize the phenomena of inequities the whole word is facing as well as the ways to solve the problem of inequities.

Further Development

1. Bill Gates is Chairman of Microsoft, the software company he founded with Paul

Allen. He is ranked consistently one of the world's wealthiest people and the wealthiest overall as of 2009. Study more about Gates and his career by consulting various resources.

2. A commencement speech is typically given to graduating students generally at a university by a notable figure in the community. Very commonly, colleges or universities often invite politicians, important citizens, or other noted speakers to come and address the graduating class. It differs from other speeches given at departing time, although the style, theme and rhetoric of the two may share something in common. Study and learn the styles of some famous commencement speeches and departing speeches by watching videos, listening to the speeches and reading texts closely. Choose your favorite one and try to readdress the class, paying attention to imitating the tone and manner.

Section B Text Two

Address to the 2005 World Summit United Nations Headquarters

By Kofi Annan

1 Majesties, Heads of State and Government, Excellencies, Ladies and Gentlemen,

2 Two years ago, speaking from this podium, I said that we stood at a fork in the road.

3 I did not mean that the United Nations, marking its sixtieth anniversary this year, was in existential crisis. The Organization remains fully engaged in conflict resolution, peacekeeping, humanitarian assistance, defence of human rights, and development around the world.

4 No, I meant that deep divisions among Member States, and the underperformance of our collective institutions, were preventing us from coming together to meet the threats we face and seize the opportunities before us.

5 ° The clear danger was that States of all kinds might increasingly resort to self-help, leading to a proliferation of ad hoc responses that would be divisive, destabilizing, and dangerous.

6 To help you, the Member States, chart a more hopeful course, I appointed the High-level Panel, and commissioned the Millennium Project. Their reports set the agenda for reform.

7 Drawing on these reports and the early reactions of Member States, as well as my own conviction that our work must be based on respect for human rights, I put forward, six months ago, a balanced set of proposals for decisions at this Summit.

8 Those proposals were ambitious. But I believed they were necessary, given the era of peril and promise in which we live. And I believed they were achievable, if the political will was there. Since then, under the able leadership of President Ping, your representatives have been negotiating an outcome document for this Summit. They have worked hard,

right up to the last minute, and yesterday they produced the document that is now before you.

9   Even before they finished their work, this Summit served as a trigger for progress on critical issues. In recent months, a Democracy Fund has been created, and a convention against nuclear terrorism has been finalized.

10 Most important of all, an additional $50 billion a year has been unleashed to fight poverty by 2010. The 0.7 target has gained new support; innovative sources of financing are now coming to fruition; and there has been progress on debt relief.

11 By your agreement on the outcome document, these achievements will be locked in. And progress on development will be matched by commitments to good governance and national plans to achieve the Millennium Development Goals by 2015.

12 Millions of lives, and the hopes of billions, rest on the implementation of these and other pledges to fight poverty, disease, illiteracy, inequality, and on development remaining at the centre of trade negotiations in the year ahead.

13 Your adoption of the outcome document will achieve vital breakthroughs in other areas as well.

14 You will condemn terrorism in all its forms and manifestations, committed by whomever, wherever, for whatever purpose. You will pledge to seek agreement on a comprehensive anti-terrorism convention in the coming year. And you will signal your support for a strategy to make sure that we fight terrorism in a way that makes the international community stronger and terrorists weaker, not the other way around.

15 For the first time, you will accept, clearly and unambiguously, that you have a collective responsibility to protect populations from genocide, war crimes, ethnic cleansing and crimes against humanity. You will make clear your willingness to take timely and decisive collective action through the Security Council, when peaceful means prove inadequate and national authorities are manifestly failing to protect their own populations. Excellencies, you will be pledged to act if another Rwanda looms.

16 You will agree to establish a Peacebuilding Commission, backed by a support office and a fund. This will mark a new level of strategic commitment to one of the most importantcontributions the United Nations makes to international peace and security. You will also agree to create a standing police capacity for the United Nations peacekeeping operations.

17 You will agree to double the budget of the Office of the High Commissioner for Human Rights and strengthen her office. You will also agree that the failures of the Human Rights Commission must be remedied by establishing a new Human Rights Council, the details of which must now be worked out during the 60th General Assembly.

18 You will strengthen early humanitarian funding, to prevent hidden emergencies remaining forgotten—as we have seen happen too often, particularly in Africa.

19 And you will put in place a framework for a far-reaching Secretariat and management reform, which must be followed up and implemented. An independent oversight committee and ethics office, on which I will be giving you more details in the

near future, will help ensure accountability and integrity, while the review of old mandates, the overhaul of rules on budget and human resources, and one-time buy-out of staff, will help re-align the Secretariat to the priorities of the Organization in the 21st century.

20   Taken together, this amounts to a far-reaching package of changes. But let us be frank with each other, and with the peoples of the United Nations. We have not yet achieved the sweeping and fundamental reform that I and many others believe is required. Sharp differences, some of them substantive and legitimate, have played their part in preventing that.

21   Our biggest challenge, and our biggest failing, is on nuclear non-proliferation and disarmament. Twice this year—at the NPT review conference, and now at this Summit—we have allowed posturing to get in the way of results. This is inexcusable. Weapons of mass destruction pose a grave danger to us all, particularly in a world threatened by terrorists with global ambitions and no inhibitions. We must pick up the pieces in order to renew negotiations on this vital issue, and we should support the efforts Norway has been making to find a basis for doing so.

22   Likewise, Security Council reform has, for the moment, eluded us, even though everyone broadly agrees that it is long overdue.

23   The fact that you have not reached agreement on these and other issues does not render them any less urgent.

24   So this package is a good start. On some issues, we have real breakthroughs. On others, we have narrowed our differences and made progress. On others again, we remain worryingly far apart.

25   We must now turn to the next stages in the reform process.

26   First, we must implement what has been agreed. The coming session of the General Assembly will be one of its most important, and we must give our support to President Eliasson as he assumes his duties. We must get the Peacebuilding Commission and the Human Rights Council up and running, conclude a comprehensive convention on terrorism, and make sure the Democracy Fund starts working effectively. And the coming years will test our resolve to halve extreme poverty by 2015, to act if genocide looms again, and to improve our success rate inbuilding peace in war-torn countries. These are the tests that really matter.

27   Second, we must keep working with determination on the tough issues on which progress is urgent but has not yet been achieved. Because one thing has emerged clearly from this process on which we embarked two years ago whatever our differences, in our interdependent world, we stand or fall together.

28   Whether our challenge is peacemaking, nation-building, democratization or responding to natural or man-made disasters, we have seen that even the strongest amongst us cannot succeed alone.

29   At the same time, whether our task is fighting poverty, stemming the spread of

disease, or saving innocent lives from mass murder, we have seen that we cannot succeed without the leadership of the strong, and the engagement of all.

30   And we have been reminded, again and again, that to ignore basic principles—of democracy, of human rights, of rule of law—for the sake of expediency, undermines confidence in our collective institutions, in building a world that is freer, fairer and safer for all.

31   That is why a healthy, effective United Nations is so vital. If properly utilized, it can be a unique marriage of power and principle, in the service of all the world's peoples.

32   And that is why this reform process matters, and must continue. No matter how frustrating things are, no matter how difficult agreement is, there is no escaping the fact that the challenges of our time must be met by action—and today, more than ever, action must be collective if it is to be effective.

33   For my part, I am ready to work with you on the challenges that remain , on implementing what has been agreed, and on continuing to reform the culture and practice of the Secretariat. We must restore confidence in the Organization's integrity, impartiality, and ability to deliver—for the sake of our dedicated staff, and those vulnerable and needy people throughout the world who look to the United Nations for support.

34   It is for their sake, not yours or mine, that this reform agenda matters. It is to save their lives, to protect their rights, to ensure their safety and freedom, that we simply must find effective collective responses to the challenges of our time.

35   I urge you, as world leaders, individually and collectively, to keep working on this reform agenda—to have the patience to persevere, and the vision needed to forge a real consensus.

36   We must find what President Franklin Roosevelt once called "the courage to fulfil our responsibilities in an admittedly imperfect world". I am not sure we have done that yet. But I believe all of us now understand that we need to do it. Precisely because our world is imperfect, we need the United Nations.

37   Thank you very much.

Independent Study Assistance

I. Words and Expressions
1. **podium** *n.*   a raised platform for a speaker, performer, or the leader of an orchestra
2. **proliferation** *n.*   quick increase in number or amount
3. **ad hoc** *adj.*   made or done without planning because of an immediate need
4. **destabilize** *v.*   to cause (something, such as a government) to be unable to continue existing or working in the usual or desired way; to make (something) unstable
5. **commission** *v.*   to order or request (something) to be made or done
6. **conviction** *n.*   a strong belief or opinion

7. **representative** *n.*   someone who acts or speaks for or in support of another person or group
8. **unleash** *v.*   to allow or cause (something very powerful) to happen suddenly
9. **fruition** *n.*   the state of being real or complete
10. **lock in**   to do something that makes you sure to get (something that could change, such as a good price, an interest rate, etc.)
11. **rest on**   to depend or rely on (someone or something)
12. **implementation** *n.*   the act of beginning to do or using (something, such as a plan); act of making (something) active or effective
13. **illiteracy** *n.*   the state of not knowing how to read or write
14. **manifestation** *n.*   one of the forms that something has when it appears or occurs
15. **unambiguous** *adj.*   clearly expressed or understood
16. **genocide** *n.*   the deliberate killing of people who belong to a particular racial, political, or cultural group
17. **cleanse** *v.*   to make (someone or something) clean
18. **manifestly** *adv.*   with being able to be seen; with being clearly shown or visible
19. **loom** *v.*   to be close to happening: to be about to happen—used especially of unpleasant or frightening things
20. **remedy** *v.*   to solve, correct, or improve (something)
21. **oversight** *n.*   the act or job of directing work that is being done
22. **integrity** *n.*   the quality of being honest and fair
23. **mandate** *n.*   an official order to do something
24. **overhaul** *n.*   a thorough examination and repair
25. **substantive** *adj.*   important, real, or meaningful
26. **legitimate** *adj.*   fair or reasonable
27. **posturing** *n.*   behavior that is intended to impress other people and that is not sincere
28. **inhibition** *n.*   a nervous feeling that prevents you from expressing your thoughts, emotions, or desires
29. **elude** *v.*   to fail to be achieved by (someone)
30. **embark** *v.*   to begin (something that will take a long time or happen for a long time)
31. **undermine** *v.*   to make (someone or something) weaker or less effective usually in a secret or gradual way
32. **utilize** *v.*   to use (something) for a particular purpose
33. **impartiality** *n.*   act or state of treating all people and groups equally
34. **vulnerable** *adj.*   easily hurt or harmed physically, mentally, or emotionally
35. **consensus** *n.*   a general agreement about something; an idea or opinion that is shared by all the people in a group

II. Referential Points

Kofi Annan (1938—)   a Ghanaian diplomat who served as the seventh Secretary-General of the United Nations from 1 January 1997 to 1 January 2007. Annan and the United Nations were the co-recipients of the 2001 Nobel Peace Prize.

United Nations (UN)   an international organization whose stated aims are facilitating cooperation in international law, international security, economic development, social progress, human rights, and the achieving of world peace. The UN was founded in 1945 after World War II to replace the League of Nations, to stop wars between countries, and to provide a platform for dialogue. It contains multiple subsidiary organizations to carry out its missions.

Member States   There are currently 192 United Nations (UN) member states, and each of them is a member of the United Nations General Assembly. According to the United Nations Charter, Chapter II, Article 4: Membership in the United Nations is open to all other peace-loving states which accept the obligations contained in the present Charter and, in the judgment of the Organization, are able and willing to carry out these obligations; the admission of any such state to membership in the United Nations will be effected by a decision of the General Assembly upon the recommendation of the Security Council. In principle, only sovereign states can become UN members, and all current members are fully sovereign states (although a few members were not fully sovereign when they joined the UN).

Security Council (UNSC)   one of the principal organs of the United Nations and is charged with the maintenance of international peace and security. Its powers, outlined in the United Nations Charter, include the establishment of peacekeeping operations, the establishment of international sanctions, and the authorization of military action. Its powers are exercised through United Nations Security Council Resolutions. There are 15 members of the Security Council, consisting of five veto-wielding permanent members (China, France, Russia, United Kingdom, United States) and ten elected non-permanent members with two-year terms. Security Council members must always be present at UN headquarters in New York so that the Security Council can meet at any time.

Peacebuilding Commission   established in December 2005 by the United Nations General Assembly and the Security Council acting concurrently. It is an inter-governmental advisory body that will help countries in post-conflict peace building, recovery, reconstruction and development.

General Assembly (UNGA / GA)   one of the five principal organs of the United Nations and the only one in which all member nations have equal representation. Its powers are to oversee the budget of the United Nations, appoint the non-permanent members to the Security Council, receive reports from other parts of the United Nations and make recommendations in the form of General Assembly Resolutions. It has also established a wide number of subsidiary organs.

Secretariat   one of the five principal organs of the United Nations and it is headed by the United Nations Secretary-General, assisted by a staff of international civil servants worldwide. It provides studies, information, and facilities needed by United Nations bodies for their meetings. It also carries out tasks as directed by the UN Security Council, the UN General Assembly, the UN Economic and Social Council, and other U.N. bodies. The United Nations Charter provides that the staff be chosen by application of the "highest standards of efficiency, competence, and integrity," with due regard for the importance of recruiting on a wide geographical basis.

Nuclear Non-Proliferation Treaty (NPT or NNPT)   a treaty to limit the spread (proliferation) of nuclear weapons, opened for signature on July 1, 1968. There are currently 189 countries party to the treaty, five of which have nuclear weapons: the United States, Russia, the United Kingdom, China and France (also permanent members of the UN Security Council).

Human Rights Council (UNHRC)   an inter-governmental body within the United Nations System. The UNHRC is the successor to the United Nations Commission on Human Rights (UNCHR, herein CHR), and is a subsidiary body of the United Nations General Assembly. The council works closely with the Office of the High Commissioner for Human

Rights (OHCHR) and engages the United Nations' Special Procedures.

Franklin Roosevelt (1882—1945) the 32nd President of the United States and the only one elected to more than two terms. He was a central figure in world events during the mid-20th century, leading the United States during a time of worldwide economic crisis and world war. Often referred to by his initials, FDR won his first of four presidential elections in 1932, while the United States was in the depths of the Great Depression. His combination of optimism and economic activism is often credited with keeping the country's economic crisis from developing into a political crisis. He led the United States through most of World War II, and died in office of a cerebral hemorrhage, shortly before the war ended.

III. Questions for Comprehension

1. How much do you know about Kofi Annan? Work out a brief report about his life and main achievements.
2. How should Kofi Annan's statement that we stood at a fork in the road be understood?
3. What actions are expected to take so as to achieve the Millennium Development Goals by 2015?
4. What challenges is the UN facing in achieving the fundamental reform?
5. What are the next stages that the UN should turn to in the reform process?
6. What are the basic principles? Why shouldn't these principles be ignored?

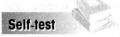

Self-test

I. Fill in the blanks with the words and expressions provided, making some change when necessary.

loom	rest on	substantive	unambiguous	integrity
mandate	fruition	elude	utilize	illiteracy
inhibition	manifestly	remedy	lock in	vulnerable

1. The plaza is _____ an elite indigenous space, centering on an imperial Inca history.
2. Subjects such as mathematics, however, are made less threatening by _____ methods such as open-book tests.
3. We Californians have, primarily through the initiative process, _____ the vast majority of spending.
4. I would hope to see a more evenhanded discussion and more _____ reasons offered by the editorial board as to why that is the case.
5. Whether or not the plan comes to _____ is largely up to Jeanty, who owns the building.
6. Specifically, participants may be unwilling to report certain information or may report such information inaccurately in an attempt to present themselves in a particular manner. As a result, these social desirability effects may compromise the _____ of conclusions derived primarily from relying on self-reports.
7. This urban community is a depressed area with high rates of unemployment, poverty, _____, and crime.

8. Our companies faced new union _____ and global cap-and-trade and the second highest corporate tax rate in the world.
9. One teacher noted that emotionally, migrant children are much more _____ than the others.
10. It is the conductor's responsibility to develop a clear, _____, and well-conceived perception of the work before the first rehearsal.
11. With the constant fear of a world war _____ over Americans' heads, many people actually believed there was an alien attack occurring!
12. This problem is easily _____ by featuring junior and senior singers in performance for the younger students.
13. The preemptive attack on Iraq was the most visible of his presidency's actions _____ that claim—actions we can't fully count because so many have been undertaken in secret.
14. I do mean that you should allow yourself the freedom and self-approval to write without _____.
15. She simply couldn't find the word. She had a loose sense for what she wanted to say, but the word itself _____ her.

II. Use the appropriate form of the words given in the brackets to fill in the blanks.

1. It was the big one, the _____ of several conjoining forks into one, unimaginable fury. (finalize).
2. The resulting competition would raise quality, lower costs, and spur _____ in both health care delivery and finance. (innovative)
3. They had not yet collapsed under the influence of teacher unions, _____ politics, and the decline of the family. (progress)
4. His luxurious life had been disrupted by a _____ turn of events in the German and American money markets. (disaster)
5. The mining town of Victor, near the Monument's southeast _____, was also believed to have been named for him. (extreme)
6. The more that government expands into industries such as health care, the more the market signals get _____, which makes it even more difficult for policymakers to pursue rational plans. (destruction)
7. Somehow, he had come to embody the spirit and independence and _____ of everyone I admired. (persevere)
8. Queries that start with "Dear Agent "or attach an entire proposal and take up server space are too general or too _____, respectively. (assume)
9. Gradually this inner voice becomes more distinct, _____ itself into units of meaning, at which point the poem begins to knock like a fist on a window. (resolution)
10. The cycle of decay and _____ is as much a part of capitalism as it is of the forest floor. (renew)

III. Translating the short paragraph into Chinese.

Second, we must keep working with determination on the tough issues on which progress is urgent but has not yet been achieved. Because one thing has emerged clearly from this process on which we embarked two years ago whatever our differences, in our interdependent world, we stand or fall together. Whether our challenge is peacemaking, nation-building, democratization or responding to natural or man-made disasters, we have seen that even the strongest amongst us cannot succeed alone. At the same time, whether our task is fighting poverty, stemming the spread of disease, or saving innocent lives from mass murder, we have seen that we cannot succeed without the leadership of the strong, and the engagement of all.

IV. Analyze difficult sentences.

1. Drawing on these reports and the early reactions of Member States, as well as my own conviction that our work must be based on respect for human rights, I put forward, six months ago, a balanced set of proposals for decisions at this Summit.
2. You will signal your support for a strategy to make sure that we fight terrorism in a way that makes the international community stronger and terrorists weaker, not the other way around.
3. We have been reminded, again and again, that to ignore basic principles—of democracy, of human rights, of rule of law—for the sake of expediency, undermines confidence in our collective institutions, in building a world that is freer, fairer and safer for all.

V. Proofread the following passage.

The pursuit of human rights was a central reason for creating the UN. World War II atrocities and genocide leading to a ready consensus that the new organization must work to prevent any similar tragedies in the future. An early objective was creating a legal framework to considering and acting on complaints about human rights violations. The UN Charter obliges all member nations to promote "universal respect of, and observance of, human rights" and to take "joint and separate action" to that end. The Universal Declaration of Human Rights, though not legally bind, was adopted by the General Assembly in 1948 a common standard of achievement for all. The Assembly regularly takes up human rights issues.

The UN and its agencies are central in upholding and implementing the principles enshrined in the Universal Declaration of Human Rights. A case in point is support by the UN for countries in transition to democracy. Technical assistance in providing free and fair elections, improved judicial structures, drafting constitutions, training human rights officials, and transforming armed movements into political parties have contributed significantly in democratization worldwide. The UN has helped run elections in countries with little or no Democratic history, including recently in Afghanistan and East Timor. The UN is also forum to support the right of women to participate fully in the political, economic, and social life of their countries. The UN contribute to raising consciousness of the concept of human rights through its covenants and its attention to specific abuses through its General Assembly, Security Council resolutions, and International Court of Justice rulings.

1. _____
2. _____
3. _____
4. _____
5. _____
6. _____
7. _____
8. _____
9. _____
10. _____

VI. Write a composition.

Review the address in groups. Summarize the main points of how to achieve the Millennium Development Goals and how to solve the problems the UN is facing. Write a composition in which you have to show how much you have known about the UN and its significant role in building a more perfect world.

Unit 5

Education

Section A

Text One Education as a Necessity of Life

Focal Consideration

1. Dewey brings to view the important role education plays in one's life. Concentration will be on the analysis of the relation between:
   a. renewal and education;
   b. transmission and education;
   c. education and communication.
2. The essay is written in a plain and simple language, yet you can have a strong sense of persuasiveness and powerfulness. We are going to explore what devices Dewey employs to achieve this effect.

Research Questions

Think about the following questions and discuss them with your group members. After your discussion, share your opinions with other groups.
1. How much do you know about Dewey? Do some research into his life, his works and his contribution to education.
2. How do you understand "renewal"? Compare your view with what is explained by Dewey in the text and justify your point of view.
3. What is the function of transmission? And how does it occur?
4. What is the relation among the ideas conveyed by the three words: common, community and communication?
5. What is the relation between education and communication? Why does the author say communication is educative? Do you agree? Demonstrate your ideas with examples.

Education as a Necessity of Life

By John Dewey

Renewal of Life by Transmission

1   The most notable distinction between living and inanimate things is that the former maintain themselves by renewal. A stone when struck resists. If its resistance is greater than the force of the blow struck, it remains outwardly unchanged. Otherwise, it is shattered into smaller bits. Never does the stone attempt to react in such a way that it may maintain itself against the blow, much less so as to render the blow a contributing factor to its own continued action. While the living thing may easily be crushed by superior force, it none the less tries to turn the energies which act upon it into means of its own further existence. If it cannot do so, it does not just split into smaller pieces (at least in the higher forms of life), but loses its identity as a living thing.

2   As long as it endures, it struggles to use surrounding energies in its own behalf. It uses light, air, moisture, and the material of soil. To say that it uses them is to say that it turns them into means of its own conservation. As long as it is growing, the energy it expends in thus turning the environment to account is more than compensated for by the return it gets: it grows... Life is a self-renewing process through action upon the environment.

3   In all the higher forms this process cannot be kept up indefinitely. After a while they succumb; they die. The creature is not equal to the task of indefinite self-renewal. But continuity of the life process is not dependent upon the prolongation of the existence of any one individual. Reproduction of other forms of life goes on in continuous sequence. And though, as the geological record shows, not merely individuals but also species die out, the life process continues in increasingly complex forms. As some species die out, forms better adapted to utilize the obstacles against which they struggled in vain come into being. Continuity of life means continual readaptation of the environment to the needs of living organisms.

4   We have been speaking of life in its lowest terms—as a physical thing. But we use the word "Life" to denote the whole range of experience, individual and racial. When we see a book called the Life of Lincoln we do not expect to find within its covers a treatise on physiology. We look for an account of social antecedents; a description of early surroundings, of the conditions and occupation of the family; of the chief episodes in the development of character; of signal struggles and achievements; of the individual's hopes, tastes, joys and sufferings. In precisely similar fashion we speak of the life of a savage tribe, of the Athenian people, of the American nation. "Life" covers customs, institutions, beliefs, victories and defeats, recreations and occupations.

5   We employ the word "experience" in the same pregnant sense. And to it, as well as to life in the bare physiological sense, the principle of continuity through renewal applies. With the renewal of physical existence goes, in the case of human beings, the recreation

of beliefs, ideals, hopes, happiness, misery, and practices. The continuity of any experience, through renewing of the social group, is a literal fact. Education, in its broadest sense, is the means of this social continuity of life. Every one of the constituent elements of a social group, in a modern city as in a savage tribe, is born immature, helpless, without language, beliefs, ideals, or social standards. Each individual, each unit who is the carrier of the life-experience of his group, in time passes away. Yet the life of the group goes on.

6   The primary ineluctable facts of the birth and death of each one of the constituent members in a social group determine the necessity of education. On the one hand, there is the contrast between the immaturity of the new-born members of the group—its future sole representatives—and the maturity of the adult members who possess the knowledge and customs of the group. On the other hand, there is the necessity that these immature members be not merely physically preserved in adequate numbers, but that they be initiated into the interests, purposes, information, skill, and practices of the mature members: otherwise the group will cease its characteristic life. Even in a savage tribe, the achievements of adults are far beyond what the immature members would be capable of if left to themselves. With the growth of civilization, the gap between the original capacities of the immature and the standards and customs of the elders increases. Mere physical growing up, mere mastery of the bare necessities of subsistence will not suffice to reproduce the life of the group. Deliberate effort and the taking of thoughtful pains are required. Beings who are born not only unaware of, but quite indifferent to, the aims and habits of the social group have to be rendered cognizant of them and actively interested. Education, and education alone, spans the gap.

7   Society exists through a process of transmission quite as much as biological life. This transmission occurs by means of communication of habits of doing, thinking, and feeling from the older to the younger. Without this communication of ideals, hopes, expectations, standards, opinions, from those members of society who are passing out of the group life to those who are coming into it, social life could not survive. If the members who compose a society lived on continuously, they might educate the new-born members, but it would be a task directed by personal interest rather than social need. Now it is a work of necessity.

8   If a plague carried off the members of a society all at once, it is obvious that the group would be permanently done for. Yet the death of each of its constituent members is as certain as if an epidemic took them all at once. But the graded difference in age, the fact that some are born as some die, makes possible through transmission of ideas and practices the constant reweaving of the social fabric. Yet this renewal is not automatic. Unless pains are taken to see that genuine and thorough transmission takes place, the most civilized group will relapse into barbarism and then into savagery. In fact, the human young are so immature that if they were left to themselves without the guidance and succor of others, they could not acquire the rudimentary abilities necessary for physical

existence. The young of human beings compare so poorly in original efficiency with the young of many of the lower animals that even the powers needed for physical sustentation have to be acquired under tuition. How much more, then, is this the case with respect to all the technological, artistic, scientific, and moral achievements of humanity!

Education and Communication

9   So obvious, indeed, is the necessity of teaching and learning for the continued existence of a society that we may seem to be dwelling unduly on a truism. But justification is found in the fact that such emphasis is a means of getting us away from an unduly scholastic and formal notion of education. Schools are, indeed, one important method of the transmission which forms the dispositions of the immature; but it is only one means, and, compared with other agencies, a relatively superficial means. Only as we have grasped the necessity of more fundamental and persistent modes of tuition can we make sure of placing the scholastic methods in their true context.

10   Society not only continues to exist by transmission, by communication, but it may fairly be said to exist in transmission, in communication. There is more than a verbal tie between the words common, community, and communication. Men live in a community in virtue of the things which they have in common; and communication is the way in which they come to possess things in common. What they must have in common in order to form a community or society are aims, beliefs, aspirations, knowledge—a common understanding—like-mindedness as the sociologists say. Such things cannot be passed physically from one to another, like bricks; they cannot be shared as persons would share a pie by dividing it into physical pieces. The communication which insures participation in a common understanding is one which secures similar emotional and intellectual dispositions—like ways of responding to expectations and requirements.

11   Persons do not become a society by living in physical proximity, any more than a man ceases to be socially influenced by being so many feet or miles removed from others. A book or a letter may institute a more intimate association between human beings separated thousands of miles from each other than exists between dwellers under the same roof. Individuals do not even compose a social group because they all work for a common end. The parts of a machine work with a maximum of cooperativeness for a common result, but they do not form a community. If, however, they were all cognizant of the common end and all interested in it so that they regulated their specific activity in view of it, then they would form a community. But this would involve communication. Each would have to know what the other was about and would have to have some way of keeping the other informed as to his own purpose and progress. Consensus demands communication.

12   We are thus compelled to recognize that within even the most social group there are many relations which are not as yet social. A large number of human relationships in any

social group are still upon the machine-like plane. Individuals use one another so as to get desired results, without reference to the emotional and intellectual disposition and consent of those used. Such uses express physical superiority, or superiority of position, skill, technical ability, and command of tools, mechanical or fiscal. So far as the relations of parent and child, teacher and pupil, employer and employee, governor and governed, remain upon this level, they form no true social group, no matter how closely their respective activities touch one another. Giving and taking of orders modifies action and results, but does not of itself effect a sharing of purposes, a communication of interests.

13 Not only is social life identical with communication, but all communication (and hence all genuine social life) is educative. To be a recipient of a communication is to have an enlarged and changed experience. One shares in what another has thought and felt and in so far, meagerly or amply, has his own attitude modified. Nor is the one who communicates left unaffected. Try the experiment of communicating, with fullness and accuracy, some experience to another, especially if it be somewhat complicated, and you will find your own attitude toward your experience changing; otherwise you resort to expletives and ejaculations. The experience has to be formulated in order to be communicated. To formulate requires getting outside of it, seeing it as another would see it, considering what points of contact it has with the life of another so that it may be got into such form that he can appreciate its meaning. Except in dealing with commonplaces and catch phrases one has to assimilate, imaginatively, something of another's experience in order to tell him intelligently of one's own experience. All communication is like art. It may fairly be said, therefore, that any social arrangement that remains vitally social, or vitally shared, is educative to those who participate in it. Only when it becomes cast in a mold and runs in a routine way does it lose its educative power.

14 In final account, then, not only does social life demand teaching and learning for its own permanence, but the very process of living together educates. It enlarges and enlightens experience; it stimulates and enriches imagination; it creates responsibility for accuracy and vividness of statement and thought. A man really living alone (alone mentally as well as physically) would have little or no occasion to reflect upon his past experience to extract its net meaning. The inequality of achievement between the mature and the immature not only necessitates teaching the young, but the necessity of this teaching gives an immense stimulus to reducing experience to that order and form which will render it most easily communicable and hence most usable.

Preview Assistance

1. **none the less** variant of nonetheless. Nonetheless, nevertheless, however, all imply an antecedent, in spite of which [whatever you next say]. Nonetheless [for that which has just been said], or not less true because of what has been said.
2. **in behalf of** for the benefit of; in the interest of

3. **subjugate** *v.*   to defeat sb/sth; to gain control over sb/sth:
4. **succumb** *v.*   not to be able to fight
5. **treatise** *n.*   a long and serious piece of writing on a particular subject
6. **antecedent** *n.*   one that precedes another; a forerunner or predecessor
7. **pregnant** *adj.*   meaningful; substantial
8. **ineluctable** *adj.*   not able to be escaped from or avoided; certain; inevitable
9. **suffice** *v.*   to be enough; to satisfy
10. **be cognizant of**   to be conscious of; to be aware of
11. **done for**   doomed to death or destruction
12. **relapse** *v.*   to slip or fall back into a previous condition or into a worse state after making an improvement or seeming improvement
13. **succor** *n.*   help that you give to sb who is suffering or having problems
14. **rudimentary** *adj.*   beginning; elementary
15. **sustentation** *n.*   a support; something that sustains
16. **with respect to**   considering or related to; with regard to
17. **dwell on**   to rest attention on; to think, speak or write at length
18. **unduly** *adv.*   more than you think is reasonable or necessary
19. **truism** *n.*   a self-evident, obvious truth
20. **disposition** *n.*   the natural qualities of a person's character
21. **in virtue of**   through the force of ; by the authority of ; because of; on account of
22. **proximity** *n.*   the state of being near sb/sth in distance or time
23. **institute** *v.*   to set up; to establish; to produce
24. **in view of**   taking into account; in consideration of
25. **consensus** *n.*   agreement in opinion; unanimity
26. **without reference to**   unrelatedly; without relation to
27. **fiscal** *adj.*   related to the treasury of a country, a company or a city, particularly to government spending and revenue ; financial
28. **meager** *adj.*   small in quantity and poor in quality
29. **resort to**   to make use of; to apply
30. **expletive** *n.*   a word, especially a rude word, that you use when you are angry, or in pain
31. **ejaculation** *n.*   a sudden shout or sound that you make when you are angry or surprised

Referential Points

John Dewey (1859—1952)   an American philosopher, psychologist, and educational reformer. Along with Charles Sanders Peirce and William James, he is recognized as one of the founders of the philosophy of pragmatism and of functional psychology. He is also a major representative of the progressive and populist philosophies of schooling during the first half of the 20th century in the USA.

Dewey's educational theories are presented in *My Pedagogic Creed* (1897), *The School and Society* (1900), *The Child and Curriculum* (1902), *Democracy and Education* (1916) and *Experience and Education* (1938). He is a relentless campaigner for reform of education, pointing out that the authoritarian, strict, pre-ordained knowledge approach of modern traditional education is too concerned with delivering knowledge, and not enough with understanding students' actual experiences. He is also the most famous proponent of hands-on learning, which is related to, but not synonymous with experiential learning. Many researchers credit him with the influence of Project Based Learning (PBL) which places students in the active role of researchers.

About the text It is an extract from *Democracy and Education*: *An Introduction to the Philosophy of Education* by John Dewey. In *Democracy and Education* Dewey emphasizes the associational and communal aspects of democracy, and finds that conscious, directed education is necessary to establish these conditions and form democratic character in children. Growth, experience, and activity are the preferred terms by Dewey to describe the trying of learning to social, communicative activity that allows for the flourishing of democratic community.

The text contains two parts, with a subtitle in each part. Attention is needed to pay to the key words in each subtitle for a good understanding of the text.

the Athenian people The Athenian people were a unique people. They believed that individuals should be free as long as they acted within the laws of Greece. This allowed them the opportunity to excel in any direction they chose. Individuality, as the Greeks viewed it, was the basis of their society. The ability to strive for excellence, no matter what the challenge, was what the Athenians so dearly believed in. This strive for excellence was the method from which they achieved such phenomenal accomplishments. These accomplishments astound us to this day. They also believed in the balance of mind and body. Although many of them strove to become soldiers and athletes, others ventured into philosophy, drama, pottery and the arts. The two most important concepts which the ancient Greeks followed were found inscribed on the great shrine of Delphi, which read "Nothing in excess" and "Know thyself". This philosophy greatly impacted the Greek civilization.

About the myths of Abraham Lincoln Many people believe the grandiose dimensions and symbol-building power of the myths people create reveal their deepest longings. This is especially true of the myths Americans have created about Abraham Lincoln, who presided over the country's greatest trial, the Civil War. However, some people argue that rather than reflect any actual truths about Lincoln the man and President, the American mythology surrounding Lincoln reflects the spiritual and psychological needs of America's culture. The Lincoln myth has imbued him with the traits Americans consider their most noble, among them honesty, tolerance, a work ethic, forgiveness, compassion, a clear-sighted vision of right and wrong, and a dedication to God and country. Thus the mythological Lincoln "carries the torch of the American dream, a dream of noble idealism, of self-sacrifice and common humanity, of liberty and equality for all."

Consolidation Work

I. Fill in the blanks with the words and expressions provided, making some change when necessary.

none the less	succumb	antecedent	suffice	with respect to	relapse
rudimentary	dwell on	truism	disposition	in virtue of	proximity
in view of	resort to	done for			

Section A

1. This is also explainable _____ the explanatory power that speech act theory has in describing conversational sequencing.
2. To this end, researchers are studying how different versions of certain genes could cause some people to _____ to infection whereas others are left relatively unscathed.
3. They need to learn more about the law and to solve the disputes through regular channels, and not _____ violence.
4. Rather than _____ painful memories, he prefers to devote his energy to bring warmth, confidence and love to disadvantaged children.
5. The expression of their demand for interest-sharing covers such a wide scope that no historical _____ could match it.
6. Her easy-going nature and down-to-earth _____, crucial to the way she deals with fame, is also part of the moral values of Chinese society.
7. Statistics show that only about two-tenths of those in the program _____ into crime, a ratio much lower than among those who are put behind bars.
8. The country had little in the way of transportation, communication or economic networks and only _____ education and health systems when it was established in 1932.
9. Rio's gesture signals its seriousness to repair relations with China, its biggest customer, _____ the long-term business advantages.
10. The achievements that China has made do not _____ to change its social nature: a developing country in the primary stage of socialism.
11. The craze for the Chinese language has brought the ancient Chinese philosopher Confucius into Russia. _____, the thriving Confucius Institutes there still can not satisfy the growing need for Chinese learning.
12. The _____ that all adults need at least eight hours of sleep a night for good health should be put to rest by mounting evidence that less may be better.
13. The use of opposing elements, such as colors, forms, or lines in _____ is to produce an intensified effect in a work of art.
14. There is another question _____ this plan that must be answered before any decision can be made.
15. The money's almost gone and we've got no results after three years' hard work. I think the project is just about _____.

II. Use the appropriate form of the words given in the brackets to fill in the blanks.

1. Not so long ago, China was weak and poor and its people have not forgotten what the accompanying shame, _____ and deprivation meant. (subjugate)
2. To _____ the achievements made so far and to attain some accomplishment in my 50s are now my main aim. (sustentation)
3. Academics should be able to express their opinions on their area of expertise, whether they be negative or positive, without people taking _____ offense. (unduly)
4. It is a _____ populated area covered by dense forest and it is difficult to conduct archaeological surveys there. (meager)
5. Success is something that most women _____ to have, not necessarily success in the public eye, but success on a personal level. (aspiration)
6. In the light of the new evidence that the court can now take _____ of, the case is dropped. (cognizant)

7. If media become an element of "smart power" and a means of national strategy, their objectiveness and impartiality would _____ suffer more damage. (ineluctable)
8. In a feat of strength to match those marvels of skill and _____, he put the Los Angeles Lakers on his back and carried them past Golden State. (endure)
9. Only in the 20th century have people become conscious of the fragility of nature and thus started to _____ resources. (conservation)
10. Following 300 years of cultural _____, Yina Silo's descendants on the mainland have settled into the ethnic Han lifestyle. (assimilate)

III. Paraphrase the following sentences taken from the text.
1. ... the energy it expends in thus turning the environment to account is more than compensated for by the return it gets...
2. As some species die out, forms better adapted to utilize the obstacles against which they struggled in vain come into being.
3. Beings who are born not only unaware of, but quite indifferent to, the aims and habits of the social group have to be rendered cognizant of them and actively interested.
4. Persons do not become a society by living in physical proximity, any more than a man ceases to be socially influenced by being so many feet or miles removed from others.
5. ... but the necessity of this teaching gives an immense stimulus to reducing experience to that order and form which will render it most easily communicable and hence more usable.

IV. Test your general knowledge.
1. The right to education has been established as a basic human right: since _____, Article 2 of the first Protocol to the European Convention on Human Rights obliges all signatory parties to guarantee the right to education.
   A. 1949   B. 1952   C. 1852   D. 1886
2. At world level, the United Nations' International Covenant on Economic, Social and Cultural Rights of 1966 guarantees _____ right under its Article 13.
   A. cultural   B. social   C. economic   D. educational
3. Education in the People's Republic of China is a state-run system of _____ education run by the Ministry of Education. All citizens must attend school for at least nine years.
   A. public   B. private   C. state   D. federal
4. In the U.S., the elementary school usually covers grades _____, and the higher school _____.
   A. 1—8, 9—10 B. 1—6, 7—12 C. 1—8, 9—12 D. 1—9, 10—12
5. Higher education in America began with the founding of _____ in 1636.
   A. Harvard   B. Yale   C. MIT   D. Princeton
6. The emergence of _____ in the United States did not happen until 1910, caused by the rise in big businesses and technological advances in factories (for instance, the emergence of electrification), that required skilled workers.
   A. elementary education   B. secondary education
   C. public education   D. higher education
7. In 1852, _____ passed the first compulsory education law in the United States, which set an example for other states to implement compulsory education.

A. Massachusetts　　　　　　　B. Washington
   C. Florida　　　　　　　　　　D. Illinois
8. American education system, through over 200 years' development, consists of three levels: elementary, secondary and higher education, among which _____ is not free and compulsory.
   A. elementary education　　　　B. secondary education
   C. public education　　　　　　D. higher education
9. Education in the United States is mainly provided by the public sector, with control and funding coming from three levels: federal, _____, and local.
   A. public donations　　　　　　B. social organizations
   C. state　　　　　　　　　　　D. schools
10. In Britain, education is compulsory for everyone between _____.
    A. 5 and 16　　　　　　　　　B. 5 and 18
    C. 6 and 16　　　　　　　　　D. 6 and 18
11. About 90% of the state secondary school population in the UK attends _____.
    A. public schools　　　　　　　B. comprehensive school
    C. college　　　　　　　　　　D. independent schools
12. Experiential education is a process that occurs between a teacher and student that infuses direct experience with the learning environment and content. _____ was the most famous proponent of experiential education.
    A. William James　　　　　　　B. Socrates
    C. Plato　　　　　　　　　　　D. John Dewey
13. For an experience to be educational, Dewey believes that certain parameters have to be met, the most important of which is that the experience has _____ and interaction.
    A. practicability　　　　　　　B. interest
    C. significance　　　　　　　　D. continuity
14. Dewey also categorizes experiences as possibly being non-educative and _____, which refers to an experience that stops or distorts growth for future experiences.
    A. mis-educative　　　　　　　B. multi-educative
    C. macro-educative　　　　　　D. micro-educative
15. An important member of the American _____ movement, Dewey carried the subordination of knowledge to action into the educational world by arguing for experiential education that would enable children to learn theory and practice simultaneously.
    A. naturalism　　　　　　　　　B. functionism
    C. pragmatism　　　　　　　　D. behaviorism

V. Proofread the following passage.

There is, accordingly, a marked difference between the education
which every one get from living with others, as long as he really　　　1. _____
lives instead of just continuing to subsist, and the deliberate educating
of young. In the former case the education is incidental; it is　　　　2. _____
natural and important, but it is not the express reason of the
association. While it may be said, without exaggeration, that the
measure of the worth of any social institution, economic, domestic,

political, legal and religious, are its effect in enlarging and improving   3. _____
experience, yet this effect is not a part of its original motive,
what is limited and more immediately practical.   4. _____

    Only gradually was the by-product of the institution, its effect upon
the quality and extent of conscious life, note, and only more gradually   5. _____
still was this effect considered as a directive factor in the conduct of
the institution. Even today, in our industrial life, apart from certain
values industriousness and thrift, the intellectual and emotional   6. _____
reaction of the forms of human association under which the world's
work is carried on receive little attention as compared with physical   7. _____
output.

    But in dealing with the young, the fact of association itself as an
immediate human fact, gains in importance. While it is not easy to   8. _____
ignore in our contact with them the effect of our acts upon their
disposition, or to subordinate that educative effect to some external
and tangible result, is not so easy as in dealing with adults. The need   9. _____
of training is too evident; the pressure to accomplish a change in
their attitude and habits is urgent to leave these consequences   10. _____
wholly out of account.

VI. Write a composition.

Summarize the author's ideas about education in the text. Comment on one of the ideas that you are for or against.

Further Development

1. Dewey defines education as a process of growth. To help you further understand this concept, we recommend Dewey's three key educational texts. Among them, *Democracy and Education* is one. The other two are: *How We Think: A restatement of the relation of reflective thinking to the educative process*, which is a brilliant and accessible exploration of thinking and its relationship to learning, and *Experience and Education*, in which Dewey seeks to move beyond dualities—such as progressive/traditional—and to outline a philosophy of experience and its relation to education. Read any of them. Based on your reading and critical thinking, write a composition about your understanding of the concept of education.
2. Dewey addresses the place of education in society, expressing his belief that both informal and formal educations are crucial elements of advanced societies. Do you agree with him? Find evidence to prove your ideas.

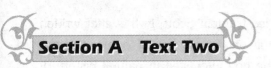

Section A Text Two

The Use of Leisure

By J. H. Badley

1   To teach a sensible use of leisure, healthy both for mind and body, is by no means the least important part of education. Nor is it by any means the least pressing, or the least difficult, of school problems.

2   "Loafing" at times that has no recognized duties assigned, is generally a sign of slackness in work and play as well; and if we do not find occupation for thoughts and hands, the rhyme tells us who will. The devils of cruelty and uncleanness will be ready to enter the empty house, and fill it at least with unwholesome talk, and thoughtless if not ill-natured "ragging". Yet work and games, whatever keenness we arouse and encourage in these, cannot fill a boy's whole time and thoughts—or, if they do, his life, whether he is student or athlete, or even the occasional combination of both, is still a narrow one and likely to get narrower as years go by. If life to the uneducated means a soulless round of labor varied by the public-house and the "pictures", so to the half-educated it is apt, except in war time, to mean the office and the club, with interests that do not go beyond golf and motoring and bridge. If our lives are emptier and our interests narrower than they need be, it is partly the result of a narrow and unsatisfying education, which leaves half our powers undeveloped and interests untouched, and too often only succeeds in giving us a distaste for those which it touches.

3   Both for the sake of the present, therefore, to avoid the dangers of unfilled leisure, and still more for the sake of the future, the wise schoolmaster does all he can to foster, in addition to keenness in the regular work and games, interests, both individual and social, of other kinds as well. He will make opportunities for various handicrafts: He will try to stimulate lines of investigation not arranged for in the class-routine; he will encourage the formation of societies both for discussion and active pursuits, for instruction and entertainment. It is the purpose of this essay to suggest what, along these lines, is possible in the school.

4   But the reasons so far given for the encouragement of leisure-time interests are mainly negative. In order to realize the full importance of this side of education, we must look rather at their positive value. From whichever point of view one looks at it, physical, intellectual, or social, this value is not small. Some of these interests contribute directly to health in being outdoor pursuits; and these, in not letting games furnish the only motive and means of exercise, can help to establish habits and motives of no little help in later life, when games are no longer easy to keep up. And even in the years when the call of games is strongest, some rivalry of other outdoor pursuits is useful as a preventive of absorption in athleticism, easily carried to excess atschool so as to shut out finer interests

and influences. It was a consciousness of this that led Captain Scott, in the letter written in those last hours among the Antarctic snows, thinking of his boy at home, and the education that he wished for him, write: "Make the boy interested in natural history, if you can; it is better than games: they encourage it in some schools."

5   Besides health, we must remember, is not only a bodily matter, but depends on mental as well as bodily activity, and on the enjoyment of the activity that comes from its being mainly voluntary—the pursuits that we are considering can do much to train skill of various kinds. The class-work represents the minimum that we expect a boy to know; but there is much that necessarily lies outside it of hardly less value. Many a boy learns as much from the hobby on which he spends his free time as from the work he does in class. Sometimes, indeed, such a free-time hobby reveals the bent that might otherwise have gone undiscovered, and determines the choice of a special line of work for the future career.

6   But the chief value of such interests lies rather in their influence on other work, and on the general development of character. In giving scope for many kinds of skill, they are helping the intellectual training; and however ready we may be to pay lip-service to the principle of learning by doing, and to admit the educational importance of the hand in brain–development, in most of our school work we still ignore these things, so far as any practical application of them is concerned. One is sometimes tempted to wonder if in the future there may not be so complete a reaction from our present ideas and methods as to make what are now regarded as mere hobbies the main matter of education, and to relegate much of the present school course, as the writing of verses has already been relegated, to the category of optional side-shows. At any rate these free-time interests can supply a very useful stimulus to much of the routine work. In these a boy may find himself for the first time, and discover, despite his experience in class, that he is no fool. Or at least he may find there a center of interest, otherwise lacking, round which other interests can group, and knowledge obtained in various class-subjects can attach itself, and so get for him a meaning and a use. And further, if we do not make the mistake of narrowing the range of choice, and allow, at any rate at first, a succession of interests, the very range and variety of these pursuits is an antidote against the tendency to early specialization, encouraged by scholarship and entrance examinations, which is one of the dangers against which we need to be on our guard. If, therefore, without mere dissipation of interest, we can widen the range of mental activities and encourage, by discussions, essays, lectures and so forth, reading round and outside the subjects dealt with in class, this is all to the good.

7   And all this has a social as well as an individual aspect. The meetings for the purposes just mentioned, as well as those for entertainment, have, like games, a real educational value, and do much to cement the comradeship of common interests and common aims that is one of the best things school has to give. And not only among those of the same age. These are things in which the example and influence of the older are particularly helpful to the younger. They can become, like the games, and perhaps to an

even greater extent, one of the interests that help to bind together past and present members of a school. And they afford an opportunity for masters to meet boys on a more personal and friendly footing, and to get the mutual knowledge and respect which are all important if education is to be, in Thring's definition, a transmission of life through the living to the living. That the organization of leisure-time pursuits is of the utmost help to the school as well as to the boy, is the unanimous verdict of the schools in which it has long been a tradition. The master who has had charge, for the past five and twenty years, of this organization in one such school writes that there they consider such pursuits as the very life-blood of the school, and the only rational method of maintaining discipline.

8   If what has here been said is admitted, it is plain that to teach, by every means in our power, the use of leisure, is one of the most important things a school has to do. We might, therefore, turn at once to the consideration of the various means for such teaching that experience has shown to be practicable in the school. But before doing so, there is yet another reason, the most far-reaching of all, to be urged for regarding this as a side of education fully as necessary, at the present time above all, as those sides that none would question. Great as is the direct and immediate value of the interests and occupations thus to be encouraged, their indirect influence is more valuable still, if they teach not only handiness and adaptiveness, but also call forth initiative and individuality, and so help to develop the complete and many-sided human personality which is the crown and purpose of education as of life. We do not now think of education as merely book-learning, nor even as concerned only with mind and body, or only as fitting preparation for skilled work and cultured leisure; but rather as the development of the whole human being, with all his possibilities, interests, and motives, as well as powers, his feelings and imagination no less than reason and will. In a word, education is training for life, with all that this connotes, and as we learn to live only by living, must be thought of not merely as preparation for life, but as a life itself. Plainly, if we give it a meaning as wide as this, a great part of education lies outside the school, in the influences of the home surroundings and, after school, of occupation and the whole social environment.

9   But during the school years, they are the most impressionable of all and it is the school life that is for most the chief formative influence; and now more necessarily so than ever. When, a few generations back, life was still, in the main, life in the country, and most things were still made at home or in the village, the most important part of education lay, except for a few, outside the school. Now it is the other way. Town life, the replacing of home-made by factory-made goods, the disappearance of the best part of home life before the demands of industry on the one side and the growth of luxury on the other—these things are signs of a tendency that has swept away most of the practical home-education, and thrown it all upon the school. And the schools have even yet hardly realized the full meaning of this change. Instead of having to provide only a part of education—the specially intellectual and, in the public schools at least, the physical side—we have now to think of the whole nature of the growing boy or girl, and, by the

environment and the occupations we provide, to appeal to interests and motives, and give occasion for the right use of powers, that may otherwise be undeveloped or misused.

10 A school cannot now consist merely of class-rooms and playing fields. This is recognized by the addition of laboratories and workshops, gymnasium, swimming-bath, lecture-hall, museum, art-school, music-rooms—all now essentials of a day school as much as of a boarding school. But many of these things are still only partially made use of, and are apt to be regarded rather as ornamental excrescences, to be used by the few who have a special bent that way, at an extra charge, than as an integral part of education for all. All the interests and means of training that they represent, and others as well, need to be brought more into the daily routine; to some extent in place of the too exclusively literary, or at least bookish, training, that has hitherto been the staple of education, but more, perhaps, since it is not possible to include in the regular curriculum all that is of value, as optional subjects and free-time occupations, though organized as part of the school course. For it is not only the few who already know their bent who need opportunity to be made for following it, but rather those who will not discover their powers without practice, or their interests without suggestion or encouragement.

11 In this respect the war has brought opportunities of no little value to the school, not only in the absorbing interest in the war itself and the desire for knowledge and readiness for effort that it awakens, but also in the demands it has made for practical work of many kinds that boys and girls can do, and the lessons of service that it has taught. Work on the land and in the shops, for those whose school time is already too short, is a curtailment, only to be made as a last resort, of the kind of learning they will have no other opportunity to acquire; but it gives to the public schoolboy the feeling of reality that most of his school work lacks. Such opportunities of doing what is seen to be productive and necessary work, are, like the making of things for those at the front, and for the wounded, both in themselves and in the motives that inspire them, a valuable part of education that should not be forgotten when the present need for them is over.

Independent Study Assistant

I. Words and Expressions

1. **sensible** *adj.* able to make good judgments based on reason and experience rather than emotion; practical
2. **by no means** (also "not by any means") not at all
3. **loaf** *v.* to spend your time not doing anything, especially when you should be working
4. **slackness** *n.* (disapproving) when a person or organization is not working as well and as hard as they should
5. **unwholesome** *adj.* unpleasant or not natural
6. **apt** *adj.* likely or having a natural tendency to do sth
7. **for the sake of** out of consideration or regard for a person or thing; for someone's or something's advantage or good

8. **along the lines of** (also on the lines of, along those lines) roughly similar in type or in keeping with
9. **furnish** *v.* to supply or provide
10. **preventive** *n.* anything that prevents, esp. anything that prevents disease
11. **bent** *n.* a natural skill or interest in sth
12. **relegate** *v.* to put someone or something into a lower or less important rank or position
13. **antidote** *n.* anything that takes away the effects of sth unpleasant
14. **on guard** very careful and prepared for sth difficult or dangerous
15. **dissipation** *n.* behavior which is enjoyable but has a harmful effect on you
16. **cement** *v.* to make a relationship, an agreement, etc. stronger
17. **footing** *n.* the position or status of sb/sth in relation to others; the relationship between two or more people or groups
18. **verdict** *n.* a decision that you make or an opinion that you give about sth, after you have tested it or considered it carefully
19. **call forth** to produce a particular reaction
20. **connote** *v.* to suggest a feeling, an idea, etc. as well as the main meaning
21. **excrescence** *n.* something considered to be very ugly
22. **hitherto** *adv.* until now; until the particular time you are talking about
23. **staple** *n.* a large or important part of sth
24. **curtailment** *n.* the activity of limiting sth or making it last for a shorter time
25. **resort** *n.* a place where many people go for rest, sport or another stated purpose

II. Referential Points

John Haden Badley (1865—1967) author, educator, and founder of Bedales School, which claimed to have become the first coeducational public boarding school in England in 1893. All Badley's initial ideas—though their later development was quite different—were taken from Reddie, the founder of Abbotsholme School. For instance the curriculum was English based, not classical, and wide—with science, art, music, French, German, and opportunities for plays and hobbies; religion was non-dogmatic and non-sectarian; boys were not crammed for exams, there were no prizes and lessons were only in the mornings; the games madness of Rugby and the conventional Public School was condemned; instead much time was spent on manual labor in fields and gardens; and the boys were also taught tailoring, boot making and cookery. He wrote a number of books which include *After the War* (1917), *Bedales: A Pioneer School* (1923), *Form and Spirit* (1951), and his autobiography, *Memories and Reflections*, published in 1955. Yet it was his last work that can be looked at as his magnum opus: *A Bible for Modern Readers* (the New Testament) in 1961 and *The Bible as Seen Today* (the Old Testament) in 1965.

Captain Scott (1868—1912) Robert Falcon Scott was a British Royal Naval officer and explorer who led two expeditions to the Antarctic regions: the Discovery Expedition in 1901—1904, and the ill-fated Terra Nova Expedition in 1910—1913. During this second venture Scott led a party of five which reached the South Pole on 17 January 1912. On their return journey Scott and his four comrades all perished from a combination of exhaustion, hunger and extreme cold.

Edward Thring British educator. He transformed Uppingham School from a small country grammar school into a large and important public school, which influenced public school education throughout England. At Uppingham, Thring opened (1859) the first school gymnasium in England, introduced wood and metal workshops, and provided a swimming pool. In academic matters he stressed sound training in mathematics, the classics, and music. His major work, *Theory and Practice of Teaching* (1883), offered critical advice on teaching and teacher education.

III. Questions for Comprehension

1. What does the word "use" indicate in the title *The Use of Leisure*?
2. Why does the author say "To teach a sensible use of leisure, healthy both for mind and body, is by no means the least important part of education"?
3. What are the related school problems according to the author?
4. What suggestions does the author provide to solve the problems?
5. What kind of view does the author indicate on school education?

Self-test

I. Fill in the blanks with the words and expressions provided, making some change when necessary.

| by no means | line | furnish | bent | antidote | on guard | relegate |
| cement | footing | verdict | call forth | excrescence | hitherto | staple |
| for the sake of |

1. It had become clear that only actual fossils would _____ incontrovertible evidence for the time at which bilaterians had emerged.
2. In the event, the only effective _____ is the truth, and it should not be withheld until it is too late.
3. Despite the challenges and difficulties, worldwide media organizations should enhance communication, _____ cooperation and accelerate development to live up to their social obligations.
4. A large group of police stand _____ as thousands of anti-war, environmental and pro-jobs groups marching through part of downtown.
5. You can't do much in the art _____ without training, for success in this field depends on, apart from talent, constant practice.
6. Once he was in full charge of the section. Now he was _____ to a role of a mere assistant. That accounted for his resignation.
7. Voters gave their _____ on the government's economic record last night by voting overwhelmingly for the opposition.
8. Thanks to government policies, millions of poorer and _____ excluded families became homeowners.
9. It is unlikely that the world would find a solid _____ for a lasting recovery unless the problem of global imbalance can be properly tackled.
10. Government support is _____ arbitrary administrative intervention with the operation of a particular cultural enterprise.

Section A

11. The appearance of name brand products is just _____ following the trend of modem elaborate works consciousness.
12. As an art form, caricature has deeps root in Poland and has become a _____ of art around the world.
13. The new office development is a/an _____ on the face of the city, which has ruined the original harmony of urban layout.
14. Knowledge can _____ equally powerful ways to destroy life, intentionally and unintentionally.
15. Because we have a/an _____ on exporting and pleasing the Western audience, our recent movies are on the whole cultural disasters.

II. Use the appropriate form of the words given in the brackets to fill in the blanks.
1. Trust and stability enable us to plan _____ and on a long term basis to bring benefit to the whole community. (sensible)
2. The doctor advised Facer to _____ up for few days, as his lifestyle was having a bad effect on his heart. (slackness)
3. Learn to feed yourself in a/an _____ way by eating a balanced diet rich in organic fruits and vegetables. (unwholesome)
4. His failed takeover attempt during the 2007-08 season was partly blamed as a factor in the club's _____ from the Premier League. (relegate)
5. The government has to let go of the state-owned performing arts troupes before the "free" culture will _____. (dissipation)
6. Ancient Musical Instrument can deepen visitors' understanding of the museum's rich cultural _____. (connote)
7. Renewable energy, especially wind power, is helping to slow China's reliance on coal and _____ emissions of global warming gases. (curtailment)
8. Teachers are, after all, the best role models for _____ young minds who spend large chunk of their time in school almost every day. (impression)
9. All through my boyhood and youth, I was known as a _____, that I was always busy on my own private end, which was to learn to write. (loaf)
10. "Next on Twilight Zone", a show that might very _____ be called a living end, and, with comparable _____, is called "Living Doll". (apt)

III. Translate the short paragraph into Chinese.
　　Work and games, whatever keenness we arouse and encourage in these, cannot filla boy's whole time and thoughts—or, if they do, his life, whether he is student or athlete, or even the occasional combination of both, is still a narrow one and likely to get narrower as years go by. If life to the uneducated means a soulless round of labor varied by the public-house and the "pictures", so to the half-educated it is apt, except in war time, to mean the office and the club, with interests that do not go beyond golf and motoring and bridge. If our lives are emptier and our interests narrower than they need be, it is partly the result of a narrow and unsatisfying education, which leaves half our powers undeveloped and interests untouched, and too often only succeeds in giving us a distaste for those which it touches.

184 Unit 5

IV. Analyze difficult sentences.

1. Both for the sake of the present, therefore, to avoid the dangers of unfilled leisure, and still more for the sake of the future, the wise schoolmaster does all he can to foster, in addition to keenness in the regular work and games, interests, both individual and social, of other kinds as well.
2. It was a consciousness of this that led Captain Scott, in the letter written in those last hours among the Antarctic snows, thinking of his boy at home, and the education that he wished for him, write: "Make the boy interested in natural history, if you can; it is better than games: they encourage it in some schools."
3. If, therefore, without mere dissipation of interest, we can widen the range of mental activities and encourage, by discussions, essays, lectures and so forth, reading round and outside the subjects dealt with in class, this is all to the good.
4. Such opportunities of doing what is seen to be productive and necessary work, are, like the making of things for those at the front, and for the wounded, both in themselves and in the motives that inspire them, a valuable part of education that should not be forgotten when the present need for them is over.

V. Proofread the following passage.

Besides all these more specially intellectual interests, and of still wider appeal, various kinds of handicrafts afford abundant occupation, some for the longer and some also for the short periods of leisure. Wood-work, carving, work in metal or leather, pottery, basket-plaiting, bookbinding, needlework and embroidery, knitting, netting hammocks and so forth—the only limit to a number of such crafts is the limit to the knowledge and energy of those who can start and direct them, and to the space available, as some can only carried on in rooms reserved for such work. So, too, with various kinds of art-work—drawing, modeling, lettering, making posters of entertainments; or music, both individual and concerted, orchestra practice, part-singing, glee-clubs and so on; or morrice and other folk-dances, now happily being widely revived. And lastly there are indoor games, some of them, like chess, have a high training value, and others afford a useful occasional outlet to high spirit; and entertainments got up by some society, or perhaps by single form, for the rest of the "house" or school, such as a concert or play or even an occasional fancy-dress dance, the preparation which will happily occupy free time for as long beforehand as is allowed, and does much to encourage ingenuity, especially if strict conditions are imposed that all which is required must be made for the purpose and not bought.

But by this time many questions will have arisen in the mind of the reader, especially if much of what has been enumerated lie outside his school experience; questions that demand an immediate answer. Even if all this free-time work and play may have a certain

1. _____
2. _____
3. _____
4. _____
5. _____
6. _____
7. _____
8. _____
9. _____

value, how can the time be found for it without encroaching on the
regular work and games which, after all, must be the main concern
of the school? And even supposing that time could be found for both,
will not all this voluntary activity and pleasure-work absorb the
interests and energies that ought to be given to the more serious,
if less attractive, studies?

10. _____

VI. Write a composition.

Badley discusses the use of leisure in the text. Summarize his main arguments and write a composition to show your reflections (agreement or disagreement) on the ideas and justify your reflections with examples.

Section B

Text One Is Rock Music Ruining Education?

Focal Consideration

Rock music is a popular music genre among the young people. The author of the text faults rock music for its bad effect on education. The discussion of the text will focus on:
1. the history of rock music and its effects on young people.
2. how rock music is related to liberal education in the author's eyes.
3. whether rock music ruins the ambition of young people and corrupts the tradition of civilization.

Research Questions

Think about the following questions and discuss them with your group members. After your discussion, work out the research report and share it with the students of other groups.
1. What kind of music do you like? Why do you like it? Analyze the underlying relationship between music and human mind.
2. Do you agree or disagree that the youth culture contradicts the tradition of our civilization? Why?
3. What is the target of liberal education? Is traditional education already out of date in modern society?
4. Why does the author think that rock music and drugs ruin ambition of the young people? Do you agree?

Is Rock Music Ruining Education?

By Allan David Bloom

1   Picture a thirteen-year-old boy sitting in the living room of his family home doing his math assignment while wearing his Walkman headphones or watching MTV. He enjoys the liberties hard won over centuries by the alliance of philosophic genius and political heroism, consecrated by the blood of martyrs; he is provided with comfort and leisure by the most productive economy ever known to mankind; science has penetrated the secrets of nature in order to provide him with the marvelous, lifelike electronic sound and image reproduction he is enjoying. And in what does progress culminate? A pubescent child whose body throbs with orgasmic rhythms; whose feelings are made articulate in hymns to the joys of onanism or the killing of parents; whose ambition is to win fame and wealth in imitating the drag-queen who makes the music. In short, life is made into a nonstop, commercially prepackaged masturbational fantasy.

2   This description may seem exaggerated, but only because some would prefer to regard it as such. The continuing exposure to rock music is a reality, not one confined to a particular class or type of child. One need only ask first-year university students what music they listen to, how much of it and what it means to them, in order to discover that the phenomenon is universal in America, that it begins in adolescence or a bit before and continues through the college years. It is the youth culture and, as I have so often insisted, there is now no other countervailing nourishment for the spirit. Some of this culture's power comes from the fact that it is so loud. It makes conversation impossible, so that much of friendship must be without the shared speech that Aristotle asserts is the essence of friendship and the only true common ground. With rock, illusions of shared feelings, bodily contact and grunted formulas, which are supposed to contain so much meaning beyond speech, are the basis of association. None of this contradicts going about the business of life, attending classes and doing the assignments for them. But the meaningful inner life is with the music.

3   This phenomenon is both astounding and indigestible, and is hardly noticed, routine and habitual. But it is of historic proportions that a society's best young and their best energies should be so occupied. People of future civilizations will wonder at this and find it as incomprehensible as we do the caste system, witch-burning, harems, cannibalism and gladiatorial combats. It may well be that a society's greatest madness seems normal to itself. The child I described has parents who have sacrificed to provide him with a good life and who have a great stake in his future happiness. They cannot believe that the musical vocation will contribute very much to that happiness. But there is nothing they can do about it. The family spiritual void has left the field open to rock music, and they cannot possibly forbid their children to listen to it. It is everywhere; all children listen to it; forbidding it would simply cause them to lose their children's affection and obedience.

When they turn on the television, they will see President Reagan warmly grasping the daintily proffered gloved hand of Michael Jackson and praising him enthusiastically. Better to set the faculty of denial in motion—avoid noticing what the words say, assume the kid will get over it. If he has early sex, that won't get in the way of his having stable relationships later. His drug use will certainly stop at pot. School is providing real values. And popular historicism provides the final salvation: there are new life-styles for new situations, and the older generation is there not to impose its values but to help the younger one to find its own. TV, which compared to music plays a comparatively small role in the formation of young people's character and taste, is a consensus monster—the Right monitors its content for sex, the Left for violence, and many other interested sects for many other things. But the music has hardly been touched, and what efforts have been made are both ineffectual and misguided about the nature and extent of the problem.

4   The result is nothing less than parents' loss of control over their children's moral education at a time when no one else is seriously concerned with it. This has been achieved by an alliance between the strange young males who have the gift of divining the mob's emergent wishes — our versions of Thrasymachus, Socrates' rhetorical adversary — and the record—company executives, the new robber barons, who mine gold out of rock. They discovered a few years back that children are one of the few groups in the country with considerable disposable income, in the form of allowances. Their parents spend all they have providing for the kids. Appealing to them over their parents' heads, creating a world of delight for them, constitutes one of the richest markets in the postwar world. The rock business is perfect capitalism, supplying to demand and helping to create it. It has all the moral dignity of drug trafficking, but it was so totally new and unexpected that nobody thought to control it, and now it is too late. Progress may be made against cigarette smoking because our absence of standards or our relativism does not extend to matters of bodily health. In all other things the market determines the value. (Yoko Ono is among America's small group of billionaires, along with oil and computer magnates, her late husband having produced and sold a commodity of worth comparable to theirs.) Rock is very big business, bigger than the movies, bigger than professional sports, bigger than television, and this accounts for much of the respectability of the music business. It is difficult to adjust our vision to the changes in the economy and to see what is really important. McDonald's now has more employees than U.S. Steel, and likewise the purveyors of junk food for the soul have supplanted what still seem to be more basic callings.

5   It is interesting to note that the Left, which prides itself on its critical approach to "late capitalism" and is unrelenting and unsparing in its analysis of our other cultural phenomena, has in general given rock music a free ride. Abstracting from the capitalist element in which it flourishes, they regard it as a people's art, coming from beneath the bourgeoisie's layers of cultural repression. Its antinomianism and its longing for a world without constraint might seem to be the clarion of the proletarian revolution, and Marxists

certainly do see that rock music dissolves the beliefs and morals necessary for liberal society and would approve of it for that alone. But the harmony between the young intellectual Left and rock is probably profounder than that. Herbert Marcuse appealed to university students in the sixties with a combination of Marx and Freud. In Eros and Civilization and One Dimensional Man he promised that the overcoming of capitalism and its false consciousness will result in a society where the greatest satisfactions are sexual, of a sort that the bourgeois moralist Freud called polymorphous and infantile. Rock music touches the same chord in the young. Free sexual expression, anarchism, mining the irrational unconscious and giving it free rein are what they have in common. The high intellectual life I shall describe in Part Two and the low rock world are partners in the same entertainment enterprise. They must both be interpreted as parts of the cultural fabric of late capitalism. Their success comes from the bourgeois' need to feel that he is not bourgeois, to have undangerous experiments with the unlimited. He is willing to pay dearly for them. The Left is better interpreted by Nietzsche than by Marx. The critical theory of late capitalism is at once late capitalism's subtlest and crudest expression. Anti-bourgeois ire is the opiate of the Last Man.

6   My concern here is not with the moral effects of this music whether it leads to sex, violence or drugs. The issue here is its effect on education, and I believe it ruins the imagination of young people and makes it very difficult for them to have a passionate relationship to the art and thought that are the substance of liberal education. The first sensuous experiences are decisive in determining the taste for the whole of life, and they are the link between the animal and spiritual in us. The period of nascent sensuality has always been used for sublimation, in the sense of making sublime, for attaching youthful inclinations and longings to music, pictures and stories that provide the transition to the fulfillment of the human duties and the enjoyment of the human pleasures. Lessing, speaking of Greek sculpture, said, "beautiful men made beautiful statues, and the city had beautiful statues in part to thank for beautiful citizens." This formula encapsulates the fundamental principle of the esthetic education of man. Young men and women were attracted by the beauty of heroes whose very bodies expressed their nobility. The deeper understanding of the meaning of nobility comes later, but is prepared for by the sensuous experience and is actually contained in it. What the senses long for as well as what reason later sees as good are thereby not at tension with one another. Education is not sermonizing to children against their instincts and pleasures, but providing a natural continuity between what they feel and what they can and should be. But this is a lost art. Now we have come to exactly the opposite point. Rock music encourages passions and provides models that have no relation to any life the young people who go to universities can possibly lead, or to the kinds of admiration encouraged by liberal studies. Without the cooperation of the sentiments, anything other than technical education is a dead letter.

7   Rock music provides premature ecstasy and, in this respect, is like the drugs with which it is allied. It artificially induces the exaltation attached to the completion of the

greatest endeavors — victory in a just war, consummated love, artistic creation, religious devotion and discovery of the truth. Without effort, without talent, without virtue, without exercise of the faculties, anyone and everyone is accorded the equal right to the enjoyment of their fruits. In my experience, students who have had a serious fling with drugs — and gotten over it — find it difficult to have enthusiasms or great expectations. It is as though the color has been drained out of their lives and they see everything in black and white. The pleasure they experienced in the beginning was so intense that they no longer look for it at the end, or as the end. They may function perfectly well, but dryly, routinely. Their energy has been sapped, and they do not expect their life's activity to produce anything but a living, whereas liberal education is supposed to encourage the belief that the good life is the pleasant life and that the best life is the most pleasant life. I suspect that the rock addiction, particularly in the absence of strong counterattractions, has an effect similar to that of drugs. The students will get over this music, or at least the exclusive passion for it. But they will do so in the same way Freud says that men accept the reality principle as something harsh, grim and essentially unattractive, a mere necessity. These students will assiduously study economics or the professions and the Michael Jackson costume will slip off to reveal a Brooks Brothers suit beneath. They will want to get ahead and live comfortably. But this life is as empty and false as the one they left behind. The choice is not between quick fixes and dull calculation. This is what liberal education is meant to show them. But as long as they have the Walkman on, they cannot hear what the great tradition has to say. And, after its prolonged use, when they take it off, they find they are deaf.

Preview Assistant

1. **consecrate** *v.* to declare, make or set a part in a special ceremony as holy; to set apart solemnly for a particular purpose
2. **martyr** *n.* a person who by his death or sufferings proves the strength of his beliefs
3. **culminate** *v.* to reach the highest point, degree or development
4. **pubescent** *adj.* of puberty
5. **throb** *v.* to beat strongly and rapidly
6. **orgasmic** *adj.* being at the highest point of sexual pleasure
7. **articulate** *v.* to declare, make or set a part in a special ceremony as holy;
8. **hymn** *n.* a song of praise
9. **onanism** *n.* masturbation
10. **masturbational** *adj.* being excited by handling the sex organs
11. **adolescence** *n.* the period between being a child and being a grown person
12. **countervailing** *adj.* acting against something with equal force
13. **nourishment** *n.* something that can cause to stay alive or grow by giving food, water, etc.
14. **assert** *v.* state or declare forcefully; to make claim to; defend in words
15. **illusion** *n.* something seen wrongly, not as it really is; a false idea

16. **grunt** *v.* make short, deep rough sounds in the throat
17. **sensuous** *adj.* being of, concerning, causing, interested in, etc, feeling esp. of pleasure by the senses
18. **sensuality** *n.* the state of being interested in or related to etc. giving pleasure to one's own body, as by sex, food and the drink
19. **nascent** *adj.* beginning to be, starting to grow or develop
20. **sublimation** *n.* the act of replacing something with socially acceptable activities
21. **sublime** *adj.* very noble or wonderful
22. **sculpture** *n.* the art of shaping solid figures out of stone, wood, clay, metal, etc.
23. **encapsulate** *v.* to enclose in
24. **esthetic** *adj.* of or concerning the sense of beauty esp. in art
25. **sermonize** *v.* try to teach moral lessons in a solemn way
26. **ecstasy** *n.* a state of very strong feeling esp. of joy and happiness
27. **induce** *v.* lead often by persuading
28. **endeavor** *n.* an effort; attempt
29. **exaltation** *n.* the joy of success
30. **consummate** *v.* make perfect
31. **faculty** *n.* natural power or ability of the mind
32. **accord** *v.* to be of the same nature or quality; be in agreement; to give; allow
33. **fling** *n.* a short time of satisfying one's own desires; wild time
34. **sap** *v.* to weaken by wearing or digging away at the base; to weaken or destroy, esp. during a long time
35. **assiduously** *adv.* carefully and attentively

Referential Points

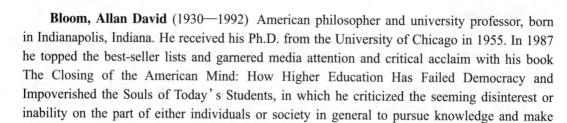

Bloom, Allan David (1930—1992) American philosopher and university professor, born in Indianapolis, Indiana. He received his Ph.D. from the University of Chicago in 1955. In 1987 he topped the best-seller lists and garnered media attention and critical acclaim with his book The Closing of the American Mind: How Higher Education Has Failed Democracy and Impoverished the Souls of Today's Students, in which he criticized the seeming disinterest or inability on the part of either individuals or society in general to pursue knowledge and make judgments about the worth of ideas and values.

Friedrich Wilhelm Nietzsche (1844—1900) a 19th-century German philosopher and classical philologist. He wrote critical texts on religion, morality, contemporary culture, philosophy and science, using a distinctive rhetorical and evocative style, displaying a fondness for metaphor, irony and aphorism. Nietzsche's influence remains substantial within and beyond philosophy, notably in existentialism and postmodernism. His style and radical questioning of the value and objectivity of truth have resulted in much commentary and interpretation, mostly in the continental tradition. His key ideas include the death of God, perspectivism, the Übermensch, the eternal recurrence, and the will to power. Nietzsche began his career as a classical philologist before turning to philosophy.

Herbert Marcuse a German philosopher, sociologist, and political theorist, associated with the Frankfurt School of critical theory. Celebrated as the "Father of the New Left," his best known works are Eros and Civilization, One-Dimensional Man and The Aesthetic Dimension. Marcuse's analysis of capitalism derives partially from one of Karl Marx's main concepts: Objectification, which under capitalism becomes Alienation. Marx believed that capitalism was exploiting humans; that the objects produced by laborers became alienated and thus ultimately dehumanized them to functional objects. Marcuse took this belief and expanded it. He argued that capitalism and industrialization pushed laborers so hard that they began to see themselves as extensions of the objects they were producing.

Aristotle (384—322 B.C.) Greek philosopher, pupil of Plato, tutor of Alexander the Great. His philosophy grew away from the idealism of Plato and became increasingly concerned with science and the phenomena of the world. His analyses were original and profound and his methods exercised an enormous influence on all subsequent thought.

Lessing (1729—1781) German philosopher, dramatist, and critic, one of the most influential figures of the Enlightenment. He was connected with the theater in Berlin, where he produced some of his most famous works, and with the national theater in Hamburg. Lessing differentiated between the poet as interpreter of time and the artist as interpreter of space; he found different aesthetic criteria applicable to each. Lessing's introduction in Germany of English literature, especially of Shakespeare, was an important contribution.

Marxism a particular political philosophy, economic and sociological worldview based upon a materialist interpretation of history, a Marxist analysis of capitalism, a theory of social change, and an atheist view of human liberation derived from the work of Karl Marx and Friedrich Engels. The three primary aspects of Marxism are: the dialectical and materialist concept of history, the critique of capitalism and Advocacy of proletarian revolution.

Michael Joseph Jackson (1958—2009) known as a superb dancer and pop singer, often conveying an androgynous image and an ambiguous sexuality, but offstage he has become known for various alleged eccentricities, for his sharp business acumen, and for a physical appearance that has changed radically over the years. As a child in the 1960s and 70s he was the dominant voice and youngest member of the Jackson Five, a pop group that included five brothers. With his solo albums Off the Wall (1979) and the even more successful Thriller (1982), which sold over 30 million copies, he became one of the world's leading pop stars. His success continued with Bad (1987) and Dangerous (1991), both of which sold over 20 million copies. In 1993 he was charged in a civil suit with sexual abuse of a minor, a charge he denied. The suit was settled out of court in 1994, and no criminal charges were filed. Jackson was indicted in another sexual abuse case in 2004. The trial, in 2005, was marked by sensational testimony and spellbound media coverage, and ended in Jackson's acquittal.

Socrates a Classical Greek philosopher. Credited as one of the founders of Western philosophy, he is an enigmatic figure known chiefly through the accounts of later classical writers, especially the writings of his students Plato and Xenophon, and the plays of his contemporary Aristophanes. Many would claim that Plato's dialogues are the most comprehensive accounts of Socrates to survive from antiquity.Through his portrayal in Plato's dialogues, Socrates has become renowned for his contribution to the field of ethics, and it is this Platonic Socrates who also lends his name to the concepts of Socratic irony and the Socratic method, or elenchus. The latter remains a commonly used tool in a wide range of discussions, and is a type of pedagogy in which a series of questions are asked not only to draw individual answers, but to encourage fundamental insight into the issue at hand.

Thrasymachus a sophist of Ancient Greece best known as a character in Plato's Republic. Thrasymachus was a citizen of Chalcedon, on the Bosphorus. His career appears to have been spent as a sophist, at Athens as far as we know, though there is no concrete evidence that he was a sophist. He is credited with an increase in the rhythmic character of Greek oratory, especially the use of the paeonici rhythm in prose; also a greater appeal to the emotions through gesture.

Rock Music a genre of popular music that entered the mainstream in the 1950s. It has its roots in 1940s and 1950s rock and roll, rhythm and blues, country music and also drew on folk music, jazz and classical music. The sound of rock often revolves around the electric guitar, a back beat laid down by a rhythm section of electric bass guitar, drums, and keyboard instruments such as Hammond organ, piano, or, since the 1970s, synthesizers. Along with the guitar or keyboards, saxophone and blues-style harmonica are sometimes used as soloing instruments. The foundations of rock music are in rock and roll, which originated in the United States during the late 1940s and early 1950s, and quickly spread to much of the rest of the world. Its immediate origins lay in a mixing together of various black musical genres of the time, including rhythm and blues and gospel music; in addition to country and western.

Consolidation Work

I. Fill in the blanks with the words and expressions provided, making some change when necessary.

consecrate	ecstasy	assiduous	penetrate	culminate
adolescence	addict	consummate	hero	articulate
in part	get over	in this respect	accord to	be confined to

1. Terms of such scientific technology _____ professional manuals and magazines.
2. The Christian term _____ means the act of solemnly dedicating or setting apart a person or thing to the service of God.
3. This newly developed programming language is the _____ of five years of work by the U.S. Department of Defense to devise a common high-order language to meet its varied requirements.
4. The new problems were concerned with the education, both general and vocational, of the returning veterans, with universal military training of youth, with the return of _____ to school.
5. There is an _____ that marks the summit of life, and beyond which life cannot rise.
6. Privileges and immunities _____ the representatives of Members, not for the personal benefit of the individuals themselves, but in order to safeguard the independent exercise of their functions in connection with the Agency.
7. Nicotine, a major constituent of tobacco smoke, is both poisonous and highly _____.
8. It was not until the U.S.-China summit that the shift toward a multipolar world structure may be said to have been _____.
9. Vocal training allows a singer to develop breath control, to regulate the degree of relaxation or tension in the body, and to resonate and _____ sound.
10. In spite of the above, his opinion may be wrong _____, simply because he hates war

in view of its severe consequences.
11. During the Second World War, the British and the Russians had shown a surprising strength and _____ equal to the task.
12. Through _____ research work in museums and libraries, some very rare drawings have been recovered for this exhibition.
13. Automobile experts have shown that halogen headlights _____ thick fog more effectively than traditional incandescent headlights and thus help to reduce accidents.
14. This research report, based on careful study of satellite data and an increase of hurricane activities in recent years, suggests that catastrophic hurricanes are due _____ to global warming. .
15. The rich woman was so upset at the loss of her beloved puppy that it was hard for her to _____ the shock.

II. Use the appropriate form of the words given in the brackets to fill in the blanks.
1. Well, it is a little late, but nine prototypes later the folks over at Martin Aircraft are releasing a _____ available jetpack. (commerce)
2. Economists who study food issues say the worldwide drop in _____ is a red flag: potential shortages of soybeans, rice, wheat and maize, the world's primary grains, are a real possibility. (produce)
3. Once a movement begins to make an impact, the role of the reformist leaders becomes increasingly _____. (contradict)
4. Variety will issue press releases and photographs announcing the _____ between the charity and your organization to relevant trade and consumer publications. (ally)
5. Gender organization of schooling and television viewing among early _____: a test of two alternative hypotheses. (adolescence)
6. He favors elaborate (often microtonal) but richly _____ textures and grand, totalizing structures. (sense)
7. The Orthodox Church offers a characteristic mix of monkish asceticism, mystical _____, and a special cult of beauty. (exalt)
8. These capabilities will deny an _____ the information advantage, preventing him from effectively employing his forces. (adverse)
9. The great story of the Catastrophe that destroyed an ancient peaceful _____ had been handed down from father to son. (civil)
10. Rejecting historicism it had a desire to enhance the _____ of German products, many of its patrons had English contacts. (compete)

III. Paraphrase the following sentences taken from the text.
1. He enjoys the liberties hard won over centuries by the alliance of philosophic genius and political heroism, consecrated by the blood of martyrs.
2. The continuing exposure to rock music is a reality, not one confined to a particular class or type of child.
3. It makes conversation impossible, so that much of friendship must be without the shared speech that Aristotle asserts is the essence of friendship and the only true common ground.
4. What the senses long for as well as what reason later sees as good are thereby not at tension with one another.

5. Without the cooperation of the sentiments, anything other than technical education is a dead letter.

IV. Test your general knowledge.

1. _____ is considered America's unique contribution to music.
   A. Rock and Roll   B. Country Music
   C. Western Music   D. Jazz
2. Rock'n' Roll was born in the _____ and it emerged from rhythm and blues, a music similar to jazz played by blacks. This kind of music started to attract white teenagers.
   A. 1920's   B. 1940'   C. 1950's   D. 1960's
3. The Blues is a typical American music, music of strong rhythm, originally sung by the Negroes in the _____ states of America.
   A. eastern   B. southern   C. western   D. northern
4. The Beatles were an English music group from _____ who were the most critically acclaimed, commercially successful artists in 1960s.
   A. Liverpool   B. Birmingham C. London   D. Manchester
5. The Woodstock Music and Art Festival was a rock festival held at Max Yasgur's 600 acre dairy farm in Bethel, New York. It is arguably and very widely viewed as the most famous rock festival ever held. It is held in _____.
   A. July   B. August   C. December   D. May
6. _____ is renowned as an early pioneer of rock music and is considered by many to be rocks greatest performer.
   A. Elvis Presley   B. Led Zeppelin
   C. the Beatles   D. Michael Jackson
7. Higher education in America began with the founding of _____ in 1636.
   A. MIT   B. Yale   C. Princeton   D. Harvard
8. Education in the United States is provided mainly by the government, with control and funding coming from _____ levels.
   A. two   B. three   C. four   D. five
9. _____ is not one of the levels which mainly fund the education in the United States.
   A. Federal   B. State   C. Local   D. parliamentary
10. Entrance into graduate programs in America usually depends upon a student's undergraduate academic performance or professional experience as well as their score on a standardized entrance exam. Which of the following tests is not of such kind?
    A. GRE   B. LSAT   C. TOFEL   D. GMAT
11. Which of the following statements about American education is NOT true?
    A. Schooling is compulsory for all children in the United States, but the age range for which school attendance is required varies from state to state.
    B. Most parents send their children to either a public or private institution, and some may also choose to educate their own children at home.
    C. Elementary school, "grade school", "grammar school", and "public school" are all interchangeable names for schools that begin with kindergarten or first grade and end either with fifth or sixth grade.
    D. Middle school runs from grades 9 through 12. It is also called "high school", and "intermediate school".

12. In 2004, the three states _____ accounted for 41 of the 100 largest public school districts?
    A. Texas, New York, and Ohio
    B. California, Texas, and New York
    C. California, Florida, and Texas
    D. California, Florida, and New York
13. Most American schools accept ACT or _____ which measures reasoning skills in mathematics and language.
    A. SAT
    B. TOFEL
    C. IELTS
    D. TOEIC
14. TOEIC is short for _____, which measures the ability of non-native English-speaking examinees to use English in everyday workplace activities.
    A. Teaching of English for International Communication
    B. Test of English for International Communication
    C. Test of English for Internet Communication
    D. Test of English International Cognition
15. State schools, also known as _____ or, in the United States and Canada, _____, are schools mandated for or offered to all children by the government, whether national, regional, or local, provided by an institution of civil government, and paid for, in whole or in part, by taxes.
    A. public schools, private schools
    B. government schools, intermediate schools
    C. government schools, public schools
    D. public schools, government schools

V. Proofread the following passage.

The average teenager today, even in the best family, wants to get away from the confines of the family and find his own individual identity. This is not necessarily something bad. The teenager wants to see whom he is himself when there is no one to define him. There is a time that he must be able to stand lonely and he wants to be prepared for this first stage of adulthood. During this preparation period, he also wants to enjoy himself. After all, it is true that he will ever be a teenager again. Half of himself in adolescence and half aim for adulthood, he sets off for his life of independence. Independence, although necessary, can be a lonely state of mind. The only ideal independence exists in a ideal world. The teenager has a gift for distorting the size of a problem. He would rather die than to get a low grade on his academic scores. The end of the world comes when his girlfriend breaks up him. He may even feel the need to get his own extra "medical help" to get the energy to cram for college entrance exams. Whether alone in a school dorm room or among his family at home, he is often consumed with feelings of loneliness and fear of rejection. But he may have his independence, the restrictions of society allow a "freedom" which takes a great deal of adjusting to. Once out of the confine of the family structure, the young person must survive the cruelties of society without being consumed by the rigid molds which it offers.

1. _____
2. _____
3. _____
4. _____
5. _____
6. _____
7. _____
8. _____
9. _____
10. _____

VI. Write a composition.

Read the text again and summarize the author's ideas about the influence of rock music on the youth. Do you agree with the author? Write down your comments.

Further Development

1. In this article Bloom gave a violent criticism of American education in the young generation of his time. He pointed out that "liberal education" is the solution. Do you agree with him? Is there any similar educational situation in China? Do some research about this issue and report it to your classmates.
2. This article is an excerpt from the section "Music" in Allan Bloom's book *The Closing of the American Mind*, in which he faults the schools and colleges for lack of moral leadership as well as for failing to teach the traditions of our civilization. You are encouraged to read through this book and comment on the far-reaching effects of entertainment industry on students' lives.

Bloom, Allan. *The Closing of the American Mind*. NY: Touchstone, 1988.

Section B Text Two

Literary Study among the Ruins

By J. Hillis Miller

1   It must be remembered and squarely faced, though it is difficult to do so for a lover of literature like me, that in spite of the lip service paid these days to literature's authority by politicians, the media, and educationists, fewer and fewer people, in Europe and America at least, actually spend much time reading "literature" in the old-fashioned sense of canonical works—Chaucer, Shakespeare, Milton, Pope, Wordsworth, George Eliot, Virginia Woolf, and the rest, in English literature. Literature has been granted enormous authority in our culture, but though that authority may still be tacitly or even explicitly acknowledged, for example by the media, no candid observer can doubt that it is no longer so pragmatically operative. If the books just stay there on the shelves, their authority is only potential. They must be read to be performatively effective.

2   If you are watching a movie or television or playing a computer game or surfing the Internet, you cannot at the same time be reading Shakespeare. People spend, all the statistical evidence suggests, more and more time doing the former. Poetry, it might be argued, does little legislating these days, unacknowledged or otherwise. Fewer and fewer people are decisively influenced by such reading as they do. Radio, television, cinema, popular music, and now the Internet—these are more decisive in shaping citizens' ethos and values, as well as in filling their minds and feelings with imaginary worlds. It is these

virtual realities rather than strictly literary ones that have most performative efficacy these days to generate people's feelings, behavior, and value judgments. To speak of literature's authority is already to speak, to some degree, of an historical epoch that began in the late seventeenth or early eighteenth century in Europe with the rise of modern democracies and their concomitant print cultures. That epoch is now perhaps rapidly vanishing, whatever teachers of literature say, write, or do. Nevertheless, if someone happens for some reason to pick up Hamlet, or Middlemarch, or Yeats's poems, these works may still exert their magic power. Literature still has great authority over me and over no doubt many others. Just what effects are the globalization of the university and the new regime of telecommunications having on literary study and on the social role of literature itself?

3 Jacques Derrida, in a striking passage written by one or another of the protagonists of La carte postale (The Post Card), says the following:

. . . an entire epoch of so-called literature, if not all of it, cannot survive a certain technological regime of telecommunications (in this respect the political regime is secondary). Neither can philosophy, or psychoanalysis. Or love letters. . .

4 Derrida's words in The Post Card perhaps generate in most readers the passions of disbelief and even scorn. What a ridiculous idea! We passionately and instinctively resist the statement that Derrida makes in such a casual and offhand way, as though it goes without saying. How could a change in something so superficial, mechanical, or contingent as the dominant means of preservation and dissemination of information, the change, to be precise, from a manuscript and print culture to a digital culture, actually bring to an end things that seem so universal in any civilized society as literature, philosophy, psychoanalysis, and love letters?

5 Derrida is claiming: the change in the "regime of telecommunications" does not simply transform but absolutely brings to an end literature, philosophy, psychoanalysis, and even love letters. It does this by a kind of death–dealing performative fiat: "Let there be no more love letters!" How in the world could this be? Insofar as Derrida's words, either those he said to the graduate student, or the words you or I read now in that book, generate the passions of fear, anxiety, disgust, incredulity, and secret desire, those words are a "felicitous" performative utterance. They do what they say and help bring about the end of literature, love letters, etc.

6 In spite of all his love for literature, Derrida's writings have certainly contributed to the end of literature as we have known it in a particular historical epoch and culture, say the last two or two and a half centuries in Europe and America. The concept of literature in the West has been inextricably tied to Cartesian notions of selfhood, to the regime of print, to Western-style democracies and notions of the nation-state, and to the right to free speech within such democracies. "Literature" in that sense began fairly recently, in the late seventeenth or early eighteenth century, and in one place, Western Europe. It could come to an end, and that would not be the end of civilization. In fact, if Derrida is right, and I believe he is, the new regime of telecommunications is bringing literature to

an end by transforming all those factors that were its preconditions or its concomitants.

7   Perhaps the most disturbing thing Derrida says in the passage I have cited is that in the power of the new regime of telecommunications to bring an end to literature, psychoanalysis, philosophy, and love letters, "the political regime is secondary." More exactly, Derrida says, "in this respect the political regime is secondary." "In this respect" means, I take it, that he does not deny, nor would I, the importance of political regimes, but that the power of the new regime of telecommunications is not limited or controlled, except in a "secondary" way, by the political regime of this or that nation.

8   Literary study certainly continues today "among the ruins" of the old nation-centered research university. Literary study, including comparative literature, is massively institutionalized in our colleges and universities. Thousands of professors have been trained and are still being trained to study literature and to teach the study of literature. Literary study seems to be safely and solidly ensconced in the curriculum. Nevertheless, in spite of the inertia that will keep what we have called literary study going for a few more years, the handwriting is on the wall. Literary study's time is up. Manifold changes are making it more and more obsolete, at least as it used to be organized, that is, as the study of canonical works, categorized by nationality and by chronological "periods," approached more or less thematically, without much exigent theoretical reflection, as an intimate part of the culture within which we dwell like bees in a honeycomb.

9   A massive paradigm shift is under way that will radically restructure literary study and make it no more than a component in new disciplinary configurations. This shift will of course occur according to different rhythms in different universities, or in different departments in the same university, or in different countries, but what is happening is irreversible.

10   Just what is bringing about these radical changes? Certain ambient factors define the placement of literary study today, just as a person's "subject position" defines the context within which he or she must act. That does not mean that we are helpless to take charge and determine the way things happen. We can devise new disciplinary configurations that will make for social amelioration, for example the empowering of women and minorities. I can choose to a considerable degree what and how I teach and do research. The circumambient changes do mean, however, that such acts will take place within the given context, in all its over determined, heterogeneous, and fluid complexity.

11   What are the salient features of this new context? Some are outside the university, some within it. The development of strong new theoretical reflection about literature, among other topics, by Bakhtin, Benjamin, Blanchot, Barthes, Foucault, Derrida, de Man, Jameson, and all the rest of that bunch (we know their names) was in part a response to a dislocation of literature that was already taking place even before World War II with the rise of a cinema— and then television—dominated culture. Instead of using literature or being used by it, unreflectively, we could now hold it at arm's length and think about it, "mention" it rather than "use" it. In part, however, the new theoretical reflection itself

brought about the displacement or marginalization of literature rather than simply mirroring it. The rise of cultural studies, impossible without that prior theoretical reflection, even though it often seems hostile to it, has delivered the second blow in the one-two punch that has knocked out old-fashioned literary study. For both theory and cultural studies literature is seen "critically," as a detached object of "study," in one way or another denatured. Seen this way, literature is deprived of the power it would have if it were taken for granted as an intimate part of a single homogeneous culture within which the citizens of a given nation live. To see literature "critically" may mean to "deconstruct" it by seeing the way it exemplifies certain theoretical presuppositions, or it may mean to see, critically, the way literature reinforces and creates an ideology—sexist, racist, nationalist, or classist—that is contested through the performative effects of its study.

12   We live now, as most people know, in the time after the end of the Cold War and the time of the globalization of economies. All the economies of the world are intertwined in new ways that have partly to do with the way markets are global, not national, just as corporations are now often transnational, not national, and partly with the way financial transactions and investments are globally intertwined. Globalization would also have been impossible without the new speed of communication and transportation. Now it is feasible to make something anywhere in the world, wherever labor is cheapest, and sell it anywhere else. The United States economy is dependent on the global economy. If economies around the world become depressed, then the global economy in which we want to be competitive no longer offers such opportunities to get rich. If we have a "downturn", that has a worldwide effect.

13   The end of the Cold War has meant that United States colleges and universities no longer have as their primary mission to make the United States better able to defeat the "Evil Empire". This now vanished mission included not only the technological side of university teaching and research but also the humanities. The National Endowment for the Humanities was explicitly founded by Congress to make the United States better in the humanities than the Soviet Union. We must be better than they in everything. Now the United States universities' mission, especially the mission of "research universities", is to help make the United States competitive in the global economy. United States universities are no longer so much covertly part of the military-industrial complex, as they were during the Cold War. They are now overtly part of a global technology complex.

14   What, one might ask, will be the role in this new university of literary study or of the humanities generally, cultural studies? The answer, I believe, is that the utility of such study will no longer be measured so much by its contribution to ideological indoctrination in national values as by its utility in helping us better understand our own country and all the others around the globe better so we can "be competitive in the global economy". Just how the study of Beowulf or Shakespeare will aid United States economic imperialism is not immediately apparent, at least not to me. Certainly the changes will give the study of English literature a radically different function from the older one that saw Shakespeare as part of our cultural heritage. One of the strange anomalies of literary

study in the United States is that, until recently at least, it was focused primarily on the literature of a foreign country that happens to speak the same language many of us do but that was a nation we defeated over two hundred years ago in a revolutionary war of independence. English literature was our basic resource for education in national values. In this respect at least, we went on acting like a colony for two hundred years after we ceased to be a colony. All that is rapidly changing now.

European Studies, Atlantic Studies, American Studies, Pacific Rim Studies, African Studies—literary study in a much-changed mode will, it appears to me, best survive in the new globalized university as a part of such new configurations. These will seem to have pragmatic value to those scientists, technicians, and bureaucrats who, to a considerable degree, run the university and to those corporate sponsors who to a considerable degree pay for it.

Independent Study Assistance

I. Words and Expressions

1. **squarely** *adv.*   fairly, justly, directly
2. **lip service** *n.*   an expression to show that sb. says he supports sth. although he does not really, especially when he does nothing to prove his support
3. **canonical** *adj.*   connected with works of literature that are highly respected
4. **tacit** *adj.*   not expressed or declared openly, but implied or understood
5. **performative** *adj.*   having to do with a statement that functions as an action
6. **ethos** *n.*   the moral ideas and attitudes that belong to a particular group or society
7. **virtual** *adj.*   of, pertaining to, or taking place in cyberspace or in virtual reality
8. **concomitant** *adj.*   happening at the same time as sth. else, especially because one thing is related to or causes the other
9. **contingent** *adj.*   depending on sth. that may or may not happen
10. **dissemination** *n.*   the act of spreading information, knowledge, etc. so that it reaches many people
11. **fiat** *n.*   an official order given by sb. in authority
12. **incredulity** *n.*   the act of showing an inability to believe sth
13. **felicitous** *adj.*   especially of words) chosen well; very suitable; giving a good result
14. **inextricably** *adv.*   impossible to separate
15. **ensconce** *v.*   to make oneself comfortable and safe in a place or position
16. **inertia** *n.*   lack of energy; lack of desire or ability to move or change
17. **manifold** *adj.*   many; of many different types
18. **exigent** *adj.*   needing urgent attention, or demanding too much from other people
19. **paradigm** *n.*   an example that serves as pattern or model
20. **configuration** *n.*   an arrangement of the parts of sth. or a group of things; the form or shape that this arrangement produces
21. **ambient** *adj.*   relating to the surrounding area; on all sides
22. **amelioration** *n.*   the state of being improved or becoming better; improvement
23. **heterogeneous** *adj.*   consisting of many different kinds of people or thing

24. **salient** *adj.*   most important or noticeable
25. **dislocation** *n.*   stopping a system, plan, etc. from working or continuing in the normal way
26. **homogeneous** *adj*   of the same or similar nature or kind
27. **feasible** *adj.*   that is possible and likely to be achieved
28. **downturn** *n.*   a fall in the amount of business that is done; a time when the economy becomes weaker
29. **indoctrinate** *v.*   to instruct, to teach
30. **covert** *adj.*   secret or hidden, making it difficult to notice
31. **overtly** *adv.*   open and observable, obviously
32. **anomaly** *n.*   departure from the regular arrangement, general rule, or usual method; abnormality
33. **configuration** *n.*   form or figure as determined by the arrangement of parts; contour; outline

II. Referential Points

J. Hillis Miller an American literary critic who has been heavily influenced by—and who has heavily influenced—deconstruction. He is Distinguished Research Professor of English and Comparative Literature at the University of California (Irvine), Chairman of the International Literary Theory Association, academician of the American Academy of Art and Science, member of the "Yale School" of deconstruction, and honorary professor of Tsinghua University. From the 1950s onward, Miller has made invaluable contributions to our understanding of the practice and theory of literary criticism, the ethics and responsibilities of teaching and reading, and the role of literature in the modern world. He has also shown successive generations of scholars and students the necessity of comprehending the relationship between philosophy and literature. His research interests are in the areas of Victorian literature, modern English and American literature of the nineteenth- and twentieth-centuries, comparative literature, and literary theory.

Chaucer (1343—1400) an English author, poet, philosopher, bureaucrat, courtier and diplomat. Although he wrote many works, he is best remembered for his unfinished frame narrative The Canterbury Tales. Sometimes called the father of English literature, Chaucer is credited by some scholars as the first author to demonstrate the artistic legitimacy of the vernacular English language, rather than French or Latin.

Shakespeare (1564—1616) an English poet and playwright, widely regarded as the greatest writer in the English language and the world's pre-eminent dramatist. He is often called England's national poet and the "Bard of Avon".

Wordsworth (1770—1850) a major English Romantic poet who, with Samuel Taylor Coleridge, helped to launch the Romantic Age in English literature with the 1798 joint publication Lyrical Ballads. He was England's Poet Laureate from 1843 until his death in 1850. Along with Coleridge and Southey, he came to be known as the "Lake Poets".

Yeats (1865—1939) an Irish poet, dramatist, and one of the foremost figures of 20th century literature. In 1923, he was awarded the Nobel Prize in Literature for what the Nobel Committee described as "inspired poetry, which in a highly artistic form gives expression to the spirit of a whole nation", the first Irishman so honored.

Jacques Derrida (1930—2004) a French philosopher born in Algeria, who is known as the founder of deconstruction. His voluminous work had a profound impact upon literary theory and continental philosophy. And his best known work is Of Grammatology.

about psychoanalysis a method, developed by Freud and others, of investigating mental processes and of treating neuroses and some other disorders of the mind: it is based on the assumption that such disorders are the result of the rejection by the conscious mind of factors that then persist in the unconscious as repressed instinctual forces, causing conflicts which may be resolved or diminished by discovering and analyzing the repressions and bringing them into consciousness through the use of such techniques as free association, dream analysis, etc.

The National Endowment for the Humanities an independent federal agency of the United States established by the National Foundation on the Arts and the Humanities Act of 1965 dedicated to supporting research, education, preservation, and public programs in the humanities.

III. Questions for Comprehension

1. What role does literature play in the society of telecommunication?
2. How much do you know about canonical works?
3. What is the function of Jacques Derrida's quotation? What does it have to do with the development of the whole essay?
4. What brings about the changes of literary study according to the author?
5. What is use of studying literary works in this competitive global economy?

Self-test

I. Fill in the blanks with the words and expressions provided, making some change when necessary.

lip service	ethos	virtual	concomitant	offhand	contingent
fiat	felicitous	inextricably	ensconce	inertia	manifold
ambient	canonical	downturn			

1. To combat the global economic _____, the government adopted a massive plan to adjust and reinvigorate the country's key industries.
2. Air temperature and _____ luminosity may fall slightly during the eclipse, but this will have little effect on daily activities.
3. The government sorted out and published the Kangyur, Tibetan _____ collection of Buddhist scriptures.
4. I looked up and saw Chang'e, and the jade hare in the moon, wondering there should be room enough to _____ the old lady with a spinning wheel who is so much a part of my own nursery lore.
5. The problems are _____ and intertwining, and have to be understood against a backdrop of historical development.
6. Naturally, he must pay _____ to the policy of the organization; otherwise, he would find himself very unpopular.
7. On a television show the Japanese prime minister even expressed formal, if _____, sympathy for "the injuries of the heart" of the comfort women.
8. Some young Chinese prefer to spend the holiday shopping online and enjoying _____ fireworks, instead of setting off firecrackers in the street.

9. _____ money has no particular value in use, not even a value in exchange except that which is decreed that it would have.
10. The author's devotion to Chinese history and literature pays off in the _____ portrayal of the bustling metropolis and tranquil countryside.
11. Many people in the middle class are uninsured and face the risks of catastrophic health care costs which can push families into huge debt with _____ suffering.
12. Urban development is all about making city life easier along with retaining its distinct cultural and historical _____.
13. Mental efficiency is _____ upon harmony; discord means confusion; therefore, he who would acquire power must be in harmony with Natural Law.
14. There should be no doubt today that climate change, agricultural land and food production are _____ linked.
15. The magnitude of the problem and the difficulty in finding a comprehensive solution for it should not force us into a state of _____.

II. Use the appropriate form of the words given in the brackets to fill in the blanks.
1. With blazing and _____ eyes she fairly withered him by demanding whatever he meant by speaking to respectable people that way. (scorn)
2. The wanton exposure of the personal lives of citizens by using immoral, even illegal behavior to _____ indecent information, is a serious violation of personal dignity. (dissemination)
3. The key operational objective of a foreign invasion and interference is first to _____ the national institutions and its unifying indigenous forces. (dislocation)
4. I _____ believed that I was taking a big risk with my health and maybe with my whole future. (covert)
5. Sea temperature _____ is a very important factor to the climate of 10-20 km high and its effect comes up to 9% of total variations. (normal)
6. From both the economical and technical point of view, it has a significant meaning to correctly and reasonably _____ the testing system and testify its specifications. (configuration)
7. People get _____ because some experts either lack or abuse the expertise they are supposed to possess. (incredulity)
8. We should build a cooperative relationship between countries that is as wide and as deep as possible so that differences may lose their _____. (salient)
9. However, because of the _____, the distribution and the dynamic of the grid, the resource management is a difficult problem. (heterogeneous)
10. Both sides will step up efforts on the _____ study on a free trade area so as to draw a good result to open a new chapter of bilateral economic and trade ties. (feasible)

III. Translating the short paragraph into Chinese.

What, one might ask, will be the role in this new university of literary study or of the humanities generally, cultural studies? The answer, I believe, is that the utility of such study will no longer be measured so much by its contribution to ideological indoctrination in national values as by its utility in helping us better understand our own country and all the others around the globe better so we can "be competitive in the global economy". Just how the study of

Beowulf or Shakespeare will aid United States economic imperialism is not immediately apparent, at least not to me. Certainly the changes will give the study of English literature a radically different function from the older one that saw Shakespeare as part of our cultural heritage. One of the strange anomalies of literary study in the United States is that, until recently at least, it was focused primarily on the literature of a foreign country that happens to speak the same language many of us do but that was a nation we defeated over two hundred years ago in a revolutionary war of independence.

IV. Analyze difficult sentences.
1. Perhaps the most disturbing thing Derrida says in the passage I have cited is that in the power of the new regime of telecommunications to bring an end to literature, psychoanalysis, philosophy, and love letters, "the political regime is secondary." More exactly, Derrida says, "in this respect the political regime is secondary."
2. Manifold changes are making it more and more obsolete, at least as it used to be organized, that is, as the study of canonical works, categorized by nationality and by chronological "periods," approached more or less thematically, without much exigent theoretical reflection, as an intimate part of the culture within which we dwell like bees in a honeycomb.
3. The development of strong new theoretical reflection about literature, among other topics, by Bakhtin, Benjamin, Blanchot, Barthes, Foucault, Derrida, de Man, Jameson, and all the rest of that bunch (we know their names) was in part a response to a dislocation of literature that was already taking place even before World War II with the rise of a cinema- and then television-dominated culture.
4. The rise of cultural studies, impossible without that prior theoretical reflection, even though it often seems hostile to it, has delivered the second blow in the one-two punch that has knocked out old-fashioned literary study.

V. Proofread the following passage.

The practice of literary theory become a profession in the 20th century, but it has historical roots that run far back as ancient Greece, ancient India, ancient Rome and medieval Iraq, and the aesthetic theories of philosophers from ancient philosophy through the 18th and 19th centuries are important influence on current literary study. The theory and criticism of literature are, of course, also closely tied to the history of literature.
The modern sense of "literary theory," however, dates only to approximate the 1950s, when the structuralist linguistics of Ferdinand de Saussure began strongly to influence English language literary criticism. The New Critics and various European-influenced formalists (particularly the Russian Formalists) had described some of their more abstract efforts as "theoretical" as well. But it was until the broad impact of structuralism began to be felt in the English-speaking academic world that "literary theory" was thought as a unified domain.

In the academic world of the United Kingdom and the United

1. _____
2. _____

3. _____

4. _____

5. _____
6. _____

States, literary theory was at its most popular from the late 1960s
through the 1980s. During this span of time, the literary theory was   7._____
perceived as academically cutting-edge, most university literature
departments sought to teach and study theory and incorporate it into
their curricula. Because of its meteoric rise on popularity and   8._____
the difficult language of its key texts, theory was also often
criticized as faddish or trendy obscurantism.Some scholars, both
theoretical and anti-theoretical, refer to the 1970s and 1980s
debates on the academic merits of theory "the theory of wars."   9._____

   By the early 1990s, the popularity of "theory" as a subject of
interest by itself was declining slightly even though as the texts   10._____
of literary theory were incorporated by the study of almost all
literature.

VI. Write a composition.

In spite of such ambient changes as globalization and telecommunications, literary study can still play its role. How well do you understand the author's ideas about literary study? Summarize his major points and write a composition to show your understanding of his ideas.

Unit 6

Man and Nature

Section A

Text One   The Obligation to Endure

Focal Consideration

1. In this now universal contamination of the environment, chemicals are the sinister and little-recognized part in changing the very nature of the world. Concentrate on the fact that chemicals kill not only so-called pests and weeds, but also potentially man himself.
2. The text sets a good example for argumentation. The author laid good foundation for people to believe that the chemicals have become a serious problem and in doing so convinced the readers that we have to make the right choice. Try to locate examples of counter-argument which are also obvious in the text.
3. The text is well-organized since all the parts are stringed under the main argument and the theme. Try to understand the author's main argument and how the author develops it in her writing.

Research Questions

Think about the following questions and discuss them with your group members. After your discussion, work out a research report and share it with the students of other groups.
1. This is an excerpt from *Silent Spring* which was a best-seller about the environment. Find out what is so special about the book.
2. The author Rachel Carson was an American marine biologist and nature writer whose writings are credited with advancing the global environmental movement. Gather information about her and try to find out her ideas on how to save our natural environment.
3. The title of the text is *The Obligation to Endure*. Why does the author think the human beings have such obligation and what are the obstacles for them to finish this task?
4. In this text, the author holds the idea that the misuse and overuse of chemicals endanger some species and even human beings themselves. What do you think of the use of

chemicals to extinguish weeds and pests? Do you think we should use the so-called pesticides? Will the use bring imbalance to our environment? Share your ideas.

The Obligation to Endure

By Rachel Carson

1 The history of life on earth has been a history of interaction between living things and their surroundings. To a large extent, the physical form and the habits of the earth's vegetation and its animal life have been molded by the environment. Considering the whole span of earthly time, the opposite effect, in which life actually modifies its surroundings, has been relatively slight. Only within the moment of time represented by the present century has one species—man—acquired significant power to alter the nature of his world.

2 During the past quarter century this power has not only increased to one of disturbing magnitude but it has changed in character. The most alarming of all man's assaults upon the environment is the contamination of air, earth, rivers, and sea with dangerous and even lethal materials. This pollution is for the most part irrecoverable; the chain of evil it initiates not only in the world that must support life but in living tissues is for the most part irreversible. In this now universal contamination of the environment, chemicals are the sinister and little-recognized partners of radiation in changing the very nature of the world—the very nature of its life. Strontium 90, released through nuclear explosions into the air, comes to earth in rain or drifts down as fallout, lodges in soil, enters into the grass or corn or wheat grown there, and in time takes up its abode in the bones of a human being, there to remain until his death. Similarly, chemicals sprayed on croplands or forests or gardens lie long in soil, entering into living organisms, passing from one to another in a chain of poisoning and death. Or they pass mysteriously by underground streams until they emerge and, through the alchemy of air and sunlight, combine into new forms that kill vegetation, sicken cattle, and work unknown harm on those who drink from once pure wells. As Albert Schweitzer has said, "Man can hardly even recognize the devils of his own creation." It took hundreds of millions of years to produce the life that now inhabits the earth—eons of time in which that developing and evolving and diversifying life reached a state of adjustment and balance with its surroundings. The environment, rigorously shaping and directing the life it supported, contained elements that were hostile as well as supporting. Certain rocks gave out dangerous radiation; even within the light of the sun, from which all life draws its energy, there were short-wave radiations with power to injure. Given time—time not in years but in millennia—life adjusts, and a balance has been reached. For time is the essential ingredient; but in the modern world there is no time. The rapidity of change and the speed with which new situations are created follow the impetuous and heedless pace of man

rather than the deliberate pace of nature. Radiation is no longer merely the background radiation of rocks, the bombardment of cosmic rays, the ultraviolet of the sun that have existed before there was any life on earth; radiation is now the unnatural creation of man's tampering with the atom. The chemicals to which life is asked to make its adjustment are no longer merely the calcium and silica and copper and all the rest of the minerals washed out of the rocks and carried in rivers to the sea; they are the synthetic creations of man's inventive mind, brewed in his laboratories, and having no counterparts in nature.

3   To adjust to these chemicals would require time on the scale that is nature's; it would require not merely the years of a man's life but the life of generations. And even this, were it by some miracle possible, would be futile, for the new chemicals come from our laboratories in an endless stream; almost five hundred annually find their way into actual use in the United States alone. The figure is staggering and its implications are not easily grasped—500 new chemicals to which the bodies of men and animals are required somehow to adapt each year, chemicals totally outside the limits of biologic experience.

4   Among them are many that are used in man's war against nature. Since the mid-1940s over 200 basic chemicals have been created for use in killing insects, weeds, rodents, and other organisms described in the modern vernacular as "pests"; and they are sold under several thousand different brand names. These sprays, dusts, and aerosols are now applied almost universally to farms, gardens, forests, and homes—nonselective chemicals that have the power to kill every insect, the "good" and the "bad", to still the song of birds and the leaping of fish in the streams, to coat the leaves with a deadly film, and to linger on in soil—all this though the intended target may be only a few weeds or insects. Can anyone believe it is possible to lay down such a barrage of poisons on the surface of the earth without making it unfit for all life? They should not be called 'insecticides', but 'biocides'. The whole process of spraying seems caught up in an endless spiral. Since DDT was released for civilian use, a process of escalation has been going on in which ever more toxic materials must be found. This has happened because insects, in a triumphant vindication of Darwin's principle of the survival of the fittest, have evolved super races immune to the particular insecticide used, hence a deadlier one has always to be developed—and then a deadlier one than that. It has happened also because, for reasons to be described later, destructive insects often undergo a "flareback", or resurgence, after spraying, in numbers greater than before. Thus the chemical war is never won, and all life is caught in its violent crossfire.

5   Along with the possibility of the extinction of mankind by nuclear war, the central problem of our age has therefore become the contamination of man's total environment with such substances of incredible potential for harm—substances that accumulate in the tissues of plants and animals and even penetrate the germ cells to shatter or alter the very material of heredity upon which the shape of the future depends.

6   Some would-be architects of our future look toward a time when it will be possible to alter the human germ plasm by design. But we may easily be doing so now by

inadvertence, for many chemicals, like radiation, bring about gene mutations. It is ironic to think that man might determine his own future by something so seemingly trivial as the choice of an insect spray. All this has been risked—for what? Future historians may well be amazed by our distorted sense of proportion. How could intelligent beings seek to control a few unwanted species by a method that contaminated the entire environment and brought the threat of disease and death even to their own kind? Yet this is precisely what we have done. We have done it, moreover, for reasons that collapse the moment we examine them. We are told that the enormous and expanding use of pesticides is necessary to maintain farm production. Yet is our real problem not one of overproduction? Our farms, despite measures to remove acreages from production and to pay farmers not to produce, have yielded such a staggering excess of crops that the American taxpayer in 1962 is paying out more than one billion dollars a year as the total carrying cost of the surplus-food storage program. And is the situation helped when one branch of the Agriculture Department tries to reduce production while another states, as it did in 1958, "It is believed generally that reduction of crop acreages under provisions of the Soil Bank will stimulate interest in use of chemicals to obtain maximum production on the land retained incrops." All this is not to say there is no insect problem and no need of control. I am saying, rather, that control must be geared to realities, not to mythical situations, and that the methods employed must be such that they do not destroy us along with the insects.

7   Much of the necessary knowledge is now available but we do not use it. We train ecologists in our universities and even employ them in our governmental agencies but we seldom take their advice. We allow the chemical death rain to fall as though there were no alternative, whereas in fact there are many, and our ingenuity could soon discover many more if given opportunity. Have we fallen into a mesmerized state that makes us accept as inevitable that which is inferior or detrimental, as though having lost the will or the vision to demand that which is good? Such thinking, in the words of the ecologist Paul Shepard, "idealizes life with only its head out of water, inches above the limits of toleration of the corruption of its own environment...Why should we tolerate a diet of weak poisons, a home in insipid surroundings, a circle of acquaintances who are not quite our enemies, the noise of motors with just enough relief to prevent insanity? Who would want to live in a world which is just not quite fatal?"

8   Yet such a world is pressed upon us. The crusade to create a chemically sterile, insect-free world seems to have engendered a fanatic zeal on the part of many specialists and most of the so-called control agencies. On every hand there is evidence that those engaged in spraying operations exercise a ruthless power. "The regulatory entomologists... function as prosecutor, judge and jury, tax assessor and collector and sheriff to enforce their own orders," said Connecticut entomologist Neely Turner. The most flagrant abuses go unchecked in both state and federal agencies. It is not my contention that chemical insecticides must never be used. I do contend that we have put poisonous and biologically

potent chemicals indiscriminately into the hands of persons largely or wholly ignorant of their potentials for harm. We have subjected enormous numbers of people to contact with these poisons, without their consent and often without their knowledge. If the Bill of Rights contains no guarantee that a citizen shall be secure against lethal poisons distributed either by private individuals or by public officials, it is surely only because our forefathers, despite their considerable wisdom and foresight, could conceive of no such problem.

9   I contend, furthermore, that we have allowed these chemicals to be used with little or no advance investigation of their effect on soil, water, wildlife, and man himself. Future generations are unlikely to condone our lack of prudent concern for the integrity of the natural world that supports all life. There is still very limited awareness of the nature of the threat. This is an era of specialists, each of whom sees his own problem and is unaware of or intolerant of the larger frame into which it fits. It is also an era dominated by industry, in which the right to make a dollar at whatever cost is seldom challenged. When the public protests, confronted with some obvious evidence of damaging results of pesticide applications, it is fed little tranquilizing pills of half truth. We urgently need an end to these false assurances, to the sugar coating of unpalatable facts. It is the public that is being asked to assume the risks that the insect controllers calculate. The public must decide whether it wishes to continue on the present road, and it can do so only when in full possession of the facts. In the words of Jean Rostand, 'The obligation to endure gives us the right to know.'

Preview Assistance

1. **lethal** *adj.*   able to cause or causing death; extremely dangerous
2. **sinister** *adj.*   making you feel that something bad or evil might happen
3. **fallout** *n.*   unpleasant result
4. **alchemy** *n.*   a type of chemistry, especially from about the years 1100 to 1500, which dealt with trying to find a way to change ordinary metals into gold and with trying to find a medicine which would cure any disease
5. **eon** *n.*   a period of time which is so long that it cannot be measured
6. **impetuous** *adj.*   likely to act on a sudden idea or wish, without considering the results of your actions
7. **tamper with**   to touch or make changes to something which you should not, usually without enough knowledge of how it works or when you are trying to damage it
8. **vernacular** *n.*   the form of a language that a regional or other group of speakers use naturally, especially in informal situations
9. **rodent** *n.*   any of various small mammals with large sharp front teeth, such as mice and rats
10. **escalate** *v.*   to make or become greater or more serious
11. **vindicate** *v.*   to prove that what someone said or did was right or true, after other people thought it was wrong
12. **resurgence** *n.*   a new increase of activity or interest in a particular subject or idea which had been

forgotten for some time
13. **crossfire** *n.*   bullets fired towards you from different directions
14. **inadvertently** *adv.*   not intentionally
15. **mutation** *n.*   a permanent change in an organism, or the changed organism itself
16. **mesmerize** *v.*   to have someone's attention completely so that they cannot think of anything else
17. **insipid** *adj.*   not having a strong taste or character, or having no interest or energy
18. **flagrant** *adj.*   (of a bad action, situation, person, etc.) shocking because of being so obvious
19. **sugar-coated** *adj.*   An announcement or promise that is sugar-coated is intended to seem positive or pleasant, although in fact it will result in something unpleasant or unacceptable.
20. **unpalatable** *adj.*   describes a fact or idea that is unpleasant or shocking and therefore difficult to accept

Referential Points

Silent Spring   A book written by Rachel Carson and published by Houghton Mifflin in September 1962. The book is widely credited with helping launch the environmental movement. The book was widely read (especially after its selection by the Book-of-the-Month Club and the *New York Times* best-seller list), and inspired widespread public concerns with pesticides and pollution of the environment. *Silent Spring* facilitated the ban of the pesticide DDT in 1972 in the United States. The book documented detrimental effects of pesticides on the environment, particularly on birds. Carson said that DDT had been found to cause thinner egg shells and result in reproductive problems and death. She also accused the chemical industry of spreading disinformation, and public officials of accepting industry claims uncritically. *Silent Spring* has been featured in many lists of the best nonfiction books of the twentieth century.

Rachel Carson   (1907—1964) was an American marine biologist and nature writer whose writings are credited with advancing the global environmental movement. Carson started her career as a biologist in the U.S. Bureau of Fisheries, and became a full-time nature writer in the 1950s. Her widely praised 1951 bestseller *The Sea Around Us* won her financial security and recognition as a gifted writer. In the late 1950s, Carson turned her attention to conservation and the environmental problems caused by synthetic pesticides. The result was *Silent Spring* (1962), which brought environmental concerns to an unprecedented portion of the American public. *Silent Spring* spurred a reversal in national pesticide policy—leading to a nationwide ban on DDT and other pesticides—and the grassroots environmental movement the book inspired led to the creation of the Environmental Protection Agency. Carson was posthumously awarded the Presidential Medal of Freedom by Jimmy Carter.

DDT   (from its trivial name, dichlorodiphenyltrichloroethane) is one of the most well-knownsynthetic pesticides. It is a chemical with a long, unique, and controversial history. First synthesized in 1874, DDT's insecticidal properties were not discovered until 1939. In the second half of World War II, it was used with great effect to control mosquitoes spreading malaria and lice transmitting typhus among civilians and troops, resulting in dramatic reductions in the incidence of both diseases. After the war, DDT was made available for use as an agricultural insecticide, and soon its production and use skyrocketed. In 1962, *Silent Spring* by American biologist Rachel Carson was published. The book catalogued the environmental impacts of the indiscriminate spraying of DDT in the US and questioned the logic of releasing large amounts of chemicals into the environment without fully understanding their effects on ecology or human health. *Silent Spring* resulted in a large public outcry that eventually led to most uses of DDT being banned in the US in 1972.

Survival of the Fittest a phrase which is commonly used in contexts other than intended by its first two proponents—British polymath philosopher Herbert Spencer (who coined the term) and Charles Darwin. Herbert Spencer first used the phrase—after reading Charles Darwin's *On the Origin of Species*—in his *Principles of Biology* (1864), in which he drew parallels between his own economic theories and Darwin's biological ones, writing "This survival of the fittest, which I have here sought to express in mechanical terms, is that which Mr. Darwin has called 'natural selection', or the preservation of favored races in the struggle for life." Darwin first used Spencer's new phrase "survival of the fittest" as a synonym for "natural selection" in the fifth edition of *On the Origin of Species*, published in 1869.

The Bill of Rights (a short title conferred by the Short Titles Act 1896, section 1 and the first schedule) is an act of the Parliament of England, whose title is *An Act Declaring the Rights and Liberties of the Subject and Settling the Succession of the Crown*. It is often called *the English Bill of Rights*. *The Bill of Rights* was passed by Parliament in December 1689 and was a re-statement in statutory form of *the Declaration of Right*, presented by the Convention Parliament to William and Mary in March 1688, inviting them to become joint sovereigns of England. It enumerates certain rights to which subjects and permanent residents of a constitutional monarchy were thought to be entitled in the late 17th century, asserting subjects' right to petition the monarch, as well as to bear arms in defense. It also sets out—or, in the view of its drafters, restates—certain constitutional requirements of the Crown to seek the consent of the people, as represented in parliament.

Consolidation Work

I. Fill in the blanks with the words and expressions provided, making some change when necessary.

lethal	lodge	impetuous	tamper with	vernacular	linger
heredity	inadvertence	mutation	mesmerize	insipid	flagrant
tranquilize	sugarcoat	sinister			

1. Mind and heart _____, and into them stepped Isabel, and she and I, hand in hand, walked fields of the west
2. She was fatally injured due to a _____ l stab to the chest.
3. She didn't _____ or offer explanations, but then again, maybe she didn't have to.
4. I mostly just loved the way they looked—but as I became more and more _____, my mind wandered into dangerously banal territory.
5. Even the English word _____ comes from the Latin sinestra, which means left.
6. The words that do creep through range from the inspired to the _____, and often work as just another texture added to the music.
7. I will never have plastic surgery and _____ God's masterpiece!

Section A

8. He was defending the Lamarckianism of Samuel Butler, who declared that our _____ was a kind of race-memory, a lapsed intelligence.
9. Smith was also fined $50,000 by the league for what it called a _____ violation of player safety rules.
10. The girl— _____, hot-blooded, excitable—poured out her love-talk like a bird singing.
11. Especially in areas of the body where cellular turnover is especially rapid, such as the digestive system, preventing DNA _____ translates into preventing cancer.
12. Speed is of the essence: the longer it _____, the more details emerge, proving this egg is rotten to the core.
13. Use of this _____ is a deliberate attempt to dehumanize and belittle. By doing so you sink to the level of those you oppose on so many subjects.
14. All the nuns seemed to her amiable, her _____ was all she needed, her food was excellent; her lessons gave her amusement.
15. If they were the effects merely of _____, and you do not, on reflection, approve of them, perhaps you may think it proper to write something for effacing the impressions made by them.

II. Use the appropriate form of the words given in the brackets to fill in the blanks.
1. _____ were a matter of indifference to them. (surround)
2. "The most commonly reported incidents were oil and chemical spills or _____, muddy or discolored water, illegally dumped rubbish and dead fish and other wildlife," the report said. (contaminate)
3. I perceived that she was _____, and yet I stood watching, watching, watching! (recover)
4. I fail to understand why somebody in science would use the word _____ which has a very definite meaning in the real world as well as in science, to characterize a time scale of a millennium. (reverse)
5. And Mr. Robinson winked _____, and the process seemed to relieve his mind and soothe his suspicions. (mystery)
6. I have struck the land of the Anakim, for the _____ are all of "tremendous" size, and indeed, "tremendous" in all their ways, more particularly in their religion. (inhabit)
7. It would seem as though the Germans had been lacking in the _____ which is so marked a feature of our modern civilization. (invent)
8. Whilst the _____ are a little scary, it's nice to see the reality of the EU painted so starkly. (implicate)
9. It was unclear whether the _____ was a final push before a ceasefire, as peace talks continued yesterday in Cairo where Israel's chief negotiator Amos Gilad arrived to hear the Hamas response to an Egyptian initiative. (escalate)
10. There have indeed been found persons who insist that the _____ was a really serious expression of the writer's own opinions. (vindicate)

III. Paraphrase the following sentences taken from the text.
1. The rapidity of change and the speed with which new situations are created follow the impetuous and heedless pace of man rather than the deliberate pace of nature.

2. Along with the possibility of the extinction of mankind by nuclear war, the central problem of our age has therefore become the contamination of man's total environment with such substances of incredible potential for harm—substances that accumulate in the tissues of plants and animals and even penetrate the germ cells to shatter or alter the very material of heredity upon which the shape of the future depends.
3. I am saying, rather, that control must be geared to realities, not to mythical situations, and that the methods employed must be such that they do not destroy us along with the insects.
4. Have we fallen into a mesmerized state that makes us accept as inevitable that which is inferior or detrimental, as though having lost the will or the vision to demand that which is good?
5. The crusade to create a chemically sterile, insect-free world seems to have engendered a fanatic zeal on the part of many specialists and most of the so-called control agencies.

IV. Test your general knowledge.

1. US president _____ created the Environmental Protection Agency?
   A. Richard Nixon   B. Franklin D. Roosevelt
   C. Jimmy Carter   D. John F. Kennedy
2. The Environmental Protection Agency banned DDT in the year _____.
   A. 1974   B. 1982   C. 1979   D. 1972
3. President _____ organized the first Earth Day.
   A. John F. Kennedy   B. Gaylord Nelson
   C. Rachel Carson   D. Al Gore
4. _____ percent of U.S. waste materials is potential compost.
   A. 11 percent   B. 23 percent   C. 47 percent   D. 72 percent
5. Transportation consumes about _____ percent of the total energy used in the United States.
   A. 10 percent   B. 25 percent   C. 33 percent   D. 50 percent
6. _____ percentage of the world's total water supply is fresh, accessible water?
   A. less than 1%   B. 5%—10%   C. 25%   D. 50%
7. The names of the primary federal and state regulatory agencies that work to protect the environment are _____,
   A. Environmental Protection Agency (the EPA) and the Department of Natural Resources' Environmental Protection Division
   B. Department of Health, Environment, and Safety (the DHES) and State Environmental Protection Agency
   C. National Environmental Agency (the NEA) and the Department of Agriculture
   D. Federal Pollution Control Agency (the FPCA) and the Department of Natural Resources' Pollution Prevention Assistance Division
8. World Environment Day (WED), established by the UN General Assembly in 1972 to mark the opening of the Stockholm Conference on the Human Environment is every _____.
   A. 5th of July   B. 6th of July   C. 5th of June   D. 6th of June
9. _____ consumes the most energy in the world.
   A. Russia   B. China   C. The United States   D. Canada
10. _____ produces the most energy in the world.
    A. Iraq   B. Saudi Arabia   C. The United States   D. Russia

Section A

11. _____ of the following is a greenhouse gas.
    A. Oxygen   B. Carbon Dioxide   C. Helium   D. nitrogen
12. The Earth is surrounded by an insulating layer of gases which protects it from the light and heat of the Sun. This insulating layer is called the _____.
    A. Hydrosphere   B. Biosphere   C. Lithosphere   D. Atmosphere
13. ENSO is a complex interaction between oceans and atmosphere that has far-reaching climatic, ecological, and climatic effects. ENSO means _____.
    A. El Niño Southern Osillation   B. El Niño Southern Oscillation
    C. El Nino Southern Oscillation   D. El Nino Southern Oscillization
14. _____ of the following has the least adverse effects to man and water life.
    A. pesticides   B. acid rain
    C. heavy metals like mercury or HG   D. heat
15. The layer of _____ protects earth from UV Rays?
    A. oxygen   B. nitrogen   C. ozone   D. hydrogen

V. Proofread the following passage.

    Under primitive agricultural conditions the farmer had few
insect problems. These arose with the intensification of agriculture—
the devotion of immense acreage to a single crop.   1. _____
Such a system set the stage for explosive increases
in specific insect populations. Single-crop farming does
not take advantage of the principles of which nature works;   2. _____
it is agriculture as an engineer might conceive to it to be.   3. _____
    Nature has introduced great variety into the landscape, but man
has displayed a passion for simplify it. Thus he undoes the   4. _____
built-in checks and balances by which nature holds the species
within bounds. One important natural check is limit on the amount   5. _____
of suitable habitat for each species. Obviously then, an insect
that lives on wheat can build up its population to much higher
levels on a farm devoted to wheat than on one in which wheat is
intermingled with other crops to which the insect is not adopted.   6. _____
    The same thing happens in another situations. A generation or   7. _____
more ago, the towns of large areas of the United States lined
their streets with the noble elm tree. Now the beauty they
hopefully created is threatened with complete construction as   8. _____
disease sweeps through the elms, carried by a beetle that would have
only limited chances to build up large populations and to spread   9. _____
from tree to tree if the elms were only occasional trees in a rich   10. _____
diversified planting.

VI. Write a composition.

    Read the text once more and summarize the author's point of view. Do you think her idea is reasonable? Write down your comments.

Further Development

1. Read Chapter One "A Fable for Tomorrow" and Chapter Eight "And No Birds Sing" from Silent Spring. Try to find out what tomorrow would be like if people continue to use some chemicals and what consequence would people face without birds singing in the future.
2. In China, people have been also using chemicals to extinguish the so-called pests and weeds. The natural environment has been damaged by those chemicals in various ways. Gather information about the chemical-using in China and compare your information with your classmates'. Do you have any suggestions on chemical-using in our country? Share your ideas with your classmates.

Section A   Text Two

The Good Earth

By Gregg Easterbrook

1 So here's the good news: Our air is cleaner, our lakes are purer, our forests are healthier, endangered species are recovering, toxic emissions are down, and acid rain has diminished dramatically. And yet, if you've looked at a newspaper or watched the evening news lately, you—like most Americans—might think our environment is under siege. Media coverage of the environment is heavy on doomsday, but the truth is not at all bleak: Nearly all environmental trends in the United States are positive and have been for years—if not decades.

2 Eco-legislation, green organizations, corporate cooperation and new inventions have all quietly steered our environment in a positive direction. We can't afford to be complacent, though—especially when it comes to greenhouse gases, since global warming is the one huge problem we haven't really tackled. But almost every measure taken by government agencies and grass-roots efforts to improve the environment has shown encouraging results—usually faster than expected and at a lower cost. Now that's good news.

3 Scientists and environmentalists think that even the worrisome fact of global warming can be ameliorated. There is a strong scientific consensus that the global warming threat requires action, but if current environmental trends persist and the reduction of most pollutants continues to be accomplished faster and more cheaply than expected, we may be able to control and reduce greenhouse gases in both affordable and practical ways.

4 Consider some of the environmental improvements the United States has witnessed over the last three decades. (Most environmental trends in Europe are positive too; the developing world, however, is a different story.)

Clean Air and Water
Improved Air Quality

5   Take a nice, big cleansing breath: According to the Environmental Protection Agency, emissions of the primary smog-causing chemicals from cars and trucks have declined 54 percent since 1970, even though the number of registered cars and trucks has more than doubled, from 108,407,000 to 230,428,000, and they are now driven one and a half times as far annually.

6   Keep breathing, because the fine particulates linked to respiratory disease, including those sometimes seen as soot, are down by about one-third since 1979 (though fewer cities were surveyed back then). The level of carbon monoxide, a dangerous odorless gas, is down 53 percent since 1970. And emissions of sulfur di-oxide, often the major culprit behind acid rain, are down 49 percent since 1970, despite the fact that the United States now burns far more coal, the main source of this pollutant.

7   These improvements have translated into better air quality for millions of Americans. Between 1976 and 1990, the Los Angeles area averaged some 150 days per year in violation of federal smog standards; in 2004, that figure dropped to just 27 violation days, the fewest ever for that city.

8   And, in case you are wondering, federal standards have become stricter, not weaker, during this period. Of course, there is more to be done—27 smog days in Los Angeles are still 27 too many, and Atlanta, Houston and other cities continue to experience air-pollution problems. But overall, air-quality trends are strongly positive. Now, exhale.

Better Water Quality

9   Other environmental trends are equally encouraging. Water quality has improved, too, and rates of waterborne disease are also in decline. It's hard to believe, but just a generation ago, factories and municipal plants actually discharged untreated wastewater directly into rivers; today, though some raw sewage often makes it to waterways, almost all wastewater in the United States is treated before discharge.

10   Even our largest metropolises have seen dramatic changes in their waterways. Remember when the filthy condition of Boston Harbor became a contentious issue in the 1988 presidential campaign? Today, Boston Harbor is sparkling again. The Potomac River, which in the 1960s literally gave off a stench, now boasts a thriving waterfront restaurant scene. And the Chicago River, a virtual open sewer in the 1960s, now hosts charming dinner cruises.

Species and Seedlings Rebound
Animals Are Back

11   While air and water quality have been steadily improving, life itself has been making a comeback. One reason many rates of cancer are declining today may be the ever-lower level of toxic chemicals to which people are exposed; toxic emissions by industry have diminished by a dramatic 55 percent since 1988.

12   But humans aren't the only creatures benefiting from an improved environment: Only one animal species is known to have gone extinct in the United States in the last 15 years, the dusky seaside sparrow. During that same period, numerous other species once described as certain to become extinct—including the Arctic peregrine falcon, the brown pelican, the gray whale, and the bald eagle, our beloved national emblem—have recovered sufficiently enough that they are no longer classified as imperiled. In the 1960s, bald eagles were rarely seen in the United States south of Alaska; now the great birds are commonly spotted in many states. Both the banning of DDT, which weakened birds' eggshells, and strict hunting laws have contributed to this success.

Forests Are Growing

13   Species are recovering partly due to the fact that the forested portion of the United States continues to remain stable, despite a recent real estate boom. High-yield agriculture has enabled millions of acres of farmland to be retired from cultivation and returned to forest.

14   For example, early in the 19th century, the state of Connecticut was 25 percent forest; today, Connecticut is fully 59 percent forested, though its population has increased twelvefold, from 275,000 to 3.46 million, since then. And Connecticut's wooded area is up even as its agricultural production has risen. Many other states show a similar dynamic of higher farm production coupled with stable forest acreage.

15   Steep reductions in acid rain have also boosted forest vitality. Twenty years ago, some people speculated that acid rain would cause a "new silent spring" in the Appalachian Mountains. These days, the health of the Appalachian forest is greatly improved, with a promising return of wild animals, including deer and black bears, and a rebound in tree cover and heartiness.

16   Steady environmental improvements have taken place across the board, regardless of which party is in the White House or controlling Congress. During the last four years, air pollution has continued to decline, improvements in technology have reduced emissions, the amount of protected lands is on the uptick, and deadly pollutants like dioxin are trending downward. And even more improvement is likely since the Bush Administration has imposed strict new rules that will reduce air pollution from diesel engines and diesel fuel.

How Did We Get Here?

17   A combination of technological inventions, government regulation, citizen activism and business innovations have, well, worked!

Innovation Goes Green

18   Invention has always been an important force in American history. When major reductions in automobile pollution were first mandated by the Clean Air Act of 1970, automakers either called the goals impossible or claimed that cars would become ruinously expensive. Then the catalytic converter was invented. This device reduces the level of many pollutants from automobile exhaust both cheaply and reliably.

19   Today, it is estimated that new cars and light trucks emit just 3 to 4 percent of the amount of pollution that a new car would have emitted in 1968, before regulation; soon cars emitting less than 1 percent could be seen driving around your neighborhood.

20   Other inventions, such as an enormous device known as the electrostatic precipitator, have reduced severe emissions from power-plant smokestacks, eliminated toxic substances from manufacturing processes, and replaced CFCs, the chemicals that cause ozone-layer depletion, with other more benign compounds. And by the way, the ozone layer appears to be restoring itself.

Legislation in Action

21   Government regulation has also been an important force in the drive to protect the environment. The reason the catalytic converter and other antipollution devices were invented in the first place is because the government required big reductions in pollution, via the Clean Air Act, Clean Water Act and other legislation. Some environmental regulation may be too cumbersome and needs to be streamlined—standards can vary wildly between regions—but there isn't any doubt that environmental regulation actually works.

Citizens for Change

22   Individual activism has been another important factor in the amazing progress we have seen in our natural world. Without the continued pressure from environmentalists, antipollution legislation would not have been enacted, and many pollution-reducing devices would not have been invented. Grass-roots organizations have been particularly essential to the ongoing creation and maintenance of new parks, wildlife refuges and protected forests.

Doing Business Better

Corporations Clean Up

23   Businesses that once resisted environmental rules now generally comply. When companies started losing lawsuits regarding their chemical emissions, the idea of toxic reduction became rather popular in corporate boardrooms. But many corporations today seem to have genuinely come to believe that environmental protection is good for the country, good for the economy and, therefore, good for business. Getting a head start on the future, several big manufacturers, such as Alcoa, Boeing and Whirlpool, have already taken steps to reduce their companies' greenhouse gas emissions.

24   Alcoa, for example, has initiated a plan to use improved technology to reduce its greenhouse gas emissions 25 percent by 2010. The company also has extensive tree-planting programs near many of its operations and service areas, and Alcoa helps fund environmental nonprofits. Boeing and Whirlpool, meanwhile, are working to meet emissions reduction targets even though no federal law yet requires this.

25   Business leaders, environmentalists, regulators and inventors working toward the same goal? That's certainly an odd mix—not clearly Republican or Democratic, not

clearly left-wing or right-wing. And maybe that's the biggest reason you rarely hear about environmental progress: Current trends do not fit any preconceived ideological notions. The political left wants to believe that industry is destroying the planet, and refuses to consider the evidence that business and the environment are making peace. The political right wants to believe that regulations are destroying the country, and refuses to consider the evidence that the longest period of economic expansion in American history occurred during the very period when pollution was in the midst of its big decline. However, today's reality—an improving environment without economic harm—does not fit with anyone's scare-tactic fund-raising or cheap-shot political campaigns.

Miles to Go...

26   Do the positive trends mean that environmental protection is no longer a concern? Absolutely not. Many problems remain, among them the loss of wildlife habitat in suburban expansion areas, chemical runoff from nearly unrestricted agriculture, and low miles-per-gallon SUVs, which cause waste by burning excessive gas. And, in the developing world, environmental problems of all sorts are at an emergency level—including lack of clean water, air pollution from unregulated cars and industry, and species loss. Beyond these setbacks stands the specter of artificially triggered climate change. Global warming may be the Super Bowl of environmental problems, since it could impact all of Earth.

27   But just bear this in mind: In every place where nations have imposed strict environmental standards, negative trends turned to positive very quickly. Earth, after all, has proved throughout the eons to be nothing if not resilient. This gives us good reason to hope that if we act to solve the environmental problems that still remain, we will achieve rapid progress against them too. Now that's a reason to say Happy Earth Day!

Independent Study Assistant

I. Words and Expressions
1. **toxic** *adj.*   poisonous
2. **emission** *n.*   when gas, heat, light, etc. is sent out
3. **siege** *n.*   the surrounding of a place by an armed force in order to defeat those defending it.
4. **bleak** *adj.*   If a situation is bleak, there is little or no hope for the future: The economic outlook is bleak.
5. **complacent** *adj.*   feeling so satisfied with your own abilities or situation that you feel you do not need to try any harder
6. **ameliorate** *v.*   to make a bad or unpleasant situation better
7. **respiratory** *adj.*   relating to breathing
8. **particulate** *n.*   an extremely small piece of dirt, especially one produced by road vehicles, which causes serious pollution
9. **odorless** *adj.*   without a smell: an odorless gas

10. **culprit** *n.* a fact or situation that is the reason for something bad happening
11. **metropolis** *n.* a very large city, often the most important city in a large area or country
12. **rebound** *v.* to bounce back after hitting a hard surface
13. **extinct** *adj.* not now existing
14. **imperil** *v.* to put something or someone at risk or in danger of being harmed or destroyed
15. **uptick** *n.* a transaction in the stock market at a price above the price of the preceding transaction
16. **mandate** *v.* to give official permission for something to happen
17. **preconceive** *v.* to conceive, or form an opinion of, beforehand; to form a previous notion or idea of
18. **specter** *n.* (the specter of sth) the idea of something unpleasant that might happen in the future
19. **eon** *n.* a period of time which is so long that it cannot be measured
20. **resilient** *adj.* able to quickly return to a previous good condition

II. Referential Points

The U.S. Environmental Protection Agency (EPA or sometimes USEPA) an agency of the federal government of the United States charged to regulate chemicals and protect human health by safeguarding the natural environment: air, water, and land. The EPA was proposed by President Richard Nixon and began operation on December 2, 1970, when its establishment was passed by Congress, and signed into law by President Nixon, and has since been chiefly responsible for the environmental policy of the United States. It is led by its Administrator, who is appointed by the President of the United States. The agency conducts environmental assessment, research, and education. It has the primary responsibility for setting and enforcing national standards under a variety of environmental laws, in consultation with state, tribal, and local governments. It delegates some permitting, monitoring, and enforcement responsibility to U.S. states and Native American tribes. EPA enforcement powers include fines, sanctions, and other measures. The agency also works with industries and all levels of government in a wide variety of voluntary pollution prevention programs and energy conservation efforts.

The Bald Eagle (the national emblem of the United States) In 1782, US Congress selected the bald eagle as the emblem of the newly formed United States, because it symbolized courage and might, and because it was indigenous only to the United States and to Canada. The national seal depicts the bald eagle with its wings spread, with one claw clutching an olive branch, and the other claw grasping arrows. The eagle, however, strikes different poses on other national depictions. The bald eagle owes its name to the early American colonists, and is bald in name only. As the white-headed American eagle differed from the European gray eagle, the colonists used their word for white, which translated into bald, in describing it. Unfortunately for the eagle, the literal translation, bald-headed, stuck like a toupee. Since ancient times, men have identified themselves with the eagle, because it creates an impression of majesty and of power while in flight. As early as 5,000 years ago, ancient Sumerians chose the eagle, in spread eagle form, as their emblem symbolizing their power. Ancient Romans followed suit, as did Emperor Charlemagne, and finally Napoleon. No doubt, Congress considered the eagle's historical pedigree as being the animal representing a nation's power, when selecting it to be the national emblem of the United States.

The Banning of DDT The pesticide DDT was banned in the United States in 1972 because it contributed to the near extinction of birds, including the bald eagle and the peregrine falcon. DDT is a persistent chemical that becomes concentrated in animal tissues, rising in concentration in animals that are higher in the food chain. It is particularly toxic to fish, aquatic invertebrates and insects (including some that are beneficial). While not immediately toxic to birds, DDT causes long-term reproductive problems by causing eggshells to weaken and crack, threatening the survival of many bird species. Because of its chemical nature, once DDT is applied in a field or other environment, it remains in an active form for decades. People throughout the United States still carry DDT and its metabolites in their bodies, 30 years after the pesticide was banned in this country. Most other developed countries have also banned DDT, but it is still used in many developing countries.

Acid Rain   rain or any other form of precipitation that is unusually acidic, i.e. elevated levels of hydrogen ions (low pH). It has harmful effects on plants, aquatic animals, and infrastructure. Acid rain is mostly caused by emissions of compounds of sulfur, nitrogen, and carbon which react with the water molecules in the atmosphere to produce acids. However, it can also be caused naturally by the splitting of nitrogen compounds by the energy produced by lightning strikes, or the release of sulfur dioxide into the atmosphere by phenomena of volcano eruptions.

Clean Air Act   A Clean Air Act describes one of a number of pieces of legislation relating to the reduction of smog and air pollution in general. The use by governments to enforce clean air standards has contributed to an improvement in human health and longer life spans. Critics argue it has also sapped corporate profits and contributed to outsourcing, while defenders counter that improved environmental air quality has generated more jobs than it has eliminated.

Clean Water Act   The Clean Water Act is the primary federal law in the United States governing water pollution. Commonly abbreviated as the CWA, the act established the goals of eliminating releases to water of high amounts of toxic substances, eliminating additional water pollution by 1985, and ensuring that surface waters would meet standards necessary for human sports and recreation by 1983.

Super Bowl   The Super Bowl is the championship game of the National Football League (NFL), the premier association of professional American football. In most years, the Super Bowl is the most-watched American television broadcast. Many popular singers and musicians have performed during the event's pre-game and halftime ceremonies. The day on which the Super Bowl is played is now considered to be a de facto American national holiday, called Super Bowl Sunday. Super Bowl Sunday is the second-largest U.S. food consumption day, after Thanksgiving Day. Exclusive television broadcast rights for the Super Bowl rotate each year among the major American television networks. Because of its high viewership, commercial airtime for the Super Bowl broadcast is the most expensive of the year. Due to the high cost of investing in advertising on the Super Bowl, companies regularly develop their most expensive (and ostensibly, best) advertisements for this broadcast. As a result, watching and discussing the broadcast's commercials has become a significant aspect of the event as well.

III. Questions for Comprehension

1. Why do you think most Americans have the impression that our environment is under siege? Do you have it? Why or why not?
2. According to the writer in Paragraph 2, what contributes to the betterment of our environment?

3. From which aspects does the writer prove his idea that our environment is getting better?
4. What improvements have translated into better air quality for millions of Americans?
5. From what facts can we tell that the Americans now have better water quality?
6. What are the two major reasons for the recovering of some species?
7. Which has the greater influence on the betterment of the environment, government regulation or citizen activism? Why?
8. Business leaders, environmentalists, regulators and inventors working toward the same goal. But in paragraph 22, the writer said "that's certainly an odd mix". Why? What do you think?
9. According to the writer, what is the biggest reason people rarely hear about environmental progress?
10. In the last paragraph, the writer stated the belief that we would achieve rapid progress against the environmental problems that still remained. How can we do that? What do you think?

Self-test

I. Fill in the blanks with the words and expressions provided, making some change when necessary.

emission	siege	complacent	ameliorate	respiratory	odorless
culprit	metropolis	extinct	imperil	mandate	comply
conceive	eon	resilient			

1. Unstructured play also helps kids manage stress and become _____, the college said in a release.
2. Instead of _____, they struck their horses with full force, and broke away from the Indians.
3. But they will _____ —if not terminate the experiment with un-backed fiat (or man-made) money that started in 1971.
4. The castle was under _____ for months.
5. Stolid and self-_____, theirs was an unquestioning faith, accepting, as they did, the Divine decrees as a Mohamedan accepts his fate.
6. It was one of the most beautiful and moving books I've read in _____, and I was sorry when it ended.
7. The facilities for a _____ should be adequate—a rich, fertile, and productive country surrounding it, with some great staple (which the world requires as a commodity) of exportation.
8. But we should find that; precisely in proportion as that slavery was _____, the power and prosperity of the country flourished.
9. It should be _____ —then we wouldn't need two or three tons of metal for protection.
10. We also know that poor exercise performance most often is associated with problems

Unit 6

involving the musculoskeletal, _____, and cardiovascular systems—these systems must be closely evaluated.

11. While power plants account for only a third of the carbon dioxide generated in the region, they're the easiest source to regulate because their _____ are already monitored in other pollution programs, said Peter Iwanowicz, director of the state Department of Environmental Conservation's Climate Change Office.

12. It is tasteless, _____, and colorless, and in high concentrations, it is a human health hazard.

13. She explains that because of GW, emperor penguins are at risk of extinction in Antarctic, apollo butterflies in Europe, harlequin frogs _____ in Central America, and so on.

14. The elegance and purity of his diction is the more remarkable as he was a Carthaginian by birth, and therefore spoke an idiom as diverse as can be _____ from the Latin in syntax, arrangement, and expression.

15. If you've been having trouble sleeping, the _____ might be your cholesterol-lowering medication.

II. Use the appropriate form of the words given in the brackets to fill in the blanks.

1. These root causes can include parasites, heavy metal _____ which is more common than you'd expect and organ congestion. (toxic)
2. The machine _____ a high-pitched sound when you press the button. (emission)
3. Your life changes _____ when you have a baby. (drama)
4. For Mr. Chesterton the _____ is all on the side of the pagans, and the beauty with the idealists. (bleak)
5. What annoys me about these girls is their _____ —they seem to have no desire to expand their horizons. (complacent)
6. This _____ is a necessary effect of the laws of nature; for, by the law of sensibility, man as invincibly tends to render himself happy as the flame to mount, the stone to descend, or the water to find its level. (ameliorate)
7. Sulphur dioxide is one of several _____ that are released into the atmosphere by coal-fired power stations. (pollute)
8. Philanthropy only dragged out the misery for those remaining in the "wild," said Caldwell; "their _____ will be a dispensation of kindness." (extinct)
9. On the other hill, two hundred yards across a somber precipice, I saw a line of high blackened stakes, showing here and there _____ —the remnants of Sheriff Ali's impregnable camp But it had been taken, though. (ruin)
10. The company said that it had always acted in _____ with environmental laws. (comply)

III. Translate the short paragraph into Chinese.

Do the positive trends mean that environmental protection is no longer a concern? Absolutely not. Many problems remain, among them the loss of wildlife habitat in suburban expansion areas, chemical runoff from nearly unrestricted agriculture, and low miles-per-gallon SUVs, which cause waste by burning excessive gas. And, in the developing world, environmental problems of all sorts are at an emergency level—including lack of clean water, air pollution fromunregulated cars and industry, and species loss. Beyond these setbacks stands the specter of artificially triggered climate change. Global warming may be the Super Bowl of environmental problems, since it could impact all of Earth.

IV. Analyze difficult sentences.
1. Media coverage of the environment is heavy on doomsday, but the truth is not at all bleak: Nearly all environmental trends in the United States are positive and have been for years—if not decades.
2. Scientists and environmentalists think that even the worrisome fact of global warming can be ameliorated.
3. Other inventions, such as an enormous device known as the electrostatic precipitator, have reduced severe emissions from power-plant smokestacks, eliminated toxic substances from manufacturing processes, and replaced CFCs, the chemicals that cause ozone-layer depletion, with other more benign compounds. And by the way, the ozone layer appears to be restoring itself.
4. The political left wants to believe that industry is destroying the planet, and refuses to consider the evidence that business and the environment are making peace.

V. Proofread the following passage.

  President Barack Obama's new Environmental Protection Agency chief Lisa Jackson has moved to put CO2 and other greenhouse gases up   1. _____
regulation by the Clean Air Act. In one of the most anticipatedly early   2. _____
actions by the new Administration, the EPA issued a proposed finding on April 17 that these gases endanger human health and well-being. When made final, this will clear to the way for regulation of vehicle exhaust,   3. _____
which is the source of about 30 percent of US carbon dioxide emissions.

  This is one of the most visibility of the climate actions springing from   4. _____
members of the President's new Cabinet, which include leading scientists   5. _____
and informed diplomats. As they took their posts, working scientists
announced in two international meetings that many factors in rapidly   6. _____
global warming were getting worse or running at rates which only a few years ago were thought to be extreme.

  Besides Jackson, who was an experienced state environment leader
before taking over EPA, Obama appointed former EPA head   7. _____
Carol Browner to a new post of White House climate and energy
chief; Nobel Prize winner Stephen Chu as Secretary of Energy; Harvard
professor John Holdren, who has been outspeaking on the dangers   8. _____
of climate disruption, as Presidential science advisor; and acclaimed
ocean scientist Jane Lubchenco as head of NOAA.

  Secretary of State Hillary Clinton replaced George Bush's
footdragging international climate negotiators with a team lead by Todd
Stern. One of his first actions was to announce at international   9. _____
climate talks in Bonn that "the science is clear, and the threat is real.
The facts on the ground are outstripping the worst case scenarios.
The costs of inaction-or adequate actions-are unacceptable."   10. _____

Unit 6

VI. Write a composition.

Write a summary about 500 words. You are suggested to follow the common steps of writing an effective summary: Read carefully; reread, label and underline; write, revise and edit.

Section B

Text One   The Story of an Eyewitness: The San Francisco Earthquake

Focal Consideration

1. There are some earthquake hazards like ground shaking, ground placement, flooding and fire. The focal points of the content will be the discussions of the hazards and effects of earthquake.
2. In a vivid first-person account, London shows how and why the 1906 San Francisco earthquake and resulting fire would be remembered as one of the worst natural disasters in U.S. history. Discussion will lie on the narrative skills London used in this text.

Research Questions

Think about the following questions and discuss them with your group members. After your discussion, work out the research report and share it with the students of other groups.

1. How much do you know about Jack London? Work out a brief report about his life experience, his major works and his influence as a writer.
2. What do you know about earthquake? Have you ever experienced or heard of another earthquake which also caused great damages to people's lives and properties? Share your story with your partner.
3. Gather information about the San Francisco Earthquake and try to understand why the 1906 San Francisco earthquake and resulting fire would be remembered as one of the worst natural disasters in U.S. history.
4. The story seems discursive. However, Jack London organized his work in a way which tied all the minor parts in a necklace. Try to work out the clue.

The Story of an Eyewitness: The San Francisco Earthquake

By Jack London

1   The earthquake shook down in San Francisco hundreds of thousands of dollars worth of walls and chimneys. But the conflagration that followed burned up hundreds of millions

of dollars' worth of property. There is no estimating within hundreds of millions the actual damage wrought. Not in history has a modern imperial city been so completely destroyed. San Francisco is gone. Nothing remains of it but memories and a fringe of dwelling-houses on its outskirts. Its industrial section is wiped out. Its business section is wiped out. Its social and residential section is wiped out. The factories and warehouses, the great stores and newspaper buildings, the hotels and the palaces of the nabobs, are all gone. Remains only the fringe of dwelling houses on the outskirts of what was once San Francisco.

2 Within an hour after the earthquake shock the smoke of San Francisco's burning was a lurid tower visible a hundred miles away. And for three days and nights this lurid tower swayed in the sky, reddening the sun, darkening the day, and filling the land with smoke.

3 On Wednesday morning at a quarter past five came the earthquake. A minute later the flames were leaping upward. In a dozen different quarters south of Market Street, in the working-class ghetto, and in the factories, fires started. There was no opposing the flames. There was no organization, no communication. All the cunning adjustments of a twentieth century city had been smashed by the earthquake. The streets were humped into ridges and depressions, and piled with the debris of fallen walls. The steel rails were twisted into perpendicular and horizontal angles. The telephone and telegraph systems were disrupted. And the great water-mains had burst. All the shrewd contrivances and safeguards of man had been thrown out of gear by thirty seconds' twitching of the earth-crust.

The Fire Made its Own Draft

4 By Wednesday afternoon, inside of twelve hours, half the heart of the city was gone. At that time I watched the vast conflagration from out on the bay. It was dead calm. Not a flicker of wind stirred. Yet from every side wind was pouring in upon the city. East, west, north, and south, strong winds were blowing upon the doomed city. The heated air rising made an enormous suck. Thus did the fire of itself build its own colossal chimney through the atmosphere. Day and night this dead calm continued, and yet, near to the flames, the wind was often half a gale, so mighty was the suck.

5 Wednesday night saw the destruction of the very heart of the city. Dynamite was lavishly used, and many of San Francisco proudest structures were crumbled by man himself into ruins, but there was no withstanding the onrush of the flames. Time and again successful stands were made by the fire-fighters, and every time the flames flanked around on either side or came up from the rear, and turned to defeat the hard–won victory.

6 An enumeration of the buildings destroyed would be a directory of San Francisco. An enumeration of the buildings undestroyed would be a line and several addresses. An enumeration of the deeds of heroism would stock a library and bankrupt the Carnegie medal fund. An enumeration of the dead will never be made. All vestiges of them were

destroyed by the flames. The number of the victims of the earthquake will never be known. South of Market Street, where the loss of life was particularly heavy, was the first to catch fire.

7   Remarkable as it may seem, Wednesday night while the whole city crashed and roared into ruin, was a quiet night. There were no crowds. There was no shouting and yelling. There was no hysteria, no disorder. I passed Wednesday night in the path of the advancing flames, and in all those terrible hours I saw not one woman who wept, not one man who was excited, not one person who was in the slightest degree panic stricken.

8   Before the flames, throughout the night, fled tens of thousands of homeless ones. Some were wrapped in blankets. Others carried bundles of bedding and dear household treasures. Sometimes a whole family was harnessed to a carriage or delivery wagon that was weighted down with their possessions. Baby buggies, toy wagons, and go-carts were used as trucks, while every other person was dragging a trunk. Yet everybody was gracious. The most perfect courtesy obtained. Never in all San Francisco's history, were her people so kind and courteous as on this night of terror.

A Caravan of Trunks

9   All night these tens of thousands fled before the flames. Many of them, the poor people from the labor ghetto, had fled all day as well. They had left their homes burdened with possessions. Now and again they lightened up, flinging out upon the street clothing and treasures they had dragged for miles.

10   They held on longest to their trunks, and over these trunks many a strong man broke his heart that night. The hills of San Francisco are steep, and up these hills, mile after mile, were the trunks dragged. Everywhere were trunks with across them lying their exhausted owners, men and women. Before the march of the flames were flung picket lines of soldiers. And a block at a time, as the flames advanced, these pickets retreated. One of their tasks was to keep the trunk-pullers moving. The exhausted creatures, stirred on by the menace of bayonets, would arise and struggle up the steep pavements, pausing from weakness every five or ten feet.

11   Often, after surmounting a heart-breaking hill, they would find another wall of flame advancing upon them at right angles and be compelled to change anew the line of their retreat. In the end, completely played out, after toiling for a dozen hours like giants, thousands of them were compelled to abandon their trunks. Here the shopkeepers and soft members of the middle class were at a disadvantage. But the working-men dug holes in vacant lots and backyards and buried their trunks.

The Doomed City

12   At nine o'clock Wednesday evening I walked down through the very heart of the city. I walked through miles and miles of magnificent buildings and towering skyscrapers. Here was no fire. All was in perfect order. The police patrolled the streets. Every building had its watchman at the door. And yet it was doomed, all of it. There was no water. The

dynamite was giving out. And at right angles two different conflagrations were sweeping down upon it.

13   At one o'clock in the morning I walked down through the same section. Everything still stood intact. There was no fire. And yet there was a change. A rain of ashes was falling. The watchmen at the doors were gone. The police had been withdrawn. There were no firemen, no fire-engines, no men fighting with dynamite. The district had been absolutely abandoned. I stood at the corner of Kearney and Market, in the very innermost heart of San Francisco. Kearny Street was deserted. Half a dozen blocks away it was burning on both sides. The street was a wall of flame. And against this wall of flame, silhouetted sharply, were two United States cavalrymen sitting their horses, calming watching. That was all. Not another person was in sight. In the intact heart of the city two troopers sat their horses and watched.

Spread of the Conflagration

14   Surrender was complete. There was no water. The sewers had long since been pumped dry. There was no dynamite. Another fire had broken out further uptown, and now from three sides conflagrations were sweeping down. The fourth side had been burned earlier in the day. In that direction stood the tottering walls of the Examiner building, the burned-out Call building, the smoldering ruins of the Grand Hotel, and the gutted, devastated, dynamited Palace Hotel.

15   The following will illustrate the sweep of the flames and the inability of men to calculate their spread. At eight o'clock Wednesday evening I passed through Union Square. It was packed with refugees. Thousands of them had gone to bed on the grass. Government tents had been set up, supper was being cooked, and the refugees were lining up for free meals.

16   At half past one in the morning three sides of Union Square were in flames. The fourth side, where stood the great St. Francis Hotel was still holding out. An hour later, ignited from top and sides the St. Francis was flaming heavenward. Union Square, heaped high with mountains oftrunks, was deserted. Troops, refugees, and all had retreated.

A Fortune for a Horse!

17   It was at Union Square that I saw a man offering a thousand dollars for a team of horses. He was in charge of a truck piled high with trunks from some hotel. It had been hauled here into what was considered safety, and the horses had been taken out. The flames were on three sides of the Square and there were no horses.

18   Also, at this time, standing beside the truck, I urged a man to seek safety in flight. He was all but hemmed in by several conflagrations. He was an old man and he was on crutches. Said he: "Today is my birthday. Last night I was worth thirty thousand dollars. I bought five bottles of wine, some delicate fish and other things for my birthday dinner. I have had no dinner, and all I own are these crutches."

19   I convinced him of his danger and started him limping on his way. An hour later, from a distance, I saw the truck-load of trunks burning merrily in the middle of the street.

20   On Thursday morning at a quarter past five, just twenty-four hours after the earthquake, I sat on the steps of a small residence on Nob Hill. With me sat Japanese, Italians, Chinese, and negroes—a bit of the cosmopolitan flotsam of the wreck of the city. All about were the palaces of the nabob pioneers of Forty-nine. To the east and south at right angles, were advancing two mighty walls of flame.

21   I went inside with the owner of the house on the steps of which I sat. He was cool and cheerful and hospitable. "Yesterday morning," he said, "I was worth six hundred thousand dollars. This morning this house is all I have left." It will go in fifteen minutes. He pointed to a large cabinet. "That is my wife's collection of china. This rug upon which we stand is a present. It cost fifteen hundred dollars. Try that piano. Listen to its tone. There are few like it. There are no horses. The flames will be here in fifteen minutes."

22   Outside the old Mark Hopkins residence a palace was just catching fire. The troops were falling back and driving the refugees before them. From every side came the roaring of flames, the crashing of walls, and the detonations of dynamite.

The Dawn of the Second Day

23   I passed out of the house. Day was trying to dawn through the smoke-pall. A sickly light was creeping over the face of things. Once only the sun broke through the smoke-pall, blood-red, and showing quarter its usual size. The smoke-pall itself, viewed from beneath, was a rose color that pulsed and fluttered with lavender shades Then it turned to mauve and yellow and dun. There was no sun. And so dawned the second day on stricken San Francisco.

24   An hour later I was creeping past the shattered dome of the City Hall. Than it there was no better exhibit of the destructive force of the earthquake. Most of the stone had been shaken fromthe great dome, leaving standing the naked framework of steel. Market Street was piled high with the wreckage, and across the wreckage lay the overthrown pillars of the City Hall shattered into short crosswise sections.

25   This section of the city with the exception of the Mint and the Post-Office, was already a waste of smoking ruins. Here and there through the smoke, creeping warily under the shadows of tottering walls, emerged occasional men and women. It was like the meeting of the handful of survivors after the day of the end of the world.

Preview Assistance

1. **conflagration** *n.*   a fire that burns over a large area and destroys property
2. **wipe out**   to wipe out something such as a place or a group of people or animals means to destroy them completely
3. **lurid** *adj.*   too bright in color, in a way that is not attractive

4. **ghetto** *n.* an impoverished, neglected, or otherwise disadvantaged residential area of a city, usually troubled by a disproportionately large amount of crime
5. **perpendicular** *adj.* forming an angle of 90 with another line or surface; upright and going straight up
6. **contrivance** *n.* something that somebody has done or written that does not seem natural; the fact of seeming artificial
7. **enumeration** *n.* the act of counting
8. **harness** *v.* to put a harness on a horse or other animal; to attach a horse or other animal to something with a harness
9. **caravan** *n.* a vehicle without an engine that can be pulled by a car or van. It contains beds and cooking equipment so that people can live or spend their holidays in it
10. **fling** *vi.* to move (oneself) violently with impatience, contempt, or the like
11. **bayonet** *n.* a daggerlike steel weapon that is attached to or at the muzzle of a gun and used for stabbing or slashing in hand-to-hand combat
12. **surmount** *v.* to mount upon; get on the top of; mount upon and cross over
13. **silhouette** *n.* any outline or sharp shadow of an object
14. **totter** *v.* to move without being stable, as if threatening to fall
15. **cosmopolitan** *adj.* composed of people from or at home in many parts of the world; especially not provincial in attitudes or interests
16. **flotsam** *n.* the floating wreckage of a ship
17. **nabob** *n.* a wealthy man (who made his fortune in the Orient)
18. **detonation** *n.* an explosion or sudden report made by the instantaneous decomposition or combustion of unstable substances
19. **mauve** *n.* a moderate purple
20. **dun** *n.* a color partaking of a brown and black

Referential Points

Jack London (1876—1916) was an American author who wrote *The Call of the Wild*, *White Fang*, and *The Sea Wolf* along with many other popular books. A pioneer in the then-burgeoning world of commercial magazine fiction, he was one of the first Americans to make a lucrative career exclusively from writing.

The San Francisco Earthquake The San Francisco earthquake of 1906 was a major earthquake that struck San Francisco, CA and the coast of Northern California at 5:12 A.M. on Wednesday, April 18, 1906. It ruptured along the San Andreas Fault both northward and southward for a total of 296 miles (477 km). Shaking was felt from Oregon to Los Angeles, and inland as far as central Nevada. The earthquake and resulting fire is remembered as one of the worst natural disasters in the history of the United States. The death toll from the earthquake and resulting fire, estimated to be above 3,000, is the greatest loss of life from a natural disaster in California's history. The economic impact has been compared with the more recent Hurricane Katrina.

The Carnegie Medal The Carnegie Medal is awarded annually to the writer of an outstanding book for children. Carnegie set up more than 2800 libraries across the English speaking world and, by the time of his death, over half the library authorities in Great Britain had

Carnegie libraries. It was first awarded to Arthur Ransome for Pigeon Post. The winner receives a golden medal and £500 worth of books to donate to a library of their choice.

Union Square Union Square is a 2.6 acres (11,000 m^2) plaza bordered by Geary, Powell, Post and Stockton Street in San Francisco, California. It also refers to the central shopping, hotel, and theater district that surrounds the plaza for several blocks. The name "Union Square" stems from the fact that the area was once used for rallies and support for the Union Army during the Civil War. Today, this one-block plaza and nearby area is one of the largest collection of department stores, upscale boutiques, tourist trinket shops, art galleries, and salons in the Western United States, which continue to make Union Square a major tourist draw, a vital, cosmopolitan place in downtown San Francisco, and one of the world's premier shopping districts. Grand hotels and small inns, as well as repertory, off-Broadway and single-act theaters also contribute to the area's dynamic, 24-hour character.

Nob Hill refers to a small district in San Francisco, California adjacent to the intersection of California and Powell streets (and the respective cable car lines). Nob Hill is an affluent district, home to many of the city's upper class families. Sometimes it is sarcastically referred to as Snob Hill (in fact, "Nob" is shortened from "nabob," a 19th century slang term synonymous with "snob"). The area was settled in the rapid urbanization happening in the city in the late 19th century. Because of the views and its central position, it became an exclusive enclave of the rich and famous on the west coast who built large mansions in the neighborhood.

Consolidation Work

I. Fill in the blanks with the words and expressions provided, making some change when necessary.

wipe out	contrivance	conflagration	harness	totter
perpendicular	lighten up	surmount	crosswise	imperial
ghetto	twitch	retreat	intact limp	

1. Every time I'd ask the question, it seemed he _____ a bit more.
2. "There are only two creatures," says a proverb, "who can _____ the pyramids—the eagle and the snail."
3. The song depicted an example of a kid's tragic fate to us, but I guess it is a miniature of all the underprivileged people, who lived in the _____ or other humble shelters.
4. In the lower part it was formed of close wood-work nailed _____, and had openings in the upper by way of windows.
5. Thus we are told how in India the mimosa is known as the _____ tree on account of its remarkable properties, being credited as an efficacious charm against all sorts of malignant influences, such as the evil eye.
6. There's nothing like a vacation to motivate yourself to _____ your "to do" list. Want nothing hanging over you.
7. Still, even with the phrase _____, the Common Article 3 restrictions against torture and "outrages upon personal dignity" were removed.
8. Government is a _____ of human wisdom to provide for human wants.

9. At length, however, after terrible destruction of property and the loss of many lives, the fury of the _____ was arrested.
10. For many dogs, a _____ is an important piece of equipment used in their everyday life.
11. Woe! woe to us all; our thrones are _____, they will surely fall if we do not ruin this evil-doer who threatens us all With a fearful groan, the queen fell fainting into the arms of Countess Ogliva.
12. Dancing is a _____ expression of a horizontal desire.
13. His lifted tail was _____, his lips were drawn back from the red gums, and I saw his great white fangs.
14. Is Tangle another hot Internet site or just a community living for itself and _____ into a religious ghetto?
15. This man descending the stairs with a _____ was the Commandant Marnier, of the 193rd Regiment, wounded in 1915, and now attached to the General Staff.

II. Use the appropriate form of the words given in the brackets to fill in the blanks.
1. But as to whether or not your _____ is accurate, I believe my point still stands. (estimate)
2. Neither the press nor the _____ was able to assess his policy critically. (oppose)
3. One of the most humiliating things in life is when another seems to offer his friendship _____, and we are unable to respond. (lavish)
4. Some are _____, with intent to list all significant articles in a subject. (enumerate)
5. He said a pickup truck with the keys in the _____ was also stolen and has not been recovered. (ignite)
6. This year's overall increase in real property value—_____, commercial and industrial—was 24 percent over the last revaluation four years ago. (resident)
7. They broke up with faint _____, and being damp with human mud, they refused to flame, and merely smoked with growing intensity. (detonate)
8. His other _____ were an ebony walking stick with a gold head and what he referred to in moments of expansion as his "library." (possess)
9. There will be no distorted or inaccurate knowing in heaven, but neither will we ever _____ know the infinite God. (exhaust)
10. He was uneducated, but he possessed that exact knowledge of mankind that makes leaders; and his _____ was the result of caution and suspicion. (shrewd)

III. Paraphrase the following sentences taken from the text.
1. Remains only the fringe of dwelling houses on the outskirts of what was once San Francisco.
2. And the great water-mains had burst. All the shrewd contrivances and safeguards of man had been thrown out of gear by thirty seconds' twitching of the earth-crust.
3. Now and again they lightened up, flinging out upon the street clothing and treasures they had dragged for miles.
4. The exhausted creatures, stirred on by the menace of bayonets, would arise and struggle up the steep pavements, pausing from weakness every five or ten feet.
5. In that direction stood the tottering walls of the Examiner building, the burned-out Call building, the smoldering ruins of the Grand Hotel, and the gutted, devastated, dynamited Palace Hotel.

Unit 6

IV. Test your general knowledge.

1. The Father of American literature was _____.
   A. Mark Twain   B. Washington Irving   C. Walt Whitman   D. Jack London
2. _____ of the following works is not written by Jack London.
   A. *Moby Dick*   B. *The Call of the Wild*   C. *White Fang*   D. *The Sea Wolf*
3. Jack London is best known for his books about _____ including *The Call of the Wild*.
   A. The east.   B. The west.   C. The north.   D. The south.
4. Jack London also designed and built a ship which sailed out of San Francisco Bay to the South Pacific in 1907. The ship's name is _____.
   A. "Snarl"   B. "Bark"   C. "Snail"   D. "Snark"
5. San Francisco is the fourth most populous city in California and the 12th most populous city in the United States, with a 2008 estimated population of 808,976. It is the _____ most densely populated major city in the U.S.
   A. second   B. third   C. first   D. fourth
6. The largest earthquake of the twentieth century occurred along the coast of the continent of _____.
   A. North America   B. Asia   C. South America   D. Africa
7. _____ of the following describes the build up and release of stress during an earthquake.
   A. the Modified Mercalli Scale   B. the elastic rebound theory
   C. the principle of superposition   D. the travel time difference
8. The first seismic instruments accurate enough to be used in the scientific study of earthquakes were invented in the 1880s in _____.
   A. United States   B. England   C. Japan   D. China
9. _____ of the following can be triggered by an earthquake.
   A. tsunami   B. intense ground shaking
   C. a landslide   D. all of the above
10. _____ developed the procedure used to measure the size of an earthquake.
    A. Charles Richter   B. James Hutton
    C. Charles Darwin   D. Henri Darcy
11. Earthquakes occur in the layer of _____.
    A. Troposphere   B. Lithosphere   C. Asthenosphere   D. Mesosphere
12. The plate of _____ in the Earth's crust causes the most earthquakes.
    A. North American plate   B. Pacific plate
    C. Eurasian plate   D. Antarctic plate
13. _____ of the United States West Coast is most due for a big earthquake.
    A. Oregon   B. Northern California
    C. Central California   D. Southern California
14. _____ of the following phenomena occurred with the 2004 Indonesian earthquake.
    A. The Indian Ocean water level dropped
    B. Sumatra became smaller in size
    C. The Earth's rate of rotation was altered
    D. The Earth's oceans became less salty
15. A typical initial earthquake lasts for _____.
    A. 10 seconds   B. One minute   C. 10 minutes   D. One half hour

V. Proofread the following passage.

At almost precise 5:12 a.m., local time, a foreshock occurred with insufficient force to be felt widely throughout the San Francisco Bay area. The great earthquake broke loose some 20 to 25 seconds later, with an epicenter near San Francisco. Violent shocks punctuated the strong shaking which lasted some 45 to 60 seconds. The earthquake was felt from southern Oregon to south of Los Angeles and inland as far as central Nevada. The highest Modified Mercalli Intensities (MMI's) of VII to IX paralleled the length of the rupture, extended as far as 80 kilometers inland from the fault trace. One important characteristic of the shaking intensification noted in Lawson's (1908)report was the clear correlation of intensity with underlying geologic conditions. Areas situated in sediment-filled valleys sustained stronger shaking than nearby bedrock sites, and the strongest shaking occurred in areas that ground reclaimed from San Francisco Bay failed in the earthquake. Modern seismic-zonation practice accounting for the differences in seismic hazard posed by various geologic conditions.

As a basic reference about the earthquake and the damage it caused to, geologic observations of the fault rupture and shaking effects, and other consequences of the earthquake, the Lawson (1908) report remains the authoritative work, as well as arguably the most important study of a single earthquake.

On the public's mind, this earthquake is perhaps remembered most for the fire it spawned in San Francisco, giving the somewhat misleading appellation of the "San Francisco earthquake".

1. _____
2. _____
3. _____
4. _____
5. _____
6. _____
7. _____
8. _____
9. _____
10. _____

VI. Write a composition.

Read the text once more and write a summary about 500 words which should be in a descriptive chronology of events.

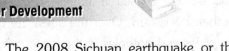

Further Development

1. The 2008 Sichuan earthquake or the Great Sichuan Earthquake was a deadly earthquake that measured at 8.0 Ms and 7.9 Mw occurred at 14:28:01.42 on May 12, 2008 in Sichuan province of China and killed at least 68,000. Compare the two earthquakes and try to find out the effects and aftermaths of great earthquakes. Write a summary of what you learn or feel from reading materials about earthquakes.
2. An earthquake can take away a lot of people's lives and properties. After the earthquake, plagues often haunt the survivors. Gather information about how to help the survivors of earthquakes to reconstruct their homes and confidence for life. Share your ideas with your classmates.

Section B Text Two

Dam Brea

By William M. Hendryx

Underwater

1   A wave of water 30 feet high spun Jerry Toops like a tornado. Debris battered and cut him. He fought to keep his head up, using all the strength in his legs and upper body to swim, angling across the ripping current toward a line of cedar trees. The night was as black as the water, the trees vague shadows against an ebony sky. As he was swept toward the cedars, Toops grabbed a limb and held on. Wood, pieces of plaster and litter slammed him, accumulating around his waist like flotsam against a pole in a breakwater. The rubble weighed him down. He was an outdoorsman with strong, callused hands, but inch by inch, the weight and force of the water pulled his hand down the tree limb, stripping the leaves.

2   Just when he could hold on no longer, the debris gave way, and Toops pulled himself into the swaying treetop. Clinging there, exhausted, wearing only his undershorts in the spitting snow and 32-degree chill, he was limp with fatigue. He was alive, but as he surveyed the rampaging water, he was certain his wife and babies were dead.

3   Bedtime came early for the Toops family at their three-bedroom brick ranch house nestled in a forested valley in Johnson's Shut-Ins State Park. At 8 p.m. Lisa Toops put the three kids to bed. She and Jerry, superintendent of the park, followed soon after. Self-reliant and religious, they were used to a work cycle that more closely followed the sun than the flow of commuter traffic. Jerry was a real "ranger type," rugged, fit, good with his hands. His outdoorsman's beard was just beginning to gray at the edges.

4   The 42-year-old naturalist loved the park, with its strange formations of igneous rock called shut-ins. A billion years ago volcanic activity caused a granite upheaval and confined, or "shut-in," the Black River in southeast Missouri. Over the ages, the trapped water carved spectacular gorges, natural water slides and potholes in the hard rock. In the summertime, the park was a magnet for swimming, camping and hiking, but now, in the weeks before Christmas, all was quiet.

5   At 4 a.m. that December 14, 2005, the baby awoke, softly crying to be fed. Lisa brushed hersandy hair away from sleepy green eyes, plucked Tucker from his crib near their bedroom and retreated down the hall to the living room sofa to nurse him. Normally, after feeding she'd put him back in his crib, but this night they both fell asleep on the couch.

6   An hour later, Lisa bolted awake. There was a booming roar—loud, then soft, then loud again—a huge tornado, she thought. She tucked the infant under one arm and jumped up. "Jerry, get the kids!" She figured the basement was their only hope. She ran

to Tanner's room. The five-year-old was climbing from his bed, awakened by the bedlam. She yelled to him to come, extending her hand, but before she could grasp him, a barrage of water rushed into the house.

7   It coursed around her ankles, her knees. In seconds the water level was above her chest. Lisa held the baby over her head as the surge filled the room. She didn't know what was happening, but tried to stay calm for her kids. "Hang on to the bed!" she called to Tanner, fighting to stay upright in the flood. The water kept rising, relentlessly. "Hold your breath, baby!" she called over the din. In the next moment, they were in liquid darkness.

8   "Jerry—!" That was all Jerry Toops had heard of Lisa's cry to "get the kids." The sharp urgency in her voice sliced through his sleep a moment before the roar cut off the rest of her sentence. The noise. It sounded like a squadron of jet aircraft flying through the house. Jerry's feet hit the floor, and in that same instant, the back wall of the bedroom exploded, slamming him back. A second later, the opposite wall blew out, heaving him and the bed in reverse. He was deep underwater.

9   Intuitively, he swam upward—10 feet, 20, 30, before surfacing in a sea of uprooted trees, Sheetrock, furniture, and granite boulders the size of SUVs. It looked like the Biblical Flood, everything destroyed. He swam to a portion of rooftop that floated nearby and climbed on. "Lisa! Tanner! Tara! Tucker!" he called, but couldn't hear his own voice above the rushing water. Praying to see just one head bob to the surface, he knew the odds were all wrong. He was strong and agile, and it had taken all he had to escape. What chance did they have?

10 It seemed forever. Underwater, Lisa Toops fought for her life and the lives of Tucker and Tanner. She had no idea where Tara, her three-year-old, was. The thought was terrible. She pushed it aside and focused.

In Shock

11 As suddenly as it had crested, the water began to recede. Lisa's head came into air. Gasping, she looked up to see the roof splinter and crack open like an eggshell. A way out where there had been none. She hugged the infant with one arm and swam toward the opening with the other. Where was Tanner? She'd lost her firstborn child amid the chaos. Kick your feet, baby, she thought, hoping he would remember the swimming lessons he'd had that summer. Kick your feet.

12 Within moments, she and the infant washed free of the crumbling house, riding what amounted to a tsunami in the wintry pitch of night.

13 Thirty seconds earlier, he'd been sound asleep. Now Jerry Toops was in a battle for his life. The section of rooftop he'd stood on buckled beneath him, and he dropped back into the swirling waves. Finally, he managed to grab onto the cedar tree and climb from the water. His body was battered and numbed by the freezing chill.

14 Toops strained his eyes in the dark night. He knew what had happened. He'd foreseen the possibility. He'd even prepared, devising an evacuation plan in case a

natural disaster ruptured the dam on the mountaintop less than two miles from their home. His job required it, but his choice to live there had put his family at risk. He blamed himself for their deaths.

15   Toops was only half-correct about the flood. The dam had ruptured, cascading 1.5 billion gallons—6 million tons—of water into a narrow valley, leveling everything in its path, including an entire hardwood forest. But it was not a natural disaster that released the monster. It was a man-made flaw.

16   Completed in 1963, the dam had concrete walls 90 feet tall. It was part of the Taum Sauk hydroelectric generating facility owned by the local utility. A fail-safe mechanism had gone awry, allowing the reservoir to overfill. Runoff eroded the soil beneath one edge of the basin, and it crumbled, washing the Toops family away.

17   Captain Ryan Wadlow of the volunteer fire department in Lesterville was just leaving for his job as a heavy-equipment operator when the emergency pager sounded around 5:50 a.m. Wadlow stood 6' 7" and weighed 327 pounds. To strangers he looked threatening; friends and neighbors knew him for his soft heart.

18   Living close by, Wadlow was first on the scene. He didn't know it, but roughly 45 minutes had elapsed since the Toops family had been swept from their home. He parked his truck and slogged through knee-deep mud and water, tracing the reflected ruin with his flashlight.

19   Everything in this valley, usually so familiar to him, was unrecognizable. Divested. Scraped away. A stretch of the elevated road was covered in six inches of sludge. A towering wall of uprooted trees had been deposited near the edge of a bridge spanning the Black River. On the opposite side of the roadway from where the family's home had been, several vehicles littered a sodden field as if they'd been dropped from the sky.

20   Just then, in the silence of predawn, came a faint cry for help. A man's voice, desperate and shaking with cold. "Where are you?" Wadlow called back. "Help," was the only reply, repeated again and again.

21   Shining a path with his flashlight, Wadlow trudged a quarter-mile through light rain and spitting snow into the field, stumbling up to his calves in muck, listening for the voice.

22   Seven minutes later, he found himself under a tree. The voice was coming from above. A man, deathly ashen, wearing only undershorts, was clinging to the upper limbs. He was bleeding and covered with silt and leaves, and appeared to be in shock.

23   Wadlow stretched to his full height, helped Jerry Toops to the ground, and gave him his coat. "Are you the park superintendent?" he asked.

24   "Yes," said Toops.

25   "Anybody with you?" asked Wadlow. Toops mumbled something unintelligible as Wadlow's two-way radio crackled. Other members of the volunteer department were now on the scene, including Chief Ben Meredith and veteran Gary Maize, looking for survivors.

"Are They Alive?"

26   Wadlow escorted Toops to the edge of the flood-scoured field and had another

volunteer take him to an ambulance. Then Wadlow returned to search. Meanwhile, Gary Maize and two others had begun hunting about a half-mile north of Wadlow and the command post.

27 With one weak flashlight between them, Maize's group inched through a minefield of slimy waste and barbed-wire fences. "Anybody out there?" Maize shouted. Then he said to the others, "Shhh! I heard something." He killed his radio and listened intently. Slowly, deliberately, he scanned the field with the light. Just ahead there was something in the rubble.

28 Wearing only a nightshirt, Lisa Toops sat limp and incoherent on the soggy ground near the far perimeter of the field about a half-mile from where her home once stood. She held the gurgling infant tightly to her chest, while five-year-old Tanner lay apparently lifeless across her legs. Neither stirred nor spoke. They had been stranded there in the rain and snow for an hour and ten minutes.

29 "Ma'am, are you all right?" Maize asked. Clearly she was not. He took the baby and cleared its air passages of mud and leaves. Another firefighter wrapped Tanner in his coat and felt for a pulse. He couldn't find one.

30 Ryan Wadlow had by now joined the others. He lifted Lisa into his arms and carried her toward rescue vehicles at the edge of the field.

31 One of the volunteers asked her, "Ma'am, how many children do you have?" Lisa was unresponsive, refusing to let go of Wadlow's neck. "How many children, ma'am?"

32 Lisa seemed to come awake. "I have three ..." she said, and then her voice trailed off into silence.

33 Somehow, in all the tumult, she'd managed to hold on to her baby. And, miraculously, she'd snagged Tanner as he washed by her, crying for help. But she had not seen or heard anything of Tara, her sweet little girl.

34 After turning Lisa over to volunteers, Wadlow slogged back to the spot where she'd been found. He stood in the stillness for a moment. Then he heard a weak whimper. A child! He followed the sound. Sloshing through mud, some 30 feet away, he came to a cedar tree. There beneath the boughs, almost invisible under silt and rubbish, lay a little girl in muddy brown pajamas. He came closer and shone his light. Her blue eyes were wide open; her breath came in shallow rasps. Wadlow swept her up and hurried to the ambulance.

35 Back down the road near the command post, an anguished Jerry Toops was being tended in the other ambulance when word filtered in that they'd "found the baby and little girl." Toops thought that meant their bodies had been found. Dreading the answer, he asked, "Are they alive?"

36 "Yes," came the reply.

37 For the first time that night, Jerry Toops wept.

38 The sun rose behind the mountains. Ten minutes later, he learned that Lisa and Tanner were also alive.

39　　　The family members were gathered like pieces of driftwood and taken to the local medical center. From there, they were transferred to Cardinal Glennon Hospital in St. Louis. All were suffering from hypothermia and were covered with cuts and bruises—except Tara, who survived without a scratch. Tanner was in the worst shape. An EMT described his condition as "not compatible with life." But the medical team kept working and after almost two hours of CPR, he was revived. Tucker and Tara were hospitalized for six days, Tanner two weeks. Everyone recovered.

Independent Study Assistance

I. Words and Expressions
1. **debris** *n.*   broken or torn pieces of something larger
2. **batter** *v.*   to hit and behave violently towards a person, especially a woman or child, repeatedly over a long period of time, or to hit something with force many times
3. **ebony** *adj.*   black
4. **flotsam** *n.*   pieces of broken wood and other waste materials found on the beach or floating on the sea
5. **rampage** *v.*   to go through an area making a lot of noise and causing damage
6. **rugged** *adj.*   (of land) wild and not even; not easy to travel over
7. **igneous** *adj.*   (of rocks) formed from magma (= very hot liquid rock that has cooled)
8. **upheaval** *n.*   (a) great change, especially causing or involving much difficulty, activity or trouble
9. **pothole** *n.*   a deep hole formed underground in limestone areas by the gradual rubbing and dissolving action of water flowing through the stone
10. **bedlam** *n.*   a noisy situation with no order
11. **squadron** *n.*   a unit of one of the armed forces, especially (in Britain) the air force or the navy
12. **intuitive** *adj.*   able to know or understand something because of feelings rather than facts or proof
13. **recede** *v.*   to move further away into the distance, or to become less clear or less bright
14. **splinter** *n.*   a small sharp broken piece of wood, glass, plastic or similar material
15. **tsunami** *n.*   an extremely large wave caused by movement of the Earth under the sea, often caused by an earthquake (= when the Earth shakes)
16. **rupture** *v.*   to (cause to) explode, break or tear
17. **cascade** *v.*   to fall quickly and in large amounts
18. **divest** *v.*   to sell something, especially a business or a part of a business
19. **sludge** *n.*   soft wet soil or a substance that looks like this
20. **sodden** *adj.*   (of something which can absorb water) extremely wet
21. **silt** *n.*   sand or soil which is carried along by flowing water and then dropped, especially at a bend in a river or at a river's opening
22. **unintelligible** *adj.*   not able to be understood
23. **escort** *v.*   to go with someone or a vehicle especially to make certain that they arrive safely or that they leave a place
24. **unresponsive** *adj.*   not responsive (= reacting quickly or positively to something)
25. **trail** *v.*   to move slowly and without energy or enthusiasm

26. **tumult** *n.*   a loud noise, especially that produced by an excited crowd, or a state of confusion, change or uncertainty
27. **whimper** *n.*   a series of small weak sounds expressing pain or unhappiness
28. **rasp** *n.*   a rough unpleasant noise, like metal being rubbed against metal
29. **anguish** *n.*   extreme unhappiness caused by physical or mental suffering
30. **hypothermia** *n.*   a serious medical condition in which a person's body temperature falls below the usual level as a result of being in severe cold for a long time
31. **compatible** *adj.*   able to exist, live together, or work successfully with something or someone else

II. Referential Points

Johnson's Shut-Ins State Park   A Missouri state park on the Black River in Reynolds County. The term "shut in" refers place where the river's breadth is limited by hard rock resistant to erosion. In these shut-ins the river cascades in many rivulets over and around igneous rocks worn smooth over many eons. It used by park visitors as a natural water park when the water is not so high as to be dangerous. One and a half billion years ago, hot volcanic ash and gases spewed into the air, then cooled, forming igneous rock. Later, shallow seas covered the rock, depositing sedimentary rock. The area was uplifted and erosion exposed the volcanic rock. Waters of the East Fork Black River became confined, or "shut-in," to a narrow channel. Water-borne sand and gravel cut deeply even into this erosion-resistant rock, carving potholes, chutes and canyon-like gorges. Most of the park, including the shut-ins and two miles of river frontage, was assembled over the course of 17 years and donated to the state in 1955 by Joseph Desloge (1889—1971), a St. Louis civic leader and conservationist from a prominent lead mining family.

The Biblical Flood   God observes that the earth is corrupted with violence and decides to destroy all life. But Noah "was a righteous man, blameless in his generation, [and] Noah walked with God," and God gives him instructions for the construction of an ark, into which he is told to bring "two of every sort [of animal] ... male and female," and their food. God instructs Noah to board the Ark with his family, and seven pairs of the birds and the clean animals, and two pairs of the unclean animals, and "on the same day all the fountains of the great deep were broken up, and the windows of heaven were opened, and the rain was upon the earth," and God closes up the door of the Ark. The flood begins, and the waters prevail until all the high mountains are covered fifteen cubits deep, and all the people and animals and creeping things and birds of the heavens are blotted out from the earth, and only Noah and those with him in the Ark remain.

Taum Sauk Mountain   In the Saint Francois Mountains is the highest point in the U.S. state of Missouri, 1,772 feet (540 m) above mean sea level. The topography of Taum Sauk is that of a somewhat flat ridge rather than a peak. While not as impressive at 1,772 feet (540 m) as other peaks, Taum Sauk and the St. Francois range are true mountains, being the result of a volcanic orogeny. Whereas vertical relief in the rest of the Ozarks region is the result of erosion of sedimentary strata, the St. Francois are an ancient Precambrian igneous uplift several times older than the Appalachians. Geologists believe that Taum Sauk and its neighbors may be among the few areas in the US never to have been submerged in ancient seas. The peaks of the St. Francois range existed as islands in the shallow seaway throughout most of the Paleozoic Era as the sandstones, limestones, and shales typical of the Ozarks were deposited. Weathering and erosion of these ancient peaks provided the clastic sediments of the surrounding rock layers.

EMT (Emergency medical technician) A term used in various countries to denote a healthcare provider trained to provide pre-hospital emergency medical services. The precise meaning of the term varies by jurisdiction, but in many countries EMTs respond to emergency calls, perform certain medical procedures and transport patients to hospital in accordance with protocols and guidelines established by physician medical directors. They may work in an ambulance service (paid or voluntary), as a member of technical rescue teams, or as part of an allied service such as a fire or police department. EMTs are trained to assess a patient's condition, and to perform such emergency medical procedures as are needed to maintain a patent airway with adequate breathing and cardiovascular circulation until the patient can be transferred to an appropriate destination for advanced medical care. Interventions include cardiopulmonary resuscitation, defibrillation, controlling severe external bleeding, preventing shock, body immobilization to prevent spinal damage, and splinting of bone fractures.

CPR (Cardiopulmonary resuscitation) An emergency first aid protocol for a victim of cardiac arrest. It can be performed by trained lay persons or by healthcare or emergency response professionals. It is normally begun on an unbreathing unconscious person and continued until action can be taken to restart the heart or otherwise diagnose the problem. CPR essentially consists of a pattern of chest compressions and rescue breaths (i.e. artificial blood circulation and lung ventilation) and is intended to maintain a trickle of oxygenated blood to the brain and the heart and thereby extend the otherwise brief window of opportunity for successfully restarting the heart without permanent brain damage. CPR itself is not intended to restart the heart but must be performed continuously until medical responders can attempt to restart the heart by other means.

III. Questions for Comprehension
1. The story seems to begin a little sudden. Paragraph 3 is a flashback. What do you think of the beginning? What are the advantages of using flashbacks?
2. From the first four paragraphs, we can have a glimpse of Jerry's character. Can you summarize it?
3. Where were the family members when the disaster happened?
4. What was Lisa doing when the water came and what was her first response?
5. In paragraph 9, the writer commented: "It looked like the Biblical Flood". Why do you think the writer used this simile?
6. What was the reason of the disaster?
7. Who was the first on the scene? What did he do when he got there?
8. How was Jerry saved?
9. Where were Lisa and the kids when they were rescued? How were they?
10. Where was the third child? How was she found?

Self-test

I. Fill in the blanks with the words and expressions provided, making some change when necessary.

debris	batter	ebony	rampage	upheaval	splinter
tsunami	rupture	cascade	elapse	sodden	escort
trail off	tumult	compatible			

1. Panelists tackled questions such as balancing the need to innovate with the need to be _____, as well as pondering.
2. He had made an early start, as he wanted to be back before the men began work, and the air hung round one and against one's cheek like a _____ blanket in the dusky dawn.
3. At ten thousand feet the pressure of gas had become so great that the silk envelope was _____, and the terrified travelers realized that they were falling rapidly.
4. She had merely run home—_____, of course, through the perils of the wood—to impart her great news and bring her mother back to lunch, which Roy persistently called "tiffin."
5. There was a momentary _____, a spasm, and a struggle; but the tightly-rolled blanket clung to the unfortunate man like cerements There was no noise, no outcry, no sound of struggle.
6. The bathing glow, like a _____ waterfall, washed clean the shame he felt in his body.
7. Among the first to be taken from the _____ was a lady, and a little girl about two years old.
8. Woods such as _____, sandalwood, cherry, brier, box, pear-tree, lancewood, and many others, are all good for the carver, but are better fitted for special purposes and small work.
9. It also revealed that rather than being a single big wave, the _____ was an initial big one followed by hours of choppy sloshing.
10. His voice _____ weakly and we could not hear the rest of what he said.
11. Amidst wars and _____, and the depredations of banditti without and around, it remains secure and inviolate and inviolable.
12. One road we could not find at all, so _____ was the countryside; and so after five and a half hours' wandering, we returned to a dinner of soup, steak, stewed fruit, and cocoa.
13. And if possible pass us a bottle of water, some minutes _____—three long, slow minutes of it—intense anxiety.
14. For the wind howled now like a _____ demon; it tore at them in hot anger; it dragged at the coat about her head, and when her clutch resisted, it flung the sand over and over her till she lay half buried and choking.
15. The wood is valuable for its toughness; it seldom _____, and will bear a greater weight than the wood of most other trees.

II. Use the appropriate form of the words given in the brackets to fill in the blanks.

1. This _____ (accumulate), which is greatest in the surface soil, is due to decaying

244 Unit 6

leaves dropped during the growth of clover, and to an abundance of roots, containing, when dry, from one and three-fourths to two per cent of nitrogen 6.

2. We understand ourselves _____ (intuition), and we understand men by study, yet we are made the receivers, not the givers; the chosen, not the choosers.
3. Other effects of the _____ (explode) were the striking of some stones and the leads of the dormer window which carries the frame of a clock, as also some small windows.
4. This _____ (mechanic) was altogether too successful, for, after using it some time, he found his third finger so badly crippled that he was forced to give up hope of ever winning fame on the concert stage.
5. Occasional slopes of the type have had the soil covering entirely removed by _____ (erode), and here, where the clay appears on the surface, the soil is very poor.
6. Down in the street below a newsboy was yelling _____ (intelligible), and in the distance a barrel-organ jangled the latest music-hall craze; but he was deep, deep in an abyss of suffering, very far below the surface of things.
7. The shadow or the _____ (reflect) is a representation of its original, but without material substance See, it lies there, wavering, on the rock, or in the water.
8. It seemed as though some string had snapped, leaving half his nature broken, _____ (respond), and dumb.
9. For the former it is necessary merely that the persons introduced have business interests in common—which are much more easily determined than social _____ (compatible), which is the requisite necessary for the latter.
10. He was _____ (recognize), with his head wrapped in his aviation cap and his face concealed by his goggles.

III. Translate the short paragraph into Chinese.

Everything in this valley, usually so familiar to him, was unrecognizable. Divested. Scraped away. A stretch of the elevated road was covered in six inches of sludge. A towering wall of uprooted trees had been deposited near the edge of a bridge spanning the Black River. On the opposite side of the roadway from where the family's home had been, several vehicles littered a sodden field as if they'd been dropped from the sky.

IV. Analyze difficult sentences.

1. He fought to keep his head up, using all the strength in his legs and upper body to swim, angling across the ripping current toward a line of cedar trees.
2. He was an outdoorsman with strong, callused hands, but inch by inch, the weight and force of the water pulled his hand down the tree limb, stripping the leaves.
3. Shining a path with his flashlight, Wadlow trudged a quarter-mile through light rain and spitting snow into the field, stumbling up to his calves in muck, listening for the voice.

V. Proofread the following passage.

The UN climate change conference, to be held in Copenhagen in December, should provide the climax to two years of international negotiations to reach to a new treaty aimed at addressing the   1. _____

causes and consequences of greenhouse gas (GHG) emissions.

A global deal on climate change, to succeed the Kyoto Protocol that expired in 2012, is urgently needed. Concentrations of carbon dioxide and other GHGsin the atmosphere have reached 435 parts per million (ppm)of CO2-equivalent, compared with about 280 ppm before industrialization in the 19th century.

2. _____

If we continue with business-as-usual emissions from activities such as burning fossil fuels and cut down forests, concentrations could reach 750 ppm by the end of this century. Should that happen, the probable rise in global average temperature, relatively to pre-industrial times, will be 5 C or more.

3. _____

4. _____

The last time the earth's temperature was that high was more than 30 million years ago. The human species, which has been around for no more than 200,000 years, would have to deal with a more hospitable physical environment than it has ever experienced.

5. _____

Floods and drought would become more intense and the sea level would be several meters higher, severely disrupting lives and livelihoods, and causing massive population movements and inevitable conflicts around the world. Some parts of the world would be under water; others would become deserts.

6. _____

Developing countries recognize and angered by the inequity of the current situation. Existing GHG levels are largely the result of industrialization in the developed world.

7. _____

Yet developing countries are the most vulnerable for the consequences of climate change, which threatens the economic growth that is necessary to overcome poverty. At the same time, emissions cannot be reduced to the required level without the central contribution of the developing world.

8. _____

9. _____

Climate change and poverty, the two defining challenges of this century, must be tackled together. If we fail on one, we will fail on the other. The task facing the world is to meet the environment's "carbon constraints" while creating the growth necessary to rise living standards for the poor.

10. _____

VI. Write a composition.

Read the article carefully, try to understand it accurately and look for main ideas. Connect your points to write a rough draft of the summary in your own words. Refer to the passage or the article only when you want to make sure of some points. Revise the rough draft, inserting transitional words and phrases where necessary to ensure coherence.

Unit 7

Science and Technology

Section A

Text One
The Tale of Albert Einstein's "Greatest Blunder"

Focal Consideration

1. The tale of Albert Einstein's "greatest blunder" is concentrated on the problem of universal expansion. Today, there are still some controversial views about the expansion of the universe. The focal points about the content will lie on the discussion of:
   a. the information of man's exploration of the cosmos
   b. the major controversies about the future of the universe
   c. the relation between Einstein's relativity and Newton's gravity, and Hawking's view of cosmos
2. This text is written in a style of popular science. Concentration will be on the characteristics of scientific style reflected in this passage.

Research Questions

Think about the following questions and discuss them with your group members. After your discussion, work out a research report and share it with the students of other groups.
1. In what way did Einstein test his theory? Do you think "thought experiment" is acceptable? Why?
2. Why did Einstein feel deeply uneasy with lambda? What is Einstein called his "greatest blunder"?
3. What is the assumption taken from Hubble's discovery and recent astronomical data?
4. What is the writer's attitude toward the inflationary model?
5. What would be the future of the universe according to some cosmologists? What is your idea?

The Tale of Albert Einstein's "Greatest Blunder"

By Neil deGrasse Tyson

1   Cosmology has always been weird. Worlds rest on the backs of turtles, and matter and energy come into existence out of much less than thin air. And now, just when you'd gotten familiar with the idea of a big bang, along comes something new to worry about. A mysterious and universal pressure pervades all of space and acts against the cosmic gravity that has tried to drag the universe back together ever since the big bang. On top of that, "negative gravity" has forced the expansion of the universe to accelerate exponentially, and cosmic gravity is losing the tug-of-war.

2   For these and similarly mind-warping ideas in twentieth-century physics, just blame Albert Einstein.

3   Einstein hardly ever set foot in the laboratory; he didn't test phenomena or use elaborate equipment. He was a theorist who perfected the "thought experiment," in which you engage nature through your imagination, inventing a situation or a model and then working out the consequences of some physical principle.

4   If—as was the case for Einstein—a physicist's model is intended to represent the entire universe, then manipulating the model should be tantamount to manipulating the universe itself. Observers and experimentalists can then go out and look for the phenomena predicted by that model. If the model is flawed, or if the theorists make a mistake in their calculations, the observers will detect a mismatch between the model's predictions and the way things happen in the real universe. That's the first cue to try again, either by adjusting the old model or by creating a new one.

5   One of the most powerful and far-reaching theoretical models ever devised is Einstein's theory of general relativity, published in 1916 as "The Foundation of the General Theory of Relativity" and refined in 1917 in "Cosmological Considerations in the General Theory of Relativity." Together, the papers outline the relevant mathematical details of how everything in the universe moves under the influence of gravity. Every few years, laboratory scientists devise ever more precise experiments to test the theory, only to extend the envelope of its accuracy.

6   Most scientific models are only half baked, and have some wiggle room for the adjustment of parameters to fit the known universe. In the heliocentric universe conceived by the sixteenth-century astronomer Nicolaus Copernicus, for example, planets orbited the Sun in perfect circles. The orbit-the-Sun part was correct, but the perfect-circle part turned out to be a bit off. Making the orbits elliptical made the Copernican system more accurate.

7   Yet, in the case of Einstein's relativity, the founding principles of the entire theory require that everything take place exactly as predicted. Einstein had, in effect, built a house of cards, with only two or three simple postulates holding up the entire structure.

That unassailable structure—the fact that the theory is fully baked—is the source of one of the most fascinating blunders in the history of science. Einstein's 1917 refinement of his equations of gravity included a new term—denoted by the Greek letter lambda—in which his model universe neither expands nor contracts. Because lambda served to oppose gravity within Einstein's model, it could keep the universe in balance, resisting gravity's natural tendency to pull the whole cosmos into one giant mass. Einstein's universe was indeed balanced, but, as the Russian physicist Alexsandr Friedmann showed mathematically in 1922, it was in a precarious state—like a ball at the top of a hill, ready to roll down in one direction or another at the slightest provocation. Moreover, giving something a name does not make it real, and Einstein knew of no counterpart in the physical universe to the lambda in his equations.

8   Einstein's general theory of relativity (GR) radically departed from all previous thinking about the attraction of gravity. Instead of settling for Sir Isaac Newton's view of gravity as "action at a distance", GR regards gravity as the response of a mass to the local curvature of space and time caused by some other mass. In other words, concentrations of mass cause distortions in the fabric of space and time. Those distortions guide the moving masses along straight-line geodesics, which look like the curved trajectories that physicists call orbits.

9   In effect, GR accounts for two opposite phenomena: good gravity, such as the attraction between the Earth and a ball thrown into the air or between the Sun and the Earth; and a mysterious, repulsive pressure associated with the vacuum of space–time itself. Acting against gravity, lambda preserved what Einstein and every other physicist of his day had strongly believed in: the status quo of a static universe. Static it was, but stable it was not. And to invoke an unstable condition as the natural state of a physical system violates scientific credo: you cannot assert that the entire universe is a special case that happens to be precariously balanced for eternity. Nothing ever seen, heard, or measured has acted that way in the history of science. Yet, in spite of being deeply uneasy with lambda, Einstein included it in his equations.

10   Twelve years later, in 1929, the U.S. astronomer Edwin P. Hubble discovered that the universe is not static after all: convincing evidence showed that the more distant a galaxy, the faster that galaxy is receding from the Earth. In other words, the universe is growing. Embarrassed by lambda, and exasperated by having thus blown the chance to predict the expanding universe himself, Einstein discarded lambda, calling its introduction his life's "greatest blunder."

11   That wasn't the end of the story, though. Off and on over the decades, theoreticians would exhume lambda—more commonly known as the "cosmological constant"—from the graveyard of discredited theories. Then, sixty-nine years later, in 1998, science exhumed lambda one last time, because now there was evidence to justify it. Early that year two teams of astrophysicists made the same remarkable announcement. Dozens of the most distant supernovas ever observed appeared noticeably dimmer than expected—a

disturbing finding, given the well-documented behavior of this species of exploding star. Reconciliation required that either those distant supernovas acted quite differently from their nearer brethren, or else they were as much as 15 percent farther away than the prevailing cosmological models had placed them.

12   Not only was the cosmos expanding, but a repulsive pressure within the vacuum of spacewas also causing the expansion to accelerate. Something had to be driving the universe outward at an ever-increasing pace. The only thing that "naturally" accounted for the acceleration was lambda, the cosmological constant. When physicists dusted it off and put it back in Einstein's original equations for general relativity, the state of the universe matched the state of Einstein's equations.

13   To an astrophysicist, the supernovas are worth their weight in fusionable nuclei. Each star explodes the same way, igniting a similar amount of fuel, releasing a similarly titanic amount of energy in a similar period of time, and therefore achieving a similar peak luminosity. Hence these exploding stars serve as a kind of yardstick, or "standard candle," for calculating cosmic distances to the galaxies in which they explode, out to the farthest reaches of the universe.

14   Standard candles simplify calculations immensely: since the supernovas all have the same wattage, the dim ones are far away and the bright ones are nearby. By measuring their brightness (a simple task), you can tell exactly how far away they are from you. If the luminosities of the supernovas were not all the same, brightness alone would not be enough to tell you which of them are far from Earth and which of them are near. A dim one could be a high-wattage bulb far away or a low-wattage bulb close up.

15   Fine. But there's a second way to measure the distance to galaxies: their speed of recession from our Milky Way, a recession that is part and parcel of the overall cosmic expansion. As Hubble was the first to show, the expansion of the universe makes distant objects race away from us faster than the nearby ones do. By measuring a galaxy's speed of recession, you can deduce its distance from Earth.

16   If those two well-tested methods give different distances for the same object, something must be wrong. Either the supernovas are bad standard candles, or our model for the rate of cosmic expansion as measured by galaxy speeds is wrong.

17   Well, something was wrong in 1998. It turned out that the supernovas are splendid standard candles, surviving the careful scrutiny of many skeptical investigators. Astrophysicists were left with a universe that is expanding faster than they had ever thought it was. Distant galaxies turned out to be even farther away than their recession speed had seemed to indicate. And there was no easy way to explain the extra expansion without invoking lambda, the cosmological constant.

18   Here, then, was the first direct evidence that a repulsive pressure permeated the universe, opposing gravity. That's what resurrected the cosmological constant overnight. And now cosmologists could estimate its numerical value, because they could calculate the effect it was having: the difference between what they had expected the expansion to be and what it actually was.

19   That value for lambda suddenly signified a physical reality, which now needed a name. "Dark energy" carried the day, suitably capturing our ignorance of its cause. The most accurate measurements done to date have shown dark energy to be the most prominent thing in town.

20   So what is this stuff? As with dark matter, nobody knows. The closest anybody has come to a reasonable guess is to presume that dark energy is a quantum effect—whereby the vacuum of space, instead of being empty, actually seethes with particles and their antimatter counterparts. They pop in and out of existence in pairs, and don't last long enough to be measured. Their transient existence is captured in their moniker: virtual particles.

21   But the remarkable legacy of quantum mechanics—the physics of the small—demands that we give these particles serious attention. Each pair of virtual particles exerts a little bit of outward pressure as it ever so briefly elbows its way into space. Unfortunately, when you estimate the amount of repulsive "vacuum pressure" that arises from the abbreviated lives of virtual particles, the result is more than 10120 times bigger than the value of the cosmological constant derived from the supernova measurements. That may be the most embarrassing calculation ever made, the biggest mismatch between theory and observation in the history of science.

22   I'd say astrophysicists remain clueless—but it's not abject cluelessness. Dark energy is not adrift, with nary a theory to call home. It inhabits one of the safest homes we can imagine: Einstein's equations of general relativity. It's lambda. Whatever dark energy turns out to be, we already know how to measure it and how to calculate its effects on the cosmos.

23   Without a doubt, Einstein's greatest blunder was having declared that lambda was his greatest blunder.

24   A remarkable feature of lambda and the accelerating universe is that the repulsive force arises from within the vacuum, not from anything material. As the vacuum grows, lambda's influence on the cosmic state of affairs grows with it. All the while, the density of matter and energy diminishes without limit. With greater repulsive pressure comes more vacuum, driving its exponential growth—the endless acceleration of the cosmic expansion.

25   As a consequence, anything not gravitationally bound to the neighborhood of the Milky Way will move away from us at ever-increasing speed, embedded within the expanding fabric of space-time. Galaxies now visible will disappear beyond an unreachable horizon. In a trillion or so years, anyone alive in our own galaxy may know nothing of other galaxies. Our—or our alien Milky Way brethren's—observable universe will merely comprise a system of nearby stars. Beyond the starry night will lie an endless void, without form: "darkness upon the face of the deep."

26   Dark energy, a fundamental property of the cosmos, will, in the end, undermine the ability of later generations to comprehend their universe. Unless contemporary

astrophysicists across the galaxy keep remarkable records, or bury an awesome time capsule, future astrophysicists will know nothing of external galaxies—the principal form of organization for matter in our cosmos. Dark energy will deny them access to entire chapters from the book of the universe.

27 Here, then, is my recurring nightmare: Are we, too, missing some basic pieces of the universe that once was? What part of our cosmic saga has been erased? What remains absent from our theories and equations that ought to be there, leaving us groping for answers we may never find?

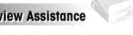

Preview Assistance

1. **cosmology** *n.*   the branch of philosophy dealing with the origin and general structure of the universe
2. **on top of**   in addition to; over and above
3. **exponential** *adj.*   of or pertaining to an exponent or exponents
4. **tug-of-war** *n.*   an athletic contest between two teams at opposite ends of a rope, each team trying to drag the other over a line
5. **tantamount** *adj.*   equivalent, as in value, force, effect, or signification
6. **wiggle** *v.*   to move or go with short, quick, irregular movements from side to side
7. **parameter** *n.*   one of a set of measurable factors, such as temperature and pressure, that define a system and determine its behavior and are varied in an experiment
8. **heliocentric** *adj.*   measured or considered as being seen from the center of the sun
9. **postulate** *n.*   something taken as self-evident or assumed without proof as a basis for reasoning
10. **precarious** *adj.*   dependent on circumstances beyond one's control; uncertain; unstable; insecure
11. **curvature** *n.*   a curved condition, often abnormal
12. **geodesic** *n.*   the shortest line between two points on any mathematically defined surface
13. **trajectory** *n.*   the path of a projectile or other moving body through space
14. **repulsive** *adj.*   tending to repel or drive off. In physics, the word means of the nature of or characterized by physical repulsion
15. **credo** *n.*   any creed or formula of belief
16. **eternity** *n.*   infinite time; duration without beginning or end
17. **exasperate** *v.*   to irritate or provoke to a high degree; annoy extremely
18. **exhume** *v.*   to remove from a grave; disinter ;to bring to light, especially after a period of obscurity
19. **discredit** *v.*   to injure the credit or reputation of; defame
20. **reconciliation** *n.*   the process of making consistent or compatible
21. **brethren** *n.*   *slang.* brother; fellow; buddy
22. **prevailing** *adj.*   encountered generally especially at the present time
23. **fusion** *n.*   also called nuclear fusion; (Physics) a thermonuclear reaction in which nuclei of light atoms join to form nuclei of heavier atoms, as the combination of deuterium atoms to form helium atoms
24. **nucleus** *n.*   (plu. Nuclei) Physics. the positively charged mass within an atom, composed of neutrons and protons, and possessing most of the mass but occupying only a small fraction of the volume of the atom

25. **luminosity** *n.* (Astronomy) the brightness of a star in comparison with that of the sun: the luminosity of Sirius expressed as 23 indicates an intrinsic brightness 23 times as great as that of the sun
26. **wattage** *n.* the amount of power required to operate an electrical appliance or device
27. **part and parcel** an essential, necessary, or integral part
28. **scrutiny** *n.* a searching examination or investigation; minute inquiry
29. **permeate** *v.* to pass into or through every part of
30. **resurrect** *v.* to bring back into practice, notice, or use
31. **moniker** *n.* a person's name, esp. a nickname or alias
32. **abject** *adj.* utterly hopeless, miserable, humiliating, or wretched
33. **nary** *adj.* (old use) not any; no; never a
34. **embed** *v.* to surround tightly or firmly; envelop or enclose
35. **saga** *n.* any narrative or legend of heroic exploits

Referential Points

Neil deGrasse Tyson American astrophysicist. Tyson earned his BA in Physics from Harvard and his PhD in Astrophysics from Columbia. Tyson's professional research interests are broad, but include star formation, exploding stars, dwarf galaxies, and the structure of our Milky Way.

Albert Einstein (1879—1955) German-born American theoretical physicist whose special and general theories of relativity revolutionized modern thought on the nature of space and time and formed a theoretical base for the exploitation of atomic energy. He won a 1921 Nobel Prize for his explanation of the photoelectric effect.

big bang the theory of the cosmic explosion that marked the origin of the universe. According to the big-bang theory, at the beginning of time, all of the matter and energy in the universe was concentrated in a very dense state, from which it exploded, with the resulting expansion continuing until the present. This big bang is dated between 10 and 20 billion years ago. In this initial state, the universe was very hot and contained a thermal soup of quarks, electrons, photons, and other elementary particles. The temperature rapidly decreased, falling from 1013 degrees Kelvin after the first microsecond to about one billion degrees after three minutes. As the universe cooled, the quarks condensed into protons and neutrons, the building blocks of atomic nuclei. Some of these were converted into helium nuclei by fusion; the relative abundance of hydrogen and helium is used as a test of the theory. After many millions of years the expanding universe, at first a very hot gas, thinned and cooled enough to condense into individual galaxies and then stars.

gravity an attractive force that pulls matter together like a rubber band. Gravity weakens over distance, when the distance between two galaxies doubles, the force between them is one-fourth as strong. As the universe expands, gravity is less and less effective at slowing the expansion.

negative gravity (also called **antigravity or dark energy**) a property of empty spacethat exerts an outward force like a compressed spring at every point in space. A given volume of space always has the same amount of dark energy, so when the distance between two galaxies doubles, the force pushing them away from each other is twice as strong. As the universe expands, the volume of space increases, which means more dark energy. By now, 14 billion years after the Big Bang, antigravity has overwhelmed gravity, so the expansion will get faster and faster.

general relativity a theory of gravity deriving almost entirely from Einstein (1916). It supersedes Newton's theory of gravitation, which is reproduced as a weak gravity, low velocity special case, and replaces the Newtonian notion of instantaneous action at a distance with the gravitational field as a distortion of space—time due to the presence of mass. For example, as the Earth moves round the Sun there is distortion of space – time by the Sun's greater mass. An analogy represents space—time as a rubber sheet distorted by a heavy ball representing the Sun; a smaller ball rolling by, representing a planet, will tend to fall into this depression, apparently attracted. General relativity is supported by experiments which measure the bending of starlight due to the presence of the Sun's mass, and also the precession of Mercury's orbit. Other predictions include black holes and gravitational waves. Using general relativity Einstein predicted the impact of the Earth's spin on other rotating objects; this effect, called frame dragging, was first reported in 1997 by observing changes in satellite orbits.

Alexsandr Friedmann (1888—1925) Russian cosmologist and mathematician. Alexander Friedman lived much of his life in Leningrad. And later became a professor in Perm State University in 1918. He discovered the expanding-universe solution to the general relativity field equations in 1922, which was corroborated by Edwin Hubble's observations in 1929. Friedman's 1924 papers demonstrated that he had command of all three Friedman models describing positive, zero and negative curvature respectively, a decade before Robertson and Walker published their analysis. This dynamic cosmological model of general relativity would come to form the standard for the Big Bang and steady state theories. Friedman's work supports both theories equally, so it was not until the detection of the cosmic microwave background radiation that the steady state theory was abandoned in favor of the current favorite Big Bang paradigm. The classic solution of the Einstein field equations that describes a homogeneous and isotropic universe is after Friedman.

Edwin P. Hubble (1889—1953) American astronomer He profoundly changed astronomers' understanding of the nature of the universe by demonstrating the existence of other galaxies besides the Milky Way. He also discovered that the degree of redshift observed in light coming from a galaxy increased in proportion to the distance of that galaxy from the Milky Way. This became known as Hubble's law, and would help establish that the universe is expanding.

cosmological term a term introduced by Einstein into his field equations of general relativity to permit a stationary, nonexpanding universe. After the discovery of Hubble redshift and the introduction of the expanding space paradigm Einstein abandoned the concept. New discoveries in the 1990s have, however, renewed interest in a cosmological constant. The termcan be positive, negative, or zero. It is the energy density of empty space: it can be thought of as the "cost" of having space. In cosmology, the value and sign are related to the expansion or contraction of the universe.

supernova a stellar explosion that produces an extremely bright object made of plasma that declines to invisibility over weeks or months. There are several different types of supernovae and two possible routes to their formation. A massive star may cease to generate fusion energy from fusing the nuclei of atoms in its core and collapse inward under the force of its own gravity to form a neutron star or black hole, or a white dwarf star may accumulate material from a companion star until it nears its Chandrasekhar limit and undergoes runaway nuclear fusion in its interior, completely disrupting it (note that this should not be confused with a surface thermonuclear explosion on a white dwarf called a nova). In either case, the resulting supernova explosion expels much or all of the stellar material with great force.

dark matter material that is believed to make up (along with dark energy) more than 90% of the mass of the universe but is not readily visible because it neither emits nor reflects electromagnetic radiation, such as light or radio signals. Its existence would explain gravitational anomalies seen in the motion and distribution of galaxies. Dark matter can be detected only indirectly, e.g., through the bending of light rays from distant stars by its gravity.

antimatter substance composed of elementary particles having the mass and electric charge of ordinary matter (such as electrons and protons) but for which the charge and related magnetic properties are opposite in sign. The existence of antimatter was posited by the electron theory of P.A.M. Dirac. In 1932 the positron (antielectron) was detected in cosmic rays, followed by the antiproton and the antineutron detected through the use of particle accelerators. Positrons, antiprotons, and antineutrons, collectively called antiparticles, are the antiparticles of electrons, protons, and neutrons, respectively. When matter and antimatter are in close proximity, annihilation occurs within a fraction of a second, releasing large amounts of energy.

"darkness upon the face of the deep" from the Genesis 1:2. "And the earth was without form, and void; and darkness was upon the face of the deep. And the Spirit of God moved upon the face of the waters."

Consolidation Work

I. Fill in the blanks with the words and expressions provided, making some change when necessary.

embed	repulsive	blunder	transient	scrutiny	assert
convince	seethe with	tantamount to	work out	embarrass	permeate
in effect	elbow one's way		part and parcel		

1. A home is not a mere _____ shelter: its essence lies in the personalities of the people who live in it.
2. Electromagnetic forces between particles can be _____ or attractive depending on whether the particles both have a positive or negative electrical charge, or they have opposite electrical charges.
3. He was glad it was to him she had revealed her secret, rather than to the cold scrutiny of Mr. Letterblair, or the _____ gaze of her family.
4. In spring, the rivers and their mighty tributaries swell and _____ the melting snows.
5. Formulated in 1823, the Monroe Doctrine _____ that the Americans were no longer open to European colonization.
6. Diplomatic misunderstandings can often be traced back to _____ in translation.
7. The statesman has pointed out that victory attained by violence is _____ a defeat, for it is momentary.

8. America lives in the heart of every man everywhere who wishes to find a region where he will be free to _____ his destiny as he chooses.
9. It is unnecessary for all the talented to _____ into officialdom. They can strive to become experts in philosophy, science and other fields.
10. The entire earth is _____ by magnetic power. All the living beings and objects that are present on this earth also have this magnetic power.
11. _____ systems are computers that do not look like computers which are "hidden" in everyday electronic devices from mobile phones and hi-fi equipment to cars and planes.
12. Jane Austen said, "Where so many hours have been spent in _____ myself that I am right, is there not some reason to fear I may be wrong?"
13. Argument structure is considered to be _____ of the information associated with lexical, syntactically atomic verbs.
14. Glamour is the power to rearrange people's emotions, which, _____, is the power to control one's environment.
15. Skeptical _____ is the means, in both science and religion, by which deep insights can be winnowed from deep nonsense.

II. Use the appropriate form of the words given in the brackets to fill in the blanks.
1. However, when a body moves in an _____ orbit, tracking its motion as a function of time is not as straightforward. (ellipse)
2. People with the so-called "warrior gene" exhibit higher levels of behavioral aggression in response to _____, according to new research. (provoke)
3. The quality of programming books between these publishers is _____ different. (notice)
4. The long-range purpose of the studies is _____: by understanding the global forces that produce climate changes, scientists hope to be able to identify early signs of climatic shifts and thereby to _____ future trends. (prediction)
5. _____ is a branch of astronomy, but the observational and theoretical techniques used by _____ involve a wide range of other sciences, such as physics and chemistry. (cosmos)
6. One of the most important techniques in production is _____, in which different firms make different kinds of products and individual workers perform specific jobs within a company. (special)
7. People suffering with an eating disorder often have a _____ perception of their body and personality. (distortion)
8. Though force can protect in emergency, only justice, fairness, consideration and co-operation can finally lead men to the dawn of _____ peace. (eternity)
9. In the last few years, _____ has become one of the "hottest" topics in the increasingly "hot" field of conflict resolution.
10. Mr. Johnson says the local insurance industry's right to access the European single market is now _____.

III. Paraphrase the following sentences taken from the text.
1. For these and similarly mind-warping ideas in twentieth-century physics, just blame Albert Einstein.

2. Every few years, laboratory scientists devise ever more precise experiments to test the theory, only to extend the envelope of its accuracy.
3. Most scientific models are only hall baked, and have some wiggle room for the adjustment of parameters to fit the known universe.
4. Off and on over the decades, theoreticians would exhume lambda—more commonly known as the "cosmological constant"—from the graveyard of discredited theories.
5. When physicists dusted it off and put it back in Einstein's original equations for general relativity, the state of the universe matched the state of Einstein's equations.
6. "Dark energy" carried the day, suitably capturing our ignorance of its cause.
7. Dark energy is not adrift, with nary a theory to call home.

IV. Test your general knowledge.
1. For his work in theoretical physics, notably on the _____, Einstein received the 1921 Nobel Prize in Physics.
   A. general relativity   B. special relativity
   C. photoelectric effect   D. cosmological constant
2. In 1916 he completed his mathematical formulation of a general theory of relativity that included _____ as a determiner of the curvature of a space-time continuum.
   A. gravitation   B. anti-gravitation
   C. dark energy   D. cosmological constant
3. Which of the following statements about Albert Einstein is true?
   A. After Hitler's rise to power, Einstein left Germany and worked from 1934 in USA. On October 1, 1940, Einstein became an American citizen. He remained both an American and a Swiss citizen until his death on April 18, 1955.
   B. In 1939, Einstein sent a letter to President Truman urging the study of nuclear fission for military purposes, under fears that the Nazi government would be first to develop nuclear weapons.
   C. In addition to the theory of relativity, Einstein is also known for his contributions to the development of the atomic bomb.
   D. Einstein spent the later part of his life attempting to establish a merger between unified field theory and his general theory of relativity.
4. Which of the following statements is not the idea belonging to the big-bang theory?
   A. At the beginning of time, all of the matter and energy in the universe was concentrated in a very dense state, from which it exploded, with the resulting expansion continuing until the present.
   B. The big bang is dated between 10 and 20 billion years ago.
   C. In the initial state, the universe was very hot and contained a thermal soup of quarks, electrons, photons, and other elementary particles.
   D. The universe has always expanded, with no beginning or end, at a uniform rate and it always will expand and maintain a constant density.
5. Newton's apple is a popular story claiming that Newton was inspired to formulate his _____ by the fall of an apple from a tree.
   A. laws of motion   B. theory of universal gravitation
   C. conservation of momentum   D. development of calculus

6. The solar system comprises the Sun and the retinue of celestial objects gravitationally bound to it: currently there are officially _____ and their 165 known moons, as well as asteroids, meteoroids, planetoids, comets, and interplanetary dust.
   A. nine stars   B. eight stars   C. nine planets   D. eight planets
7. Which theory concluded that the expansion of the universe is approximately uniform and the greater the distance between any two galaxies, the greater their relative speed of separation?
   A. The Big-Bang theory   B. The Big-Rip theory
   C. The Steady-State theory   D. Hubble's Law
8. At the end of the 20th century, the study of very distant supernovas led to the belief that the cosmic expansion was accelerating. To explain this cosmologists postulated a repulsive force, _____, which counteracts gravity and pushes galaxies apart.
   A. black hole   B. dark energy   C. universal constant   D. cosmic force
9. Stephen Hawking showed that if the general theory of relativity was correct the universe must have a _____, or starting point, in space-time.
   A. singularity   B. black hole   C. dark matter   D. boundary
10. Which of the following statements is NOT true?
    A. According to Einstein's special theory of relativity, which is a geometric interpretation of gravitation, matter produces gravitational effects by actually distorting the space about it.
    B. In 1687, Newton used the Latin word *gravitas* (weight) for the force that would become known as gravity, and defined the law of universal gravitation.
    C. Edwin Hubble, American astronomer, was the first to offer observational evidence to support the theory of the expanding universe.
    D. In 1971 Hawking, British theoretical physicist, provided mathematical support for the big-bang theory of the origin of the universe.
11. The galaxy we live in is called the Milky Way. It is shaped approximately like_____.
    A. a round ball   B. a doughnut   C. a pretzel   D. a flat spiral
12. Unlike most other fish, sharks have no _____.
    A. bones   B. teeth   C. gills   D. liver
13. Alexander Graham Bell is best known for inventing the telephone, but he was a man of many interests. Another product for which he received patents was_____.
    A. a cement-burning kiln   B. a hydrofoil boat
    C. a "magic lantern" projector   D. a vacuum cleaner
14. It is now believed that dinosaurs became extinct because of _____.
    A. viral diseases   B. hunting by early humans
    C. a worldwide period of climatic cooling   D. a meteorite impact
15. Kinetic energy is _____.
    A. life energy, possessed only by living organisms
    B. only important at subatomic distances
    C. energy of movement
    D. a rare form of energy sometimes observed in deep space

V. Proofread the following passage.

   As scientific advances bring cloning out of the realm of

science fiction and into the domain of medical reality, concern
is growing what the possible implications will be. Many fear that   1. _____
it could have disastrous consequences. Will experiments gone awry
result to deformed human beings? Will people replicate themselves   2. _____
for egomaniacal reasons? Will the concept of human identity
drastically change? "Life is a creation, not a commodity," President
Bush argued last month in a speech before Congress, and as for such,   3. _____
he emphasized, it should not be manufactured through cloning
as though it was some kind of specialty good.   4. _____
But many also argue that an important distinction needs to be
recognized between "reproductive cloning," in which the goal is
the creation of a full-fledged human being, and "therapeutic cloning,"
in which the goal is the creation of a several-day-old embryo which   5. _____
undifferentiated stem cells can be harvested and potentially used to
cure a variety of devastated diseases. Those who believe that human   6. _____
life begins with the very existence of an embryo cannot countenance
a procedure that involves an embryo's creation and destruction, even
on a very early stage. But those who believe that human life does not   7. _____
begin at least when an embryo's cells have begun to differentiate   8. _____
themselves into distinctly human tissue feel that prohibiting such   9. _____
research—which could save the lives of many people for cancer,   10. _____
diabetes, heart disease, and other illnesses—would in itself be
reprehensible and disrespectful of human life.

VI. Write a composition.

Review and compare different theories of the universe in groups. Write a composition in which you have to show how much you have known about gravity, antigravity, and dark energy.

Further Development

1. Students are required to watch the documentary film "Einstein's Greatest Blunder" and do the following tasks:
   A. Tell each other what you have known about gravity and antigravity.
   B. How much do you know about Einstein's repulsive idea and try to make a brief description of them.
2. In the forest of great figures of science in the 20th century, two men stand out, as their thoughts in quest of the laws of the physical world have changed our views about space, time and the universe tremendously, and reoriented the course of modern science. They are Albert Einstein and Stephen Hawking. Look up reference books or visit websites for more information about them. Prepare a class presentation on the basis of your knowledge about one of the two great scientists and his contributions to human history.

3. *A Brief History of Time* is a popular science book written by Stephen Hawking. It became a best-seller and has sold more than 9 million copies. It was also on the *London Sunday Times* best-seller list for more than four years. *A Brief History of Time* attempts to explain a range of subjects in cosmology, including the Big Bang, black holes and light cones, to the non-specialist reader. Its main goal is to give an overview of the subject but, unusual for a popular science book, it also attempts to explain some complex mathematics. In this task you are going to read this book and write a book review about 500 words.

Section A Text Two

Cosmology and 21st-Century Culture

By Nancy Ellen Abrams and Joel R. Primack

1   We like to think of our generation in this Information Age as the smartest and most knowledgeable that has ever lived. Yet most people in modern Western culture have no idea what our universe looks like or how to begin to think about the way we humans may fit into the cosmos. Every traditional culture known to anthropology has had a cosmology—a story of how the world began and continues, how humans came to exist, and what the gods expect of us. Cosmology made sense of the ordinary world by defining a larger context and grounding people's sense of reality, their identity, and their codes of behavior in that grand scheme. Like modern science, it embedded everydayness in an invisible reality: Modern science explains by means of countless molecules; African cosmologies explain by means of countless spirits. Ordinary people in traditional societies accepted responsibility for maintaining the cosmos itself by ritually reenacting the creation stories for every generation. This is how they knew who they were. The absence of a cosmology was as inconceivable as the absence of language. Their pictures of the universe were not what anyone today would consider scientifically accurate, but they were true by the standards of their culture.

2   Science undermined all traditional pictures of the universe in the Renaissance, centuries before it was in a position to create one of its own. A cosmology can only be taken seriously if it is believable, and after the scientific revolution our standards of believability were forever changed. For four centuries, scientific cosmology was not taken seriously because the ratio of theory to data was almost infinite. However, science now appears to be closing in on an origin story that may actually be true—one that can withstand the most rigorous tests and will still be accepted hundreds of years from now, as Newton's theory remains valid for the solar system (within known limitations). This is the highest grade of truth possible in modern science.

3   Modern cosmology is in the midst of a scientific revolution. New instruments are producing the first detailed data about the distant universe. Since light travels at a finite

speed, looking out in space is the same as looking back in time. We can now observe every bright galaxy in the visible universe, and even look back to the cosmic dark ages before galaxies had formed. In the patterns of the subtle temperature differences in the cosmic background radiation in different directions we are learning to read the Genesis story of the expanding universe.

4   The resulting origin story will be the first ever based on scientific evidence and created by a collaboration of people from different religions and races all around the world, all of whose contributions are subjected to the same standards of verifiability. The new picture of reality excludes no one and treats all humans as equal. The revolution in scientific cosmology today may open the door to a believable picture of the larger reality in which our world, our lives, and all our cultures are embedded.

5   In Biblical times when people looked up at a blue sky, they understood the blue to be water, held up by a hard, transparent dome that covered the entire flat Earth. In the King James translation, the dome was named the "firmament." According to the first creation story at the beginning of Genesis, by creating this dome on the second day, God divided the waters "above" from the waters "below" and held open the space for dry land and air.

6   At about the same time as the Genesis story took the form in which we know it, Greek philosophers were living in a different universe in which the Earth was not flat and domed but a round celestial object. By the Middle Ages, the Greek image of concentric spheres, and not the Bible's flat domed Earth, had become the unquestioned universe for Jews, Moslems, and Christians alike.

7   Thus, on a clear night in Medieval Europe, a person looking up into the sky would have seen hard, transparent spheres nested inside each other, encircling the center of the universe, the Earth. Each sphere carried a planet, the moon, or the sun. Heaven itself was immediately outside the most distant sphere, which carried the "fixed stars." The hierarchies of church, nobility, and family mirrored this cosmic hierarchy. Every thing and every creature in the universe tended toward its proper place for love of God.

8   The stable center was torn out of the Medieval universe at the beginning of the 17th century, when Galileo's telescope observations showed that the Ptolemaic Earth-centered picture was wrong. Galileo ridiculed the prevailing cosmology, but the Catholic Church forced him to recant and held him under house arrest for the rest of his life. This was a frightening and sobering event for scientists all over Europe. Eventually, following the lead of Bacon and Descartes, science protected itself by entering into a de facto pact of noninterference with religion: Science would restrict its authority to the material world, and religion would hold unchallenged authority over spiritual issues. By the time Isaac Newton was born in 1642, the spoils of reality had been divided. The physical world and the world of human meaning were now separate realms.

9   The new picture portrayed the universe as endless empty space with stars scattered randomly in it. It never fully replaced the Medieval universe in people's hearts, partly

because it felt so incomplete. There was no particular place for humans, no place for God, and no explanation of the universe's origin. In the mid-17th century, Blaise Pascal expressed a sentiment unheard of in the Middle Ages: "engulfed in the infinite immensity of spaces whereof I know nothing, and which know nothing of me, I am terrified...The eternal silence of these infinite spaces alarms me." Newtonian cosmology was the first that had nothing to say about humans, and believers in science could no longer even conceptualize the ancient ideal of humans living in harmony with the universe.

10 Why should an origin story matter today? "The universe" is irrelevant to most people in the West, except as a fantasy outlet. The universe plays no part in mainstream religions, except perhaps to demonstrate the glory of a creator. How many people recognize the possibility of a sacred relationship between the way the expanding universe operates and the way human beings ought to behave? What religion teaches that this could be a source of harmony among humans?

11 Instead, most educated people in the 21st century live in a cosmology defined by a 17th-century picture of cold, still, empty space, along with fragments of traditional stories and doubts about what is real. Many have not fully absorbed the discovery nearly a century ago of the great age and size of the universe; indeed, controversies between science and religion often center on conflicting origin stories. The current cosmological revolution may provide the first chance in 400 years to develop a shared cosmology. There is, however, a moral responsibility involved in tampering with the underpinnings of reality, as scientific cosmology is now doing. How well the emerging cosmology is interpreted in language meaningful to ordinary people may influence how well its elemental concepts are understood, which may in turn affect how positive its consequences for society turn out to be. Will the new scientific story fuel a renaissance of creativity and hope in the emerging global culture—or will it be appropriated by the powerful and used to oppress the ignorant, as the Medieval hierarchical universe was used to justify rigid social hierarchies? Will news of new discoveries about the universe just be entertainment for an educated minority but, like science fiction or metaphysics, have little to do with the "real world"?

12 All possibilities are still open because the meaning of this new cosmology is not implicit in the science. Scientific cosmology, unlike traditional cosmologies, makes no attempt to link the story of the cosmos to how human beings should behave. It is the job of scholars, artists, and other creative people to try to understand the scientific picture and to perceive and express human meanings in it. A living cosmology for 21st-century culture will emerge when the scientific nature of the universe becomes enlightening for human beings.

13 This will not happen easily. The result of centuries of separation between science and religion is that each is suspicious of the other infringing on its turf. In 1999 the AAAS Program of Dialogue on Science, Ethics, and Religion sponsored a 3-day public conference that asked: Did the universe have a beginning? Was the universe designed?

Are we alone? Not surprisingly, no consensus was reached on any of these questions. Although the goal was "constructive dialogue" between science and religion, some of the participants complained that the dialogue went one way—science always demanding that religion adapt to new discoveries. Naturally, science is not about to change its methods to accommodate religious concerns. But a cosmology that does not account for human beings or enlighten us about the role we may play in the universe will never satisfy the demand for a functional cosmology that religions have been trying to satisfy for millennia.

14   There is space in this article for only one of many possible examples of how the emerging scientific cosmology could provide a basis for a living, functional cosmology for the 21st century that, like ancient cosmologies, can help guide humanity.

15   Standard Big Bang theory explains the creation of the light elements in the first 3 minutes, but it does not explain what preceded or what has followed. Gravity alone could not have created the complex, large-scale structures and flows of galaxies that are observed to exist. If matter were absolutely evenly distributed coming out of the Big Bang, gravity could have done nothing but affect the rate of the overall expansion. Consequently, either some causal phenomenon such as "cosmic strings" acting after the Big Bang formed the giant structures we observe today—which looks increasingly dubious because such theories conflict with the new observations of the cosmic background radiation—or else gravity must have had some differences in density to work with from the beginning. Cosmic Inflation could have caused such primordial differences.

16   The theory of Cosmic Inflation was proposed by Alan Guth, Andrei Linde, and others. It is the only explanation we have today for the initial conditions that led to the Big Bang. It says that for an extremely small fraction of a second at the beginning of the Big Bang, the universe expanded exponentially, inflating countless random quantum events in the process, and leaving the newly created spacetime faintly wrinkled on all size scales. All large structures in the universe today grew from these quantum fluctuations, enormously inflated in scale.

17   Inflation is also the controlling metaphor of our culture in the present epoch. Not only is the human population inflating; so too are the average technological power and the resource use of each individual. The human race is addicted to exponential growth, but this obviously cannot continue at the present rate. In a finite environment, inflation must end, however cleverly we may postpone or disguise the inevitable.

18   The single most important question for the present generation may be how global civilization can make the transition gracefully from inflating consumption to a sustainable level. But the cosmic transition from inflation to the slow and steady expansion that followed the Big Bang shows that ending inflation does not mean that all growth must stop, even though many people trying to save the planet assume so. Inflation transformed to expansion can go on for billions of years. Processing information, which occupies more and more of the world's population, does not need to be environmentally costly. Human life can continue to be enhanced as long as our creativity in restoring the Earth stays ahead of our material growth.

Independent Study Assistant

I. Words and Expressions

1. **anthropology** *n.*   the scientific study of the origin, the behavior, and the physical, social, and cultural development of humans
2. **make sense**   to be understandable
3. **ground** *v.*   to supply with basic information; to instruct in fundamentals
4. **scheme** *n.*   an internal representation of the world; an organization of concepts and actions that can be revised by new information about the world
5. **molecule** *n.*   (physics and chemistry) the simplest structural unit of an element or compound; (non-technical usage) a tiny piece of anything
6. **ritually** *adv.*   in a ceremonial manner
7. **reenact** *v.*   to enact or perform again; to act out
8. **inconceivable** *adj.*   not conceivable; unimaginable; unthinkable
9. **rigorous** *adj.*   rigidly accurate; allowing no deviation from a standard
10. **collaboration** *n.*   act of working jointly
11. **verifiable** *adj.*   capable of being verified
12. **transparent** *adj.*   transmitting light; able to be seen through with clarity
13. **dome** *n.*   a geologic structure, usually of relatively large dimensions, whose flanks slope gradually away from the center
14. **celestial** *adj.*   of or relating to the sky or the heavens
15. **concentric** *adj.*   having a common center or center point, as of circles
16. **nest** *v.*   to put snugly together or inside one another
17. **encircle** *v.*   to form a circle around; surround; encompass
18. **hierarchy** *n.*   any system of persons or things ranked one above another
19. **ridicule** *v.*   to deride; to make fun of
20. **recant** *v.*   to formally reject or disavow a formerly held belief
21. **sober** *v.*   to make or become serious; to become more realistic
22. **de facto** *adj.*   existing in fact whether with lawful authority or not
23. **conceptualize** *v.*   to form a concept or concepts of, and especially to interpret in a conceptual way
24. **irrelevant** *adj.*   having no bearing on or connection with the subject at issue
25. **fragment** *n.*   a piece broken off or cut off of something else
26. **tamper with**   to interfere or meddle, especially in a harmful way
27. **underpinning** *n.*   (oft. underpinnings) a foundation or basis
28. **appropriate** *v.*   to take possession of
29. **metaphysics** *n.*   the branch of philosophy that treats of first principles, includes ontology and cosmology, and is intimately connected with epistemology
30. **infringe** *v.*   to encroach or trespass (usually fol. by on or upon)
31. **consensus** *n.*   majority of opinion
32. **primordial** *adj.*   constituting a beginning; giving origin to something derived or developed; original; elementary

II. Referential Points

Nancy Ellen Abrams a lawyer, writer, and performance artist, and her husband Joel R. Primack is a professor of physics at the University of California, Santa Cruz. They have been teaching a course at UCSC on Cosmology and Culture for 6 years. Primack currently serves on the executive committee of the American Physical Society Division of Astrophysics and chairs the advisory committee to the AAAS (American Academy of Arts and Sciences) Program of Dialogue on Science, Ethics, and Religion.

Renaissance a term used to describe the development of Western civilization that marked the transition from medieval to modern times. The Italian Renaissance of the 15th century represented a reconnection of the west with classical antiquity, the absorption of knowledge—particularly mathematics, the focus on the importance of living well in the present (e.g. Renaissance humanism), and an explosion of the dissemination of knowledge brought on by printing. In addition the creation of new techniques in art, poetry, and architecture led in turn to a radical change in the style and substance of the arts and letters. The Italian Renaissance was often labeled as the beginning of the "modern" epoch.

King James (1566—1625) The first Stuart king of England (1603—1625), also king of Scotland (1567—1625) as James VI, born in Edinburgh, EC Scotland, UK, the son of Mary, Queen of Scots, and Henry, Lord Darnley. On his mother's forced abdication, he was proclaimed king, and brought up by several regents. When he began to govern for himself, he ruled through his favorites, which caused a rebellion and a period of imprisonment. In 1589 he married Anne of Denmark. Hating Puritanism, he managed in 1600 to establish bishops in Scotland. On Elizabeth's death, he ascended the English throne as great-grandson of James IV's English wife, Margaret Tudor. At first well received, his favoritism again brought him unpopularity.

The English translation of the Bible commissioned by James I and accomplished by a panel of leading scholars of the day is widely called the King James Bible. They used Greek and Hebrew texts, but were indebted also to earlier English translations. Noted for its literary excellence, the "Authorized Version" gained wide popular appeal after its first publication in 1611, but was never formally 'authorized' by king or Parliament.

Galileo Galilei (1564—1642) Astronomer and mathematician, born in Pisa, Italy. He entered Pisa University as a medical student in 1581, and became professor of mathematics at Padua (1592—1610), where he improved the refracting telescope (1610), and was the first to use it for astronomy, discovering the four largest satellites of Jupiter. His bold advocacy of the Copernican theory brought severe ecclesiastical censure. He was forced to retract before the Inquisition, and was sentenced to indefinite imprisonment—though the sentence was commuted by the pope, at the request of the Duke of Tuscany. Under house arrest in Florence, he continued his research, though by 1637 he had become totally blind. Among his other discoveries were the law of uniformly accelerated motion towards the Earth, the parabolic path of projectiles, and the law that all bodies have weight. The validity of his scientific work was formally recognized by the Roman Catholic Church in 1993.

Ptolemaic the adjective is formed from the name Ptolemy. This adjective is usually used to describe the writings of Claudius Ptolemaeus, the 2nd century AD geographer and astronomer. The Ptolemaic Earth-centered picture refers to the planetary system described by Claudius Ptolemaeus. It is Earth-centred, with the planets moving in circular orbits. To represent the observed positions of the planets as closely as possible, each planet is allowed to move on a small circle (the epicycle) which in turn travels along a larger circle (the deferent). It can predict positions to within 1° or so, and was widely used as the definitive description of the Solar System until overthrown by Copernicus in 1543.

Francis Bacon (1561—1626) English philosopher, essayist, and statesman, born in London, educated at Trinity College, Cambridge, and at Gray's Inn. Bacon belongs to both the worlds of philosophy and literature. Bacon's contribution to philosophy was his application of the inductive method of modern science. He urged full investigation in all cases, avoiding theories based on insufficient data. However, he has been widely censured for being too mechanical, failing to carry his investigations to their logical ends, and not staying abreast of the scientific knowledge of his own day. In the 19th century, Macaulay initiated a movement to restore Bacon's prestige as a scientist. Today his contributions are regarded with considerable respect.

René Descartes (1596—1650) also known as Cartesius, a noted French philosopher, mathematician, and scientist. Dubbed the "Founder of Modern Philosophy" and the "Father of Modern Mathematics," he ranks as one of the most important and influential thinkers of modern times. For good or bad, much of subsequent western philosophy is a reaction to his writings, which have been closely studied from his time down to the present day. Descartes was one of the key thinkers of the Scientific Revolution in the Western World. He is also honored by having the Cartesian coordinate system used in plane geometry and algebra named after him.

Blaise Pascal (1623—1662) Mathematician, physicist, theologian, and man-of-letters, born in Clermont-Ferrand, France. He invented a calculating machine (1647), and later the barometer, the hydraulic press, and the syringe.

III. Questions for Comprehension
1. What is your idea about the formation of our universe before reading this article?
2. The writers say that every traditional culture has had a cosmology. What is the cosmological idea in China?
3. In the writer's opinion, what is the significance of cosmology? What is its relation to culture?
4. What is your understanding of the writer's remark that the absence of a cosmology was as inconceivable as the absence of language?
5. How do you define truth in modern science? What factors may change our standards of believability? And how?
6. What do the writers mean by saying in Paragraph 7 that "science would restrict its authority to the material world, and religion would hold unchallenged authority over spiritual issues"?
7. What can be reflected in the change of human conception about the origin of the universe?
8. What kind of definition of the universe should people have in the 21st century?

Self-test

I. Fill in the blanks with the words and expressions provided, making some change when necessary.

> collaborate   ridicule   exclusion   ignore   noninterference   ritually
> scheme   adapt to   fantasy   hold up   controversy   make sense
> take the form   conflict with   tamper with

1. Greenpeace activists create an _____ zone outside the Parliament building to highlight the hazards of lifting the state bans on genetically engineered (GE) food crops.
2. It might be of signal advantage to one, _____ as I, to hear the opinions and experience of a master in the art.
3. It is required that proposals for papers should _____ of abstracts, in either English or Chinese.
4. In line with its idea of Purity and Tranquility, Daoism advocates _____, which refers to conformity to nature in administration and to the objective laws of human behavior.
5. In a chaotic and increasingly incomprehensible world, the family provides a small relatively stable universe where "things _____."
6. Anyone who takes himself too seriously always runs the risk of looking _____; anyone who can consistently laugh at himself does not.
7. A key to understanding certain Biblical passages is knowing about ancient concepts of _____ purity.
8. A further 18 workers _____ after flights to and from the US were suspended, but they eventually arrived at the last minute.
9. My upbringing _____ my admiration for this singer who pranced around the stage like a gazelle, with his glittering, seductive dancers.
10. Underlying the whole _____ of civilization is the confidence men have in each other, confidence in their integrity, honesty and their future.
11. Officers went to the store and found a jar that had been _____ and had white powder inside.
12. All the works of man have their origin in creative _____. What right have we then to depreciate imagination?
13. China is getting more _____ global trade rules, as exemplified in its recent complaint to the WTO on an anti-dumping dispute with the European Union (EU).
14. The ultimate measure of a man is not where he stands in moments of comfort, but where he stands at times of challenge and _____.
15. So far, more than twenty new, high level technology enterprises _____ with more than 10 countries and regions to establish 78 foreign-invested enterprises.

II. Use the appropriate form of the words given in the brackets to fill in the blanks.

1. The change has been so great that transformations utterly _____ to people of the older generation have come into being amid fire and thunder. (conceive)

2. This method can help the information user evaluate the value and _____ of the information. (believe)
3. Knowledge without know-how is sterile. We use the word "academic" in a pejorative sense to _____ this limitation. (identity)
4. I feel that he is justified in looking into the future with true assurance because he has a mode of living in which I find the joy of life and the joy of work _____ combined. (harmony)
5. I have _____ people to thank for their well-wishes and of course, for making my twentieth such a memorable one. (count)
6. The _____ of the antagonists in fact represents the conflict between determinism and freewill. (portray)
7. As a professor, he says that the Bible is _____ to the modern world and therefore should not have any impact upon our lives. (relevant)
8. The truth is that there is nothing noble in being superior to somebody else. The only real _____ is in being superior to your former self. (noble)
9. What is _____ in any given time or place? It is what the majority then and there happen to like and _____ is what they dislike. (moral)
10. Freud rebuts Wittgenstein's criticism that his theory of the unconscious is speculation, not science, because it is not subject to _____. (verify)

III. Translate the short paragraph into Chinese.

Einstein's special and general relativity theories made the astonishing assertion that time, space and matter could be squeezed and stretched like so much rubber. Using the Hubble Space Telescope to find and study a distant supernova, astronomers found that the expansion of the universe was actually speeding up as if some kind of force were pushing it out. This unknown force was simply being called "dark energy". Scientists assumed that this energy, functioning as a kind of antigravity, is just what Einstein called cosmological constant. While the force of gravity between galaxies falls as they move farther apart, dark energy is a property of space and gets stronger as the universe expands, which just matches Einstein's repulsive idea. However, the observations we have made still go a long way toward confirming that dark energy is real, and there is room for improvement in human understanding of dark energy.

IV. Analyze difficult sentences.

1. Cosmology made sense of the ordinary world by defining a larger context and grounding people's sense of reality, their identity, and their codes of behavior in that grand scheme.
2. Ordinary people in traditional societies accepted responsibility for maintaining the cosmos itself by ritually reenacting the creation stories for every generation.
3. Their pictures of the universe were not what anyone today would consider scientifically accurate, but they were true by the standards of their culture.
4. The resulting origin story will be the first ever based on scientific evidence and created by a collaboration of people from different religions and races all around the world, all of whose contributions are subjected to the same standards of verifiability.
5. Science would restrict its authority to the material world, and religion would hold unchallenged authority over spiritual issues.
6. How well the emerging cosmology is interpreted in language meaningful to ordinary people may

influence how well its elemental concepts are understood, which may in turn affect how positive its consequences for society turn out to be.

V. Proofread the following passage.

To professional physicists, the terms "antigravity" and "gravity shielding" are like the sound of fingernails scratching a blackboard. Both ideas, they hasten to remind journalists, are completely forbid by the known laws of science.

1. _____

Despite of the mainstream scientific community's insistence that defeating gravity is beyond the realm of science, two of the world's largest aerospace companies are believed to be pushing forwards with research into what can most accurately be described as "gravity modification." Europe's BAE Systems, the company created by the merger of British Aerospace and Marconi Electronics Systems, have acknowledged a speculative research effort called Project Greenglow. In the United States, the Boeing Phantom Works (BPW) has issued a qualifying denial that it is taking part in a similar program called GRASP, for "gravity research applied to space propulsion." BPW denies it is funding the project with company money, and acknowledges it cannot comment on "black projects."

2. _____

3. _____

4. _____

5. _____

6. _____

Both projects, as well several private efforts, are believed to be building on fundamental research by Ning Li, a former University of Alabama researcher, who was first to successfully construct a superconducting disc considered to be essential to creating a gravity-altering force.

7. _____

8. _____

Will the projects succeed? The answer will come soon—and somewhat indirect—from NASA. NASA is scheduled to launch the most sensitive gravity-measuring instruments ever built—the orbiting Gravity Probe B experiment. If Li's theory about a link for electromagnetic fields and the gravitation force is correct, it will be confirmed by NASA data.

9. _____

10. _____

VI. Write a composition.

Consider carefully the following excerpt and the assignment below it. Then plan and write an essay that explains your ideas as persuasively as possible. Keep in mind that the support you provide—both reasons and examples—will help make your view convincing to the reader.

People sometimes refuse to acknowledge or learn from the lessons of history. Holocaust survivor Elie Wiesel writes, "You'll try to incite people to learn from the past and rebel, but they will refuse to believe you. They will not listen to you." But many believe that understanding the past is necessary to life in the present. Swiss Philosopher of History Jacob Burckhardt notes that historical knowledge is not "to make us more clever the next time, but wiser for all time."

Assignment: What is your opinion of the claim that without adequate knowledge of the past, we cannot truly understand the present? In an essay, support your position by discussing an example (or examples) from literature, the arts, science and technology, history, current events, or your own experience or observation.

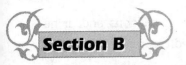

Section B

Text One A Century of Science

Focal Consideration

1. This text is written in the style of popular science. English for science and technology (EST) covers the areas of English for academic and professional purposes and of English written for occupational purposes, including the often informally written discourse found in trade journals and in scientific and technical materials written for the layman. So the focus will lie on the analysis of the main characteristics of EST highlighted in this text and the benefit of such an organization.
2. There is an opinion that the advanced science and technology might bring about disaster beyond imagination. Our focal consideration will lie on the discussion of this view.

Research Questions

Think about the following questions and discuss them with your group members. After your discussion, work out a research report and share it with the students of other groups.
1. What is the writer's purpose of listing a number of discoveries and inventions of the 20th century in the first paragraph?
2. How do you understand that "all discoveries are equally important"?
3. What is the conspicuous development in the genetic engineering?
4. What other great discoveries and inventions in the last century do you know? Share them with your classmates.

A Century of Science

By Jim Wilson

1   If ever there was a moment when our mastery of nature seemed complete, it was at the eve of the 20th century. Using little more than copper wire and magnets, physicists had tamed the mighty power of lightning into a humble servant. Electricity illuminated homes, cooked meals and turned the wheels of industry. It carried voices between cities and telegraphic messages beneath seas.

2   Meanwhile, chemists had perfected anesthesia and antiseptics, making surgery both painless and survivable. Biologists had unlocked the secrets of vaccines to vanquish the scourges of smallpox and rabies. Engineers compressed time with transcontinental railroads that reduced to risk-free days a harrowing journey that had taken months and

lives. Architects expanded space with skyscrapers. Man could fly in balloons and, if he were more adventurous, in gliders. So much had been discovered, so many things had been invented, it genuinely seemed there was little left to do.

3   Looking back on the sheer volume of innovation that took place during the century, it seems reasonable to ask which one of the several million scientific discoveries was the most important. And who better to ask than Stephen Hawking, the physicist regarded as the most brilliant thinker since Albert Einstein. "It's a stupid question," says Hawking through his computer-assisted speech synthesizer. "All discoveries are equally important." In the ivory towers of science, Hawking is most certainly correct. In the workaday world, sorting winners from losers isn't only possible, but most of the time quite necessary. As it is here in a magazine with finite space available to tell the tale of 100 years of scientific innovation. But we can explore some breakthroughs that we believe exerted the greatest influence.

Into Space

4   While the invention of airplanes can be precisely dated to the moment the Wright Flyer briefly slipped the bonds of gravity, no one really has the slightest idea when the rocket was created. Purists point to 13th century Chinese battle plans that refer to rocket-powered arrows and incendiary bombs. The assumption is that the idea for rocket propulsion is considerably older. By the time this century began, British engineer William Hale had already solved the vexing problem of keeping these projectiles on track. He fit his rockets with angled exhaust tubes that made them spin like bullets shot from a rifle as they flew toward their targets.

5   All of these early rockets used what we now call solid-fuel motors. Fuel and oxidizer to support combustion are mixed. When someone "lights the candle," as the saying goes, the fuel burns until it is exhausted. This permits a greater energy release in a shorter time than would be possible with jet engines, which burn their fuel only when oxygen is available in the air.

6   True rocket science emerged in the early part of this century when American rocket pioneer Robert H. Goddard worked out the details of a practical liquid-fueled motor. Unlike the solid-fuel rocket, this motor could be turned on and off at will. With this feature came a degree of control that, among other things, would allow satellites to be lofted into precise orbits and spacecraft to rendezvous. His first successful flight on March 16, 1926, launched the space age, although it would be nearly 30 more years before a rocket placed a satellite in orbit. By 1969, men would walk on the moon.

7   Shortly after becoming president, John F. Kennedy upped the tempo of the space race froma marathon into a sprint. In May 1961, he issued to NASA the challenge of completing a manned round trip to the moon within the decade. On July 20, 1969, Neil A. Armstrong and Edwin E. Aldrin Jr. did the seemingly impossible. With the touchdown of Apollo 11, mankind lived the ancient dream that had simmered in its soul since the first human lifted his eyes toward the moon. And then, after a dozen men had walked on the

barren lunar wasteland, the Apollo program was canceled. The task of staying alive in space had proved too expensive. The future belonged to robots.

8 As automated probes ventured to Mars, Venus, Jupiter and beyond, manned space exploration moved into low-Earth orbit with the launch of the American space station, Skylab. Meanwhile, rocket scientists turned their attention to America's next big spacecraft. Unlike the Saturn V that had lifted the Apollo missions to the moon, it would be a space shuttle, a reusable rocket that could fly again and again. The first of this fleet of space utility vehicles, Columbia, would launch from the Kennedy Space Center in Florida on April 12, 1981.

9 Soviet space achievements became scarce as the Cold War lingered. Several catastrophic rocket failures, which remained undisclosed for years, forced it to abandon its moon program on the eve of the Apollo landing. In 1999, Russia, which had inherited the Soviet Union's space program, retired its Mir space station and became a future tenant on the NASA-led international space station, which may be operational in a few years.

10 Despite the enormous differences between the two technologies, the close of the 20th century finds aircraft and rockets merging into a radically new form of transportation, the X-33 space plane. In the decades to come, the machines crafted in its image will literally fly us to the moon, and quite possibly beyond.

Into the Atom

11 In fact, as the 20th century began many scientists really believed that, aside from adding another decimal point to the precision of physical constants, there really wasn't much work to be done. Physics, which would occupy the role of the prince of sciences for most of this century, was then considered mostly good preparation for work in electrical engineering.

12 Of course, not everyone was convinced we had reached the end of the scientific road. A small cadre of physicists believed something of earthshaking importance might be lurking in the curious results of some of their more subtle experiments. Attempts to measure the impossibly fast speed of light, for example, showed that it never varied, whether you moved toward or away from a light source. This was deeply troubling because it defied the mathematics that describes the behavior of waves, and light was then thought to travel in waves. Another difficulty involved the light emitted from high-temperature furnaces. Simply put, it was the wrong color.

13 Initially, skeptics dismissed these anomalies as sloppy lab work. But as round after round of experiments produced similar results, a disturbing notion began to take hold. Perhaps the descriptions of nature that had produced so much progress in the 19th century were really incomplete—the tip of the iceberg. Efforts to probe beneath the surface would lead to the twodefining scientific breakthroughs of the 20th century—relativity and quantum theory.

14   Relativity theory would redefine our conception of matter, energy, space and time. Quantum theory would be even harder to digest. It would suggest, among other things, that the rules of reality are variable. Those rules that apply in the human-scale realm become null and void in the heart of the atom. By the halfway point of the century, the notion of the equivalence of mass and energy embodied in relativity theory would be put to work in weapons and power plants. By the three-quarter mark, quantum mechanics would touch our personal lives, chiefly through the application of the transistor, which would be used by the handful in radios and televisions, and by the millions in personal computers. Before the end of the century, a companion technology spurred on by quantum theory, the laser, would prove to be one of the most versatile tools of all time. In its various incarnations, it would be used to cut through steel, record music and quite literally mend broken hearts.

15   In spite of our enormous progress, one significant mystery remains. Relativity theory does an excellent job of explaining the very large, the play of gravitational forces across the cosmos. Quantum theory explains the realm of the very small, the distances inside the atom. What is missing and what physicists hope the experiments of the 21st century will lead to, is a theory of everything. The grand prize of this insight would be the ability to use electromagnetism to manipulate gravity, turning it on and off as though it were the light from a lamp.

Into the Cell

16   The progress made in medicine over the course of the 20th century was built on a deep and rich collection of descriptions of the natural world compiled by biologists during the preceding 200 years. These careful observations led to the discovery of antibiotics that proved to be magic bullets against infections, and vaccines that virtually eradicated polio. The largest gap in our knowledge of living systems was also filled, with the discovery of DNA. Building upon this new knowledge, biologists at long last had a cohesive theory to explain how life works.

17   Proponents of genetic engineering often present it as a technologically enhanced variation of what gardeners and farmers have been doing for centuries. After all, selective breeding of plants and animals has long produced prize-winning roses and blue ribbon bulls.

18   With the discovery that genetic heritage is passed along in a particular part of the cell, it became possible to move selective breeding from the barnyard to the laboratory. In 1953, James Watson and Francis Crick decoded the blueprint that every living thing carries within its cells—its DNA. By the early 1970s, molecular biologists had learned enough about the basic mechanics of life to go into that blueprint and selectively alter it. A new term entered the scientific and then popular language—recombinant DNA.

19   With their new technique, genetic engineers would be able to move genes. The promise was enormous. If your body was missing a gene needed to produce a particular

enzyme, a replacement for the defective gene could be cloned using a common bacteria, then "installed" in your cells. Nature would do the rest, incorporating it into the DNA, correcting a smudge on the blueprint of life as it were. In detail, these processes are, of course, far more complex. But their net effect is that genetic engineering has given humans mastery over the very essence of nature, the ability to create life.

20   Initial experiments in altering crops to resist weed killers have proved less successful in the field than in the laboratory. What's more, there are some hints that altering a group of genes to produce one desirable characteristic may produce unintended consequences, such as diminishing a food's nutritional content. By 1999, the backlash against genetically modified crops had grown to the point where foreign governments were threatening to ban American crops.

21   The public's growing demand that genetically modified foods be identified on their packaging—a move the U.S. government and biotechnology industry staunchly oppose—may reflect more than an interest in nutrition. It suggests a growing unwillingness to blindly accept the benefits of modern science. And this isn't a bad thing. If the changes of the next 100 years are even half as stunning as those of the past 100 years, a healthy dose of old-fashioned skepticism may be just what we need to prepare ourselves for life in the 21st century.

Preview Assistance

1. **anesthesia** *n.*   (Medicine) a drug, administered for medical or surgical purposes, that induces partial or total loss of sensation and may be topical, local, regional, or general, depending on the method of administration and area of the body affected
2. **antiseptic** *n.*   a substance that inhibits the growth and reproduction of disease-causing microorganisms
3. **vanquish** *v.*   to conquer, defeat or overcome
4. **scourge** *n.*   a whip or lash, esp. for the infliction of punishment or torture
5. **rabies** *n.*   an infectious disease of dogs, cats, and other animals, transmitted to humans by the bite of an infected animal and usually fatal if prophylactic treatment is not administered, caused by an RNA virus of the rhabdovirus group; hydrophobia
6. **harrowing** *adj.*   extremely distressing; agonizing
7. **glider** *n.*   a motorless, heavier-than-air aircraft for gliding from a higher to a lower level by the action of gravity or from a lower to a higher level by the action of air currents
8. **ivory tower**   a place or attitude of retreat, especially preoccupation with lofty, remote, or intellectual considerations rather than practical everyday life
9. **purist** *n.*   someone who insists on great precision and correctness
10. **incendiary** *adj.*   of or containing chemicals that produce intensely hot fire when exploded
11. **propulsion** *n.*   the act or process of propelling
12. **vexing** *adj.*   extremely annoying or displeasing
13. **projectile** *n.*   an object fired from a gun with an explosive propelling charge, such as a bullet, shell, rocket, or grenade

14. **oxidizer** *n.*   a substance that oxidizes another substance, especially one that supports the combustion of fuel; an oxidizing agent
15. **combustion** *n.*   a process in which a substance reacts with oxygen to give heat and light
16. **rendezvous** *n.*   a place designated for a meeting or assembling
17. **touchdown** *n.*   a landing (as the wheels touch the landing field); especially of airplanes
18. **simmer** *v.*   to cook or cook in a liquid at or just below the boiling point
19. **lurk** *v.*   to lie in wait, lie in ambush, behave in a sneaky and secretive manner
20. **skeptic** *n.*   one who instinctively or habitually doubts, questions, or disagrees with assertions or generally accepted conclusions
21. **anomaly** *n.*   deviation from the normal or common order or form or rule
22. **sloppy** *adj.*   marked by a lack of care or precision; slipshod
23. **quantum** *n.*   (Physics) the smallest quantity of radiant energy, equal to Planck's constant times the frequency of the associated radiation
24. **null and void**   without legal force or effect; not valid
25. **spur on**   to goad or urge ahead
26. **versatile** *adj.*   capable of or adapted for turning easily from one to another of various tasks, fields of endeavor, etc.
27. **incarnation** *n.*   an incarnate being or form
28. **electromagnetism** *n.*   the phenomena associated with electric and magnetic fields and their interactions with each other and with electric charges and currents
29. **polio** *n.*   poliomyelitis. an acute viral disease marked by inflammation of nerve cells of the brain stem and spinal cord
30. **recombinant** *adj.*   of or resulting from new combinations of genetic material
31. **enzyme** *n.*   any of several complex proteins that are produced by cells and act as catalysts in specific biochemical reactions
32. **backlash** *n.*   a movement back from an impact
33. **staunch** *adj.*   firm and dependable especially in loyalty

Referential Points

NASA   National Aeronautics and Space Administration (NASA), agency of the United States government responsible for developing space exploration and research initiatives, as well as coordinating various communications-related projects. NASA also administers the space shuttle program and a variety of other endeavors, which include improving the performance of airplanes and rockets (aeronautics), conducting scientific experiments in space, improving data-tracking technology, increasing international alliances for space activities, and establishing partnerships between private companies and government agencies in the aeronautics industry.

Stephen Hawking (1942—   )   British theoretical physicist and mathematician whose main field of research has been the nature of space and time, including irregularities in space and time known as singularities. Hawking has also devoted much of his life to making his theories accessible to the public through lectures, books, and films.

Wright Flyer   the Wright Flyer was the third plane built in 1905 by the Wright Brothers. It was the world's first fully practical airplane. It could bank, turn, circle, make figure eights, and remain in the air for as long as the fuel lasted, up to half an hour on occasion.

"Light the candle" a Chinese proverb "Don't curse the darkness—light a candle." It was used by Adlai Stevenson (1900—1965), praising Eleanor Roosevelt in an address to the United Nations General Assembly in 1962—"She would rather light candles than curse the darkness, and her glow has warmed the world."

Apollo 11 was the first lunar-landing mission. Launched on July 16, 1969, the crew of Neil A. Armstrong, Edwin E. Aldrin, Jr., and Michael Allen Collins flew the spacecraft Columbia (CSM) and Eagle (LM). The spacecraft departed lunar orbit over two days after arrival. This eight-day mission landed and was recovered safely in the Pacific Ocean. As a precautionary measure, the astronauts were quarantined for 14 days.

Saturn V Saturn (rocket), family of rockets used to launch some of the most famous space flights in history, including Apollo 11, the 1969 mission that carried American astronauts Neil Armstrong and Edwin "Buzz" Aldrin to the surface of the moon. The most powerful rockets of their time, Saturn rockets were developed by NASA, an agency of the United States government, for use in the Apollo space exploration program.

Kennedy Space Center There are five main branches of NASA: the Office of Aero-Space Technology, the Office of Earth Science, the Office of Space Flight, the Office of Life and Microgravity Sciences and Applications, and the Office of Space Science. NASA employs thousands of scientists, engineers, and technicians at its major installations across the country. These facilities include the John F. Kennedy Space Center in Merritt Island, Florida; the Lyndon B. Johnson Space Center in Houston, Texas; the Goddard Space Flight Center in Greenbelt, Maryland; and the George C. Marshall Space Flight Center in Huntsville, Alabama.

DNA Deoxyribonucleic Acid (DNA), genetic material of all cellular organisms and most viruses. DNA carries the information needed to direct protein synthesis and replication. Protein synthesis is the production of the proteins needed by the cell or virus for its activities and development. Replication is the process by which DNA copies itself for each descendant cell or virus, passing on the information needed for protein synthesis. In most cellular organisms, DNA is organized on chromosomes located in the nucleus of the cell.

blue ribbon In symbolism, blue ribbon is a term used to describe something of high quality. The usage came from The Blue Riband, a prize awarded for the fastest crossing of the Atlantic Ocean by passenger liners. The spelling blue riband is still encountered in most English-speaking countries, but in the United States, the term was altered to blue ribbon, and ribbons of this color came to be awarded for first place in certain athletic or other competitive endeavors.

Consolidation Work

I. Fill in the blanks with the words and expressions provided, making some change when necessary.

enhance	vary	intend	seem	adventure	catastrophic
defect	lurk	radical	genuine	on and off	null and void
take hold	work out	at will			

Unit 7

1. The scholar declared that this plan would never _____ with the voters and the candidate should reconsider it.
2. The common law doctrine of employment _____ holds that, unless specified otherwise, the employment relationship can be terminated for any reason.
3. An _____ activity can lead to gains in knowledge, such as in the case of the numerous pioneers who have explored and charted the Earth and, in recent times, traveled into space and to the Moon.
4. Remember that fear always _____ behind perfectionism. Confronting your fears and allowing yourself the right to be human can make you a far happier and more productive person.
5. In a perfect world, this would be sufficient, but computers and software can crash, power can fail, and other unpredictable, _____ events can conspire to erase your work.
6. There were indications that federal energy planners were beginning to give more serious consideration to _____ recovery projects to boost domestic crude oil production.
7. The officials were very pleased that they had been able to _____ an agreement to let this important legislation move to a vote in the House.
8. The warranty claims that in no event will the company be liable for incidental or consequential damages resulting from a _____ unit or improper assembly or use.
9. Involved in this study are the determination of the earth's gravitational field and observation of _____ in the earth's rotation, the location of the poles, and tides.
10. The Chelsea Theater Center created a _____ thrilling event with its adaptation of *Leo Tolstoy's Strider*.
11. On the same day a small group of residents gathered on the steps of Town Hall a few weeks ago declared the courts decision _____.
12. Minkowski's galactic research has revealed 212 new planetary nebulae, _____ concentrated toward the galactic center.
13. The view of contemporary society presented by Cox is opposed _____ to Vahanian's pessimism.
14. He said that a U.S.-Soviet working group would be set up to study ways to avert _____ confrontations between the two countries.
15. You can turn the handheld mode and wireless mode _____ independently.

II. Use the appropriate form of the words given in the brackets to fill in the blanks.

1. There is no harm in doubt an _____, for it is through these that new discoveries are made. (skeptical)
2. Regardless of the fact that South Africa no longer has any legal right to Namibia, it continues, as illegal _____, to be answerable before the international community for all of its actions in the territory. (occupy)
3. An apprentice carpenter may want only a hammer and saw, but a master craftsman employs many _____ tools. (precise)
4. The happiness of a man in this life does not consist in the absence but in the _____ of his passions. (master)
5. When we seek for connection, we restore the world to wholeness. Our _____ separate lives become meaningful as we discover how truly necessary we are to each other. (seem)

6. The research report may have predicted something that was _____, rather than theoretically, impossible at the time. (technology)
7. No _____ engineered animals, however, have yet been approved by the government to be eaten. (gene)
8. A white house spokesperson reports that the president was taken to an _____ military hospital following the crash. (disclose)
9. Techniques of genetic _____ allow scientists to change an organism's genetic code to create a plant or animal that never before existed. (modify)
10. Most conscientious researchers would be reluctant to make such an unequivocal statement at all, but if they did it would only be after an _____ examination of the evidence. (exhaust)

III. Paraphrase the following sentences taken from the text.
1. Engineers compressed time with transcontinental railroads that reduced to risk-free days a harrowing journey that had taken months and lives.
2. In the workaday world, sorting winners from losers isn't only possible, but most of the time quite necessary.
3. With the touchdown of Apollo 11, mankind lived the ancient dream that had simmered in its soul since the first human lifted his eyes toward the moon.
4. A small cadre of physicists believed something of earthshaking importance might be lurking in the curious results of some of their more subtle experiments.
5. Those rules that apply in the human-scale realm become null and void in the heart of the atom.

IV. Test your general knowledge.
1. Who proved that lightning and electricity are identical by means of kite experiment in 1752 and subsequently invented the lightning rod?
   A. James Watson.   B. Thomas Edison.
   C. Benjamin Franklin.   D. Orville Wright.
2. The following units are commonly used in the system of unit to measure electrical quantities. Which one is the unit of charge?
   A. Ampere.   B. Volt.   C. Ohm.   D. Coulomb.
3. The Wright brothers are generally credited the first controlled, powered, heavier-than-air flight on _____. In the two years afterward, they developed their flying machine into the world's first practical fixed-wing aircraft, along with many other aviation milestones.
   A. December 17, 1803   B. December 17, 1843
   C. December 17, 1903   D. December 17, 1943
4. _____ was NASA's second Space Shuttle orbiter to be put into service. Its maiden voyage was on April 4, 1983, and it made eight further round trips to low earth orbit before breaking up 73 seconds after the launch of its tenth mission, on January 28, 1986, killing all 7 crew members.
   A. Enterprise   B. Columbia   C. Challenger   D. Endeavour
5. Which of the following statements about atom is NOT true?
   A. The atom is the smallest unit of a chemical element having the properties of that element.
   B. The atom consists of a central, negatively charged core, the nucleus, and positively

charged particles called electrons that are found in orbits around the nucleus.
C. Almost the entire mass of the atom is concentrated in the nucleus, which occupies only a tiny fraction of the atom's volume.
D. The nucleus of an atom consists of neutrons and protons, the neutron being an uncharged particle and the proton a positively charged one.

6. Periodic table is the chart of the elements in which the elements are arranged in columns and rows according to _____.
   A. initial letters of elements
   B. increasing atomic number
   C. chronological time of element being found
   D. a random way

7. Acid rain can contaminate drinking water, damage vegetation and aquatic life, and erode buildings and monuments. It is so harmful because it contains high levels of _____.
   A. carbon dioxide   B. vitriol
   C. hydrochloric acid   D. sulfuric or nitric acids

8. The discovery of penicillin is usually attributed to Scottish scientist Alexander Fleming in 1928. Today penicillin is still one of the most important antibiotics because of its _____.
   A. antagonistic effect on bacteria
   B. effective reduction of blood pressure
   C. lessening of pain
   D. promotion of blood circulation

9. In 1996 experiments in cloning resulted in the development of an animal from a cell, and scientists named it Dolly. Actually Dolly is a _____.
   A. sheep   B. pig   C. cat   D. rat

10. Thomas Edison was one of the greatest and most productive inventors of his time. Which of the following things is not his invention?
    A. Incandescent lamp.
    B. Telephone.
    C. Peep-show machine.
    D. The transmitter and receiver for the automatic telegraph.

11. What is the correct description of a gene?
    A. A section of a protein.
    B. A section of an enzyme.
    C. A collection of enzymes.
    D. A section of DNA in the nucleus.

12. The Internet evolved from a secret feasibility study conceived by the U.S. Dept. of Defense in _____ to test methods of enabling computer networks to survive military attacks.
    A. 1965   B. 1967   C. 1969   D. 1970

13. The metal mercury is _____.
    A. the hardest known metal   B. a liquid at room temperature
    C. highly radioactive   D. extensively used in aircraft construction

14. Each computer that is directly connected to the Internet is uniquely identified by a _____ called its IP address.
    A. 16-bit binary number   B. 32-bit binary number
    C. 16-bit binary number   D. 32-bit decimal number

15. Which in the following techniques can be used to defend data in transit between systems, reducing the probability that data exchanged between systems can be intercepted or modified?
    A. firewall   B. encryption   C. authentication   D. anti-virus software

V. Proofread the following passage.

    Many discoveries have happened by accident. The Wright brothers discovered flight because of an accident—actually two accidents. The first occurred during the winter of 1885-86 that a hockey injury forced Wilbur, the elder Wright, to postpone college. Recovered at home, he consumed the content of his father's library and became intrigued by newspaper and magazines accounts of the German aeronaut Lilienthal. It was news of Lilienthal's death in an August 1896 glider crash that spurred the brothers to continue the quest.

    Like Lilienthal, the Wrights attacked the problem scientifically, in their case by accumulating data from a wind tunnel constructed in their bicycle shop. They realized the key difficulty achieving heavier-than-air flight was not in creating lift to elevate the aircraft, but in maintaining control once it was airborne. Their solution, while not elegant, was truly inspired. The pilot lied on the bottom wing with his hips in a cradle that was connected to a "wing-warping" system. Moving the hips to the right and left increased the angle of attack on one wing while reducing it on the other. Linkage to the rudder counteracted yaw. The net effect was to allow the pilot to roll the plane to its longitudinal axis so that it could "bank" into turns much as a bicycle allows its rider to lean into a curve. Eventually, ailerons, small flaps on the trailing edge of wings, would obsolete wing-warping. And until the Wright brothers struck upon this solution, flight remained an impossible dream.

    In the years that were followed their fateful Dec. 17, 1903, flight in Kitty Hawk, N.C., the Wright brothers refined the design of their craft. They developed the first practically flying machine in 1905. A model capable of flying for one hour at an average speed of 40 mph was purchased by the U.S. Army Signal Corps in 1909. Within 10 years, the military's experimentation and experience with aircraft would make planes as essential to future arsenals as guns or explosives.

1. _____
2. _____
3. _____
4. _____
5. _____
6. _____
7. _____
8. _____
9. _____
10. _____

VI. Write a composition.

    Choose a specific scientific breakthrough that interests you, that you want to learn about, or with which you have some familiarity either academically or personally. Write a research paper and then give a presentation in class. In your presentation you should consider the following:

    1. Carefully explain what you know of the actual breakthrough, how scientists arrived at it, and what it revealed. If you do not know that much about your topic, explain the research strategies you will use. What types of sources will you consult? Why?

    2. What opposition (if any) has this breakthrough encountered? Tell us if you know, speculate if you don't.

3. Argue how this breakthrough has shaped our experiences in the last century and how it will function as stepping stone in this century (what other benefits can come of this?)

Further Development

Students are required to do a research on the following topics:
1. What is science in nature? How does it relate to our lives and other aspects of our social and cultural communities?
2. What is our own role in and responsibility for the future? Can empirical inquiry help with such questions?

Section B Text Two

Is Science Evil?

By Karl Jasper

1 No one questions the immense significance of modern science. Through industrial technology it has transformed our existence, and its insights have transformed our consciousness, all this to an extent hitherto unheard of. The human condition throughout the millennia appears relatively stable in comparison with the impetuous movement that has now caught up mankind as a result of science and technology, and is driving it no one knows where. Science has destroyed the substance of many old beliefs and has made others questionable. Its powerful authority has brought more and more men to the point where they wish to know and not believe, where they expect to be helped by science and only by science. The present faith is that scientific understanding can solve all problems and do away with all difficulties.

2 Such excessive expectations result inevitably in equally excessive disillusionment. Science has still given no answer to man's doubts and despair. Instead, it has created weapons able to destroy in a few moments that which science itself helped build up slowly over the years. Accordingly, there are today two conflicting viewpoints: first, the superstition of science, which holds scientific results to be as absolute as religious myths used to be, so that even religious movements are now dressed in the garments of pseudoscience. Second, the hatred of science, which sees it as a diabolical evil of mysterious origin that has befallen mankind.

3 These two attitudes—both nonscientific—are so closely linked that they are usually found together, either in alternation or in an amazing compound.

4 A very recent example of this situation can be found in the attack against science provoked by the trial in Nuremberg of those doctors who, under Nazi orders, performed deadly experiments on human beings. One of the most esteemed medical men among

German university professors has accepted the verdict on these crimes as a verdict on science itself, as a stick with which to beat "purely scientific and biological" medicine, and even the modern science of man in general: "this invisible spirit sitting on the prisoner's bench in Nuremberg, this spirit that regards men merely as objects, is not present in Nuremberg alone—it pervades the entire world." And he adds, if this generalization may be viewed as an extenuation of the crime of the accused doctors, that is only a further indictment of purely scientific medicine.

5   Anyone convinced that true scientific knowledge is possible only of things that can he regarded as objects, and that knowledge of the subject is possible only when the subject attains a form of objectivity; anyone who sees science as the one great landmark on the road to truth, and sees the real achievements of modern physicians as derived exclusively from biological and scientific medicine—such a person will see in the above statements an attack on what he feels to be fundamental to human existence. And he may perhaps have a word to say in rebuttal.

6   In the special case of the crimes against humanity committed by Nazi doctors and now laid at the door of modern science, there is a simple enough argument. Science was not needed at all, but only a certain bent of mind for the perpetration of such outrages. Such crimes were already possible millennia ago. In the Buddhist pali canon, there is the report of an Indian prince who had experiments performed on criminals in order to determine whether they had an immortal soul that survived their corpses: "You shall—it was ordered—put the living man in a tub, close the lid, cover it with a damp hide, lay on a thick layer of clay, put it in the oven and make a fire. This was done. When we knew the man was dead, the tub was drawn forth, uncovered, the lid removed, and we looked carefully inside to see if we could perceive the escaping soul. But we saw no escaping soul." Thus there were experiments on human beings before modern science.

7   Better than such a defense, however, would be a consideration of what modern science really genuinely is, and what its limits are. Science, both ancient and modern, has, in the first place, three indispensable characteristics:

8   First, it is methodical knowledge. I know something scientifically only when I also know the method by which I have this knowledge, and am thus able to ground it and mark its limits.

9   Second, it is compellingly certain. Even the uncertain—i.e., the probable or improbable—I know scientifically only insofar as I know it clearly and compellingly as such, and know the degree of its uncertainty.

10   Third, it is universally valid. I know scientifically only what is identically valid for every inquirer. Thus scientific knowledge spreads over the world and remains the same. Unanimity is a sign of universal validity. When unanimity is not attained, when there is a conflict of schools, sects and trends of fashion, then universal validity becomes problematic.

11   This notion of science as methodical knowledge, compellingly certain, and universally valid, was long ago possessed by the Greeks. Modern science has not only purified this

notion; it has also transformed it: a transformation that can be described by saying that modern science is indifferent to nothing. Everything—the smallest and meanest, the furthest and strangest—that is in any way and at any time actual, is relevant to modern science, simply because it is. Modern science wants to be thoroughly universal, allowing nothing to escape it. Nothing shall be hidden, nothing shall be silent, and nothing shall be a secret.

12   In contrast to the science of classical antiquity, modern science is basically unfinished. Whereas ancient science had the appearance of something completed, to which the notion of progress was not essential, modern science progress into the infinite. Modern science has realized that a finished and total world-view is scientifically impossible. Only when scientific criticism is crippled by making particulars absolute can a closed view of the world pretend to scientific validity—and then it is a false validity. Those great new unified systems of knowledge—such as modern physics—that have grown up in the scientific era, deal only with single aspects of reality. And reality as a whole has been fragmented as never before; whence the openness of the modern world in contrast to the closed Greek cosmos.

13   However, while a total and finished world-view is no longer possible to modern science, the idea of a unity of the sciences has now come to replace it. Instead of the cosmos of the world, we have the cosmos of the sciences. Out of dissatisfaction with all the separate bits of knowledge is born the desire to unite all knowledge. The ancient sciences remained dispersed and without mutual relations. There was lacking to them the notion of a concrete totality of science. The modern sciences, however, seek to relate themselves to each other in every possible way.

14   At the same time the modern sciences have increased their claims. They put a low value on the possibilities of speculative thinking, they hold thought to be valid only as part of definite and concrete knowledge, only when it has stood the test of verification and hereby become infinitely modified. Only superficially do the modern and the ancient atomic theories seem to fit into the same theoretical mold. Ancient atomic theory was applied as a plausible interpretation of common experience; it was a statement complete in itself of what might possibly be the case. Modern atomic theory has developed through experiment, verification, refutation: that is, through an incessant transformation of itself in which theory is used not as an end in itself but as a tool of inquiry. Modern science, in its questioning, pushes to extremes. For example, the rational critique of appearance (as against reality) was begun in antiquity, as in the concept of perspective and its application to astronomy, but it still had some connection with immediate human experiences. Today, however, this same critique, as in modern physics for instance, ventures to the very extremes of paradox, attaining a knowledge of the real that shatters any and every view of the world as a closed and complete whole.

15   So it is that in our day a scientific attitude has become possible that addresses itself inquisitively to everything it comes across, that is able to know what it knows in a clear

and positive way, that can distinguish between the known and the unknown, and that has acquired an incredible mass of knowledge. How helpless was the Greek doctor or the Greek engineer! The ethos of modern science is the desire for reliable knowledge based on dispassionate investigation and criticism. When we enter its domain we feel as though we were breathing pure air and seeing the dissolution of all vague talk, plausible opinions, haughty omniscience and blind faith.

16   But the greatness and the limitations of science are inseparable. It is a characteristic of the greatness of modern science that it comprehends its own limits. Scientific, objective knowledge is not a knowledge of Being. This means that scientific knowledge is particular, not general, that it is directed toward specific objects, and not toward Being itself. Through knowledge itself, science arrives at the most positive recognition of what it does not know.

17   Scientific knowledge or understanding cannot supply us with the aims of life. It cannot lead us. By virtue of its very clarity it directs us elsewhere for the sources of our life, our decisions and our love.

18   Human freedom is not an object of science, but is the field of philosophy. Within the purview of science there is no such thing as liberty.

19   These are clear limits, and the person who is scientifically minded will not expect from science what it cannot give. Yet science has become, nevertheless, the indispensable element of all striving for truth, and it has become the premise of philosophy and the basis in general for whatever clarity and candor are today possible. To the extent that and it succeeds in penetrating all obscurities and unveiling all secrets, science directs to the most profound, the most genuine secret.

20   That modern science, like all things, contains its own share of corruption, that men of science only too often fail to live up to its standards, that science can be used for violent and criminal ends, that man will steal, plunder, abuse, and kill to gain knowledge—all this is no argument against science.

21   To be sure, science as such sets up no barriers. As science, it is neither human nor inhuman. So far as the well-being of humanity is concerned, science needs guidance from other sources. Science in itself is not enough—or should not be. Even medicine is only a scientific means, serving an eternal ideal, the aid of the sick and the protection of the healthy.

22   When the spirit of a faithless age can become the cause of atrocities all over the world, then it can also influence the conduct of the scientist and the behavior of the physician, especially in those areas of activity where science itself is confused and unguided. It is not the spirit of science but the spirit of its vessels that is depraved. Count Keyserling's dictum—"The roots of truth seeking lie in primitive aggression"—is as little valid for science as it is for any genuine truth seeking. The spirit of science is in no way primarily aggressive, but becomes so only when truth is prohibited; for men rebel against the glossing over of truth or its suppression.

Independent Study Assistance

I. Words and Expressions

1. **hitherto** *adv.*   up to this time; until now
2. **impetuous** *adj.*   having great impetus; moving with great force; violent
3. **disillusionment** *n.*   the disappointed feeling a person has when he discovers that someone or something is not as good as he had believed
4. **pseudoscience** *n.*   any of various methods, theories, or systems, as astrology, psychokinesis, or clairvoyance, considered as having no scientific basis
5. **diabolical** *adj.*   having the qualities of a devil; devilish; fiendish; outrageously wicked
6. **extenuate** *v.*   to represent (a fault, offense, etc.) as less serious
7. **indictment** *n.*   Law. a formal accusation initiating a criminal case, presented by a grand jury and usually required for felonies and other serious crimes
8. **rebuttal** *n.*   an act of rebutting, as in a debate
9. **ground** *v.*   to provide a basis for (a theory, for example); justify
10. **unanimity** *n.*   a consensus or undivided opinion
11. **antiquity** *n.*   the quality of being ancient; ancientness
12. **speculative** *adj.*   of, characterized by, or based upon contemplative speculation
13. **verification** *n.*   evidence that establishes or confirms the accuracy or truth of something
14. **plausible** *adj.*   having an appearance of truth or reason; seemingly worthy of approval or acceptance; credible; believable
15. **paradox** *n.*   a statement or proposition that seems self-contradictory or absurd but in reality expresses a possible truth
16. **ethos** *n.*   the fundamental character or spirit of a culture; the underlying sentiment that informs the beliefs, customs, or practices of a group or society; dominant assumptions of a people or period
17. **omniscience** *n.*   total knowledge; the state of knowing everything
18. **purview** *n.*   the range of operation, authority, control, concern, etc.
19. **candor** *n.*   the state or quality of being frank, open, and sincere in speech or expression; candidness
20. **atrocity** *n.*   appalling or atrocious condition, quality, or behavior; monstrousness
21. **dictum** *n.*   an authoritative, often formal pronouncement
22. **gloss over**   to make attractive or acceptable by deception or superficial treatment

II. Referential Points

Karl Jaspers   One of the founders of modern Existentialism, the philosophic trend that has attracted so much attention of late, Karl Jaspers has since the downfall of Hitler become a spokesman of Germany's highest conscience. He was born in Oldenburg in 1883, and began his career as a psychiatrist; his investigations, however, brought him up against the philosophical problems to which he soon began to devote his full attention; and thus he became a lecturer on philosophy and eventually professor of philosophy at Heidelberg, where he still lives, though now formally in retirement. Since 1945 Professor Jaspers has resumed his activities, at least as a lecturer. The present article was part of a lecture he delivered at Geneva on September 13, 1946, in the course of the Rencontres de Genève on which Stephen Spender reported in the January

1947 COMMENTARY. Professor Jaspers' latest book, *Die Schuldfrage*, on the question of German guilt, will soon appear in English. This article was translated by E.B.Ashton.

Nuremberg Trials   a series of military trials, or military tribunals, most notable for the prosecution of prominent members of the political, military, and economic leadership of Nazi Germany after its defeat in World War II. The trials were held in the city of Nuremberg, Germany, from 1945 to 1946, at the Palace of Justice. The first and best known of these trials was the **Trial of the Major War Criminals** before the International Military Tribunal **(IMT)**, which tried 22 of the most important captured leaders of Nazi Germany. It was held from November 21, 1945 to October 1, 1946. The second set of trials of lesser war criminals was conducted under Control Council Law No. 10 at the US Nuremberg Military Tribunals (NMT); among them included the Doctors' Trial and the Judges' Trial. This article primarily deals with the IMT; see the Subsequent Nuremberg Trials for details on those trials.

the Buddhist pali canon   The Pāli Canon is the standard collection of scriptures in the Theravada Buddhist tradition, as preserved in the Pali language. It is the only completely surviving early Buddhist canon, and one of the first to be written down. It was composed in North India, and preserved orally until it was committed to writing during the Fourth Buddhist Council in Sri Lanka in the 1st century BC, approximately three hundred years after the death of Shakyamuni. The Pali Canon was first printed in the nineteenth century, and is now also available in electronic form and on the Internet.

III. Questions for Comprehension

Think about the following questions and discuss them with your group members. After your discussion, work out a research report and share it with the students of other groups.

1. What is the main argument of this article? How does the author support his argument?
2. Can scientific understanding solve all problems and do away with all difficulties? Give your reasons.
3. The author points out two conflicting viewpoints about science at his times. What are they? Do they still exist nowadays?
4. What are the merits and demerits of modern science, as compared with classical science?
5. What does the author mean by saying that "Instead of the cosmos of the world, we have the cosmos of the sciences" in paragraph 13?
6. What are the differences between ancient atomic theory and modern atomic theory?
7. How do you understand the view that the greatness and the limitations of science are inseparable?
8. Why does the author say that "science is neither human nor inhuman"? Is this statement a paradox?

Unit 7

Self-test

I. Fill in the blanks with the words and expressions provided, making some change when necessary.

excessive	paradox	perpetrate	problematic esteem	compelling
plausible	inquisitive	gloss over	live up to	strive for
as such	in comparison with		fit into	by virtue of

1. While taxis are available in most United States communities, the fares charged for short distance transportation are high _____ taxi fare rates in most other countries.
2. The newspaper said that the _____ of the crime by the accused was proved to the satisfaction of the court.
3. Scientists have found _____ evidence that the Sun has a baby brother, a dark star whose eccentric orbit is responsible for periodically showering the Earth with comets and meteorites.
4. Recent concerns about global climate change, especially the impact of human activity on these changes, have sent scientists scrambling to discover how current climate trends _____ the larger picture of climate change throughout Earth's history.
5. Vigorously challenged yet widely ignored, the theory had languished for half a century, primarily due to its lack of a _____ mechanism to support the proposed drift.
6. Life is a _____ for it enjoins us to cling to its many gifts even while it ordains their eventual relinquishment.
7. We trust that you will find something among our designs which will suit your requirement, and we await your _____ order.
8. No one doubts the need for such regulations, but their _____ or discriminatory use can be implicitly protectionist.
9. The protons, bring positively charged, repel one another _____ their electrostatic interactions.
10. As every country is _____ a knowledge-based economy, the rivalry to win over people with expertise and skills has been intensifying.
11. Both cultural and linguistic differences have proved _____ for the traditional means of the machine translation.
12. To them, botany, _____, has no name and is probably not even recognized as a special branch of "knowledge" at all.
13. The right-wingers in Japan are attempting to _____ the country's ugly past with revised secondary textbook.
14. *Curiosity killed the cat* is a proverb used to warn against being too _____ lest one comes to harm.
15. If it's true that size doesn't matter, then these giants still earn points for longevity. These trees can _____ three thousand years.

II. Use the appropriate form of the words given in the brackets to fill in the blanks.

1. Claiming something is true misses the point, while presenting _____ fact proves its correctness. (verification)
2. The American writer's novel typified the _____ and bohemianism among a generation of post—World War I Americans. (illusion)
3. Quantum mechanics and relativity have revealed the boundaries of _____ of classical mechanics. (valid)
4. The novel is a powerful _____ of the capitalistic economy and a sharp criticism of the southwestern farmer for his imprudence in the care of his land. (indict)
5. The idea of cultural preservation and the teaching of humanities are _____. However, there has been a long-standing lack of emphasis on the latter. (separate)
6. The debate team must prepare the position, _____ and closing in advance, or at least major parts of it. Different students should be responsible for different parts. (rebut)
7. He wore a pair of round silver rimmed-glasses which gave him at first glance a studious or, at least, a _____ appearance. (method)
8. People with a taste for fiction experienced dreams that contained more _____ events, and their dreams were more emotionally intense. (probable)
9. Whatever critics felt about the merits of the film, the actor enjoyed nearly _____ raves for his work. (unanimity)
10. Each Member State undertakes to respect the _____ international character of the responsibilities of the Secretary-General and the staff and not to seek to influence them in the discharge of their duties. (exclude)

III. Translate the short paragraph into Chinese.

What we today think of as science is for the most part not science at all, but applied science, that is, technology. The machinery of modern science is so elaborate, and the building of it requires so much ingenuity—requires, indeed, so much science—that we naturally confuse the thinking with the doing. The great particle accelerator at CERN, for example, is for us the very image of modern science: a vast and inconceivably expensive machine built to perform minute and unimaginably complex operations whose results can be interpreted only by a handful of physicists. But we are willing to pay the cost of building these machines, are willing to allow the physicists their arcane rules and specialized language, because we believe that they are getting their hands into the very bowels of nature. And at some point, we believe, they will bring forth news of another advance, another boiled-down version of the world's variousness, another $E=mc$, only bigger and better. Perhaps, this time they may even discover the final equation, the Grand Theory of Everything.

IV. Analyze difficult sentences.
1. Anyone convinced that true scientific knowledge is possible only of things that can he regarded as objects, and that knowledge of the subject is possible only when the subject attains a form of objectivity.
2. In the special case of the crimes against humanity committed by Nazi doctors and now laid at the door of modern science, there is a simple enough argument.
3. When unanimity is not attained, when there is a conflict of schools, sects and trends of fashion, then universal validity becomes problematic.

4. Only when scientific criticism is crippled by making particulars absolute can a closed view of the world pretend to scientific validity—and then it is a false validity.
5. They put a low value on the possibilities of speculative thinking, they hold thought to be valid only as part of definite and concrete knowledge, only when it has stood the test of verification and hereby become infinitely modified.

V. Proofread the following passage.

Modern technology is problematic because it has become such an important factor in social change. Major technological changes are introduced in the belief that they will help to solve problems, and they often do so quite successfully. But in solving problems of the one kind, technological changes sometimes generate new and different problems, including some that were not foreseen. The response for this situation is called the technological fix—the use of technology to solve problems, including those that prior technology has created. The result may be a complex cycle which one new technology after another is applied to an ever more complicated situation, with the whole process takes us further and further from the original problem and its solution.

Significant technological innovation also causes economic dislocation, for it makes existing products, processes, or sometimes workers obsolete. Modern industry is becoming increasingly dependent on automation, the replacement of workers by human means of production. To be replaced in one's job by a machine can be a humiliated experience, but to employers, automated labor often makes economic sense: machines can work almost continuously, without break for food and sleep, and they require no pension plans or medical benefits. It is hardly surprising, therefore, human bank-tellers are being replaced by automated tellers, or that assembly-line welders are yielding their jobs to robots. The transition from a industrial to a postindustrial society is causing a wave of "creative destruction" in which old industries and technologies are replaced by new ones. Despite of the dislocation it causes, technological innovation creates many new occupations and opportunities—although this is small consolation to millions of workers whose jobs and sometimes careers have been destroyed.

1. _____
2. _____
3. _____
4. _____
5. _____
6. _____
7. _____
8. _____
9. _____
10. _____

VI. Write a composition.

At present there exist two conflicting tendencies towards the development of science and technology. One is that modern science has not brought blessings to human beings but the possibility to lead them to the very edge of disaster and peril. The other belief is that the crises facing human beings today are the natural consequences of the development of science, and the solution to which lies in the further development of science. What is your opinion? Write an essay based on your understanding of the issues above.

《英语综合高级教程》(上)参考答案信息

尊敬的老师：

您好！

为了方便您更好地使用《英语综合高级教程》(上)，我们特向使用该书作为教材的教师赠送参考答案。如有需要，请完整填写"教师联系表"并加盖所在单位系(院)或培训中心公章，免费向出版社索取。

北京大学出版社

教 师 联 系 表

教材名称	《英语综合高级教程》(上 册)		
姓名：	性别：	职务：	职称：
E-maill:	联系电话：	邮政编码：	
供职学校：		所在院系：	（章）
学校地址：			
教学科目与年级：		班级人数：	
通信地址：			

填写完毕后，请将此表邮寄给我们，我们将为您免费寄送《英语综合高级教程》(上)参考答案，谢谢合作！

北京市海淀区成府路205号
北京大学出版社外语编辑部　　李颖
邮政编码：100871
电子邮箱：evalee1770@hotmail.com

邮 购 部 电 话：010-62534449
市场营销部电话：010-62750672
外语编辑部电话：010-62767315